RAB

by the same author

THE MAKING OF THE PRIME MINISTER (with Richard West)

THE CROSSMAN DIARIES: SELECTIONS (ed.)

RAB

The Life of R. A. Butler

Anthony Howard

JONATHAN CAPE
THIRTY-TWO BEDFORD SQUARE
LONDON

First published 1987

Jonathan Cape Ltd, 32 Bedford Square, London WC1B 3EL

British Library Cataloguing in Publication Data

Howard, Anthony
Rab: the life of R. A. Butler.
1. Butler, Richard Austen Butler, *Baron*
I. Title
941.085′092′4 DA566.9.B89

ISBN 0-224-01862-0

Photoset in Linotron Times by
Rowland Phototypesetting Ltd
Bury St Edmunds, Suffolk
Printed in Great Britain by
Butler & Tanner Ltd,
Frome and London

For C.A.H.

Contents

Illustrations

PLATES

CARTOONS

Preface

It was towards the end of 1979 that the late Lord Butler, greatly to my astonishment, first broached the subject of my writing his official life. I had gone to see him with a rather different proposal – that he might allow me to include him in a volume of four political portraits I was then contemplating. I had written to him in advance, giving notice of my request, and was mildly nettled when, having summoned me to his flat in Whitehall Court, he made it clear that it was not an idea he was prepared to entertain.

I was just taking my leave, expressing a slightly false sense of gratitude for his courtesy in communicating the decision to me personally rather than in writing, when he delayed my exit by remarking, 'There is something else that I would rather like to put to you.' He then explained that, although he had no interest in co-operating in a study that would include three other politicians – they were intended to be Hugh Gaitskell, Richard Crossman and Iain Macleod – he had different feelings about a full-scale biography of himself alone.

Typically, nothing was settled that day. He merely murmured – on my intimating that such a project would, indeed, interest me – that he would 'consult with my friends'. Fortunately for me, at least two of them, the late Lord Boyle of Handsworth and Sir William Rees-Mogg, also happened to be friends of mine.

It was, therefore, not wholly a surprise when a month or so later, in January 1980, the news was given to me that I could go ahead. (I have always believed that I was lucky in the coincidence that, almost simultaneously, an announcement had surfaced in the Press that Alistair Horne had been engaged to write an authorised one-volume biography of Harold Macmillan.)

Nevertheless Lord Butler's decision was an illustration of his independent spirit. He was under no illusion that I was a supporter of, or even a sympathiser with, the Conservative Party: he had, in fact, as he confirmed to *The Times* on 31 January 1980, deliberately chosen to make 'an unorthodox choice'.

Elsewhere it was undoubtedly seen as an eccentric one. As a political reporter, I had observed Rab Butler only in the last half-dozen years of his parliamentary career. I cannot pretend that everything I wrote about him was complimentary (or probably even fair): indeed, until in 1963 he sent me a message through my editor (then John Freeman of the *New Statesman*) that my work would be much improved if I actually went to see him, I had never presumed to seek an audience with him.

From the Press Gallery I had none the less watched Rab Butler as often as I could. He fascinated but at the same time mystified me – which was one reason why the idea of writing his biography so strongly appealed to me.

It soon proved an intimidating task. At Trinity College, Cambridge alone there were some 200 boxes containing his papers, both official and personal. I started working through them in the autumn of 1980 and also then began interviewing Lord Butler's surviving political colleagues and associates.

It is, I know, normal in this age of 'oral history' for any biographer to provide a list of all those to whom he has talked. I hope I shall be forgiven for breaching that convention: it is not only that there were many who wished to remain anonymous; it has also been, consistently, my experience that there is no more flawed source for recalling the events of yesterday than human recollection. In every case, where a conflict arose, I chose to prefer contemporary documentary evidence to personal memory. To contradict point by point what I had often been both confidentially and confidently told struck me as discourteous. I have, therefore, confined myself to giving attribution only to the quotations from interviews that actually appear in the text.

To some extent, Lord Butler himself provides an exception to that rule. He was very generous with both the time and attention he gave me during the last three years of his life – and his widow, Mollie, Lady Butler, fully maintained that tradition of co-operation after his death on 8 March 1982. I owe an enormous debt to both of them.

A number of other individuals deserve my gratitude. My secretary, Isabel Maycock, impeccably typed every word of the manuscript – too many of them, I fear, more than once. The Master and Fellows of Trinity College, Cambridge afforded me their hospitality for more weekends and (latterly) weeks than they or I had probably at first anticipated. The staff of Trinity College Library were unfailingly helpful and I could never have finished this book even in six years without the invaluable work of Alex Saunders in cataloguing the whole collection of Butler Papers. William Keegan, economics editor of the *Observer*, kindly read Chapter 12 on the Treasury and offered most constructive comments and advice, as did David Clarke (former director of the Conservative Research Department) on Chapter 11.

Only two people cheerfully sentenced themselves to reading the entire manuscript. Lord Fraser of Kilmorack, whose thirty years in both the Research Department and the Central Office provides one of the few threads of continuity in post-war Tory politics, freely made available to me the whole benefit of his wisdom and experience. I owe as much to him as to anybody, except perhaps for my *Observer* colleague, Simon Hoggart, who not only read but annotated the whole MS with forthright criticisms of my prose style. Any infelicities that remain are entirely my own responsibility – as, of course, are all inaccuracies, misjudgments and failings of understanding.

ANTHONY HOWARD
October 1986

Acknowledgments

For permission to reproduce illustrations the author and publishers would like to thank: Associated Press (nos 20, 22, 25); BBC Hulton Picture Library (nos 10, 12–13, 33); Lady Butler of Saffron Walden (nos 9, 11, 14, 16–19, 24, 26, 29, 32, 38, 40); *Cambridge Evening News* (no. 36); *Daily Telegraph* (no. 41); Neil Libbert (no. 35); London Express News and Features Services (nos 27, 28, 30, and for 'The Last of England' by Vicky); *New Statesman* (for 'The Inimitable Jeeves' by Vicky); the *Observer* (for 'I become Prime Minister' by Trog); Photo Source (no. 21); Mrs Iris Portal (nos 1–8); Press Association (nos 15, 31, 37); *Scottish Daily Record and Sunday Mail* (no. 39); Sport and General Press Agency (no. 23); Thomson Newspapers (no. 42); Universal Pictorial Press (no. 34).

1 *Founding Fathers*

Richard Austen Butler was almost but not quite a Victorian. He was born in 1902 – the year after the old Queen died – but could claim, at least so far as his background was concerned, to be a product of the Victorian era. In fact, the Butlers might well be taken as exemplars of the age in which the middle and professional classes emerged as the backbone not just of Britain but of the Empire as well.

The family's involvement in public service came, however, only towards the end of the nineteenth century. Before that, the Butlers were predominantly academics, and exceptional ones. The first member of the family to become a Cambridge don was Richard Austen Butler's great-grandfather, George Butler, who, as Senior Wrangler, was elected a Fellow of Sidney Sussex in 1794 – and who started the connection with Cambridge that runs right through the Butler family's history.[1]

But George Butler did not merely found an academic bloodline (his father, though a London clergyman and headmaster of a Chelsea private school,[2] had not attended a university): he also, before even the days of Dr Arnold, bore witness to the growing preoccupation of the nineteenth century with education. In 1805, at the age of thirty-one (just in time to have Lord Byron as a pupil), he became headmaster of Harrow – staying there for twenty-four years and eventually dying as Dean of Peterborough in 1853, six years too soon to see the youngest of his four sons follow in his footsteps as headmaster of Harrow.*

* This same son, Henry Montagu Butler, was, in turn, nearly thirty years later to set another family precedent, eventually to be followed by his great-nephew, by becoming in 1886 Master of Trinity, in which office he remained until his death at the age of eighty-four in 1918.

Nor was that the only evidence that a quite remarkable family had come into being. Another of George Butler's four sons, Arthur Gray Butler, one of the very few members of the family to go to Oxford rather than Cambridge, also became a public school headmaster – this time of one of the proud products of Victorian educational reform, Haileybury. Although he subsequently had a nervous breakdown, he ended his career back at Oxford, first as Chaplain and Vice-Provost and then as an Honorary Fellow of Oriel.

The eldest of Dr Butler's four sons, named George after his father, also brought further distinction to the family, if only by reinforcing the clerical connection. After a lifetime of university and public school teaching, this second George, like his father, the Dean of Peterborough, before him, died as a dignitary of the Church of England, in his case as a Canon of Winchester (though his enduring claim to fame remains probably his marriage to the Victorian social reformer and pioneer of women's emancipation, Josephine Butler).

If there was a disappointment among 'the founding father's' four sons, it was perhaps the second son (and Richard Austen Butler's own grandfather), Spencer Perceval Butler. Named after the Prime Minister shot in the Lobby of the House of Commons in 1812 – two of the Prime Minister's sons had been pupils at Harrow and it had fallen to the great Dr George, while headmaster, to break the news of their father's death to them – Spencer Perceval Butler's very burden of Christian names perhaps presaged a life rather overshadowed from the start; and so, indeed, it turned out.

Such things, of course, are always relative, but in a family that had grown to admire worldly achievements being the first representative of the direct male line in three generations not to rate an entry in the *Dictionary of National Biography* tends to carry its own posthumous reproach. Spencer Perceval, though, fulfilled his Butler obligations in one respect: he went up to Trinity College, Cambridge, where he read Classics (being listed fifth in the Tripos – certainly the equivalent of a First today) and only strayed from the normal family *cursus honorum* by choosing the law rather than teaching or the Church as a profession. Alas, at the Bar he achieved little distinction, ending up not as a judge or a leading Chancery barrister but merely as Conveyancing Counsel to the Office of Works, before retiring to a somewhat gloomy house in Oxford, where he died just after the outbreak of the First World War.

In one sense, however, it was Spencer Perceval Butler who provided the bridge between the nineteenth-century academic Butlers and the twentieth-century public service ones. Having married at the age of thirty-five into a Cornish family with a long tradition of political service behind it, he and his wife, Mary Kendall (who, at the time of the marriage, was only seventeen), went on to have thirteen children (eleven of whom survived infancy). Nine were sons and four of them were ultimately to receive knighthoods (with three redeeming their father's failure by securing their own entries into the *DNB*).*

Thus by the beginning of the twentieth century, and at the time of R. A. Butler's birth, the course of the Butler family had been fairly firmly set. At Trinity College, Cambridge, in the Master's Lodge, there still reigned the patriarchal figure of Henry Montagu Butler – the same man who at the age of twenty-six in 1859 had succeeded the great Dr Vaughan as headmaster of Harrow and who, when he left a quarter of a century later, was said to have made the school into 'a miniature Parnassus';[3] still surviving at Oxford, though having just resigned his official Fellowship at Oriel, was the other ex-headmaster, from Haileybury, Arthur Gray Butler, with perhaps his most valuable work in bringing the munificence of Cecil Rhodes to the service of his college, the university and the Empire still to be done; up in Northumberland, though now living in virtual seclusion since the death of her husband at Winchester in 1890, was Josephine Butler with a tireless record of social and penal reform behind her; while toiling away at conveyancing in Lincoln's Inn was the uncelebrated Spencer Perceval Butler[4] – ironically, however, the somewhat improbable second 'founding father' of the Butler dynasty.

* The four sons of Spencer Perceval Butler honoured with knighthoods were: Sir Cyril Butler, who made a successful career in the City, Sir Harcourt and Sir Montagu Butler, both of whom joined the Indian Civil Service rising to be provincial governors and Sir Geoffrey Butler, a Fellow of Corpus Christi College, Cambridge for seventeen years and an MP for Cambridge University, 1923–9. The last three are in the *Dictionary of National Biography*.

2 *Child of the Empire*

Whatever money Spencer Perceval Butler managed to earn at the Bar must, it seems, have been spent on his children's – or rather his sons' – education. Although the first two of his sons went to Harrow (where their uncle was still headmaster), of the remaining seven boys two went to Rugby, three to Haileybury, one to Clifton, and one to the Royal Naval College, Dartmouth. There is some sign, indeed, that more importance may have been attached, in the best Victorian tradition, to the character-building qualities of a good public school than to the mere intellectual attainments of a university – since three of Spencer's sons, including the eldest, Cyril, enjoyed the former without the latter (it is only fair, perhaps, to add that Cyril turned out to be the only one of the nine brothers to go on to a career of wealth).

Montagu Butler, the third son and the father of Rab* (as I shall from now on call him), was, however, a faithful apprentice to the family tradition. Not only did he proceed on a scholarship from Haileybury to Pembroke College, Cambridge: he also covered himself with glory there, gaining a double First in Classics (with a special distinction in Part II) as well as winning the Presidency of the Union. Not surprisingly, he was immediately offered at the age of twenty-two a fellowship by his college – which he at first took up, only to relinquish it a year later (in 1896) on passing top in the Indian Civil Service examinations. The decision to leave Cambridge was not an easy one and was, no doubt, influenced by the fact that his older

* According to Lord Butler's own memoirs, his Christian names – Richard Austen – were deliberately chosen by his father in order to provide him with 'a useful sobriquet for life'. *The Art of the Possible* (Hamish Hamilton, 1971), p. 9.

brother, Harcourt,* had already followed the same path to India (though without any equivalent academic distinction) six years earlier. If sacrifice was involved – and it certainly was in Monty Butler's case – then it only serves to indicate that priorities within the Butler family were already beginning to change.

Monty Butler's distinguishing characteristic was, in fact, a highly developed sense of duty – a stern, unbending quality which his marriage in 1901 to an altogether more extrovert figure, Ann Smith (the daughter of a Scottish Presbyterian family with Indian connections reaching back over two generations), could occasionally dent but never quite destroy. It was, though, as things turned out, an extremely happy and wholly complementary match which was to survive for over fifty years until the two partners died within a year of each other in 1952–3, when their elder son was already Chancellor of the Exchequer.

Rab (Richard Austen) arrived before the marriage was two years old, on 9 December 1902. He was born in a rest-house attached to the fort at Attock guarding the junction of the Indus and the Kabul Rivers and separating the North-West Frontier Province from the Punjab. There Monty Butler, though still under thirty, was the revenue official (or Settlement Officer) – though it was hardly into any grand imperial lifestyle that the baby was introduced. His maternal uncle, Sir James Dunlop Smith, may have been Private Secretary to the Viceroy – but Calcutta (then the capital of British India), or even Simla, were many days' journey from the Punjab, where conditions remained very primitive (though not as primitive as Kotah State, where Monty Butler moved next as Settlement Officer in 1904). Nor was it in any way an affluent household into which the first child of the marriage was born. Of course, since it was India and the turn of the century, there were servants – of whom an austere Aberdonian nanny and a majestic Hindu bearer were to have the most direct impact on the boy's early childhood: but household staff was then the rule rather than the exception – and economy was to be the watchword throughout the upbringing of all four of Monty Butler's children.

If any one of them was spoiled it was possibly Rab, as what was known in those days as 'the son and heir'. Certainly, his sister, Iris – born just over two years after him – would complain even in her old age that, whereas she was regularly smacked by their formidable

* Sir Harcourt Butler, whose ICS career always tended to overshadow that of his younger brother, eventually became Governor both of the United Provinces and of Burma (twice). He died in London in 1938.

Scottish nanny, 'Rab never was';[1] and there seems little doubt that no other member of the family – there were eventually two sons and two daughters – was ever to replace the first-born in at least their mother's affections.

It is hard, if not impossible, nowadays to summon back the strange home life led by children of the Empire. In most cases the earliest years were normal enough, since there were never any inhibitions about children being born in India; the harsh decisions about separation, dictated by what was believed to be the debilitating effect of the climate on the young but rather more, in fact, to do with the imperative of acquiring an English education, came later, generally about the ages of six or seven. Then, inevitably, a choice had to be made and nearly always the duty of a wife was placed before that of a mother. The children of the relevant age were simply shipped home – normally into the care of various relatives (through whose hands they would be passed like a parcel during the school holidays) – while the wife continued with her social and child-bearing activities at her husband's side.

However, in Monty Butler's family the separation turned out to be less abrupt than it was in most cases.* Not only were the two elder children kept rather longer in India than was customary – Monty Butler had been promoted to be Deputy Commissioner at Lahore in 1909, where conditions were a good deal more 'Westernised' than they had been in Kotah State; but when the ultimate break had to come, it was made in a much more gradual way than usual. Indeed, for four years between 1912 and 1916, the entire family was able to live, if peripatetically, in England. This was due to Monty Butler's appointment as Secretary to the Royal Commission on Public Services in India – or what was known at the time as the Islington Commission, after its chairman, the first Baron Islington, who subsequently became Under-Secretary of State for India.

A year or two before that, however, the first shadow had fallen over the young Deputy Commissioner's household. Every spring, following the Indian Civil Service custom, Ann Butler took her children, their nanny and sundry other domestics up to the Viceregal hill-town of Simla in order to avoid the summer heat of the plains. It was there, when he was six, that an accident took place which was to have an enduring impact on Rab's career.

The story is perhaps best told in Rab's mother's own words,

* c.f. Philip Williams, *Hugh Gaitskell* (Jonathan Cape, 1979), p. 5. 'Apart from one exceptional year, Hugh's entire childhood from the age of two and a half was spent boarded out with relations or at boarding schools.'

writing to her husband still down in the plains. The accident took place on Sunday 22 July 1909 and the very next day Ann sent a report on it to Monty:

> Just after I'd written to you yesterday Austen [the sobriquet had plainly not yet stuck] got a toss from the pony and has broken his right arm in all three bones. I have very nearly not told you – you have so much to worry you and I long to spare you but I think you would be vexed not to know. Besides, you need not worry. If it had to be, it has been in the most fortunate way . . . . Austen was trotting so well and getting quite keen so he told the syce 'chords' [meaning 'Let go the reins'] and then, as he explained it, 'Prince went one way and I went another.'[2]

The Aberdonian nanny behaved very sensibly, taking Rab straight to the Walker Military Hospital, where, after an hour's delay – waiting for the arrival of a doctor – the arm, with the aid of chloroform, was set in all three places and put into wooden splints. That same afternoon the doctor reported, according to Ann's letter to Monty, 'there won't possibly be permanent injury'.[3]

He spoke, alas, too soon. The arm did not heal even when the splints were taken off and replaced by a plaster cast; worse, blisters caused by the unwise application of a hotwater bottle at the hospital had left bad, red sores. Three weeks later Ann had to break the news to her husband that 'some bone is pressing on the nerves of the hand so that A has no feeling beyond the wrist'. Even more alarmingly, the Army doctor was now admitting 'he has not got the arm quite straight so we are to tie a 1 lb weight to his hand'.[4]

Perhaps predictably, given such primitive medical methods, the arm never fully recovered and the hand was thereafter to hang limply at the wrist, making not just orthodox games-playing but any form of military service out of the question. When the degree and permanent nature of the injury became apparent, the sorrow initially seems to have been more the father's than the son's;* but it was a heavy handicap for any man to carry through life – and a particular liability, perhaps, for a politician since the hand that hung awkwardly was the right one and handshakes (part of the stock-in-trade of the glad-handing politician) always afterwards posed a problem.

* 'My father's sorrow was terrible. He was brought up in the public school tradition and felt that my whole future as an athlete would be prejudiced. Indeed this proved to be so.' *The Art of the Possible*, p. 7.

It was not, however, the accident that prompted Ann Butler to bring her three children (a second daughter, Dorothy, had been born at Lahore) home to England in 1911. That move was necessitated by the need to place Rab at a prep school – and such schools traditionally began their pupils' training at the age of eight. The Butlers were sufficient believers in education not to wish to miss any of its benefits for their own son – and accordingly at the beginning of 1911 Rab left India, not to return for another fifteen years. He was next to see the country of his birth on his honeymoon.

Everything, though, was done to make his acclimatisation to an entirely new environment as easy as possible. Although Monty Butler remained for the time being at his post in Lahore, the rest of the family (including nanny – the newest addition to the family meant she had a fresh baby to look after) sailed from Bombay together. When they arrived in England, their first task was to settle Rab into his prep school, and that, again, was done with a kindness and gentleness perhaps unusual for that age. The chosen scholastic forcing-ground was a school called The Wick at Hove run by a brother and sister, Laurence and Mary Thring, who were related to the famous headmaster of Uppingham. To aid her son's adjustment to educational methods far more formal than any he had known before, Ann Butler – whom India seems to have turned into a much less conventional character than most Edwardian mothers – promptly took a house in Hove to oversee the assimilation process. She soon made personal friends of the Thrings (her second son would be sent to the same school ten years later) and was frequently to be found playing the piano or otherwise lending a hand at school theatricals or concerts.

The children were, in fact, lucky in their mother, who, though she had a tendency to be impulsive, especially when it came to renting not altogether suitable holiday homes, was always able to provide the warmth and affection that their father found it difficult to show. She was thirty-five when she brought her family back to England and it was, perhaps naturally, to their Scottish relatives that the children were first introduced. In Edinburgh lived their maternal grandfather, George Smith, who himself had gone out to India to teach over half a century earlier and who had gone on to be editor of a Calcutta paper then called the *Friend of India* and today the *Statesman*: for fifteen years he had been *The Times*'s correspondent in India and, back at home in Edinburgh, was now an occasional leader-writer for the *Scotsman*. As well as his daughter, Ann, George Smith had nine other children – two or three of whom were to play influential parts in the 'wandering minstrel' lives of Rab, his sisters and (eventually) his younger brother.

In Aberdeen, where he was Principal of the University, there was George Adam Smith, later to be Moderator of the General Assembly of the United Free Church of Scotland, and a renowned Old Testament scholar. His home – Chanonry Lodge in Old Aberdeen – was to be over the next dozen years a regular point of pilgrimage, especially during the summer holidays. Then in London were a Smith uncle and two Smith aunts – Uncle Dunlop who had been Secretary to the Earl of Minto when he was Viceroy and who, having been a widower since 1902, lived with his sister, Aunt Minnie, at 25 Ovington Square; and, on the other side of the Park, at 21 Ladbroke Square, Aunt Kate, married to Bernard Townsend (whose father, Meredith, had been editor of the *Spectator*). All three of these houses were to become very familiar refuges to the Butler children as they grew up, with Ovington Square, in particular, operating as their London base.

There was another family house, however, which – perhaps more than any other – they regarded as home. If the second and third sons of Spencer Perceval Butler had gone to India to seek their fortunes, the eldest son, Cyril, had (as we have seen) stayed in England – where he, rather more successfully, found his. Like his father, he was called to the Bar but thereafter sought a career in the City, where he prospered. Married to an heiress, Mary Pease ('Aunt May') the only daughter of wealthy parents from the famous Darlington Quaker family, he was able, while a comparatively young man, to buy a landed estate at Bourton, near Shrivenham, in Berkshire. It was there that Ann Butler, after initial stays at Cambridge and Hove and a visit to Scotland, took her brood of children even before her husband had arrived from India to begin his duties with the Islington Commission.

They did not, however, stay in the great house. Instead they were loaned a small property in the village which, having formerly been the home of the local Nonconformist Minister, was known as 'The Manse'. It was a small and inconvenient house and, once Monty had arrived from India and the fourth (and last) child, John Perceval, had been born in 1914, it became a tighter and tighter squeeze for the entire family to fit in. Maybe that is why, at least in Rab's own memories in later years, 'The Manse' tended to be elided into the broad and rolling acres of his uncle's own estate across the road.[5] Nevertheless, once Monty (who went first) and then mother, nanny and the two young children had returned to India in November 1916,

Bourton House itself did become, at least for the two elder children, their nearest approach to a home in England – even if Rab's sister, Iris, does recall once asking to be allowed to take away a doll and being firmly told, 'No, darling, you see it is not yours.'

Just how much the sense of separation, and the simple feeling of not really belonging anywhere, affected successive children of the Empire must always remain a matter for psychological conjecture. From Rab's own childhood, an easier one than many, the most marked legacy appears to have been an astonishing degree of early maturity. Even as a prep schoolboy – when his mother (and, later, his father) were still in England – his letters to them tended to be a good deal more serious-minded than one might expect in a boy of eleven or twelve. In those that survive, written from The Wick between 1914 and 1916, the emphasis is very much on lectures delivered at the school rather than on athletics or games (his damaged arm, of course, though it did not prevent him playing both soccer and rugby, could in itself be an explanation for that). None the less they do provide evidence of a strange sense of detachment of the kind that many years later was to typify, and even thwart, his political career. His only apparent reaction, for example, to the outbreak of the First World War was the announcement that on a drive, taken after a spell in the school sanatorium, 'we saw some recruits shooting and others punching bags with their bayonets – they looked awfully funny'.[6] A year later, however, the drama of the war does seem to have impinged even on a twelve-year-old's consciousness. Included in the Butler Papers at Cambridge is a short note from Monty Butler headed simply 'In France', and announcing that the former Secretary of the Islington Commission (its work ended in 1914) had 'had a great time here and seen a lot'.[7] It was the only letter from his father – complete with the envelope marked 'Field Post Office' and the stamp 'Passed by Censor' – that the young Rab was to preserve from his schooldays.

3 *Marlborough and Cambridge*

Rab left The Wick in July 1916. An effort to win an Eton Scholarship having come to nothing* – the school had apparently advised against it but Rab, encouraged by his mother,† persisted in the attempt all the same – he was finally settled at Marlborough. The choice was a surprising one. Marlborough had never been one of the Butler family schools – though his cousin on his mother's side, the First World War poet, Charles Sorley (killed in action in the Battle of Loos in 1915), had just been there. It was also conveniently near Bourton and that seems to have been counted a substantial factor in its favour. The main ground for the choice was, however, negative rather than positive. Rab had all along been intended for Harrow – where, indeed, a place had been kept for him in a house presided over by a Butler family connection and where two Butler cousins were already established. Even the best-laid parental plans can, though, often go adrift, and this one did; although not yet fourteen, Rab had his own feelings about the two Butler cousins concerned and resolutely refused to go to Harrow if it meant joining them (with the younger of them, who had been with him at The Wick, he was

* There is a touching tale of this rather sad episode in Rab's own memoirs. 'I fancied myself for an Eton Scholarship, and so did my mother, but my schoolmaster was very discouraging. However, I went up and sat the papers. At the end of the second day a man in a gown read the names of those who were requested to stay and continue. Mine was not included. I went and spoke to him, asking if there had been a mistake; he said there had not.' *The Art of the Possible* (Hamish Hamilton, 1971), p. 9.

† Ann Butler, who supportively accompanied him to Eton, gave an affecting description of their son's disappointment in two letters to Rab's father, already back in India, predicting falsely as events turned out, 'I think he will not do anything big in the exam line, ever.' Family Papers held by Dorothy Middleton, letter dated 10.6.1916.

originally booked to share a study). It was a small, though significant, rebellion – and one which Rab, in later life, was always to look back upon with a certain amount of pride (the fact that he carried the day, however, was almost certainly more due to his mother's characteristic support than to any lonely resolution on his part).

In any event, the outcome was far from fortunate. Marlborough, in the middle of the First World War, was a school where academic standards had tended to slip and where what motivation survived from the pre-war era centred on a rather rugged form of athleticism; the school had just been through a difficult nine-month interregnum between headmasters and the new Master of Marlborough, Dr Cyril Norwood[1] (who was later to do great things after a formidable battle with the Governing Body), arrived in only the same term as Rab. Schoolboys' letters being what they are, there is little direct evidence that Rab was actively unhappy during his five years there, but he made singularly little mark on the school (and the school, in turn, appears to have had remarkably little enduring impact on him).*

It was not the easiest period of his life. Solicitous as always, his mother had remained in England long enough to see him into his public school,† but he had barely been at the school two months before, at the age of thirteen, he learned for the first time just what it meant to be 'a son of the Raj'. His mother sailed for India at the beginning of November and he was not to see her again – or his younger brother and sister – for another two and a half years. If he found consolation, it was perhaps in developing a certain wry, amused outlook on life. Thus his earliest surviving letter from Marlborough includes the announcement, 'Today is another half-hol. on account of some sportsman – St Luke, the evangelist, I believe.'[2] And that spirit of irreverence is maintained throughout most of his correspondence with his parents during his entire Marlborough career.

Some eight months later, for example, a further letter sent to India contains a splendidly ironic description of a school field day (though some might find its tone surprising, given that it was written during a war in which militarism seldom came under question):

* Somewhat to his chagrin, Rab, even in the years of his great political distinction, was never invited to become a Governor of Marlborough, although he served on the governing bodies of two other public schools, Felsted and Westminster.

† A full year later she was to recall in a letter from Campbellpore, India, how 'when I left you at the gate across the fields, I went on to the station for town and India. The whole place looked so lovely and I often wonder now how ever I'd the courage to leave you.' Butler Papers, Trinity College, Cambridge, A65, letter dated 'Boxing Day' 1917.

> Last Wednesday Colonel Mangle from the War Office came down to inspect the corps; this was the real inspection from the War Office. We had it upon the Common again and marched in triumph through the town. He said that we were very 'steady' on parade ('steady' is a stock word for generals inspecting, it means 'kept very still') and he also said that we were very good in marching past. He made us do crowds of things. The Junior Company and C Company had to take a wood, where there was nobody. We advanced in open order to within about 400 yards, then our platoon, which was in support with one other, doubled up to reinforce and we all set up as much noise as we could and charged the wood. He seemed quite pleased – such is a general![3]

Not many Marlburians of that wartime period would, one suspects, have been capable of that particular brand of flippant cynicism. And at school, that may, of course, have been part of Rab's undoing. Indeed, a letter from his housemaster to his father was later to speak of his 'not being ambitious enough'[4] (a cardinal sin in the public school ethic), while a subsequent school report was to be dismissed by his mother as 'a hollow fraud, it must have been meant for the other Butler, anyhow it doesn't matter'.[5]

Not that Rab was a total failure at school. One of Cyril Norwood's innovations was to make Marlborough one of the first public schools to adapt its curriculum to the system of external joint-board examinations; and in August 1918 Rab effortlessly passed his School Certificate, gaining credits in History, Latin, French, Elementary Mathematics and the English Essay (it is also possibly worthy of record, given his former scepticism about the corps, that before he left in 1920 he also passed top in the whole School in the OTC Certificate 'A' examination). Nor was he himself fully inoculated against the public school ethos. One of his letters, written on 11 November 1918, having disposed of the Armistice, goes on to reveal that 'a boy's father has just brought down four most awful pictures – such as you might see in the schoolroom of any board school';[6] while, when the time came for Confirmation, his message to his parents was, again, resignedly conformist – 'I think it would be best for me to be done with all the others next term'.[7]

Allowing for all that, though – and, indeed, for the fact that he finally, if only in his last term, became a School Prefect – it is hard to resist the conclusion that Rab, like Osbert Sitwell before him, was really educated in the holidays. To begin with, there is no doubt that Uncle Dunlop's house in London had a great influence; if

Bourton provided opulence, Ovington Square offered education. Conditions there were certainly spartan – Rab, unlike his sister, Iris, who was given a bedroom of her own, had to sleep on a camp-bed in his Uncle Dunlop's den; but it was still a house full of echoes of India. On Sunday evenings, Indian Princes would come to supper in their war uniforms with turbans on their heads and the two children would be allowed to stay up and meet them. Even on ordinary evenings, Uncle Dunlop would read aloud from Kipling and explain to his two juvenile listeners more perhaps than they had ever previously understood about India.[8]

Rab's interests, however, were already spreading beyond the sub-continent in which he was born. At about the time he was sadly confessing, after failing to get his House hockey colours and pulling a stomach muscle in a cross-country run, 'I am already realising that if one is not meant to be a gamester, one is not',[9] he was also beginning to turn his mind to a future beyond the playing-fields of a public school. The first indication of a genuine notion about his career intentions (beyond a juvenile fancy to join the Sappers and become an Army Engineer) surfaces in a surprisingly mature, and slightly priggish, letter he wrote to his parents, now back in England, shortly before his eighteenth birthday, 'Although you make money in business, the idea of the Diplomatic and HM Service appeals to one as finer somehow than being an individual on one's own wearing a dark grey suit and butterfly collar and knowing the purlieus of the City by heart.'[10] To a pre-eminently public-spirited proconsular father – with more than a trace of contempt for the ways of business (as symbolised by his eldest brother's wealth) – that was not the kind of hint to go unheeded. A week after his eighteenth birthday, Rab had left Marlborough and arrangements had been made for him to spend the next five months (as was the custom in those days for aspirants to the Diplomatic Service) learning French in the household of a Protestant pastor in Abbeville near Amiens, in northern France. Rab's cosmopolitan education had begun.

The first stage of it, admittedly, does not appear to have been particularly enjoyable. Even after the rigours of Marlborough, there were immediate complaints about the food and the living conditions: the sanitary arrangements were found 'pretty disgusting' and there was shock at being allowed 'only one hot bath a week in a dirty tin bath'.[11] From this rather bleak existence, however, Rab was eventually rescued by securing a post as tutor to the eleven-year-old son of Baron Robert de Rothschild, a pillar of the French banking family. The contrast between the austere way of life at Abbeville and the sybaritic environment of Deauville, where the Baron had a holiday home, could hardly have been sharper; and, once again, the early letters to his mother still at home register culture shock – 'Money is here in everything you see or touch, but if they take a taxi, they would argue with the man if too much . . . To call them the "nouveau riche" or "Jew" type would be rot, but they certainly keep a firm hold of it.'[12] The Rothschild son, Alain,* proved a cheerful, if somewhat recalcitrant, pupil – but Rab himself appears to have been a great success with the family, being invited back the succeeding summer, though this time more as a guest than as a tutor. The admiration also seems to have been mutual: certainly by the time the first stay with the Rothschilds ended even the initial reservations are banished and Rab is to be found simply announcing, 'One thing quite certain is that there is nothing in this house and family I would wish to scoff at.'[13]

The most important business of the summer of 1921, though, took place at home rather than abroad. In June, between his two very different stays in France, Rab returned to England to take the scholarship exam at his father's old college, Pembroke. It was, in his own words, 'a big, long affair' stretching over a full weekend from a Friday to a Monday; but it ended in success with the award of an Exhibition, secured principally by a sterling performance in the French papers (in its own way, no doubt, a tribute to the five rugged months spent under the pastor at Abbeville). It was just as well that Rab did not come away from the exam empty-handed: not only were Butlers expected to win awards; even more to the point, despite his rising distinction within the ICS (he had just been appointed President of the Punjab Legislative Council), Monty Butler's prime preoccupation continued to be money, or rather the need to husband it carefully. In fact, the very first letter Rab received from his father, on taking up residence at Pembroke in October 1921, was concerned with very little else – as, indeed, was the second one (which, quaintly, included the observation, 'I always think what Kitchener of Khartoum must have enjoyed most in his Sudan campaign was doing it all within the money allotted to him – a thing few generals ever do').[14] Certainly, Monty Butler had the full Victorian belief in thrift; indeed, he was inclined to elevate it into the Queen of the Virtues. When his son had almost finished at Cambridge he was still insisting that 'Keeping within one's income is the really

* Later Baron Alain de Rothschild, a recognised leader of the French Jewish Community. He died in New York in October 1982.

important thing' (adding, for good measure, the somewhat chilly rider, 'Then, if misfortune comes, one can always keep within a lesser income.')[15]

Fortunately, Rab turned out not to share his father's parsimonious – not to say pessimistic – outlook on life, though the Cambridge years (before all such problems were solved for him) were certainly something of a struggle. He was given an allowance of just £300 a year which was meant to cover everything – and there were, not surprisingly, occasional complaints as to just how expensive holidays could prove for a young man left on his own. (His mother returned to India, taking his older sister Iris with her, leaving him in charge of the two youngest children, who were now at English schools, in September 1922.) Not that he was entirely without means of family support even within the university: his uncle, Geoffrey Butler, was a Fellow of Corpus Christi College, another uncle-by-marriage, William Ritchie Sorley (the father of the First World War poet) was a Fellow of King's while a cousin, James Ramsay Montagu Butler, was a Fellow of Trinity and just on the point of being elected to the House of Commons as an Independent Member for the university. It was, in fact, through this last kinsman – or at least on his coat-tails – that the young Rab was to make his first mark on the Cambridge Union (as the dutiful scribe of the *Cambridge Review* recorded in his report on a debate about Ireland held on 8 November 1921), 'Mr J. R. M. Butler, ex-President, made a very lucid and reasoned speech and advocated the removal of our troops from Northern Ireland. This speech was attacked by a relative of his from Pembroke in a good maiden.'[16]

It was perhaps bad luck for the aspiring Union office-holder that his very first contribution to a Union debate should have been preserved for posterity in that semi-anonymous fashion; but he himself was delighted by the whole experience, writing excitedly to his father that same night, 'I leapt up just after Jim . . . and it was quite a success. I got several people to realise who I was.'[17]

In fact Rab, who had already confided to his father his intention to try and win the Presidency if he could, got off to a flying start in the Union, gaining favourable mentions for his subsequent speeches both in *Granta* and the *Cambridge Review* ('Mr Butler should go far,' the latter reported after his first 'paper' speech, adding magisterially, 'His delivery already leaves but little to be desired').[18] By the end of his first year he was successful in the elections for the Union Committee, and a year later had got himself on the guaranteed

1 Outpost of the Empire: Rab with his sister, Iris (on pony), in Kotah State

2 An imperial outing: Rab, Iris and their Aberdonian nanny

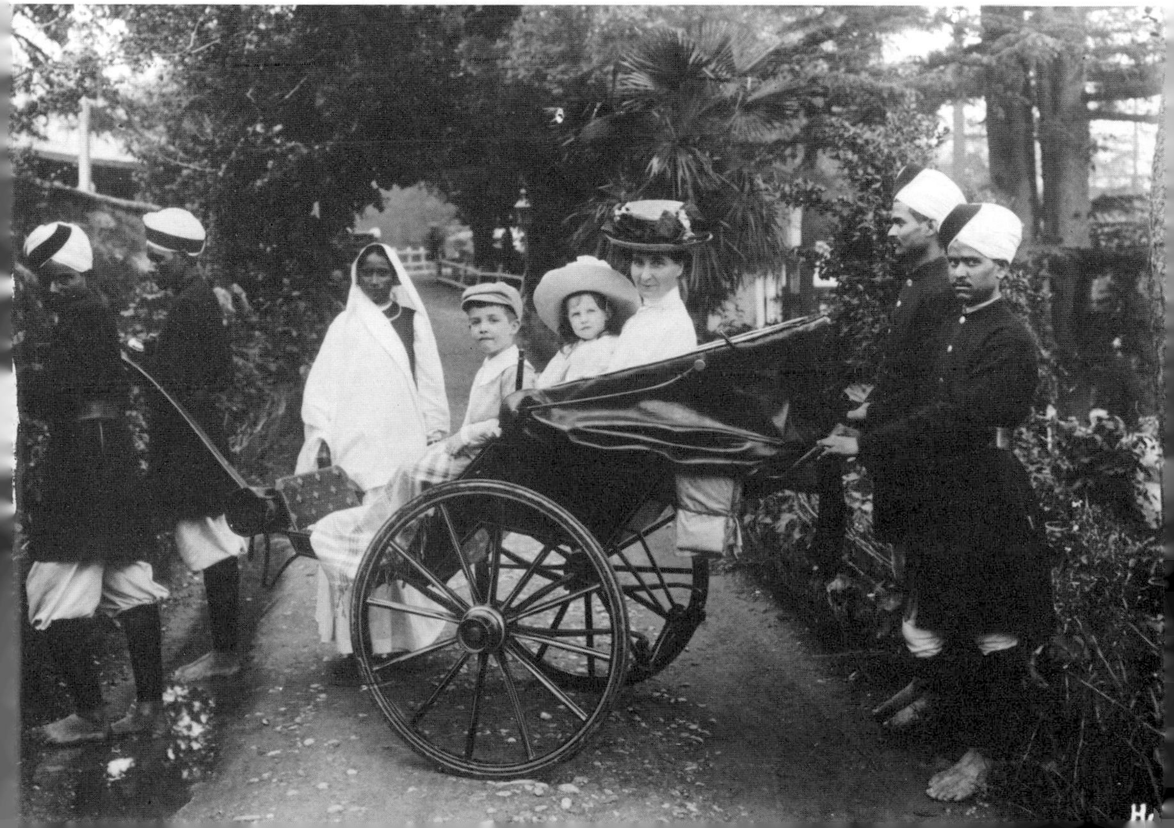

3 The frontiersman: Rab at the age of six, playing with soldiers just before his accident

4 Fancy-dress party at Viceregal Lodge, Simla. Rab is sitting on the chair with his sister, Iris, the little girl with her hair up, on his right

path to the President's chair by winning, at his second attempt, the Secretaryship (the only office normally contested in Cambridge), if by a lucky margin of ten votes out of 500.

Perhaps surprisingly, given his slightly irreverent schoolboy past, Rab emerged from the beginning in university politics as a Conservative; the whole weight of his family tradition was, of course, on that side and it may simply be that it never occurred to him to question the values which he had inherited. Nevertheless his sceptical spirit – and in particular his mischievous sense of humour in face of more conventional Conservative attitudes – was apparent even as an undergraduate. One of his greatest successes in the Union – and a speech that he always believed was instrumental in getting him elected to the Secretaryship the following term – came in a debate on 6 March 1923 in which he championed the cause of British agriculture against the assaults of the 'cheap food' Free Traders. He reported on the occasion to his parents in India without any undue modesty – 'I got over agriculture satisfactorily last night' – but then (in a typical Butlerian shaft) could not resist adding, 'Opinions now only differ as to the amount of land I really do own in Berkshire.'[19]

It was not only politically, however, that Rab was growing up. That particular debate was important for quite another reason: sitting listening to him in the gallery was one of his Scottish cousins, Kathleen (Adam) Smith,* the second of the four daughters of the Principal of Aberdeen University. Rab had already written to his parents in February 1923 announcing that the Adam Smith family were due to make 'joint and separate invasions of the Granta's banks'[20] – but there had been little, or no, forewarning of where his own interests lay. Indeed, when Kathleen Smith first arrived at the beginning of February to stay at the home of her aunt, Janetta Sorley, the wife of the Fellow of King's and Knightbridge Professor of Philosophy, the references to her are disarmingly casual ('K is coming on Wednesday and Thursday, which will prove a pleasant distraction');[21] but by the following month, when Rab delivered his Union speech, things had clearly progressed apace. 'K', as Rab always called her, was accompanying him everywhere – from local steeplechases to the Pitt Club Ball; and, even more ominously, her own letters to Rab's mother had begun to display a distinctly possessive tone – in fact on the day of, and the day after, the Union

* Isabel Kathleen Buchanan Smith, though she never used her first name. Born in 1900, she married in 1924 and died in 1941.

speech she wrote two separate letters, each betraying a good deal more than a simple cousinly affection.[22]

If, however, the alarm bells ever began to ring in Lahore, they were soon to be muffled. For only four days later Rab himself was to write an uncharacteristic letter to his mother in which, for once, he abandoned flippancy and dwelt on his genuine feelings. The letter is also illuminating in that it gives a rare glimpse of the sense of loneliness of a twenty-year-old left to cope with responsibilities well beyond those of most of his contemporaries. It is, therefore, worth quoting almost in full:

March 11 1923

Dearest M.,

I have such heaps to tell you and to talk to you about and the medium of vellum, pen and ink is not sufficient. I do wish you could all be here and mix in, or that these distances could be lessened. I sometimes feel so awfully responsible alone, whether it be in big undertakings, in adventures or in little incidents. I feel I am devouring life at a rate.

Aunt J [Janetta Sorley] said at lunch today that she had a great sheaf of news to send you. I often wonder what impression you get of me and my doings from correspondence which does not emanate from me. I cannot hope to tell you all I feel and see and do . . .

Tomorrow I dine with Uncle Will [William Ritchie Sorley]. He and Aunt J have looked on with great mercy and compassion as I whirl in my vortex. They were good in letting me see so much of K. K and I have got beyond the usual compromise and found something better. It is hard to make you understand on this bit of paper. It is the last thing one wants on the house-tops. We both like big things and have many affinities. We have come to a wonderful 'parceque c'est toi, parceque c'est moi' understanding, as Montaigne says in his 'Essais'.

She is a dear and things had got so deep that I am sure someone was meant to help. I cannot analyse it any more. I am only crudely writing this to you, Mother, as we must try and bridge the distance somehow and you can help by understanding. We have both decided that we are going forth on a higher and better quest and we have both been much helped. It has been a wonderful experience and I am no longer a Puritan and she has realised that people can understand, though nobody really seemed to before . . . You don't know how perfectly calm we both felt when we

> said goodbye at Ely. I feel everything is more worthwhile, I have a greater appreciation of Beauty and I feel so much surer; recriminations have passed . . .

That was not, however, true of regrets – and there seems little doubt that, in Rab's case at least, the intense, if brief, love affair with K was to leave something of a scar. And the same may have been true of Kathleen herself. Why, then, did the relationship so swiftly break up? The main difficulty apparently arose from the complication that they were cousins* – though the fact that Kathleen was over two years older than Rab and that he was in no position to contemplate even getting engaged may have played its part. When sixteen months later Kathleen did get engaged, to a man eight years older than herself (G. P. Thomson, the distinguished scientist son of the then Master of Trinity, J. J. Thomson), Rab received a letter warning him of the engagement three days in advance. He passed the news on to his mother bleakly, with the barest comment. Thereafter he tended to deflect all invitations to stay with his uncle and aunt in Aberdeen.

Meanwhile his Cambridge career continued to prosper. In June 1923 his election to the Secretaryship of the Union was almost immediately followed by his getting a First in Part I of the French Tripos. His college, Pembroke, promptly awarded him an £80 scholarship, while his father managed to manifest his pleasure by dispatching a cheque for just £10. Not that that in any way tempered Rab's understandably buoyant mood. 'I shall', he wrote to his father, for once risking a boast, 'be glad to be able to fulfil your wish for a three-year Cambridge and President of the Union thrown in.'[23] Alas, one part of that prophecy was not to come true.

* The Butlers were great believers in eugenics – in fact a lateral connection, Sir Francis Galton (1822–1911), who had married one of the daughters of the original George Butler, was the founder of the science.

4 *The Courtauld Connection*

Rab spent his second Cambridge summer vacation in Austria as the paying guest of a German aristocratic family called Stolberg-Stolberg.* Although their own estates were in Germany, they had sought refuge across the border after the First World War and were now, like the pastor in Abbeville, seeking to eke out their modest subsistence by taking in English students. Rab's motive for going to them was, indeed, much the same as that which had led him to France two years earlier (he was now proposing to make German his subject in the second Part of his Tripos). A letter to his father, written from Austria, provides clear enough evidence of how at the time he viewed his future:

> You know how keen I am on the Diplomatic . . . I definitely do not want to do schoolmastering, my talents are not in that line. They are in mixing with great and interesting people and seeing life and getting the best out of it. I am fired by national as well as personal temperament and would be happiest in the reverberation and interclash of nations.[1]

The commitment to the Diplomatic Service was sufficiently firm for him to react warily to his father's alternative suggestion that, with a First in Part I of the Tripos behind him and a college scholarship already under his belt, he might wish to consider becoming an academic:

> You mention the chance of a Pembroke Fellowship. What am I

* Baron Robert de Rothschild had not invited Rab back because one of his schoolgirl daughters had developed a slightly embarrassing crush on him the previous year.

> to say? No one can really tell how great a possibility of this, I suppose the greatest prize of the University career, but in Pembroke do they not mean you to be one of the teaching staff? I repeat there is no means for R. A. Butler in Upper Austria, who had previously not considered this contingency as possible, to know whether thirteen well-rooted thoroughly British gentlemen have a pew to spare or would wish Mr Butler to occupy it.[2]

Yet all that, it soon transpired, was something of an evasion, for the letter went on rather more brutally:

> Then the same Mr Butler has tremors about the roots. Though capable of writing books and having, as is natural at the age of 20 years, several in the making, yet he is strongly opposed to writing a treatise on the Popes at Avignon in 1351 or discovering whether Charles VIII's admiration for Padua was founded on an aesthetic or erotic basis. Dad, I must do something active, something which is going to help the world of today and not that of yesterday . . . Pembroke dons are sleek and affable and content themselves with saying that the modern world is dirty. It may be, but there is much to be done.[3]

Eventually, of course, Rab did become a don – though only briefly and not in the end at Pembroke at all. The explanation for that, however, and, indeed, for his never even taking the Diplomatic Service exams, was to be found in a chance meeting at the beginning of his third year with an undergraduate at Newnham who, having met him just once, promptly asked him to tea on the second Sunday of term.[4]

Sydney Elizabeth Courtauld was not merely the only daughter but the sole child of Samuel Courtauld, who for more than twenty-five years ran the famous textile firm of that name.[5] In the early 1920s women were not accepted as full members of the university, but it was characteristic of Samuel Courtauld (an industrialist always rather in advance of his time) and of his wife, Lillian (who had a great interest in the arts, particularly in music) that they should have thought it the proper and natural thing for their daughter to become a graduate. Sydney had, in fact, been brought up to a belief in independence – remarkably, for that time, she always called her parents by their Christian names. At Newnham, though she was not outstandingly academically successful (taking a 2:2 in both parts of the History Tripos), she was regarded by her contemporaries very much as a leader of a modern-minded and determined women's generation.

Rab owed his first acquaintance with her to a couple of friends of his from prep school days – two brothers called John and Arthur Pedder – who, being her cousins, took him over in the summer of 1923 to the Courtauld family home, Stanstead Hall in Essex.* Initially, however, his interest in her appears to have been only cursory (the next mention of her after the tea-party is a slightly condescending reference to her as 'the cheery Sydney Courtauld up at Newnham')[6] – though that could have been merely the consequence of Rab by now being fully occupied with university politics. During the summer vacation he had attended a great international gathering of students in London which, in turn, led to him becoming involved in a surprisingly radical bid to get the Cambridge Union Society to affiliate to Britain's own National Union of Students. Predictably, it was a proposal that ran into a good deal of opposition within the Cambridge Union[7] – and it seems to have required all of Rab's developing powers of persuasion to overcome the 'diehards' and carry the day for his own recommendation. By the middle of November, however, he had succeeded in his objective, though not without some cost in personal strain to himself; his college insisted on his being put under the care of a doctor and his letters to his parents betray signs of his being on the brink of a breakdown. In fact, the same letter in which he proudly announces his victory on the NUS issue also includes an uncharacteristic passage disclosing a rare sense of resentment against Cambridge life itself:

> I wish I could get away from all this, and I will do. It's just the continual presiding and being present – all of it compulsory. I want to have a time when life isn't a continual vista of jumps and exams and after Cambridge I'm determined to stop the avalanche and say 'What's the hurry?'[8]

Until the end of that term, however, the avalanche continued and, indeed, tended to increase in momentum – with an NUS Congress at Birmingham (at which Rab found himself elected a Vice-President), heightened activity in the University Conservative Association at the time of the 1923 general election (in which Rab's uncle, Sir Geoffrey Butler of Corpus, was elected one of the two burgesses for

* In 1934, after the death of Sydney's mother, Stanstead Hall was to become Rab's own country home and remained so until he became Master of Trinity in 1965.

the University, defeating his cousin J. R. M. Butler of Trinity), to say nothing of Rab's own twenty-first birthday (which he celebrated with a dinner party for six, costing nearly all of £10, at London's Savoy Hotel).*

Eventually the Christmas vacation saw Rab back at Bourton, reunited with his younger brother and sister – whom, not surprisingly, he had not found time to visit at all during the term. It did not, however, turn out to be a particularly cheerful holiday, since just before Christmas Rab suffered what was first thought a physical but was later diagnosed as at least partially a nervous collapse. Initially treated merely by a local GP – who prescribed a strict regimen of diet, walks and rest – he was subsequently sent by his uncle, Cyril Butler, to see a specialist in Bristol who promptly ruled that any serious academic work over the next few months must be considered out of the question. In other families that verdict might well have been easily enough accepted: it says something, no doubt, about the Butlers' concept of duty that among them, and especially by Rab's father, Monty, it was not only resented but actively resisted. The problem, of course, was that, if serious work was ruled out for the next few months, then no full-time honours degree could be taken in June; and that, inevitably and inescapably, meant extra expense.

Certainly, the initial reaction to Rab's request to be allowed to stay up for a fourth year more than fulfilled the forebodings that he plainly felt in putting it forward. It was not so much that anyone doubted the specialist's ruling; rather was it a lurking suspicion (on Rab's side almost as much as his father's) that he might be pursuing an easy option where a more demanding alternative could be said to exist. In the end, however, the business was settled on the understanding that Rab would abandon the History Part II Tripos that he had been pursuing at his college's urging. He would revert to a less taxing ordinary degree in German and, depending on a number of things (including, at least perhaps in Monty's mind, the result of that German examination) return for a possible fourth year to pick up the threads in History.

Interestingly, the one suggestion that does not appear to have crossed anyone's mind was that, in order to take his work at a more

* There was another perhaps more lavish celebration of Rab's birthday a few days earlier given at the Carlton Hotel by Sydney Courtauld. In a letter to his mother Rab described the occasion as 'gay and invigorating' but ascribed the hospitality generically to 'the Courtaulds' and did not mention Sydney specifically by name. Butler Papers, Trinity College, Cambridge, D48 Part 6, letter dated 12.12.1923.

leisurely pace, Rab should simply abandon his Union career – where, at the beginning of the Lent Term of 1924, he was already Vice-President and due to assume the mantle of President at the end of that same term. The fact that this option was not even considered may simply be explicable in terms of filial piety – in the Union Rab was, after all, merely emulating his father's progress to the presidency of thirty years earlier; on the other hand, it could be said to suggest that in the eyes of the Butler family worldly trophies had by now come to mean every bit as much as academic distinction.

Nor perhaps is it easy to fault them in that judgment. For it was, in fact, through the Union – indeed, on the occasion of the very first debate over which he presided as President – that the young Rab first met the man who was to be the mentor of at least the early part of his political career. The motion chosen for the change-of-officers debate on 11 March 1924 was 'That this House has the highest regard for rhetoric' and it had been intended as a battle of the Titans with Winston Churchill speaking in support and Stanley Baldwin opposing. At the last moment Churchill withdrew but Baldwin duly turned up accompanied by a new opponent, Mitchell Banks, a celebrated KC who was also Conservative MP for Swindon.

The main contemporary interest in the occasion turned out to lie in the fact that the Union voted absolutely evenly – 297 votes for the motion and 297 against – and it, therefore, fell to Rab, as the new President, to give a casting vote (which he delivered, slightly against the traditional rules of chairmanship, in favour of the proposition). It always amused him in his later years to ruminate on that event and to recount how Baldwin had got his own back on him the next morning by buying 'a shocker' at the station bookstall and presenting it to him with the reminder that 'the sin of intellectualism is worse than death'.[9]

That might, uncharitably, be said to be a typical Butler anecdote in that it had clearly matured with the years. For, according to the letter he wrote to his mother two days after the debate, the 'shocker' was P. G. Wodehouse's *Something Fresh*; it was given to him not just by Baldwin but by Banks and Baldwin together; and their reason for doing so was his own announcement that he had never read a single one of Wodehouse's works.[10] Old men, perhaps, do not just forget: they have also been known to embellish, if not to invent.

Not that Rab should be begrudged his fun – certainly there was not much of it in his youth. If he frequently seemed older than his age, it was hardly surprising; for he was carrying a much greater burden of responsibility than most of his contemporaries. There still survives, for example, a revealing letter, written to his father on the day he became President of the Union. After a tactful last paragraph remarking, 'Everybody is saying what a pity it is that you could not be present today', there follows a rather poignant family PS: 'I sent a camera for Jock's [his younger brother's] birthday from you and mother, a pencil box from Iris and sweets from me. Told shops to put "By request of Mrs Monty Butler, Delhi, India" inside and wrote to Jock, in which I said "I understood" you were getting Cambridge shops to do deed.'[11] In Rab's case anyway being a 'child of the Empire' evidently meant having to assume parental duties at a remarkably precocious age.

Nor was there always instinctive or immediate understanding from his father, now President of the Council of State in New Delhi (and due at last to be knighted in that summer's Birthday Honours). The year had started badly for Monty Butler when he did not receive his hoped-for promotion to be Home Member of the Viceroy's Council, and the consequences and repercussions of Rab's Christmas collapse evoked something less than a wholly sympathetic reaction from a man who had sailed through his own Cambridge career with effortless ease. When the time came for Rab to announce in June that he had attained only a 2nd in German, the news – though imparted cheerfully enough – was received in Simla in a somewhat more severe spirit. The best that Monty Butler could manage by way of congratulation was a letter beginning:

> So you are a BA 30 years after me and 130 years after your great grandfather. On thinking it over, I take comfort in the 2nd. You will remember that your first year you took a 2nd only in Mays [the Cambridge preliminary exams] and then recovered in your second year. The experience of your third year will surely produce a 1st in your fourth. Directly you are yourself again, you must get down to it. You can't do your history on what you know already, like your French. I would like you to get a 1st, if only to disprove the Master's theories. I think he considers that anyone who has done Modern Languages *ipso facto* suffers from softening of the brain.[12]

In a family that had grown to look upon academic achievement as its birthright, there was not perhaps too much to complain about in the tone of that letter; but certainly no one could say that it erred on the side of generosity. To be fair to Monty Butler, however, a second disagreement, quite apart from the initial reservations over the question of staying up for a fourth year, had recently arisen between his son and himself. He had formed the firm view that the answer to Rab's nervous troubles was to come out and spend the Long Vacation in India and was not at all amused when his son insisted instead on joining a seven-week-long Cambridge Union debating tour of the United States and Canada. So nettled, indeed, was Sir Monty by this act of rebellion that it is possible that his constant recriminations over it may have helped to induce a relapse in Rab's condition, which occurred without warning towards the end of July.

All the signs had, in fact, been that Rab, aided by his undoubted enjoyment of his term as President of the Union, had made a complete recovery. At the beginning of the vacation he had again been out with the Courtaulds – this time to a dinner at their home in Berkeley Square and then on to an A. A. Milne farce called *To Have the Honour*, starring Gerald du Maurier and Madge Titheradge. He had enjoyed the occasion, though once more his private report to his family concentrated on the parents ('I was impressed by Sam Courtauld . . . Mrs chatted in the most delightful way on many tangents')[13] rather than the daughter, about whom he said nothing. There was, however, probably no reason why he should. For a month later, after hearing the news of Kathleen Buchanan Smith's engagement to G. P. Thomson,* he was to blurt out in a letter to his parents, 'I miss somebody to share my interests with';[14] it would seem fairly clear that Sydney Courtauld, whatever her 'cheeriness' or 'gaiety', was not yet filling that bill.

It is difficult to resist the conclusion that it was the *fait accompli* of K's impending marriage to Professor Thomson of Aberdeen (combined perhaps with the difficulties his father was creating) that had cast Rab back into the slough of despond. Fortunately, on this occasion the 'mental *crise*' (as he now frankly termed it) did not last long – indeed in the same letter in which he referred to his loneliness he was to be found announcing briskly, 'You will find me somewhat changed, harder perhaps, when you return'; and, as if to prove the point, he proceeded to write, for him, an unusually testy letter to his father:

> I just ask you to be content with my conduct of affairs so far and to be pleased with any decision or achievement in the future. I ask you only to make due allowance for this rotten ill health, for

* Later Sir George Paget Thomson (1892–1975). Master of Corpus Christi College, Cambridge, 1952–62.

a plethora of responsibilities . . . for a certain sudden weariness owing to an existence packing twice a week and so on and owing to a somewhat important event to me which I mention at the beginning of Mother's letter.* I shall go to America in order to fulfil a commitment and return a free man in every way.[15]

So far as Sydney Courtauld was concerned, there was certainly no question but that was true. He appears not to have written to her at all in the seven weeks he was in North America; and, though that may not have been surprising (given the hectic nature of the tour's time-table), his silence after returning to Cambridge perhaps was. Certainly, it is not hard to detect a tone of veiled reproach in the note Sydney wrote, acknowledging an eventual Christmas letter, from Rapallo in Italy where she was staying with some cousins:

Christmas Eve 1924

Dear Rab,

A letter was certainly far more appreciated than a snow-storm would have been. The last I heard of you was in America with your portrait in all the illustrated press. I am glad it was a success and amusing.

After three months in Rome I've decided that I'm not an archaeologist and that London is the only fit place to live in. I shall be back in a week . . . and if you are in London about 5 January, I shall be at 14 Vicarage Gate. I don't know when term begins so I dare say you will have gone up.

Is the Tripos to be History again? Thank heaven, I've not got to take another.

All good wishes for the New Year, especially with the Tripos.

Yours,

SYDNEY E. COURTAULD[16]

Far from being the letter even of a friend, it reads (even allowing for the more formal manners of a different age) much more like that of a distant acquaintance – by no means sure whether there was any point in meeting again at all.

Yet meet they ultimately did – and, indeed, within three months were involved in an almost daily correspondence (some of it conducted, a little coyly, in French).

* By the same post Rab had written to inform his mother of Kathleen's engagement, curiously characterising it as 'something fundamental'.

They had always, of course, had interests in common – the University French Society, the NUS, even (not to be unkind to Rab) the presence in the background of Sydney's father and mother, exactly the sort of 'great and interesting people' with whom he had confessed two years earlier he wanted to mix. Yet at Cambridge they had somehow kept their distance and it was only when Sydney Courtauld moved out of her parents' house in Berkeley Square and set up in a flat of her own in Vicarage Gate, Kensington, that they began to get to know each other at all closely. Leaving home was perhaps an unusually daring thing for an unmarried girl of twenty-two to do at that particular time but then Sydney was never much of a believer in convention. That may well indeed have formed part of her attraction for Rab. Certainly, by the spring of 1925 their friendship had begun to blossom (with Sydney herself writing to suggest that she came on a visit to Cambridge on the very eve of Rab's finals).[17]

That did not turn out to be a particularly happy piece of timing – though they did meet briefly for lunch. The strain of working very hard had once again begun to take its toll on Rab's health. The difficulty this time was purely physical. Rab was, slightly belatedly, diagnosed as suffering from jaundice and was looked after throughout the examination week by the wife of one of his tutors: no sooner had he finished his exams than his always protective mother (who had arrived back in England the previous winter) scooped him up from Cambridge and bore him off to a Scottish hydro at Strathpeffer in Ross and Cromarty. It was there in the third week of June that he got the news that he had, after all, triumphed in the History Tripos, gaining not only a First but also (a special distinction that Cambridge has since abandoned) being placed in the first division of the whole Tripos. It had been – as his father, noting that Rab's 1:1 matched his own of thirty years earlier, wrote from Pachmarhi in the Central Provinces (where he was now the Governor) – 'a fine effort':[18] yet, typically, Sir Monty saw no reason to depart from his normal practice so far as any financial recognition was concerned – 'Lloyd's Bank will credit you with £10 as a thank offering.'[19]

Fortunately for Rab, however, he was soon to become financially independent at last. On the strength of his performance in the Tripos, he was promptly offered a fellowship by his Uncle Geoffrey's college, Corpus, which gave him a much greater measure of independence than he had ever known before. He had also been invited, before his illness, to join the Courtaulds on a family holiday in Norway.

At first, Rab seems to have been very much in two minds about taking up the invitation; but viewed from the rigours of a Scottish hydro, even if he was for one week there accompanied by a Cambridge friend, Patrick Devlin,* it suddenly seemed far more attractive than prolonged convalescence at a Highland Spa. Accordingly – with just a little chuntering from Sir Monty ('I do not understand', he wrote cautiously from India, 'whether you are entertaining the Courtaulds or they you in Norway')[20] – Rab sailed for Oslo at the beginning of August. The following fortnight, though he himself appears to have had absolutely no premonition of it, was to determine the shape of his life for the next thirty years.

Initially, the Courtauld house party, assembled in a white and green farmhouse in a valley among the northern fjords, consisted of just four people – Sydney, her mother 'Lil', a distinguished London doctor, Sir John Atkins, and Rab. Perhaps inevitably, they paired off by age, with Sydney and Rab being thrown more and more into each other's company. Not that Rab was in any mood to complain about that: indeed, before he had been there a week he was to write to his father, 'Sydney's company is quite enough for me alone all day and we even find the others irksome at times.'[21] Nor did the pattern significantly change once Sydney's father, Sam, arrived accompanied by the manager of the Covent Garden opera, Colonel Bloys. By the time in mid-August Rab journeyed down with Sydney to Copenhagen, where he took the night-ferry home and she attended to some NUS business, they were, in fact, privately and unofficially engaged.

At the age of twenty-three, Rab was, of course, already a bright, up-and-coming young man – with, as has been noticed, his own strong ideas about pursuing a career of public service. It remains, though, difficult to exaggerate the difference that the Courtauld connection made to his prospects. In the first place, it removed what had been until then the main restriction on his freedom of action – the financial limitations that had caused his father to worry over even his son's desire to join the Diplomatic Service, on the ground that to pursue such a career successfully would 'require at least £300 a year of private income'.[22] But, perhaps even more important than that, the family association with the Courtaulds launched Rab at once into the world of the important and the influential after which he had always, by no means secretly, hankered. Not for nothing, in

* Patrick Arthur Devlin (1905–). Justice of the High Court 1948–60. Lord Justice of Appeal 1960–1. Lord of Appeal in Ordinary 1961–4. Created life peer 1961.

writing to his father from Norway, had he gone out of his way to compare Sam Courtauld to Baron Robert de Rothschild – or to describe him as 'the greatest power in business in England'.[23] There was always a distinctly 'worldly' side to Rab and when he wrote of the Courtaulds from Norway 'I am very lucky to be among them',[24] there can be no doubt that he genuinely meant it.

At first, admittedly, things moved slowly – not so much out of any direct reluctance on the Courtauld side, more because of the dread with which they regarded any form of Press publicity. In September 1925 Sydney, who ranked as one of the great heiresses of England, was summoned down to Devon to meet Rab's mother, who had taken a holiday house there for the benefit of her two younger children before returning to India. The meeting passed off successfully – as did a subsequent, more formal, encounter between Lady Butler and Sydney's mother in London. No announcement, however, was made publicly until January 1926 – though news of the engagement was privately passed around both families. Characteristically, the only tension seems to have been provoked by the financial provision that Samuel Courtauld had made it known that he was ready to make for his prospective son-in-law. At £5,000 a year tax-free for life (a very considerable sum in the 1920s, indeed the exact equivalent of a Cabinet Minister's salary) it was a remarkably handsome settlement; and it was perhaps predictable that to Sir Monty Butler it should appear little short of profligate. 'I am amazed', he wrote to his son from India, 'at the generosity of the treatment you are to get' – though his evident shock did not inhibit him from rallying and reverting to a familiar favoured maxim: 'You have learnt to manage money on a small scale, so will not lose your head, I know, over the big scale.'[25]

To begin with, though, there was certainly very little change in Rab's own life-style. In October he had moved into his bachelor don's rooms in Corpus; but the only real alteration in his circumstances lay in his proud possession of a small bull-nosed Morris motor-car that he had inherited from his mother on her return to India. At Corpus he had a dozen pupils (half of them freshmen), and he also gave a university lecture once a week on modern French history, in particular on the politics of the Third Republic. Each weekend he either drove to London or Sydney came up to Cambridge, though they usually avoided the town and the university and went out into the country, if only to avoid provoking gossip. One difficulty over the engagement – quite apart from the Courtauld family's own preference for reticence on the subject – was that Rab had only just been elected to his fellowship; and that election had gone forward on the understanding that he was a single man. It was, in fact, the desire of the Senior Tutor of Corpus, Will Spens, that nothing at all should be said on the subject until Rab had completed at least a full year of teaching at the college. Even then a fairly broad hint was given that a change in his marital status might well involve his having to move to another college.

In the end, however, it was Rab's own decision that effectively ended his twelve-month association with Corpus (he was to remain a non-resident Fellow until 1929). Even if he had been content to wait, Sydney was not; and the wedding was finally fixed for 20 April 1926, at the end of the Easter vacation. It was a somewhat strange, secretive affair – held very quietly (ostensibly on the grounds of Sydney's mother's precarious health but in reality because of the Courtauld family's loathing of Press intrusion) in the City church of St Mary Abchurch, then a Corpus living. Only Sydney's parents, two Courtauld cousins, Rab's Uncle Cyril and Aunt May from Bourton, the Townsends from Ladbroke Square and Geoffrey Butler of Corpus (who served as best man) attended. After the ceremony, conducted by the Master of Corpus, Dr Edmund Pearce, there was a lunch at the Ritz Hotel and then the newly married couple were dispatched in the Courtauld Rolls back to Cambridge, where they had found a rented property in Bentley Road. It was their first home – but they were to stay in it only for a matter of months, since that autumn, as an earnest of their intention to apprentice themselves to the life of politics, Rab and his bride launched themselves on a year-long world tour. 'So', wrote Rab on the day they packed up the house in Bentley Road, 'Cambridge is behind and the world in front.'[26] It was to be nearly forty years before that order was to be reversed – and Cambridge once more was to lie in front, with the world (at least of politics) left behind.

5 *The Road to Westminster*

The most notable evidence of the change in Rab's fortunes brought about by his engagement and marriage was the general assumption that he was now destined for a parliamentary career. Whereas his former aspiration to the Diplomatic Service might, it was feared, overtax the family's resources, it was now taken for granted, even by Sir Monty Butler, that his passage into the House of Commons was assured. Indeed, in opposing what he typically called 'this all-the-world-in-a-year-stunt' Rab's father did so specifically on political grounds:

> You see, no one nowadays can expect to get preferment in politics until he is well over 30. If you exhaust the world by the time you are 25, you will fret at the long waiting . . . You will find it a great help, I am sure, to have fresh fields to explore each year or every other year until the time comes for you to take office in some Ministry.[1]

Neither Rab nor Sydney was, however, to be deterred, and at the beginning of September 1926 they started on their twentieth-century version of 'the Grand Tour' which was to take them to most of the major territories proudly painted pink on the world globe. India, where they stayed three whole months, understandably, provided the centre-piece of their journey. When Rab had left the land of his birth fifteen years earlier his father had been merely a Deputy Commissioner: now Sir Monty was Governor of one of India's nine provinces with all the panoply that attached to such an office.

Sailing from Egypt through the Red Sea to 'the Gateway of India' at Bombay, Rab and his bride went straight up by train to his father's summer camp at Pachmarhi. This was very much Kipling country and Rab – who, whatever his other sporting deficiencies, had become a good shot – distinguished himself by shooting both a tiger and a panther. Christmas was spent with Sir Monty and Lady Butler at Government House, Nagpur, the capital of the Central Provinces. The New Year found the young couple in Delhi where, as house guests of the Viceroy's Private Secretary, they were soon caught up in the social round which centred on Viceregal Lodge. (It was here in New Delhi in January 1927 that Rab first met the man – then Lord Irwin, but later Viscount Halifax – under whom just over a decade later he was to serve at the Foreign Office.) From Delhi Rab insisted on a filial pilgrimage to the place of his birth, Attock Fort in the Punjab (which, fortunately, Sydney thought offered 'the finest scenery we have seen in India').[2] After that they went on to Lahore, the first Indian city of his childhood, and then finally to Peshawar, the capital of the North-West Frontier, the most exposed outpost of what was then Britain's Indian Empire.

The letters that survive from the rest of the world tour tend to suggest that Sir Monty's original judgment may well have been correct. Certainly from Australia, New Zealand, to say nothing of the islands of the South Seas, there are frequent complaints of weariness, sea-sickness, even of occasional boredom. Only Canada – reached after a voyage across the Pacific of over a month – seems to have fulfilled expectations; but then by the time Rab and Sydney reached Vancouver in July 1927, they found a piece of news awaiting them as exciting as it was clearly welcome. It came in the shape of two separate letters written within a week of each other: one from Sydney's second cousin, William Courtauld of Halstead, Essex, and the other from Rab's uncle, Sir Geoffrey Butler, his former colleague at Corpus and the MP for Cambridge University. Both were direct and to the point and concerned the intentions of William Foot Mitchell, the then Conservative Member of Parliament for the Saffron Walden division of Essex.

Since each throws a light on the way Conservative politics worked in the 1920s, they are worth quoting virtually in full. William Courtauld's, as was only fitting for a businessman, was the brisker of the two and, though it was the second to be written, may, therefore, properly be quoted first:

Penny Pot, Halstead, Essex
20.6.27

Dear Rab,

I have just seen Foot Mitchell, MP for the Saffron Walden

Division. If his health permits, he will carry on until the general election but will not then seek re-election: this is in *strict* confidence and is not to be generally known.

He says that he does not see why the local Conservative Association should not favourably consider you as a candidate; and as soon as you return home he would like to see you about it. He says that, apart from your personal capabilities etc, it is absolutely essential that you (or any local candidate) should have a house in the division. The division does not want a 'carpet bagger'; but if it was to have one, it would have the choice of many who already had parliamentary experience and in that way would be preferable to you. Also he says that it is necessary to spend money; and that it costs him, apart from actual election expenses, about £1,000 a year in the way of subscription, charities etc. This seems to be expected of a Conservative candidate who may be supposed to have money behind him. Also, of course, it would be necessary for you to become well acquainted with the people in every part of the division, which would take a great deal of time and hard work.

The effect of all this is that if you wish to offer yourself as a candidate for this division, he wants to see you as soon as he can . . .

I send this to Vancouver on the chance that it may reach you.

Yours sincerely,

W. J. COURTAULD[3]

Sir Geoffrey Butler's letter, written almost a week earlier, was more whimsical, though no less revealing:

House of Commons Library
14 June 1927

My dear Sydney and Rab,

Yesterday Foot Mitchell took me aside and, after histing and swearing me to secrecy a good deal, told me he was bound to give up pretty soon and thought it had best be soon rather than late, if his successor was to get a chance of becoming known to the constituency. I made appropriate noises at the proper places. He then said he had been approached by a Mr Courtauld with reference to one whom he thought I might know. Might he ask some questions? These he did. He then told me something about the constituency – it is largely agricultural, it is very large and, therefore, makes a good deal of demands on any candidate . . .

I do hope it will come off. I can't tell you what ill-luck I have wished that dear old man in my prayers; but I was deadly afraid that I had overdone it and he would die (when I should be sorry for he is a very nice old man) or that I should underdo it and he would only get gout or German measles or a tickling in the throat. Now my black prayers have seemed to get pretty near the mark . . .

Yours,

GEOFFREY BUTLER[4]

It was perhaps an early indication of Rab's life-long belief in the maxim 'the patience of politics' that, even in the light of such letters, he made no effort at all to hurry back and that he and Sydney simply continued with their pre-ordained stately progress across Canada; after Vancouver they spent time at a resort in the Rocky Mountains, stopped off in Calgary and Winnipeg, visited Ottawa and finally Montreal before sailing for home on the *Empress of Australia* from Quebec City on 31 August. But once safely back in London (they returned to Sydney's flat in Vicarage Gate which had been rented during the summer to Rab's parents now on leave from India) they certainly displayed no inclination to let the grass grow under their feet. Despite some rumblings of dissatisfaction from Sydney's father, Sam[5] – who seems to have resented having to learn of the planned coup from his cousin and another neighbour at Halstead rather than from his own son-in-law – the considerable weight of the Courtauld family as the main employer in the division was promptly mobilised on Rab's behalf. That 'very nice old man' William Foot Mitchell (destined to live until 1947 and, possibly coincidentally, consoled with a knighthood on his departure from Parliament in 1929) was firmly 'guided' to meet the young aspirant candidate: before October was out, his forthcoming retirement had been publicly announced and Rab had been swiftly and painlessly nominated in his place (there was not even a rival at the selection conference).

Such was the deferential nature of Conservative county associations at the time that Rab's selection at the age of twenty-four for a seat which had been held by the Conservatives for the past three elections appears to have provoked no protest. Over four decades later Rab himself was to refer to 'considerable doubt about my tender age and attainments'[6] but whatever reservations may have been privately felt never surfaced publicly[7] – and in any case were probably stilled by Rab's faithful following of W. J. Courtauld's advice in volunteering a pledge that he and his wife would look for a home in which to live in the constituency. This they duly did – and within six months, having left Sydney's old flat in Vicarage Gate, were installed in their first Essex home, Church Hall, Broxted. Although Rab inherited a Conservative majority of 5,949, Saffron Walden, with a traditional Nonconformist allegiance and a past Liberal history, by no means ranked as a safe Tory seat; and a good proportion of the next eighteen months was to be spent in nursing it assiduously.

For a young man with a donnish, almost aloof, manner from the beginning Rab showed a surprising aptitude for constituency campaigning. He certainly took it very seriously: at least once a week he was out in one of the eighty villages or five small towns of the constituency – not making speeches but showing films of his world tour on his mobile cinematographical unit. It was an essentially non-partisan approach to politics that in those simple, far-off days worked wonders in the still waters of East Anglia, even provoking one young constituent to break into, if not verse, then at least doggerel:

Our new prospective candidate's a man of great renown,
He knows the British Empire, for he's toured it up and down.
To India and the Jubilee of Canada he went,
At Canberra with the Duke of York some time he spent,
Now when the next election comes, he'll go to Parliament.[8]

Of course such a 'broad imperial horizons' approach did have its dangers – and it was not surprising that the local Liberals were soon to be heard suggesting that the young don in their midst, though no doubt a very able man, perhaps knew 'more of the open spaces of Australia than he did of the problems of the Motherland'.[9] But Rab was too canny to be caught out like that: he lost no time in finding a genuine local issue and for the next three years he was to run with it constantly both in the constituency and, eventually, in Parliament.

Saffron Walden, like most other East Anglian seats, was primarily an arable farming constituency; and it was typical of Rab's resourceful political mind that he should very early on have spotted one anomaly – that, of the two main ingredients of beer, hops were protected by import duties whereas barley was not. This piece of seeming discrimination – hops, after all, came principally from Kent and Worcestershire, whereas cereals, like barley, were the staple product of East Anglian farming – provided him with a good earthy issue rooted, as it were, in the local soil; and in the days of a rather more relaxed interpretation of the law on election expenses, Rab certainly knew how to make the most of it. By December 1928, he was sending out this circular letter to every working-men's club in the division:

19 December 1928

Dear Mr Secretary,

I forward to your members a cask of *pure British beer* at Christmas time.

I should like as many as possible to have a taste of its excellence to show you what such a beer is like and show you how a *barley policy*, based on such a product, might help the agricultural industry.

The contents are pure Ipswich malt and British hops (Kents or Worcesters). There is no sugar included and the beer is brewed within the Division. With best wishes for Christmas to you all.

Yours sincerely,

R. A. BUTLER[10]

Whatever the vulnerability of such conduct today under the provisions of the Representation of the People Act, in the more Eatanswillish atmosphere of the early twentieth century it was, no doubt, common enough; and (unlike, for example, the Conservative candidate's wife in Stepney who went around promising, 'Oh, I'll give you all such a lovely party if only you'll send my husband to the House of Commons'),[11] Rab could at least claim to be making a serious political point. The safeguarding of barley from the threat posed by 'dumping' from the Soviet Union was very much in a rural constituency's interests; and Rab, showing at an early age his grasp on the practicalities of politics, had swiftly concluded that the best way of doing that was to campaign for a preferential excise duty on beer made from purely British products.

Not all of Rab's early political education took place, however, at the grass-roots. In gaining the Saffron Walden nomination he had, as we have seen, already had a helping hand from his uncle, Sir Geoffrey Butler, the MP for Cambridge University, who was to come to his aid again even before he reached Westminster. Although he never held any ministerial office himself, Sir Geoffrey was on friendly terms with a number of leading figures in the 1924–9 Baldwin Government – and with none more so than the Secretary of State for Air, Sir Samuel Hoare (whom he served from 1925 as Parliamentary Private Secretary). Through the intervention of his uncle, who was already conducting a losing battle with ill health, Rab was invited by Sir Samuel Hoare early in 1929 to become his unpaid Private Secretary. A letter Rab wrote to his father in March 1929, just two months before the general election that was to take him to Parliament, fully revealed his sense of excitement at finding himself already at least on the periphery of the circle of executive power.

Air Ministry, Gwydyr House, Whitehall, SW1
March 26 1929

Dear Dad,

I am now parked here for this morning and use HM's notepaper for the first time since leaving your house in India. It is a thrilling event which ties us closer together and here I am as Private Secretary to the Minister who put it through. My task, though optional, is none the less pleasant and gives me an *entrée*. Alas, that the turmoil of the general election will change so much . . .[12]

When that election finally came on Thursday 30 May, it changed Rab's own fortunes, and hardly for the worse. After a year that had seen the birth of his first son on 12 January 1929,* Rab found himself on Friday, 31 May 1929 carried shoulder-high through the streets of Saffron Walden by his ecstatic Tory supporters, proudly proclaiming, 'We'll make you Premier, or your baby.'[13]

In a general election that saw Labour become, for the first time, the largest Party in the House of Commons he had won a highly creditable victory for a party that was now, after nearly five years, to be driven from office. In gaining a majority of 4,919, or a drop of only just over 1,000 votes on the victory won by his predecessor in the far more favourable Conservative climate of October 1924, he had not only done well:† he had also, though he was hardly to know that at the time, forged an unbreakable link with a constituency that would loyally return him to the House of Commons through nine elections in the next thirty-five years.

* Richard Clive Butler, President of the National Farmers' Union, 1979–86. Knighted 1981.

† The figures were R. A. Butler (U.) 13,561, W. Cash (Lab.) 8,642, A. M. Mathews (Lib.) 8,307.

6 *A Pro-Baldwin Back-bencher*

The House of Commons which Rab entered at the age of twenty-six in June 1929 was – if nothing like as revolutionary as that which assembled in August 1945 – at least one which marked a fair political upheaval. The Labour Government, swept from office only five years earlier over the Campbell prosecution,* was now restored to the Treasury Bench, though still without an overall majority: in the election it had gained no fewer than 137 seats.† On this occasion, unlike January 1924, when the Conservatives remained the largest single Party, Stanley Baldwin did not wait to be defeated on the floor of the House of Commons before offering his Government's resignation. After a weekend spent at Chequers, he surrendered thc seals of office at Windsor on 4 June to King George V, who the next day summoned Ramsay MacDonald to the Castle to kiss hands, for the second time, as the King's First Minister.

For Rab, as a young MP, joining an Opposition Party was not without its advantages. There are few more profitless parliamentary roles than that of being a junior back-bencher in a Party already in office – and at least Rab found himself spared that. Always more suited to defence than attack, he can hardly be said to have made much mark as an assailant of the Labour Government. He waited until October to make his maiden speech and, when it came, it was, fairly predictably, on agriculture and was a non-partisan call for an international conference on commodity prices and the gold

* The failure of the 1924 Labour Government to carry through the prosecution of John Campbell, editor of the *Workers' Weekly*, had led to the fall of Ramsay MacDonald's first administration.

† In 1929 the Labour Party attained the highest vote it had ever had (8,389,512), though the Conservatives, with twenty-eight fewer parliamentary seats, still had a nearly 300,000 plurality in the aggregate vote.

standard.[1] It was, however, well received by *The Times*, which described it as 'a good maiden',[2] and even by the *Sunday Express* which, on the Sunday after its delivery, referred in its Cross-Bencher column to 'a fresh and flowing style'.[3]

Almost from the beginning Rab had, in effect, cast his lot as the type of politician who hugs the inside track rather than one who goes recklessly for the outside rails. Before he had been in the House of Commons a year there was to be a striking public proof of this trait. The first serious internal upheaval for Ramsay MacDonald's Labour Government came with the protest resignation over unemployment by its Chancellor of the Duchy of Lancaster, Sir Oswald Mosley, in May 1930. It was scarcely the type of quarrel that one might normally have expected a junior Conservative back-bencher to get involved in – but Rab had only himself to blame for becoming implicated.

The occasion for his intervention was, admittedly, a slightly curious one. The news of Sir Oswald Mosley's resignation – over the rejection of his own plan for combating unemployment by a vote of 210–29 at a meeting of the Parliamentary Labour Party – had, on the whole, been received by both Conservative politicians and the Conservative Press with a certain degree of satisfaction, if with very little sympathy (before deserting the Labour Government, Sir Oswald had, after all, deserted the Conservative Party, in whose interest he had first been elected to the Commons). That was not, however, the view taken by a young ex-Tory MP, and son-in-law of the Duke of Devonshire, defeated a year earlier at Stockton-on-Tees. In an impassioned letter to *The Times* he nailed his colours unapologetically to the doctrine of 'the mandate' and boldly suggested that Sir Oswald's only offence had been actually to believe in the 'pledges and promises' on which 'the Socialist Party obtained power'. It was, in fact, a curiously radical letter – foreshadowing the theory forty years later to be put forward by R. H. S. Crossman that the election mandate is 'the battering ram of radical change'[4] – and it concluded with an eloquent protest (worthy even of Mr Tony Benn) against what the letter-writer plainly regarded as the essential cynicism of the British political system:

> It may be . . . that we are always to have a party of the left speaking and obtaining office by means of extravagant political promises which only its most naïve supporters expect to see fulfilled, alternating with a party of the right, which will for ever operate an equally effective and perhaps more subtle technique,

> fighting its elections on the basis of a programme which is either self-contradictory or obscure, confident that when it has obtained power it cannot hope to emulate a more inspiring example than that of the reactionary immobility of parties alleged to be progressive.

Then, always a vulnerable tactic in terms of controversy, came the irony:

> I suspect that this is the real way the game ought to be played. Only, if these rules are to be permanently enforced, perhaps a good many of us will feel that it is hardly worth bothering to play at all. Sir Oswald Mosley thinks the rules should be altered. I hope some of my friends will have the courage to applaud and support his protest.[5]

The signature to the letter was that of Harold Macmillan, in the House of Commons five years before Rab but now out as a result of the 1929 election.* The very next day a crushing rejoinder to it, picking up Macmillan's final metaphor, appeared on *The Times*'s letters page. It ran as follows:

> Sir – We have read with interest and some surprise Mr Harold Macmillan's letter published in your issue of today. When a player starts complaining 'that it is hardly worth while bothering to play' the game at all it is usually the player, and not the game, who is at fault. It is then usually advisable for the player to seek a new field for his recreation and a pastime more suited for his talents.[6]

That riposte – all the more devastating for its brevity – bore the signatures of four newly elected Conservatives. They were those of Viscount Lymington (MP for Basingstoke 1929–34 and later Earl of Portsmouth), Harold Balfour (MP for Isle of Thanet 1929–45, subsequently Lord Balfour of Inchrye), Michael Beaumont (MP for Aylesbury 1929–38) and R. A. Butler.

R. A. Butler's was, in fact, the last signature but, quite apart from

* Harold Macmillan (1894–). Conservative MP, Stockton-on-Tees 1924–9 and 1931–45, Bromley 1945–64. Minister Resident, North-West Africa 1942–5. Secretary of State for Air 1945. Minister of Housing and Local Government 1951–4. Minister of Defence 1954–5. Foreign Secretary 1955. Chancellor of the Exchequer 1955–7. Prime Minister 1957–63. Created 1st Earl of Stockton 1984.

any becoming modesty on the part of the actual author, it hardly requires any great knowledge of Rab's debating technique, founded on the art of the put-down ('It is then usually advisable for the player to seek a new field for his recreation . . .') to be satisfied that his was the moving spirit behind it. Certainly that was the conclusion that Harold Macmillan soon reached – with consequences that were eventually to play their part in the leadership struggle within the Conservative Party nearly thirty years later. Even allowing for the fact that the letter may have been little more than a juvenile *jeu d'esprit* on the part of a young man (not yet twenty-eight), it was destined to prove one of those political 'teases' that are never perhaps quite forgiven.

At the time, however, there can be little doubt that it did Rab nothing but good. From the beginning he was looked on with favour both by Stanley Baldwin (who, remembering their Cambridge Union encounter, had singled him out when he first came to the House of Commons) and by Neville Chamberlain (to whom Sam Hoare had introduced him at a lunch party even before his election for Saffron Walden): few young MPs can have had a more propitious start in terms of official Party Leadership approval. Yet, given the post-1929 Tory climate, that was not necessarily an advantage. There were many Conservative voices, especially in Fleet Street, only too eager to blame Baldwin for having led the Party to defeat in the 1929 election; and a young back-bencher, with an eye to his future, might well have thought twice before lining up quite as firmly as Rab did behind the type of Conservatism represented by Baldwin's 1929 election slogan of 'Safety First'. There is no evidence at all, however, to suggest that Rab himself was ever tempted to join the then fairly crowded Conservative 'Cave of Adullam'. Baldwin, as Rab was openly to declare half a century later, was the Conservative Leader to whom he had always 'felt nearest';[7] and it was Baldwin whom he now proposed not only to follow but to defend.

As a newly elected Conservative back-bencher, Rab was, of course, far too junior to have any direct knowledge of the various intrigues by which Baldwin's rivals – supported by the Press barons, Beaverbrook and Rothermere – sought to dislodge him from the Conservative Leadership between 1929 and 1931. But among the lobby fodder of the Party Baldwin had few more loyal supporters. Rab quarrelled with other members of the 'Boys Brigade'* (his three

* A rival loyalist body to the 'YMCA'. The latter comprised Conservative Members first elected in 1923–4 owing allegiance to Anthony Eden – otherwise, and more rudely, known as 'the Glamour Boys'.

co-signatories to the anti-Macmillan letter, Lord Lymington, Harold Balfour and Michael Beaumont) when they first wavered and then deserted Baldwin: he himself voted for his Leader at both the Party meetings in the Caxton Hall, held respectively on 24 June and 30 October 1930 (finding himself, on the first occasion, on a question of policy over a 'free hand' with tariffs, among a modest majority of some 150–80 and on the second, concerned directly with the Leadership, a contributor to a more resounding victory of 462–116). Even Rab's own personal allegiance to Sam Hoare – the man who had appointed him his private secretary in the final months before his arrival in the Commons – seems to have come under slight strain when he learned from his Essex neighbour, H. A. Gwynne, the editor of the *Morning Post*, that Hoare had been touting himself for the Leadership[8] (his doubts, however, were put at rest when an old Cambridge friend, Geoffrey Lloyd,* who had previously served as Hoare's secretary, assured him that his former master had too 'good a sense of realities' to entertain any such ambitions).[9]

Yet Rab's own attitude was not just determined by his admiration for Baldwin.† He also had a great contempt for what he termed 'the conspirators' – notably for Lord Beaverbrook, who sat near him at the second Caxton Hall meeting and whom he found 'green and apeish'.[10] The rebels who signed the letter calling for the Party meeting at Caxton Hall on the Leadership he spoke of openly as 'the Forty Thieves' – and his feeling even for his more conventional back-bench colleagues ('Brigadier-General this and Colonel that')[11] stopped some way short of charity.

Before he had been in Parliament for even two years, there were, in fact, signs of disillusion with the Commons setting in – with Rab comparing it to 'a form of Riding School, in which individual horses prance around but in which the ultimate decision and march of events is left to the Riding Master in the shape of the Government'.[12] And at that stage any prospect of Rab getting a foot-hold even on the outer ramparts of Government as a PPS seemed pretty remote. Ramsay MacDonald's Labour Government may not have been doing

* Geoffrey William Lloyd (1902–84). Conservative MP, Ladywood 1931–45, King's Norton 1950–5, Sutton Coldfield 1955–74. Minister of Information 1945. Minister of Fuel and Power 1951–5. Minister of Education 1957–9. Life peer 1974.

† Initially not entirely reciprocated. After his fourth speech in the Commons, delivered on the Finance Bill on 26 July 1930, Rab was approached by his leader in the Members' Lobby. 'That was a good speech, Rab,' Baldwin began, 'but I got damn bored. You went too fast. You need not think everyone has got quick brains.' Forbearingly, Rab chose to characterise this 'as a good lesson'. Butler Papers, Trinity College, Cambridge, D48 Part 14, diary notes 5 August 1930.

particularly well but, with the Liberal Party very much at sixes and sevens and in no mood to precipitate an election, the omens for a Conservative early return to power did not look particularly favourable.

Fortunately, though, there was consolation for Rab in his home and social life. The year before his entry into the Commons had been a fairly gloomy one in family terms. His Aunt Minnie – the sister-consort to Uncle Dunlop in the Ovington Square days of his childhood – had, in February 1928, after the death of her brother, committed suicide by throwing herself under an underground train at Victoria Station; his uncle by marriage, Bernard Townsend of Ladbroke Square, had also died that spring after losing his reason; while his paternal uncle, Geoffrey Butler of Corpus and the MP for Cambridge University, had finally lost his battle with ill-health, dying just four weeks before the 1929 election. It had been left to Rab, as the English viceroy of the 'Monty Butlers', to cope with all these three domestic tragedies; he had done so with compassion and competence – but it was perhaps just as well that he was now beginning to develop a family life of his own.

In the summer of 1929 he and Sydney acquired a new London flat, at North Court, Wood Street, Westminster, and, though they still went to Broxted at weekends, this soon became a focal point for their friends both in the arts and politics (Sydney lived up fully to her parents' interest in the arts and even their glass dining-table in London was designed by Francis Bacon). In those days the life of a Commons back-bencher was hardly energetic and Rab and Sydney had plenty of time for socialising – not least as part of the musical and modern art circuit based on the Courtaulds' imposing new town house in Portman Square. Sydney's father, Sam, had begun to take a definite interest in his son-in-law's life-style, even advising on such matters as the choice of a motor-car (he recommended a Rolls-Royce while Rab, more modestly, preferred a Humber Snipe).[13] Even that latter choice, however, posed problems in terms of the constituency and Rab, displaying not for the first time a countryman's shrewdness, insisted on keeping his old Wolseley for electioneering purposes.[14]

One claim that cannot be made on Rab's behalf is that he showed, at least until the very last moment, any special foresight into the economic difficulties that were to bring about the fall of the 1929 Labour Government and would lead eventually to the 'Doctor's Mandate' general election of October 1931. His principal worry during the late summer of 1931 appears to have been whether, given his *in loco parentis* position, it was wise to allow his younger brother,

Jock (now, in turn, a Marlborough schoolboy) to go on holiday to France, considering the shaky economic conditions, not so much in Britain, as in Europe. In the end the decision went in favour of the trip on the ground that 'the most prosperous part of Europe at present is Northern France'.[15] As for Britain, Rab found reassurance in the fact that 'fortunately we have so preponderatingly large a proportion of long-term over short-term loans that, although there may conceivably be every appearance of a financial crisis, fundamentally the matter should right itself, provided drastic economies are introduced before the next Budget'.[16]

If that represented a surprising lack of foresight on the part of a young man who had trained himself for the life of politics, the explanation perhaps lay in the fact that, once the novelty had worn off, the attractions of back-bench parliamentary life had soon begun to pall. Like his father, Rab saw politics as the art of administration* and he never wanted, as he put it, 'to be a sniper or a schemer very much'.[17] But, from 1929 to 1931, 'sniping and scheming' were very much what Tory politics were about and Rab did not really feel at all in his element – though, right through to the economic crisis that finally brought Ramsay MacDonald's Labour Government down, he continued to throw his own youthful weight within his Party on the side of Baldwin. Comparing the Conservative Leader's enemies to 'the hosts of Midian who prowl and prowl around',[18] the young Conservative Member for Saffron Walden did his humble but courageous best to smite them: he even took an active part in the famous St George's, Westminster by-election of March 1931, reporting on the event with some satisfaction to his father in Nagpur (whose own interest in British politics had been revived by the controversy over the Simon Commission's proposals for Indian constitutional reform):

> Last night I went with Michael [Beaumont] and two others. We tried to get into Beaverbrook's meeting at the Aeolian Hall, but were denied entrance. We accordingly staged a meeting in Bond Street which was extremely successful. Two hundred people rapidly assembled and gave a vote of confidence in Mr Baldwin . . . It must be the first time that British agriculture was discussed there.[19]

* One of Rab's favourite sayings even in old age was (with a naughty reference to Lord Home), 'I may never have known much about ferrets or flower-arranging but one thing I did know was how to govern the people of this country.'

But agriculture, as Rab was beginning to recognise, was no longer the central issue of Tory politics. After Lord Irwin's Declaration of 31 October 1929 that 'the natural issue of India's constitutional progress is Dominion Status' alarm bells had begun to ring throughout the Conservative Party. At Westminster a special India Committee of Conservative MPs and peers had been established with the specific brief of preserving the imperial connection and safeguarding it from any threat which might emanate from the First Round Table Conference launched by Ramsay MacDonald towards the end of 1930. Rab himself was pretty scathing about the India Committee's work, though he was by no means blind to its potential for stirring up trouble:

> The barons of the late Imperial Trade Committee, who planned the Caxton Hall meeting and who are now 'specialising' on India, have again been losing their heads with childish vigour, and under the guise of the India Committee have had two meetings in as many days. Baldwin is to speak on India at Newton Abbot on Friday. I expect his calm delay will have enabled the Viceroy and Gandhi to come to a decision, which will be some positive answer to the India Committee. The public, meanwhile, inflamed by the press, has very much the attitude of the lift man in our block of flats. On India they feel that those 'niggers' are slippery black men, and must not be let out of our sight or our control because they cannot possibly manage their own affairs. Churchill's sibilant disclamour of Gandhi striding up the steps of Government House clad in a blanket has touched their hearts.*[20]

Not that Churchill's typically robust attitude can have provoked total horror or outrage in Rab's own household. In fact, the previous summer his own wife, Sydney, had included in a letter sent to her mother-in-law in India the wry forecast, 'Soon I suppose we shall have Gandhi wandering about London in a loin cloth. I shall pray for snow and sleet if he does.'[21] As it turned out, however, Gandhi did not arrive in London till the Second Round Table Conference of September 1931 – by which time there had been a decisive change in Rab's own political fortunes.

* Churchill's actual words, delivered to the Council of the West Essex Conservatives on 23 February 1931, were, 'It is alarming and also nauseating to see Mr Gandhi, a seditious Middle Temple lawyer, now posing as a fakir of a type well known in the East, striding half-naked up the steps of the Viceregal Palace, while he is still organising and conducting a definite campaign of civil disobedience, to parley on equal terms with the representative of the King-Emperor.'

7 *Apprenticed to India*

Rab was no more than a passive spectator to the traumatic events that led in August 1931 to the fall of the Labour Government and its replacement virtually in the course of a single Monday morning by a National Government still headed by the same Prime Minister, Ramsay MacDonald. Indeed, Rab confessed as much in a letter scribbled to his father from Liverpool Street Station after attending the Kingsway Hall meeting on Friday 28 August at which Baldwin explained to his followers (in the words of the telegram-whip dispatched to all Tory MPs) 'the reasons which caused him to decide it was his duty to take part in the formation of a National Government to carry the urgent financial reforms required by the current national emergency'.

The letter from Liverpool Street contained, however, even more exciting news than that. After the meeting of Conservative MPs, peers and candidates, Rab lunched at Buck's with his friend from Cambridge days, Geoffrey Lloyd, who had been serving as a member of Baldwin's secretariat since his own defeat at Ladywood in 1929. It was from him that Rab learned that 'there is a chance that Sam Hoare may ask me to help with the India Conference as sort of ADC'.[1] Although there was no disguising the pleasure that the news had given Rab, the business of imparting it to his father was plainly overshadowed by a certain nervousness. That was hardly surprising: from the moment there had been even the prospect of his son getting into Parliament, Sir Monty's advice to Rab had been wholly consistent. He had started off in 1926 by baldly announcing, 'No one in England is the least interested in India and never will be. Anyone who speaks *re* India in Parliament is regarded *ipso facto* as a bore – I would not specialise on her.'[2] The same refrain had been repeated time and again since, most recently in a letter sent from Government House, Nagpur towards the end of 1929.

> I do not want you to touch India, partly for my own sake as anything you say may be used against me, but mainly for yours as no one can touch India without loss. Simon came out to prepare for the Viceroyalty and where is he? It has been the same all through – Islington, Linlithgow, Birkenhead and so on. There are only two ways to serve India. Either you must give your life to her, as I have done and not regretted it, or you must come in at the top as Governor or Viceroy for five years untrammelled by previous actions or utterances. Your birth in India, and my record, will be ample introduction to you if you do become later on a Governor of a Presidency or Viceroy. Until then keep clear. Do not be drawn to Indian Committees or into the India Office is my advice.[3]

Little wonder that Rab's announcement of what was still only a rumoured opening rather than an actual appointment was accompanied by a nervous 'I do hope you will not mind' – and a plea as to the advantages such experience would bring 'as I have none administratively'.[4] When the offer was finally made – and indeed improved by being translated into a full invitation to serve the new Secretary of State, Sir Samuel Hoare, as his PPS – Sydney's voice was promptly added to lend persuasive weight to that of her husband:

> Rab has just been offered the Private Parliamentary Secretaryship [sic] by Samuel Hoare. You will remember Geoffrey Butler held it when SH was at the Air Ministry. I am terribly pleased as it is the first step on the ladder if Rab does well. He will have a lot to do with the Conference, I expect. We knew SH was considering Rab for this but feared he would choose someone older – possibly with a title.[5]

That subtle, feminine form of flattery seems to have done the trick. Certainly, the ultimate reaction from the Governor's camp in the Central Provinces turned out to be relatively benevolent – 'Now you have your foot on the ladder, the best of luck to you' – though even then a characteristic note of warning was struck, 'The India Office officials always used to be jealous of outsiders like the Political ADC or the PPS. You have doubtless allowed for this.'[6]

Allowed for or not, Sir Monty's diagnosis proved to be an accurate

5 Homeward bound: the first voyage to England in 1911. Rab, nanny, Iris (*right*) and friend on deck before sailing from Bombay

6 The prep schoolboy at The Wick

7 The young don: Rab was elected a Fellow of Corpus Christi in 1925

8 The Cambridge Union Society Committee in Easter Term, 1924. Rab, as President, is seated in the centre of the front row. His friend, and future Cabinet colleague, Geoffrey Lloyd, is on his left

one. When Rab finally arrived at the India Office on Monday 7 September, he discovered that the PPS had no separate room of his own and that the best that was on offer was 'the side of a desk'.[7] However, things soon looked up and the new PPS, who obviously meant to take his job seriously, found himself installed in the Under-Secretary's room (shared, on the rare occasions when the actual holder of the office put in an appearance, with the Liberal Marquess of Lothian). Rab himself, though, was not to enjoy his new much-prized view over St James's Park all that frequently. The second session of the India Round Table Conference was now in full swing and Rab, as the eyes and ears of Sir Samuel Hoare, was expected to be there every morning at eleven o'clock and to stay for most of its deliberations. Away in the Central Provinces, Sir Monty Butler (who had originally much wanted to be an official delegate to the Conference) was by now sceptical of its success; and it was certainly in no wide-eyed mood that the new youthful 28-year-old apprentice to Indian affairs repaired daily to St James's Palace.

Somewhat to the chagrin of his father, he was immediately impressed by the figure who was now emerging as the star of the proceedings. Indeed, his first full report on the Conference sent out to Government House, Nagpur made Gandhi its centre-piece:

> Just in front of me, on the left of the Lord Chancellor, was Gandhi. Then, at the right of the Lord Chancellor, the British delegates, with the Princes on their right hand. 'It is strange', said Gandhi in a quiet voice speaking very slowly, 'that this small country should have gained ascendancy over the vast continent of India.' William IV, decked in the insignia and robes of royalty, looked down over his chubby gartered calf at the ''alf naked nigger', which is what my constituents call the Mahatma. Nevertheless Gandhi's utterance was impressive. He was quick to introduce the economic argument, saying that a free India would be more helpful to an England, struggling with her economic difficulties.[8]

It was not perhaps quite the impression that Winston Churchill, who only ten days earlier had referred to Rab's selection as a PPS as 'a curious, and it may be fortunate, coincidence',[9] could have expected his 'half-naked fakir' to make on the scion of a well-known Indian Civil Service family. But then nor perhaps was it quite the message that his own family expected to hear back in the Central Provinces – whence, indeed, his father had only recently written, apropos the Mahatma, 'All this slobber over him disgusts me.'[10]

Fortunately though for Rab, Sir Monty's own indignation was now largely reserved for the outgoing Viceroy, Lord Irwin, whose pact with Gandhi he had greatly deplored and at whose door he was now more than ready to lay most of the blame for all the communal troubles that had befallen India. Here there was a clear conflict of view between father and son though, with tact perhaps deployed rather more on Rab's side than Sir Monty's, it never seems to have come to an open clash. Rab had not, in fact, been personally impressed by Irwin when he appeared before the Conservative India Committee in the summer of 1931 – finding the Viceroy's presentation of his case much less commanding and convincing than that of Sir John Simon the following week.[11] But that could not alter the fact that by becoming the political factotum of Sam Hoare, Rab had for the next four years at least committed himself to being the servant of Irwin's – and, therefore, Baldwin's – liberal approach to the Indian problem. There is no evidence that this ever put any form of strain on Rab's own beliefs (he had been an upholder of 'Dominion Status' from the beginning): there are some indications, however, that it did involve something of a tug of loyalty with his father – if only because Sir Monty, as he grew older, seems also to have grown distinctly more reactionary. Certainly, defiant statements sent from the Central Provinces along the lines of 'There is nothing like a cut across the buttocks for checking religious emotion – I have ordered whipping for the low class people caught at this game'[12] appear generally (and, no doubt, wisely) to have been ignored by their recipient, already one of the chief opponents of the Indian 'diehards' of the Tory Party.

Rab's parliamentary existence was not yet entirely dominated by India; from the moment he secured his PPS post he had never been in any doubt that he would be operating in essentially a twilight political world. Geoffrey Lloyd had told him at their August lunch together that it was unlikely the new National Government would last more than two or three months – and so, indeed, it proved, with Ramsay MacDonald eventually bowing to Tory pressure and calling a general election for Tuesday 27 October 1931. For Rab this was marginally inconvenient as Sydney was expecting their second child some time around the second week in October. His reaction, however, was philosophic – 'I am glad she will be out of it'[13] – and, as things turned out, their second son* was conveniently born at a

* Adam Samuel Courtauld Butler (1931–). Conservative MP for Bosworth since 1970. PPS to Leader of the Opposition 1975–9. Served as Minister of State in three Government Departments 1979–85. Knighted 1986.

weekend (on Sunday 11 October) – when Rab was able to be in London. Yet if that had caused a minor personal complication, there were few, if any, political ones. The campaign in Saffron Walden opened with the Liberal candidate, who had come a very close third in 1929, announcing that he was standing down and inviting his supporters to vote for 'the Conservative National candidate, Mr R. A. Butler'. As if that were not bonus enough, it was promptly followed by the announcement of the withdrawal of the Labour candidate for 'reasons of pressure of business'. The local Labour Party, with less than three weeks to go to polling day, found itself compelled to nominate its agent, S. S. Wilson, as candidate,* who, rather quaintly, announced he was taking on the job as much out of loyalty to the former candidate as to the Labour Party. On top of all this, Rab was fortunate enough to be made a present of a £1,000 'election fund' by his father-in-law in addition to his regular allowance of £5,000 a year. Not surprisingly, when the ballot boxes were opened on the day after polling, they revealed the most extravagant Conservative victory Saffron Walden had ever seen: Rab had amassed 22,501 votes while his poor Labour opponent had managed to scrape together just 6,468, yielding an unprecedented Conservative majority of 16,033.

For Rab, the most welcome by-product of the election was a hand-written 'PS' to a note he received from Sam Hoare congratulating him on his result and saying simply, 'I am assuming, I hope rightly, that you will go on as my PPS. *Do*.'[14] Matters, it soon transpired, were not to prove quite as simple as that – but Rab was certainly touched by this initial mark of confidence. On his return to London for the opening of the new Parliament on Tuesday 3 November, he immediately established that other more elaborate schemes had a part in Sam Hoare's mind:

> He said that he had one or two friends, such as Knatchbull, the new Member for Ashford, and another one, whom he would like to help by showing them the inside of a Government Office. He asked if I would mind if they came in. I said no, but it was no use unless we had a proper room, and set up a sort of Secretariat or Kindergarten, which I would run. It is not really a good idea but if he wants it, it is not up to me to mind. Geoffrey Lloyd, who is always a good ally, is going to tell him that it is stupid to have

* That agent, Stanley Wilson, was to turn out to be Rab's main rival in two subsequent elections, nearly defeating him in 1945, and becoming a much admired local figure, not least as wartime Mayor of Saffron Walden.

more than one PPS and I think he sees that. Anyway I have clear seniority.[15]

In the end Hoare took on no new PPS, not even the new Member for Ashford, Michael Knatchbull (later, as Lord Brabourne, Governor of Bombay and Bengal and until his early death in 1939, one of Rab's closest friends). But the whole experience had plainly been an unsettling one and may have had something to do with the alacrity with which Rab, two months later, sacrificed his foothold on the PPS ladder to accept an invitation to join the Franchise Committee, one of three constitutional bodies sent out to tour India as part of the legacy of the Second Round Table Conference. It was in some ways a strange and unexpected assignment for a rural Conservative Member to take on; and, true to form, Rab took pains to ensure that his decision was explained to his constituents – writing a careful letter to the local paper to justify his absence from Parliament over the next three or four months.[16] Fortunately, the general reaction seems to have been that their local Member had been 'done an honour'. Anyway, sitting now on a majority of 16,033, Rab had little cause for electoral anxiety.

There was, however, a definite cause of domestic anxiety before he and Sydney finally sailed for India on the P & O mailboat *Mooltan* on 14 January 1932. Sydney's mother had fallen seriously ill in December 1931 and was to die before the end of the year. She had never been particularly close to her daughter and Sydney's principal concern appears to have been for her father, Sam. It was, however, at his insistence that the trip – their first travels outside Europe since their honeymoon 'world tour' of 1926–7 – went ahead; and Rab and Sydney duly arrived once again in Bombay on 29 January 1932 with the other members of the three Round Table Committees. The Franchise Committee, headed by the India Office Under-Secretary, Lord Lothian, had a pronounced liberal tinge to it; it ended up by recommending that the electoral roll for the Indians should be increased from a base-line of seven million to one of thirty-six million.

For Rab himself the main attraction of the assignment was probably as much personal as political. No sooner had he and his wife arrived than they hurried off to spend the first weekend of their tour of India with Sir Monty and Lady Butler at Government House, Nagpur – a visit suitably commemorated in the indigenous version of the 'Court Circular' that the *Times of India* then carried.[17] (The gubernatorial and parental roof was, once more, to provide a shelter for Rab on his last day in India in May, though by then Sydney had returned home: he was also to pay another pilgrim's visit to the place of his birth, Attock Fort in the Punjab, though on this occasion without Sydney.) Whether, apart from the satisfactions of nostalgia, the experience added anything to Rab's own political equipment must be open to doubt: no other member of the Franchise Committee, who (apart from their chairman) all sailed back together on the SS *Rawalpindi* on 7 May, went on to achieve anything in British politics. The conclusions of their report, published on 13 June, can hardly be said to have shaken the world or, as matters turned out, to have shaped the political future of the sub-continent.

Nevertheless, at least in Rab's own eyes, the visit had clearly been worthwhile. His own knowledge of the land of his birth had never been particularly extensive: between the ages of eight and twenty-four he had never set foot in India – and, despite a sentimental attachment which tended to grow with age, he always had much less direct connection with life on the sub-continent than, for example, his two sisters. In that sense at least, his renewal of acquaintance with his family's roots in political India may well have represented not just a gesture to the past but an investment in his future. Just how valuable an investment it was to prove he can hardly have guessed when he returned to England on Saturday 21 May 1932.

The general election of 27 October 1931, which had given Rab his record majority at Saffron Walden, had also provided the biggest parliamentary landslide in British political history. No fewer than 473 Conservatives were returned to the House of Commons, compared to only 52 Labour Members. Nor was that the whole story of the National Government's triumph, since 35 National Liberals and 33 Samuelite Liberals, along with 13 members of the Prime Minister's own rump Party, National Labour, also supported the Ramsay MacDonald 'national unity' administration. Altogether, the new Government found itself with an almost embarrassing majority of 500 over its collective Commons opponents – 'an invitation', as someone remarked at the time, 'to dictatorship'.

But the new National Government, still nominally headed by Ramsay MacDonald, was in reality a fragile creation, very much subject to strains and stresses from within. It had proved quite unable to fight the election on one united manifesto and held together only on an eventual 'agreement to differ', in particular on the question of tariffs (still resolutely opposed by the Samuelite Liberals and, indeed, by the pre-election National Labour Chancellor, and subsequent Lord Privy Seal, Philip Snowden).

Before the October general election Ramsay MacDonald had been more or less able to call the tune – allowing the Conservatives, for example, only four places in his Emergency Cabinet of eleven (otherwise made up of four representatives of National Labour and three Liberals). However, once the ballot boxes had revealed the true nature of the Government's electoral mandate, his power was necessarily circumscribed – though it remained a political imperative of Baldwin's to preserve the fiction that the Government remained a 'National' one. Thus, not only did he refuse to make any effort to displace MacDonald himself: he also disappointed many of his own followers by insisting that the Government's non-Tory supporters in the new House of Commons receive a disproportionate allocation of offices. The post-election Cabinet had, admittedly, a preponderance of Conservatives – eleven as against four for National Labour, two for the National Liberals and three for the old Free-Trade Liberal Party. But if that represented a curiously lopsided picture of the true Party position in the House of Commons, the distribution of junior offices (in those days much more limited than they are today) did remarkably little to redress the balance. When these latter appointments were announced on 10 November 1931, out of a total of thirty jobs only nineteen were found to have been awarded to Conservatives.

The outlook for Rab was, therefore, hardly promising. He had dutifully kept in touch with his former patron, Sam Hoare, throughout his service on the Indian Franchise Committee – sending him regular reports from the sub-continent and receiving grateful, if slightly stilted, acknowledgments by way of reply – but the final letter he found waiting for him from his erstwhile ministerial chief on arriving back in England could hardly have been counted encouraging. In it Sam Hoare explained that he had found the new Conservative Member for Ashford, Micky Knatchbull (Rab's successor as PPS), 'extremely efficient, whilst you have been away, with the routine work of the House of Commons', and went on to suggest that 'it would be wisest to continue to let him do this work'.[18] There was, it is true, a saving clause – 'There is no reason why you should not, if you so wish, revert to the post of Parliamentary Private Secretary, and he should be Assistant Private Secretary',[19] but, even from so inhibited a person as Sam Hoare,* that could scarcely be

* In his own memoirs Rab was to write of Sam Hoare, 'I was amazed by his ambitions; I admired his imagination; I shared his ideals; I stood in awe of his intellectual capacity. But I was never touched by his humanity. He was the coldest fish with whom I ever had to deal.' *The Art of the Possible* (Hamish Hamilton, 1971), p. 57.

considered a pressing invitation. Rab, however, was not to be discouraged: this time he consented to run in double harness with Knatchbull as PPS and by the late summer of 1931 was again substantially in charge of Sam Hoare's private office. Indeed, he had virtually assumed the duties of the Secretary of State's political manager. For example, he insisted successfully that Hoare should attend that October's Conservative Party Conference at Blackpool, where the agenda contained three resolutions on India, including one critical of the Government's policy intended to be moved by Churchill.[20]

But before the Party Conference took place, Rab had been the beneficiary of one of those strokes of luck in politics, all the more fortunate for being entirely unforeseen. The unresolved conflict between Free Traders and Protectionists within the National Government came to a head over the Ottawa Economic Conference of August 1932, where an agreement made on imperial preference managed to raise, at least for the Liberals, all the old hobgoblins from the past. Baldwin tried earnestly to keep the National Government together – they had all, as he characteristically put it, 'signed on for the voyage'[21] – but without success. In late September the two surviving Liberal members of the Cabinet, Sir Herbert Samuel and Sir Archibald Sinclair (the third, Sir Donald Maclean, father of the notorious Foreign Office traitor, had died in June) resigned, accompanied by that old, unrepentant National Labour Free Trader, Philip Snowden. More to the point for Rab, the junior Liberal members of the administration went too. They included (after an initial period of hesitation)[22] the Under-Secretary at the India Office, the Marquess of Lothian.

In those more hierarchical days, a 29-year-old back-bencher – who had been in the House of Commons barely over three years and who had only just completed an interrupted twelve-month apprenticeship as a PPS – would not normally have been considered for immediate promotion. But Lothian's departure left Sir Samuel Hoare with a problem. The Third Round Table Conference on the Indian Constitution was about to meet in London. It was plain that a White Paper (to be followed by a Bill) would have to be produced soon, and, in Sam Hoare's own words, 'There was no time to train an ignorant newcomer and no place for anyone who did not already understand something of Indian Problems.'[23] So at the outset of his career Rab found himself, as he was not always later to do, in exactly the right place on the political chequerboard at precisely the right time. His appointment did not, however, come about without a struggle. According to Hoare, he had to fight off the opposition of the Conservative Whips,[24] while Rab himself was more inclined to give the credit to Baldwin, who apparently had to overcome some resistance on the part of the Prime Minister, Ramsay MacDonald, in order to push it through.[25] But once the announcement was made – along with four other junior Government changes on 29 September 1932 – the reception, on the whole, was favourable. True, the fact that Rab was now by some years the youngest member of the Government tended to be highlighted – but only the *Daily Express* found that a cause for criticism. Its front-page story declared that the promotions had caused 'utter astonishment and bewilderment' in the Conservative Party. Particular attention was paid to Rab himself, who was said to be regarded by his colleagues 'as an extremely fortunate young man'.[26]

And in one sense, of course, he was. As more than one of the many congratulatory letters he received pointed out, it was not merely a matter of his having got into the Government (thereby defying his father's forecast) before he was thirty: it was also a signal achievement, given the vast array of Conservative back-benchers in the 1931–5 Parliament, to have been plucked out for preferment with only some three years' service in the House behind him. In all the correspondence that Rab received arising out of his appointment as Under-Secretary at the India Office there was only one sour note. It was struck in a telegram from his wife's uncle, Major Jack Courtauld,* a fellow Member of Parliament and a great supporter of Winston Churchill. This baldly announced, 'Congratulations to India, Indians and Gandhi on appointment of able, industrious but loopy Under Secretary of State.'[27] Churchill's own reaction – sent in response to a letter of sympathy Rab had written to him over an attack of paratyphoid to which he had fallen victim earlier in September – was, by contrast, a model of courtly good manners. Having offered his congratulations on Rab's elevation to ministerial office, Churchill went on to express the hope that, although they would, no doubt, find themselves opposed in parliamentary debate, 'our personal relations will remain upon the agreeable footing to which you have raised them'.[28]

Churchill, who had early in 1931, before the formation of the National Government, broken with Baldwin over the Conservative Leader's support of Lord Irwin's policy in India, was already clearly

* Major J. S. Courtauld MC (1880–1942). Conservative MP for Chichester 1924–42.

identified as the most formidable opponent the India Office faced in its pursuit of constitutional reform. That was something which Rab himself readily acknowledged in the first speech he made as Under-Secretary – a speech delivered during a three-day debate at the end of March 1933 asking the Commons to approve the establishment of a Joint Select Committee of both Houses, charged both with the task of examining the Government's White Paper and of bringing forward proposals on which a Bill could be drafted. In parliamentary terms that March debate represented a great set-piece engagement – and Rab, as was only fitting for an Under-Secretary, was left to bring up the Government's light artillery on the final day. By common consent, he did so extremely effectively – not least by dramatising his own predicament and skilfully contriving to personalise the issue. He was the opening Government speaker on the same last day of the debate that Churchill himself was to speak, and he chose to capitalise on that:

> Many a time I have sat in the jungle in central India watching a bait, in the form of a bullock calf* tied to a tree, awaiting the arrival of the lord of the forest, and put there as a trap to entice him to his doom. On this occasion I have exactly the same feelings as those of the miserable animal whom I have so often looked upon in that position, and if I may compare myself to that bait, I may compare my Rt. Hon. Friend, the Member for Epping [Churchill] to the tiger. I hope that Hon. Members, and the Rt. Hon. Gentleman himself, will remember, however, that there is waiting for the tiger a pair of lynx eyes and a sure and safe rifle to ensure his ultimate fate.[29]

The battle over India would continue to dominate the Conservative Party over the next two-and-a-half years. Rab could claim from the outset to have got one thing right. It was a conflict that was kept in being almost entirely by the determination, tenacity and sheer oratorical power of Churchill. In that early debate the Conservative Member for Epping and his 'diehard' followers could muster only

* The only 'criticism' in the mail he received following his speech came, perhaps characteristically, from within the family circle. His sister, Iris, while sending a message of 'Hooray, hooray', could not resist pointing out that his analogy was in one respect false: in India 'you mustn't sit up over calves or bullocks because of Hindu religious prejudices – goats and buffaloes are more generally used but I don't suppose the H of C minded about that!' Butler Papers, Trinity College, Cambridge, B8, letter dated 5.4.1933.

42 votes against 475 for the Government in the division lobbies – but Churchill refused to allow that in any way to deflect him. If the battle could not be won outright in the Commons, then he would simply carry it forward into the constituencies – something that he proceeded very effectively to do, through the new umbrella 'diehard' organisation, the India Defence League, over the next two-and-a-half years.

Again, it seems to have been Rab who first sensed just how much of a threat to the Government's policy this extra-parliamentary revolt might constitute. Certainly, it was at his instigation in May 1933 that a rival body was formed calling itself the 'Union of Britain and India'. If Churchill's was a genuine grass-roots pressure group – and there seems little doubt that the India Defence League did enjoy considerable support among the Tory Party's constituency militants (particularly those with an Indian military background) – then, it has to be said, Rab's rival organisation was a more artificial growth. Indeed, he confessed as much in a letter to his father:

> I have been very busy during the last fortnight or three weeks trying to organise some publicity campaign in opposition to Winston. This has been very difficult. We started with the idea of having a façade of distinguished ex-Governors and so forth. But they have all refused to undertake anything in the nature of a concerted letter to the papers deploring the effect of the Winston ramp. We have now fallen back on the idea of a smaller publicity committee with John Thompson as chairman and Sir Alfred Watson and E. Villiers* as the other two officers. We are taking a room and hope to organise counter-propaganda and to arrange meetings.[30]

The truth, of course, was that the Union of Britain and India, formally launched with newspaper advertisements on 20 May 1933, was nothing but a 'front organisation' for the Government. It was funded initially by the Conservative Central Office, the Chief Conservative Agent put it on its feet and its driving force throughout was the Under-Secretary at the India Office, Rab himself.[31] Nor did its provenance deceive many people at the time. A letter addressed

* Sir John Thompson (1873–1935), a member of the Indian Civil Service, ended his ICS career as Chief Commissioner of Delhi 1929–32. Sir Alfred Watson (1874–1967) was editor of the *Statesman*, Calcutta, 1925–33. Sir Edward Villiers (1889–1967) was a member of the Bengal Legislative Council 1924–6.

by Sir John Thompson to Rab's uncle-by-marriage, Jack Courtauld, drew, for example, this stinging response:

> In reply to your letter of the 18th instant, I may say that I am definitely opposed to the policy which is being advocated by the UBI, and therefore you will understand that neither I nor my Agent, who is *not* a servant of the Central Office, but of my local Association, will be inclined to assist you in my constituency.
>
> I do not know whether the UBI is receiving support in any way from the Conservative Central Office. If so, I admit I consider the position most irregular. If not, I would suggest that it should appeal to the Liberal and Socialist Associations in the constituencies, from whom it will probably receive more sympathy. I note with interest that your Treasurer has also been appointed Governor of Bombay.[32]

That Parthian shot of Major Courtauld's was a reference to the fact that 'Micky' Knatchbull (who had succeeded his father as Lord Brabourne the previous February and whom Rab, now his friend's PPS duties were necessarily over, had put in as the first Treasurer of the organisation) had just been announced in the Press as the next Governor of Bombay. To those supporting Churchill's rebellion over India it was yet further proof* that only those who sympathised with Sir Samuel Hoare's policy were being appointed to the plum jobs within the Indian Civil Service.

That was a point of view with which Rab's own father, Sir Monty Butler, had by now a good deal of sympathy. Indeed, only a year earlier, having been passed over for two major Governorships, he was to be heard protesting that he no longer had any interest in such matters – 'My advice has not been listened to all through, hence most of the trouble.'[33] Fortunately, though, for Sir Monty, and possibly also for his son, his hour of deliverance from India was rapidly approaching. On 1 May 1933, following some fairly intensive lobbying by Rab of both the Palace and the Home Office, the appointment of Sir Monty Butler as Lieutenant-Governor of the Isle

* Churchill had in his speech in the Commons on 29 March 1933 specifically referred to his suspicion that 'the high personnel of India has been arranged, continuously arranged, with a view to securing men who will give a modern and welcome reception' to the Government's White Paper proposals. In the view even of some of his parliamentary sympathisers, this had blunted the force of the rest of his attack. Martin Gilbert, *Winston Churchill*, vol. v (Heinemann, 1976), pp. 472–3.

of Man appeared in the *London Gazette*: he was not actually to take up the office until November but with Sir Monty about to depart from India, at least one form of pressure on the youthful Under-Secretary at the India Office was removed.

It was replaced almost immediately by another. Throughout most of his parliamentary career Rab enjoyed excellent relations with his constituency Party. It is some indication of the convulsion that the India controversy created in the Conservative Party during the early 1930s that they should, for the only time, have come under strain over this last dying kick of old-fashioned imperialism. The first open sign of conflict came in a resolution passed on 13 May 1933 by the annual meeting of the Saffron Walden Conservative Association (unusually held in private) which, while reaffirming confidence in its Member, went on to 'express great apprehension lest the granting of self-government to India, to such an extent as that contemplated in the White Paper, may be injurious to the British Empire'.[34] To the ordinary Conservative MP supporting official Government policy, a resolution couched in such relatively temperate terms might well have seemed little more than a slap on the wrist; to the Under-Secretary at the India Office, who was now regularly attending the Joint Select Committee as one of the four official Government delegates, it necessarily appeared much more like a slap in the face. Little wonder if that summer Rab was to be found reflecting on the kind of local nabobs who made up his constituency organisation in cynical and disenchanted tones:

> I am in a state of deep depression, having been to the Essex Club dinner last night. I find the Essex county gentry cause tears to roll in majestic flow down my cheeks. One was able to say that the partridges have done well, and I repeated this backwards and sideways until I am sure every partridge was out of the egg, and meanwhile, as I have said, rivulets of boredom were coursing down my cheeks. I like them very much but when involved in political intrigue, such as they were all engaged in during and after dinner, and after a heavy day's work, with an Indian reception to follow, I found them almost unbearable, and one wonders whether one human being can bridge the gulf between the Essex countryside and the vast continent of India, of which they know nothing whatever.[35]

It was a mood which was to cling to Rab throughout the entrenched battle with the Tory diehards: indeed, it set in even before the troubles broke out in his own constituency. A letter he wrote to his parents in the spring of 1933, following his attendance at a women's conference of the Eastern Area, at least allowed his old sense of fun full play:

> A woman from Bedford with a determined voice said it was wrong to give votes to naked men with bows and arrows instead of keeping all the power in the hands of the British Government. She was followed by a woman who declared she had just got up from a bed of laryngitis, which appealed strongly to the women's audience. She rejoiced in the old English name of Lock. She was in turn succeeded by a woman of the name of Tennant, of athletic disposition, who lived up to her name by saying that Britain had always persecuted the Irish, and obviously were persecuting India, and so must clear out. This, from a speaker against a resolution condemning any sort of progress in India, was greeted with vociferous howls. Blood was seen streaming from the ears of several of the audience, and at this juncture a loud-voiced and broad-bosomed Irish woman leapt up on the *montagne*, that is the high benches at the side, saying that the whole of Ireland would be delighted to be forever under the British heel and that they demanded nothing better. The audience was now in a state of ecstasy.[36]

As in his schooldays, irreverence had become the armour Rab chose to wear against irritation – but there was no doubt of his sense of despondency as he confronted the legions of the right within his own Party. Nine months later, writing to his friend and former colleague, Lord Brabourne, who had arrived in Bombay towards the end of 1933, he made no effort to hide his disillusion:

> We have started the autumn with the Conservative Conference. I attended the whole of yesterday and found myself more out of sympathy with Conservative principles (?) than I have been for some time, although the tendency has been growing. The audience would have been a credit to the Zoo or wild regions of the globe were they populated by mouldy and unattractive fauna. No ray of enlightenment shone on a single face except the shining pate of Sir Henry Page Croft,* who has the merit of looking fairly well washed.[37]

* Henry Page Croft (1881–1947). Conservative MP, Christchurch 1910–18 and Bournemouth 1918–40, was one of Churchill's principal lieutenants in the battle over the India Bill. He became the 1st Baron Croft in 1940.

Part of the trouble, no doubt, stemmed from the continuing unrest in his constituency – at one stage Rab had even had to receive a deputation of aggrieved association officers in his room at the India Office[38] – but there was perhaps a deeper cause than that. Even when defending Government policy successfully at the Despatch Box, Rab's lifelong sense of detachment made it impossible for him to disregard the primitive reflexes of many of his colleagues. Thus in reporting to Lord Brabourne that the new Governor's handling of a mill strike in Bombay had gone down well in the Commons, he could not resist adding, 'There was quite a cheer when I answered a question of David Grenfell's – they always like to hear that people have been locked up or firm action has been taken.'[39] It might have been easier if Rab had had a genuine regard for his chief at the India Office, Sir Samuel Hoare; but his feelings for him had always stopped some way short of idolatry. Accordingly, when in April 1934, Sam Hoare came under his greatest peril in the whole Indian controversy – arising out of Churchill's (wholly justifiable) charge that Hoare and Lord Derby* had influenced the evidence that the Manchester Chamber of Commerce originally proposed to submit to the Joint Committee – Rab found it quite impossible, at least in private, to rush chivalrously to his chief's defence. He reported to Lord Brabourne that their former common mentor had been in 'very bad form' when Churchill raised the matter as a question of privilege on the floor of the House, adding the somewhat bleak rider that he was inclined to think that the whole incident 'will do Winston down, whatever effect it has on Sam'.[40] Nor was he much more charitable as the case progressed before the Committee of Privileges: thus a week later he was to be found again writing to Lord Brabourne, 'I think you are right in saying that, thanks to his name being coupled with that of Lord Derby, he will emerge from it without incurring the great disapproval of the public'.[41] Even between friends that hardly rated as a resounding vote of confidence in the merits of Sam Hoare's defence – and perhaps Rab gave away more than he may have realised when he commented, once the Committee of Privileges had ruled against Churchill, that his chief was 'obviously much relieved'.[42]

There can, however, be no doubt that Rab believed in the National Government's liberating scheme for Indian constitutional reform – tepid and ineffective as it later came to seem. He certainly played his full part in negotiating its passage through the Commons, filling

* The 17th Earl of Derby (1865–1948), a hereditary Conservative grandee, sometimes known as 'the King of Lancashire'.

in the end even more columns of *Hansard* than his own Secretary of State, who fell ill in the later stages of the India Bill, so leaving the principal burden on Rab's shoulders. He acquitted himself remarkably well, earning a generous tribute on the Bill's Third Reading from the man who throughout had been his most formidable opponent, Winston Churchill.* Typically, he was not, however, blind to the great defect in the Bill that the Indian Princes' sudden withdrawal from any co-operation in a federal solution, decided at a secret conference held in Bombay on 25 February 1935, had opened up. The delay between offering autonomy to the provincial legislatures and the establishment of an 'All India' federal Government in Delhi had been spotted by Rab from the beginning as 'the Achilles heel of our cause'[43]; and now the withdrawal of the princely states threatened to turn what had been intended as a transitional phase into a permanent arrangement. Not surprisingly, the Congress politicians were markedly unenthusiastic about the 'half a loaf' that the British Government finally offered them; in six provinces the Congress Party was to cause a major crisis in 1937 by refusing to take office at all. In retrospect, it is difficult to resist the conclusion that the whole protracted struggle over the Government of India Act 1935 was a classic example of a mountain labouring to produce a mouse – though given the toll the battle had exacted from the Conservative Party (both in the House of Commons and the constituencies), that was not the verdict at the time.

For Rab the placing of the Bill on the Statute Book in the late summer of 1935 represented a personal triumph – not least because Sir Samuel Hoare had left the India Office to become Foreign Secretary before the passage of the Bill was completed; it had, therefore, been left to Rab to steer the last stages of the measure (including the consideration of the Lords amendments) through the Commons. It was, no doubt, partly in recognition of this that in July Rab received a signal mark of official favour. Baldwin, who had succeeded Ramsay MacDonald as Prime Minister in June, agreed to come to Rab's constituency – and, indeed, to his own home, Stanstead Hall, Halstead (to which the family had moved from Broxted in 1934) – to address a 'Grand Fête and National Demonstration'. It was very much a full-dress occasion with five constituencies participating in its

* 'The Secretary of State has had the support of several able colleagues on the front bench – and particularly the Under-Secretary who has distinguished himself greatly and has established a parliamentary reputation of a high order.' *Hansard* (5 June 1935), col. 1911. Churchill conspicuously refrained from paying any equivalent tribute to Sam Hoare himself.

organisation, a dozen MPs on the platform* and some 8,000 people in the audience. More to the point, though, for Rab personally was the advantage of having the Prime Minister (and Leader of his Party) for two days running under his own roof.

As weekend guests the Baldwins (the Prime Minister had come accompanied by his wife, Lucy) appear to have felt immediately at home. There was one small disaster when the Prime Minister was bitten on the finger by one of the family dogs on the morning of the meeting, but Baldwin contrived tactfully to dismiss the incident by remarking that he quite understood how the dog felt, 'I want to do that to every supplementary question in the House at this time of year.' He then, according to Rab's own account written at the time,[44] calmly reached into his pocket, produced an iodine pencil and proceeded to paint the scratch. Before his speech he insisted on being left alone, but once it had been safely delivered on the Saturday evening expanded a good deal – talking freely of senior figures in the Party including Churchill ('a military adventurer who would sell his sword to anyone'). His single direct reference to Rab's own place within the Party came only on Sunday morning while he was waiting for the train to take him back to London. As they strode up and down the platform together, the Prime Minister announced to his host, 'I am so glad to have seen you at home in the country. You must go on coming down every weekend. Life in the country makes one see things clearly and will enable you to steer, as I have done, between Harold Macmillan and John Gretton.'†

If Rab had hoped, as he might well have felt justified in doing, that such a notable mark of confidence and favour would soon lead to preferment within the Government (now headed by Baldwin) he was to be disappointed. Even after the general election of 14 November 1935 – which Rab effortlessly negotiated in Saffron Walden‡ – he was left at his junior post at the India Office under

* The only Essex Conservative MP not to attend was the Member for Epping, Winston Churchill, but he at least sent a cordial message. Five years later the fact that he had been personally invited by Rab was to yield a surprise dividend. In May 1940, in explaining to Rab the political reasons why he wished him to remain as Under-Secretary at the Foreign Office, Churchill rather surprisingly added a personal note: 'Besides you once invited me to your country home.' BBC Radio Profile, June 1978.

† The Rt Hon John Gretton (1867–1947), a brewer and one of the right-wing stalwarts of the Tory Party. He was MP for Burton 1907–43 and was created the 1st Baron Gretton in 1944.

‡ The figures were R. A. Butler (U.) 19,669, Mrs C. D. Rackham (Lab.) 9,633. Unionist majority 10,036.

the new Secretary of State, the Marquess of Zetland.* The only overt sign that Rab *was* disappointed appeared in a letter he wrote a fortnight after the election to Lord Brabourne, who, now that Sir Monty was settled nearer home in the Isle of Man, had become his main direct contact with India and his principal epistolary confidant. To the Governor of Bombay he was quite open about a certain feeling of dissatisfaction, even if it did stop short of actual discontent:

> All the changes appear to have been made in the Government, and the junior posts, as usual, survive storm and strain and just carry on. It is remarkable how little one hears in a junior post of the Government at all. There is no cohesive influence; one is never together with one's colleagues, and Parliaments may come and Parliaments may go or reshuffles may occur, but if one sits tight one has security of tenure. There doesn't appear to be any invitation to proceed. In any case, I am in clover.[45]

The main reason why the grass at the India Office looked full of clover was that Rab's new chief was in the House of Lords – which meant that Rab now had the sole duty of representing the Department in the Commons. No longer did he have to make complaints about the Secretary of State on the Treasury Bench 'always joining in just as the responsibility appears to be being taken by oneself'.[46]

Rab, nevertheless, did not find his new chief wholly congenial. There were soon different sorts of complaints – this time about the formality, not to say starchiness, that the Marquess brought to the running of the India Office. Zetland had previously served as Governor of Bengal and he remained every inch the pro-consul – indeed, in his own memoirs published nearly forty years later, Rab was to characterise him as being 'too punctilious to be informal and too straitlaced to be communicative'.[47] Nor was that simply a retrospective judgment: in the first six months of his service under him Rab was to write wryly to his friend Brabourne, 'I am now the one and only person in the office who has any touch at all with the ordinary man or woman'[48] – and there can be little doubt that he did not find it easy to adjust to a regime whereby even the Parliamentary Under-Secretary was required to seek an appointment in writing if he wished to see his chief.[49] It was hardly surprising that Rab began

* The Second Marquess of Zetland (1876–1961) was Secretary of State for India 1935–40. He had served on the Islington Commission, of which Rab's father was joint Secretary, as long ago as 1912.

to look back even on Sam Hoare's inclination to interfere with something approaching nostalgia.

Necessarily, there was also some sense of anti-climax. Once the India Bill had been placed on the Statute Book, the affairs of the sub-continent no longer held the centre stage at Westminster and, although there was still a good deal of tidying up to be done (during his last year at the India Office Rab was responsible for negotiating no fewer than forty-two draft Orders-in-Council through the Commons), little of it was of a dramatic or headline-catching nature. Indeed, when Rab's name did surface before the public, it tended to be only as a result of slightly off-beat activities. Thus towards the end of 1935 he was an official delegate on behalf of India to the London Naval Conference called by the British Government in an effort to limit the size of the world's navies: the impact of his début on the international stage was, however, muffled somewhat by his own characteristic confession that he represented a rather diminutive force, lacking entirely in the kind of vessels that were the Conference's primary concern. Perhaps predictably, this held him up to some scorn in the Indian Press, where one cartoonist unkindly portrayed him as 'Admiral Butler' commanding a small dinghy, with a gagged Indian woman at the oars, lying alongside a fleet of mighty dreadnoughts.[50]

Rab was to have another, equally anomalous, walk-on part at the time of the Abdication a year later. The fact that he was the sole representative of the India Office on the Treasury Bench meant that his was one of the eight signatures attached to the Bill of Abdication laid before the Commons on 10 December 1936: he thus found himself promoted, at least for one historic garment-touching moment, into the company of such Government grandees as the Foreign Secretary, the Chancellor of the Exchequer and even the Prime Minister himself.

Of the Abdication itself Rab took, perhaps not surprisingly, a typical Middle England view. Too junior to play much part in the life of the Court and never a member of the old Prince of Wales set, Rab's own mind as to the inevitability of the departure of Edward VIII was made up early on. At the beginning of December he was confiding in Brabourne that he regarded the new King as 'a congenitally weak man – with great personal charm, publicity sense and some cunning – in the hands of a clever, adventurous foreigner'. More remarkably, he added his own forecast that Edward VIII would abdicate – and that Baldwin's handling of the crisis would see to it that, although the royal successor would inevitably be 'a dull dog who will hold the declining influence of the Church and whose fortunes will be linked with that of the middle class', the monarchy would be saved until the time came 'to pass on the sceptre to a Queen'.[51] It is only fair to add that at this stage Rab's one meeting with the Duke of York (who was to become King George VI on 10 December) had been in Australia on his and Sydney's honeymoon world tour ten years earlier and that he was very soon to revise his estimate of the new monarch.*

In any event, probably of more immediate personal concern to Rab had been the fall of his first political mentor exactly one year earlier over the affair of the Hoare–Laval Pact. Foreign Secretary for barely six months, Sir Samuel Hoare had been forced into resignation when, in face of a public outcry, the Cabinet repudiated an agreement he had made in Paris with the French Foreign Minister, Pierre Laval, over the proposed cession of Abyssinian territory to Mussolini's Italy. There was no doubt of Rab's personal sympathy for his initial sponsor – 'Sam's resignation is, of course, a great blow to me', he had written to Brabourne on the day the Foreign Secretary resigned, 'since he was my patron in politics and I owe him a great deal;'[52] but there was equally no concealment that on the policy issue Rab found himself entirely unable to endorse his former chief's stand. 'The sudden volte-face six weeks after the election has aroused almost unanimous dissatisfaction,' he added in that same letter, going on to speak of it revealing 'a division in principle between the older and the younger generation'. Whatever was to be alleged later, it was, therefore, apparent that, at least at the outset, Rab did not place himself automatically in the appeasement camp. Indeed, rather the reverse – for, slightly callously, Rab was eventually to announce that he found consolation in the reflection that morality should still be strong enough for 'Parliament and public opinion to have sacked a Foreign Secretary and a King within a year.'[53]

Any Cromwellian echoes in that comment were, however, misleading – if only because Rab had become by now not so much a village Hampden as a thoroughly conventional country squire. Installed for the past two years in his father-in-law's former home, Stanstead Hall, he had recently acquired shooting rights on a neighbouring estate from the left-wing Countess of Warwick and had even taken to regular riding – an activity which, he readily confessed, he was beginning to find preferable to his somewhat humdrum life at Westminster and in Whitehall. 'I feel', he wrote to Brabourne (whom

* See Chapter 8, p. 79.

he had just asked to be godfather to his third son),* 'that I am marking time in politics' – adding that the recompense was that at least it gave him more time in the country on horseback.[54] One reason for his restiveness lay, no doubt, in the fact that he had fallen progressively out of sympathy with what he regarded as the 'negativism' of the policy being pursued both by Zetland and by the new Viceroy, the Marquess of Linlithgow: alone among the India Office hierarchy he was, as he wrote to Brabourne that spring, in favour of reopening talks with the Congress Party, and in particular with Gandhi.[55]

Fortunately, however, for Rab's political future his sense of unease – and, indeed, his uncharacteristic feeling of withdrawal from his official work – did not pass without notice. As early as the beginning of March 1937 he had been approached by Sir Geoffrey Fry, a member of Baldwin's secretariat, and told that there was a plan in the wind for him to be moved to the home front. After nearly six years at the India Office (the last two as the Department's sole spokesman in the Commons) Rab could have been forgiven for hoping that he might be promoted to a Ministry of his own, if a relatively minor one outside the Cabinet: but it was soon made clear to him that that was not what was on offer. Instead he found dangled in front of him the prospect of going to the Ministry of Labour, or possibly the Board of Trade, again as an Under-Secretary. It was, understandably, not a change that initially excited Rab – though the more he thought about it, the more inclined he became to see advantages in the transfer. Strangely, the negotiations seem to have been conducted mainly with Sir Horace Wilson,† the industrial adviser to the Government and shortly to become the real power behind both the Government's domestic and foreign policy, once Neville Chamberlain had taken over from Stanley Baldwin in Downing Street following the Coronation in May.

With a new Prime Minister in office, Rab – along with all other members of the Government – was expected to submit his resignation; and this he duly did, according to the required protocol of those days, to his own Secretary of State, the Marquess of Zetland. It was, however, in his case no more than a pure formality – demonstrated by the fact that on the same day he wrote his resig-

* Samuel James Butler born 13 December 1936. He became a TV producer.

† Sir Horace Wilson (1882–1972). Permanent Secretary, Ministry of Labour 1921–30. Chief Industrial Adviser to HM Government 1930–9. Seconded to Treasury for service to the Prime Minister 1935. Permanent Secretary to Treasury and official head of Civil Service 1939–42.

nation letter to his principal at the India Office, he wrote another – this time to the new Prime Minister – accepting appointment as Parliamentary Under-Secretary at the Ministry of Labour. Both letters were written from Stanstead, since Rab's new penchant for riding had led him into a second tumble* which had broken his collar-bone – a mishap which had kept him at home since the middle of May. At least it enabled him from the beginning to establish something more than a mere official relationship with the new Prime Minister, whose handwritten letter to Rab inviting him to join his Government opened with the statement, 'I was very sorry to hear of your accident and hope you are making a good recovery.'[56] Rab promptly replied in kind assuring him that the break 'had been a simple one' and that he would be available for duty the following week. He also made all the expected noises, intimating that he regarded the opening offered to him as 'a great opportunity of acquiring fresh experience' and expressing his gratitude for the chance 'to come into closer contact with the most intimate, internal problem of this country' – meaning, of course, unemployment.[57]

As a model of tact and diplomacy from an aspiring and rising politician (still not yet thirty-five) it was hard to fault. The impression it was designed to make upon Chamberlain would perhaps have been slightly dulled if the Prime Minister had been able to read another, rather more candid, letter that Rab wrote the same day to his father in the Isle of Man. In this he made no pretence. 'The offer is not an exciting one', he wrote, finding comfort only in the reflection 'that most of my contemporaries are receiving no better'. To his father Rab was prepared to blurt out the real truth:

> I am also exceedingly glad in my inner self to have escaped from the India Office before a period of what looks like repression . . . It appears that British policy is determined not to try and back up the Hindu front by political handling so if it is to be broken up by a straight bat, I would rather not be in the team.[58]

If rather different in tone from the official letter of acceptance sent to Downing Street, that private note at least represented the honest and refreshing expression of a political attitude – an attitude that, for better or for worse, was to characterise the rest of Rab's political and ministerial career.

* This fall seems effectively to have ended Rab's riding career. It was left to Sydney to instil a love of horses into their children.

8 *Appeasement and the Foreign Office*

The Ministry of Labour was to prove little more than a way-station for Rab. He remained there only nine months – and though he may have been exaggerating when, in the immediate aftermath, he described the whole episode as 'a sordid period',[1] his heart does not seem to have been in his new work in the same way as it was (at least initially) at the India Office.

Part of the reason for that may well have lain in the character of his new ministerial chief. Certainly, Ernest Brown* presented a sharp enough contrast with the Marquess of Zetland: a fisherman's son from Cornwall, he was a lifelong ardent Baptist whose whole outlook on life was heavily influenced by his evangelical zeal. With that very much in mind, Rab had artfully included in his first communication to him – a wire sent in reply to a letter of welcome from his new chief – a biblical reference about outflanking the Philistines from the Second Book of Samuel. This, according to his own account in a letter to his parents,[2] led to the political evangelist being found in 'a state of ecstasy' when they first met officially on Monday 31 May.

There was, though, a slightly ominous undertone to the wording of the Minister's own invitation to 'come along and have a yarn':[3] Ernest Brown was in fact a compulsive talker and Rab was to

* Ernest Brown (1881–1962). Liberal MP Rugby 1923, Leith 1927–31 (Liberal National 1931–45). Minister of Labour 1935–40. Secretary for Scotland 1940–1. Minister of Health 1941–3. Chancellor of the Duchy of Lancaster 1943–5. Minister of Aircraft Production 1945.

find his new chief's stentorian voice* and staunchless eloquence something of a trial. Indeed, when, some six months later, a groundless rumour circulated that Rab had gone down with laryngitis, he jokingly wrote to his friend Brabourne that he could only attribute its currency to 'my attempts to talk to Ernest Brown'.[4]

Yet the volubility of his new departmental head was not the sole reason for Rab's lack of happiness. Years later he was to write of how dispiriting he had found the Ministry of Labour experience. 'We toured the depressed areas of South Wales, Cumberland and the North-East, and for ever afterwards I remembered what Montagu Norman's† deflationary strictness at the Bank of England meant in human terms.' More than that, in his own memoirs, Rab went on to recall how in his own days as a post-war Chancellor, he had once rounded on the apostles of the old-style economics and told them sharply that 'those who talked about creating pools of unemployment should be thrown into them and made to swim'.[5] It was a rare moment of acerbity for Rab and it perhaps serves to demonstrate what a profound impression the vision of patient, shuffling men in shabby macintoshes outside Labour Exchanges had made on him.

His new job also brought Rab into far closer contact with Labour Members in the Commons than his old post at the India Office had ever done – and he seems to have made a conscientious effort to get to know each and every Opposition MP (thereby perhaps laying the foundations for what was later to be his striking cross-Party appeal). Being now on the home front, he began, too, to take a more active part in the policy-making machinery of his own Party, becoming chairman of its Central Education Committee on 1 July 1937 (and thus acquiring not only an *ex officio* seat on the Executive of the National Union of Conservative and Unionist Associations but also, far more importantly, forging the link that was later to bring him the chairmanship of the Conservative Research Department). Yet, try as he might, Rab did not at this time find it easy to focus his interests exclusively on domestic matters. His correspondence with Brabourne, for instance, during this period contains far more refer-

* A probably apocryphal anecdote of the time had it that on one occasion Stanley Baldwin, while Prime Minister, inquired the source of a terrible noise disturbing the calm of No. 10. On being told by a Private Secretary, 'Mr Ernest Brown is talking to Birmingham,' he is supposed to have replied, 'But why can't he use the telephone?'

† First Baron Norman of St Clere (1871–1950). Governor of the Bank of England 1920–44.

ences to the storm clouds gathering over Europe than to his work at the Ministry of Labour. In particular, Rab emerges from these letters as a stout defender of the controversial visit of Halifax, then Lord Privy Seal, to Hitler at Berchtesgaden in November 1937 – viewing it as a chance 'to further the spirit, which is in evidence here, in favour of agreement and negotiations'[6] and firmly denying (inaccurately as events turned out) that it had caused any distress to Anthony Eden,* who had succeeded Sir Samuel Hoare as Foreign Secretary after the *contretemps* of the Hoare–Laval Pact in December 1935.

When Eden's resignation finally came on 20 February 1938 – admittedly on the separate issue of Chamberlain's private contacts with Mussolini – Rab was clearly taken by surprise. Only eight days beforehand he had been writing to Brabourne in fulsome praise of the Foreign Secretary, 'Anthony, who has been so long patient and moderate, is certainly in good form and in strength with the party.'[7] The tribute was all the more remarkable since Rab (a founder member of the Boys' Brigade, as opposed to the YMCA or the Glamour Boys)† had never been counted among the most constant of Eden's admirers: indeed, a year earlier in the wake of Eden's original appointment he had gone on record (if only privately) with the view that 'There is considerable doubt about whether Anthony is not too amenable and polite and "in" with the Foreign Office officials.'[8] Once Eden resigned, however, Rab lost no time in reverting to his original judgment:

> He has always been impressionable and it appears that people have been getting at him for the past few weeks and, in particular, Winston Churchill. He seems also to have been influenced by a backing of a certain section of the Press and, in a mood of resentment, at Neville Chamberlain's great interest in foreign affairs, taken a course of action which it is extremely difficult to justify rationally.[9]

Whether it could be justified rationally or not, it certainly opened

* Robert Anthony Eden (1897–1977). Conservative MP, Warwick and Leamington 1923–57. Parliamentary Under-Secretary Foreign Office 1931–3. Lord Privy Seal 1934–5. Minister without Portfolio 1935. Foreign Secretary 1935–8. Secretary of State for Dominions 1939–40. Secretary of State for War 1940. Foreign Secretary 1940–5, Leader of the House of Commons 1942–5. Foreign Secretary 1951–5. Prime Minister 1955–7. Made Knight of the Garter 1954 and created 1st Earl of Avon 1961.

† See p.42.

up an exciting vista for Rab. Eden had not, after all, resigned alone: with him had gone his subordinate at the Foreign Office, Viscount Cranborne, later the Marquess of Salisbury.* Rab's initial apprehension seems to have been that Eden would simply be replaced by another figure in the Commons, in which case the Under-Secretaryship would presumably remain in the Lords; but he spotted almost at once a possible alternative scenario in which the top job would go to Halifax, and in that event 'one of us will be Under-Secretary though it is difficult to see who'. It was not really all that difficult, as Rab himself was to make half-clear by going on to add, 'I was delighted to sense the dust of battle again last night.'[10]

The scent did not mislead him. The next morning he was sent for by Chamberlain and, in the Cabinet Room of No. 10 Downing Street, found himself offered the Under-Secretaryship at the Foreign Office. According to his own contemporary account, Chamberlain was 'very short and to the point', although the Prime Minister did apparently find time to say that the offer showed that his 'work on India had been appreciated'.[11] No compliment could have been more calculated to commend itself to Rab: only three months earlier he had been ruefully comparing the enthusiasm that he had brought to the preparation of the India Bill with the relative listlessness he felt in trying to master the provisions of a new Unemployment Bill due that session.[12] Yet Rab was to pay a price for his dramatic promotion. On the sidelines at the Ministry of Labour his growing sympathies with Chamberlain's appeasement policy may have gradually become obvious enough to his friends; but at least they were never advertised to the public. Now, however, he had been promoted to an office in which he was, necessarily, in a very exposed position – the more so, since the new Foreign Secretary was in the Lords and, for the second time in his ministerial career, Rab found himself the sole spokesman for his Department in the Commons.

However, at the age of thirty-five, it was hardly to be expected that he would operate in the Commons as an entirely free agent. Even the way the Press eventually announced his appointment was slightly unusual. Eden's resignation had been a 'scoop' for the

* The 5th Marquess of Salisbury (1893–1972). He was to go on to have a wide and varied ministerial career, serving in the Churchill, Eden and Macmillan Governments. He resigned, for a second time on a matter of policy, from the Macmillan Cabinet in 1957 in protest against the release of Archbishop Makarios from detention and never held office again.

Sunday Pictorial, then edited by the youthful Hugh Cudlipp,* on Sunday 20 February – but in those more leisured days it took a little time for the machinery of Government changes to creak into action. When the formal announcement came in a communiqué from No. 10 on Friday 25 February, the news of Rab's new post as Foreign Office Under-Secretary was accompanied by a strange coda, plainly bearing all the hallmarks of a Lobby briefing, 'As the new Foreign Secretary [Halifax] will be a member of the House of Lords, the Prime Minister proposes himself to deal with all important aspects of foreign affairs which are the subject of debate or question in the House of Commons.'[13] And so, indeed, things tended to work out – both at Question Time and in major debates in the House of Commons.

For Rab there were both advantages and disadvantages in this somewhat novel constitutional arrangement. The advantages, at least in the short term, centred on the closeness of the association it gave him with the Prime Minister and Leader of his Party. He became far more of an *habitué* of No. 10 than any other junior Minister – required to be present and in touch, if not with the Prime Minister himself, then at least with his *éminence grise*, Sir Horace Wilson, whenever there was a possible challenge to the Government's foreign policy on the floor of the House of Commons. (Inevitably, in the era of the Spanish Civil War – and of the British Government's somewhat hypocritical support of a 'Non-Intervention Policy' – there were not a few of those.) The disadvantages, as Neville Chamberlain might have foreseen, stemmed from a general feeling of resentment, at least on the Opposition benches, whenever the monkey rather than the organ-grinder was left to provide the music. Rab's early days on the Treasury Bench dealing with Foreign Office matters were, accordingly, dogged with angry cries of 'Where's the Prime Minister?' or loud injunctions to 'Fetch him in.'

Eventually, though, this rather anomalous division of parliamentary responsibility did begin to show benefits. Rab had lost none of the skill he had displayed while at the India Office, offering soft answers that turned away wrath. By the end of that summer's session – which had seen not only growing indignation over Chamberlain's blind eye to the clearest evidence of both German and Italian intervention in support of General Franco in Spain but also virtually bipartisan outrage at Hitler's *Anschluss* with Austria – Rab's bland,

* Hugh Cudlipp (1913–). Editor, *Sunday Pictorial* 1937–40 and 1946–9. Chairman Daily Mirror Newspapers 1965–8. Chairman International Publishing Corporation 1968–73. Created life peer 1974.

emollient demeanour at the Despatch Box had come to be seen as the perfect foil to the Prime Minister's naturally far more abrasive manner. When the House rose at the end of July, it was not only the *Daily Mail* which judged that the new Under-Secretary at the Foreign Office had proved one of 'the two outstanding successes' of the Chamberlain Government.[14]

That success had, however, been bought at a cost. The days of 'the Boys' Brigade' had gone for good and Rab, whether he liked it or not, was now firmly identified with 'the Old Gang'. If he had been, at least in the most discreet sense, a heretic against Party orthodoxy over India, he had become a total conformist to the predominant Party faith on appeasement. The doubts that assailed figures normally as disparate in the party as Winston Churchill, Anthony Eden, Leo Amery* and even his own senior ministerial colleague, Duff Cooper,† were not for him: he was now acknowledged as one of the main apologists for the Chamberlain Government's appeasement policy.

There is not the slightest evidence that, even in private, this role caused Rab any discomfort. True, at this stage his regular personal correspondence, in which he had always reflected with total candour on both political and diplomatic questions, tends to tail off. In the autumn of 1937 his father, Sir Monty Butler, had left the Lieutenant-Governorship of the Isle of Man in order to become, to his great delight, Master of his (and his son's) old college, Pembroke, Cambridge. From now on contact between father and son would seem to have been principally by telephone rather than by letter. In addition, early in 1939, Lord Brabourne, his closest friend and for the past six years his principal confidant by correspondence, died suddenly at the age of forty-three in Calcutta, less than two years into his second Indian Governorship of Bengal. The documentary sources for Rab's private feelings at the time are, therefore, inevitably somewhat haphazard; but there is certainly nothing in the letters from this period that survive to suggest that Rab was in any other mood than that of John Henry, Cardinal Newman, for whom ten thousand difficulties did not make a doubt.

* L. S. Amery (1873–1955). MP for Sparkbrook, Birmingham 1911–45. Held a variety of Government offices culminating as Secretary of State for India and Burma in Churchill's wartime coalition.

† Alfred Duff Cooper (1890–1954). Conservative MP for Oldham 1924–9 and St George's Division of Westminster 1931–45. Secretary of State for War 1935–7. First Lord of the Admiralty 1937–8. Minister of Information 1940–1. Chancellor of the Duchy of Lancaster 1941–3. Ambassador to France 1944–7. Created 1st Viscount Norwich 1952.

If anything the more the difficulties multiplied, especially with Hitler's Germany, the more Rab's faith in appeasement seems to have been reinforced. Through his somewhat reckless appointment of Henry ('Chips') Channon* as his PPS within a week of his arrival at the Foreign Office, he had become in much closer touch than before with what passed at the time for the world of the English social scene. He was, as a consequence, soon to be pursued by various assorted noblemen pressing upon him the necessity of reaching an accommodation with Hitler, virtually at any price. To all such importunings Rab, as one would expect, returned much the same evasive answers as he contrived to give to his critics from the opposite end of the spectrum on the floor of the House of Commons – though he may perhaps have dropped his guard a little when, characteristically, in a family letter written to his own cousin, he rashly blurted out:

> I am fairly hopeful about the future, although we must not underestimate the strength or designs of Germany. Why we should be jealous of her developing her economic strength I am uncertain. After all, Harrods and Selfridges flourish in London, and so do a lot of other small shops as well. There should be room for us all in the world.[15]

In retrospect that cannot help seeming a strangely naïve – not to say (given Hitler's treatment of the Jews) insensitive – statement;† and the only possible defence of it is perhaps that it was written in the aftermath of the Munich Agreement between Chamberlain and Hitler of September 1938. Rab himself played no part at all in negotiating even the preliminaries to that Agreement, since he spent almost the whole of September leading the British delegation at the 19th Assembly of the League of Nations in Geneva. His experience there, almost to his own surprise, he seems to have found highly agreeable – writing to his mother from the *Palais des Nations*, 'It really has been extraordinarily interesting here, although I'm sure

* Sir Henry Channon (1897–1958). Conservative MP Southend 1935–50, Southend West 1950–8. His faintly scandalous Diaries, entitled *Chips: The Diaries of Sir Henry Channon*, ed. Robert Rhodes James (Weidenfeld & Nicolson, 1967), were published only after his death.

† Rab had been an early purchaser of the English edition of *Mein Kampf*, making surprisingly neutral notes upon it while still living at Church House, Broxted – that is before 1935. From what he scribbled about it on two sides of Broxted writing paper his main interest seems to have lain in the Hitler Youth Movement, which he found characterised by 'public spirit'.

we haven't appreciated the intense drama that has been going on in England, and your anxiety.'[16] That was a veiled reference to the wave of near-panic that had swept Britain when the prospect of war over Czechoslovakia had appeared not only inevitable but immediate – a threat lifted only when Neville Chamberlain returned from Munich waving his famous piece of paper and proclaiming, 'Peace for our time.'

Whatever unhappiness the Munich Settlement, involving the dismemberment of the Czech nation, provoked elsewhere in the Conservative Party,* it was seen by Rab as little short of a triumph for the Prime Minister and his appeasement policy. He was, admittedly, perfectly entitled to claim a vein of consistency in his outlook: always a critic of the Versailles Treaty of 1919, he had written to Brabourne early in 1938 suggesting that its disregard of the principle of self-determination made it treacherous ground for any Government to take its stand upon – and certainly Rab saw nothing objectionable in allowing the Sudetenland Germans to determine their own destiny. Alas, however, in his speech to the House of Commons on 5 October 1938, winding up the third day of the debate on the Munich Agreement, he went well beyond such arguable historical points and threw all caution to the winds. Certainly, he was in untypically forthright form, as his peroration demonstrated:

> It seems to me that we have two choices – either to settle our difference with Germany by consultation, or face the inevitability of a clash between the two systems of democracy and dictatorship. In considering this I must emphatically give my opinion as one of the younger generation. War settles nothing and I can see no alternative to the policy upon which the Prime Minister has so courageously set himself.[17]

The trouble with robust sentiments of that kind is that they pre-empt any room for second thoughts. If Rab's subsequent defence of his role throughout the appeasement years never entirely carried conviction, it was partly because in developing his case he tended to neglect the number of hostages he had given to fortune. It was not simply that Rab was an open and avowed champion of the Munich

* It was Munich that finally drove Duff Cooper out of Chamberlain's Cabinet – leading to his forty-minute resignation speech on 3 October 1938. This was generally considered an impressive performance, but Rab dismissed it with the comment, 'Duff's veins stood out and he was very rude.' (Brabourne Collection, F97 22B, letter dated 12.10.1938.)

Agreement: much more damagingly, he defended it at the time on grounds that had nothing whatever to do with the justifications he tended to advance in his later years.* Nowhere in his private letters is there the slightest indication that he regarded the Munich Settlement as a means of buying time to enable Britain to build up her armaments – though that became the main burden of the defence he offered in his own autobiography.[18] He may have been on somewhat surer ground in suggesting that the country was more united in its attitude to the war in 1939 than it would have been in 1938 – though whether that was an appropriate argument to come from a man who had announced in 1938 'War settles nothing' is perhaps open to question.

Admittedly, at the time Rab could hardly have been expected to foresee how rapidly Chamberlain's policy would collapse. Indeed, so popular had the Prime Minister become as a direct result of the Munich Settlement that Winston Churchill actually found it necessary to warn him in the Commons against 'the constitutional indecency' of going for what he described as 'a sort of inverted khaki election'.[19] There was probably never any real danger of that – Chamberlain expressly repudiated any such intention in that same post-Munich debate[20] – but there was no doubt that, at least within the Conservative Party, the Government immediately after Munich held the upper hand over its critics. The boldest of these found themselves reduced to lending slightly surreptitious support to Independent candidates in two by-elections that autumn at Bridgwater and Oxford City. In the former Rab joined in the campaign on behalf of the National Conservative candidate, going out of his way to reply to the Government's critics who insisted that Hitler's word could not be trusted, 'I tell you that the one bargain he has made with us, that the German Navy should be one third of the size of the British Navy, he has kept, and kept loyally.'†[21] This assurance even from the Under-Secretary at the Foreign Office appears to have been treated with a certain degree of scepticism by the people of Somerset – when the figures were announced on 18 November, they showed an upset victory for the Independent, the journalist

* A devastating critique of Rab's defence of his appeasement role, as given in *The Art of the Possible*, is to be found in Paul Strafford's article, 'R. A. Butler at the Foreign Office 1938–9', *Historical Journal*, vol. 28, 4 (December 1985), pp. 901–22. Patrick Cosgrave offers only a slightly less rigorous treatment of the same topic in *R. A. Butler: An English Life* (Quartet, 1981), pp. 41–63.

† Unfortunately for Rab, Hitler was to announce less than five months later, on 27 April 1939, that he no longer considered Germany bound by the 1935 Anglo-German Naval Agreement.

Vernon Bartlett, against the Government candidate, P. G. Heathcoat-Amory.*

An isolated reverse of that sort was hardly, however, going to undermine the Government – or, indeed, to dent Rab's own rising career prospects. In 1938 he was to enjoy something of an *annus mirabilis*, both personally and politically. In March, a month after his appointment to the Foreign Office, he and Sydney moved from their Wood Street flat in which they had lived almost since their marriage to a grand, if somewhat gloomy, London house at 3 Smith Square, Westminster; if Stanstead remained the family's home, at least the one surviving successful member of the original 'Boys' Brigade' now had a London residence appropriate to his new position and standing within both the Government and the Party. That standing was also soon reflected in an invitation that clearly brought both Rab and his wife great pleasure. In April they were both bidden to Windsor Castle to spend a Saturday night with the new King and Queen – whom they found 'informal and pleasant'.[22] The only untoward note during the visit appears to have been struck by the King's Private Secretary, Alexander Hardinge,† who seized the opportunity of having a Minister of the Crown (if a junior one) as a captive audience, late at night after the Royal couple had gone to bed, to register his reservations about 'the lack of morality' in the Government's foreign policy. Although tactfully remarking that 'it was interesting to have such a definite criticism' Rab stoutly felt it his duty 'to answer back and to inquire whether he really felt there was anything in Labour's foreign policy'. At least the exchange seems to have broken no bones, for the next day Rab was able to report that at breakfast 'Hardinge was much calmer' – and that the whole visit had been an 'inspirational experience'.[23]

There were signs, indeed, that the Butlers' social life, originally based on Sydney's inheritance of artistic and musical connections from her mother, was now moving into an altogether higher gear. Part of this was, no doubt, due to the newly established connection with 'Chips' Channon – of whom Rab was to write in his own autobiography 'he attached a first-class restaurant car to the

* The figures were Vernon Bartlett (Ind.) 19,540, P. G. Heathcoat-Amory (Con.) 17,208. Three weeks earlier the Conservatives had retained their seat at Oxford with Quintin Hogg getting 15,797 votes against 12,363 for A. D. Lindsay, the Master of Balliol, also standing as an Independent.

† 2nd Baron Hardinge of Penshurst (1894–1960). Assistant Private Secretary to King George V 1920–36. Private Secretary to King Edward VIII 1936. Private Secretary to King George VI 1936–43.

train'.[24] But there was more to it perhaps than the pulling-power of Channon's *salon* in Belgrave Square. Certainly by the autumn of 1938 shooting-party weekends at Stanstead had become an integral part of the autumn social season – to the point where Rab often found it difficult to accommodate his own parents if they suddenly expressed a wish to come over from Cambridge and stay at Stanstead. Possibly the most revealing document of all among Rab's private papers is an unfinished letter he wrote to his three sons when, early in 1939, even he seems temporarily to have formed the judgment that war might, after all, be unavoidable. It speaks volumes for the aspirations with which he had started out and for the fulfilment which he already felt he had achieved:

> Dear Boys:
>
> We can't go on living in this uncertainty before a possible European and World War in which all this must change. In case we are in face of those Napoleonic times, but on a world scale, and that your father cannot devote the time and future that he should to you, here is a short letter which should suffice to explain his view of the continuance of family tradition.
>
> When I was young we had none too much to live on but I was brought up in the sub-country house atmosphere at Bourton. Thinking of Aunt May and the Kendalls, whom you will find described in Gilbert's *History of Cornwall*, I always wanted to set up the standard of an English country house. This your Mother and I have done now here for five years.
>
> All the time I have been busy on Government work – India, Labour, Foreign – but half my mind has been on you and Stanstead. Mama says I've been too easy with you* but you're, none of you, quite old enough yet to be taken out of irresponsibility. I know, from your riding and sham boxing with me, that you won't be irresponsible when troubles come.[25]

If it was not in any sense a boastful letter, it was also one in which it was possible to detect a real sense of pride in achievement. And the achievement had, of course, been no mean one. Within a dozen years of taking his Finals at Cambridge, Rab had established himself not just as a rising London politician but as a traditional rural country

* Rab, though an affectionate, was not a demonstrative parent. One of his sons is unable to recall ever being hugged or cuddled by him.

9 The young politician: Rab was elected to the House of Commons when he was only twenty-six

10 Stanley Baldwin as Prime Minister making his way to the House of Commons in less security-conscious days

11 Rab as Under-Secretary at the Ministry of Labour touring the depressed areas

squire* with, as he saw it, a firm stake in the continuing ordered structure of society. It was hardly surprising if the prospect of a major upheaval – threatening not only all he stood for but everything he had managed to build up – filled him with foreboding. He was certainly never part of the more insalubrious pro-Nazi elements of London's social scene who gathered round such figures as the German Ambassador, von Ribbentrop; but, equally, he never saw a challenge to the dictators as an inescapable national obligation.

Professionally, too, he had by now everything to lose by it. Nominated by the Prime Minister to the Privy Council at the age of thirty-six in the New Year's Honours of 1939 (the youngest Privy Councillor since Churchill at thirty-two in 1907) Rab had begun to be spoken of as a future Leader of the Party – possibly even the eventual successor to Chamberlain, if grander figures, like Churchill and Eden, continued to stay outside the Government. The young man who had entered Parliament a mere decade earlier in 1929 had become, if not a pillar, then at least a supporting buttress of the Tories' *ancien régime*. Not that Rab's own eyes were altogether on the past. During the summer of 1938 he devoted a good deal of his time and attention (even correcting proofs when he was at Geneva in September) to a new Conservative Central Education Committee propaganda booklet entitled *A National Faith*. Rab was not its author (it was written by the future Conservative Minister, then a young lecturer at the Conservative College at Ashridge, C. J. M. Alport)† but he was in every sense its midwife – steering the project through the party bureaucracy and even finding a publisher, Faber & Faber. Today its main interest probably lies in the *nom de plume* under which it was published. At Rab's insistence, its author was described simply as 'A Modern Conservative'.

Despite the alliances he had painstakingly built up within the pre-war Conservative Party, there is no question but that Rab continued to see himself in this light. And here his chairmanship of the Conservative Central Education Committee provided him with a useful power base – quite separate and distinct from his identity as a Foreign Office Minister. He lost no time in entirely changing the Central Education Committee's traditional, rather leisurely

* Revealingly the local vicar at Greenstead Green always addressed him as 'Dear Squire' in any letters he wrote to him.

† Cuthbert James McCall Alport (1912–). Director of the Conservative Political Centre 1945–50. Conservative MP for Colchester 1950–61. Minister of State, Commonwealth Relations Office 1959–61. High Commissioner in the Federation of Rhodesia and Nyasaland 1961–3. Created life peer 1961.

approach – producing even by the autumn of 1937 a whirlwind of meetings and courses up and down the country. By the end of 1938 he had founded the Conservative Political Circle, the forerunner of the Conservative Political Centre of the post-war era; and, although he was not yet involved in any way in the work of the Conservative Research Department (which Neville Chamberlain kept rather jealously to himself), he had undoubtedly marked himself down, not least in the all-seeing eyes of the party organisation, as the kind of politician who was 'a doer' and not just 'a blower'.

His main work, however, in the last year of peace necessarily continued to centre on the Foreign Office. Here he soon established an amiable *modus vivendi* with Halifax – who had an appropriately aristocratic attitude to the chores of the Department. It therefore fell to Rab to conduct most of the routine business of the office – the seeing of Ambassadors, the oversight of administration and, above all (since Halifax in the Lords was sheltered from these) the preparation of answers for parliamentary questions which in those days were a regular Foreign Office fixture in the Commons every Wednesday afternoon. There were, however, areas where Rab willingly learned from Halifax. He was particularly impressed, for example, with the Secretary of State's methods of compiling a speech (and, indeed, in later years, was to adopt them very much as his own). This is his contemporary account of how he first witnessed the process in action:

> I was up until one o'clock last night drafting a statement for the House, which the PM is to make on Thursday. Halifax and I had arranged to see the PM at ten o'clock. He gave us one of his usual ink MSS and then went off to bed. Halifax asked me to get a pair of scissors and pins and then proceeded to concoct a statement out of the PM's MS, an MS of his own, a typed sheet from the office and some notes of mine. The final production was truly noble.[26]

It is not easy to unravel the exact relationship between Butler and Halifax.* In his memoirs, published over thirty years afterwards, Rab was inclined to give his chief the credit for steering the Prime Minister away from the policy of appeasement during the course of 1939 and for urging him, particularly after Hitler's march into the

* Remarkably, Rab's name is not even mentioned in Halifax's own autobiography – *Fulness of Days* (Collins, 1957).

rest of Czechoslovakia in March of that year, to face the prospect of war.[27] As an account of the attitudes of the two men (to say nothing of the outlook and stance of the young Minister who served them both), this does not seem wholly satisfactory – and is, indeed, contradicted by a private memorandum which Rab wrote, for his own purposes, some three months before the Second World War started. In what he called 'a character study of those with whom I have worked', apparently set down in June 1939, Rab is at pains to deny that there had been any significant divergence of view between his two masters:

> Looking back upon the past 18 months, it is possible to say that any difference of opinion between the Foreign Office and No. 10 has been so considerably reduced as to be almost imperceptible. There remains the difference of character between the two principal personalities concerned, but barely any difference in design. The PM's main objective is to bring British policy back to surer and more realistic grounds. The Foreign Secretary's main objective is to preserve national unity, to keep in play all sections of public opinion and to 'get us through'.[28]

Nor is there much indication, at least in this contemporary document, of Halifax being the agent of any major change in the Government's policy:

> The best insight into Halifax's character is that he is a Master of Foxhounds. Many of his metaphors come from the chase. He advises one not to jump into a field until one can see a way of jumping out. On the other hand, it is occasionally necessary to do so. In the case of the Polish guarantee a jump from a dangerous main road had suddenly to be made over a high hedge in cold blood.[29]

But the Polish guarantee of 31 March 1939 – though it was not all that it seemed, since, as *The Times* spotted, it guaranteed Poland's independence and not its frontiers[30] – was Chamberlain's own handiwork. The only real evidence of any difference between the Prime Minister and his Foreign Secretary arose over a question not of policy but of personnel. Rab was by no means alone in suspecting that Halifax was a good deal more favourably disposed towards the notion of broadening the whole basis of the Government – and in particular of bringing back Churchill and Eden into the Cabinet –

than was the Prime Minister. On this issue, despite what he was prepared to indicate afterwards,[31] it seems safe to assume that Rab's own views coincided more with those of the head of the Government than with the characteristically ecumenical approach of his own departmental chief.

Only on one point of policy does Rab himself seem to have even come near to imperilling the personal confidence Chamberlain had in him. When on 7 April Mussolini's Italian troops invaded Albania, Rab hurried up from Stanstead and presented himself at No. 10, even though it happened to be Good Friday. He found the Prime Minister surprisingly unperturbed and almost resentful, as it were, of his intrusion. When, somewhat rashly, Rab began to wax eloquent about a possible general threat to peace in the Balkans, he was dismissed with the comment, 'Don't be silly. Go home to bed.'[32] It was, not surprisingly, the last time that summer that Rab was to venture any personal foreign policy initiative of his own.

On the major diplomatic effort of that summer – the somewhat half-hearted bid to persuade the Soviet Union to join in a Triple Alliance with both France and Britain – Rab, like the Prime Minister, seems to have been a less than enthusiastic participant. Certainly, in recording his own reservations about the project, Neville Chamberlain, in a private note written to his sister, was specifically to refer to Rab as 'the only supporter I could get for my views' (adding, unkindly, 'and he was not a very influential ally').[33] Rab, nevertheless, did most of the donkey-work on the negotiations – having become something of a friend of the Soviet Ambassador in London, Ivan Maisky, whom the Foreign Secretary, Lord Halifax, for high-minded Christian reasons, found it distasteful to meet. Although the notion of the alliance was popular with the public – and had rather more attractions for the French Government than it did for the British – it was probably doomed to failure from the moment that Neville Chamberlain turned his face against it, on the ground that any such formal alliance would make negotiations with the Axis powers even more difficult. The talks with the Russians nevertheless dragged on into July – with Rab handling the London end and a Foreign Office official, William Strang,* conducting the talks in Moscow. However, all that ultimately came out of this protracted effort was a declaration on the part of the three powers of their intentions to act in concert if certain threats arose – and even

* First Baron Strang (1893–1978). A career diplomat who ended up as Permanent Under-Secretary of State at the Foreign Office from 1949 to 1953.

this, of course, was promptly made nonsense of by the bombshell announcement of the Nazi-Soviet Pact of 23 August 1939.

Rab appears to have been considerably less taken aback by this development than anyone else within the Government. Indeed, he had taken a predominantly sceptical view from the start – believing that the original joint British-French guarantee to Poland back in March had relieved Russia of any real anxiety about Germany's designs on her own frontier. To his original memorandum of June 1939, incorporating character studies of the Prime Minister and the Foreign Secretary, he subsequently added this scribbled note, 'I never liked the Polish guarantee. It gave Russia just the excuse not to defend herself against Germany, since we had gratuitously planted ourselves in East Europe. It thus led to Russia going in with Germany.'[34] That may have been pitching matters a bit strong – but at least Rab was to prove consistent in his view. On his return from holiday in the south of France on 24 August 1939 (there was nothing odd or complacent about that – Winston Churchill himself had taken an identical French holiday that same month, returning only a day earlier), he was immediately involved in the discussions both at the Foreign Office and No. 10 that led to the raising of the original guarantee into a formal Treaty of Alliance with Poland, signed on 25 August. For once, parting company with both the Prime Minister and the Foreign Secretary, Rab opposed the move on the grounds that it 'would have a bad psychological effect on Hitler and would wreck any negotiations'.[35] Coupled with his curious belief that Goering was still 'working for peace', there could hardly be more eloquent testimony of Rab's faithfulness to the appeasement cause, right to the end.

For the next few days, caught up in the hurly-burly of drafting statements for Parliament and composing replies for a now thoroughly rattled British Government to send to Hitler, Rab can have had singularly little opportunity to reflect. Later, however, he left a note of his activities at the time – and at least it can be said on its behalf that it is a thoroughly honest document. There was no effort to disguise, for example, his own personal conviction that the entire Polish business, which was now provoking the occasion for war, had been ineptly handled from start to finish – 'I still believe', Rab unrepentantly wrote, 'that Germany might have negotiated had we influenced the Poles earlier in the summer.' Nor did he hesitate to put the blame for this want of effort down to what he termed 'an inhibition in the Foreign Office' – the result, in his own words, 'of the shame engendered in some breasts by Munich'. Worse than that, he went on to adjudicate that Polish diplomacy had not been 'clever and that they brought much of the trouble on their own heads'. As for the House of Commons, at its meeting of Saturday 2 September when even Chamberlain was forced to recognise that his own supporters were clamouring for war, it had – in Rab's view – 'behaved disgracefully'.[36]

Perhaps not surprisingly, in the light of all that, Rab was the only non-Cabinet Minister to be with Chamberlain in Downing Street just before he made his broadcast at 11.15 a.m. on the morning of Sunday 3 September announcing, almost in heart-broken tones, that 'this country is now at war with Germany'. In fact, it was Rab, at 11.10 a.m., who by pre-arrangement alerted the Service Departments to the announcement that was coming – later that morning getting a rocket from Leslie Hore-Belisha,* the Secretary of State for War, for not communicating directly with him. The rest of that bleak day is perhaps best told in Rab's own words:

> When we had finished listening to the PM's broadcast we went back into the Secretary's room and then into the Cabinet Room. The PM had hardly said 'How did we like it?' when the long wail of an air raid warning started. After about half-a-minute the PM said quite calmly, 'That is an air raid warning.' We all laughed and said 'It would be funny if it were.' He said several times very slowly and definitely, 'That *is* an air raid warning,' and then everybody began to leave to go through the basement of No. 10 to the War Room. Mrs Chamberlain appeared with a large basket containing books, gas masks and other aids to waiting. They all disappeared and I found myself alone in the Cabinet Room. As the terrible wail went on, a few people were scurrying across Horse Guards to try to take shelter. I decided that I had better die in the Foreign Office, and so walked across Downing Street, which was by then deserted, and finally finished up in the basement of the Foreign Office, where members of the staff had assembled. An officious warden told me that he did not anticipate the immediate use of gas. We sat on the floor of the basement, there being no furniture, thinking what a happy beginning to the war this was.[37]

* First Baron Hore-Belisha (1893–1957). MP (Lib-Nat 1923–42, Ind. 1942–5) Devonport. Parliamentary Secretary Board of Trade 1931–2. Financial Secretary, Treasury 1932–4. Minister of Transport 1934–7. Secretary of State for War 1937–40. Minister of National Insurance 1945.

For Rab, of course, it was anything but that – in fact, for him, as for Chamberlain and Halifax, it represented the loss of all their hopes and the waste of all their labours over the past many months. Once again, though, he was not the man to shirk the truth. That evening he journeyed down to Stanstead – where, according to his sister, Iris, so many bottles of champagne were dismally drunk over dinner that they had to be thrown afterwards into the moat surrounding the house for fear of the servants seeing the 'empties'.[38] It was a cool, moonlit night and, with the bottles cast away, Rab, his wife and his sister lingered among the long grass staring into the cold, black water. 'As we watched the reflections dancing upon it,' wrote Rab, 'we could hardly believe that things had gone so badly.'[39]

Whatever else might be said against him, the last apostle of appeasement could not be accused of seeking to deceive himself.

9 *Churchill Comes to Power*

In retrospect the most curious aspect of the outbreak of war was how little dislocation it caused at first to the life of the nation – even less to that of politics and Government. Some MPs immediately joined the Colours and went off to training camps; but Rab, by reason of his age (now nearly thirty-seven) and his damaged arm was, for the time being at least, hardly a candidate for enlistment.* The first impact the war made on his own way of life was more domestic than official. In pre-war days Stanstead had been maintained in some style – the staff comprised not merely a cook and a parlour-maid but a groom and gardeners, to say nothing of a butler and a footman as well. All Rab's forebodings of the social upheaval war would bring were, no doubt, fulfilled when half-way through the second week of the war he received this letter:

Oak Tree Cottage, Stanstead Hall, Halstead, Essex
14 September 1939

Sir,

As Mrs Butler may have informed you I have obtained a post as full-time Air Raid Warden, thus terminating my service as butler. I am extremely sorry that the years of service seem to be so lightly cast away, but in these modern days I suppose it is the colour of things. It is very sad to me that men's minds must turn

* In May 1941 Rab, along with his Cambridge contemporary, Geoffrey Lloyd, did register for military service as their age-group had been reached under the provisions of the National Service (Armed Forces) Acts. Their action as Ministers of the Crown was reported by Ernest Bevin, the Minister of Labour, to the Prime Minister, Winston Churchill. He minuted in reply, 'I feel strongly that they should not leave their present important duties, which bring them just as much under the fire of the enemy as training for the Army.' Butler Papers, Trinity College, Cambridge, G13.

to the Blood Lust in the futility of war, when there is so much good store for us all.

Thanking you, Sir, for past favours and wishing you all success in your efforts for Peace.

I am, Sir,

Yours respectfully,

R. KNIGHT[1]

Mr Knight was not the first member of the household staff to go – the footman had already left to join the Army and others were shortly to follow. For Rab the war inevitably meant that he had to spend more time in London and, with petrol very swiftly rationed, it was by no means every weekend that he managed to get home to Stanstead. The decision, however, seems to have been taken early on that it was there that Sydney would stay with the family – already extended by the addition of Rab's sister's two daughters (she was shortly to return to India to join her husband serving in the Indian Army) and very soon added to further by a six-year-old Polish refugee, Kris Balinski, who, with his family, had managed to escape after the German invasion.

It would be quite wrong to pretend that there was hardship at Stanstead – there was nothing of the sort. The family probably felt the pinch of the war years much less markedly than most: people living in the country always tended to fare better under rationing than did those living in towns and in any case the 'shoot' at Stanstead underpinned the domestic economy at least for the winter months. It was only perhaps grandeur that had departed – though Rab, ironically, was far more inclined to mourn the passing of that than was his wife, Sydney, who had been brought up to it.

For a Tory politician, especially one representing a rural constituency, easily the greatest postbag problem at the beginning of the war arose from the strains and stresses inflicted on local communities by the arrival of evacuated children from the cities. In middle-class homes 'the billeting officer' became a figure of real dread – a dread in no way mitigated by the presence in the background of 'a tribunal' before which the billeting officer's decisions could be appealed against. Sitting for an Essex constituency, conveniently sited to receive the overflow from the schools of London's East End, Rab promptly found himself surrounded by a rising tide of middle-class resentment and indignation. He needed all his gifts of tact and diplomacy to persuade his protesting constituents – many of whom were normally to be found among his most active supporters – that the Government had not, after all, resolved to celebrate the outbreak of war by deliberately adopting the methods of its totalitarian opponents. Eventually, with the return of most of the children to their homes during the period of the 'phoney war', the controversy subsided. The fact that it had left its scars was revealed by a letter Rab received as late as the second Christmas of the war from his own constituency chairman, 'May we soon have peace, but what a socialistic mess we shall have to clear up!'[2]

As for the affairs of the Government in London, Rab – once war had been formally declared – inevitably found his role circumscribed and his influence diminished. A modest restructuring of the Government had been announced by Chamberlain on the very day war broke out and, though the appointment of Churchill to the Admiralty (combined with a seat in the War Cabinet), and of Eden to the Dominions Office, had little direct relevance to Rab's own sphere, the implication that 'the Old Gang' was no longer in sole charge was not lost on anyone. Rab, indeed, found himself encouraged to devote his own efforts to the field of information and to the preparing of a formal statement of Government war aims; within the Foreign Office he was also given specific responsibility for the work of the British Council, of Chatham House (removed for the duration of the war to Balliol College, Oxford) and of an organisation called the British Association for International Understanding. It may not have been work without value or merit; but it certainly represented a sharp contrast with the drama of high international politics in which he had been fully engaged only a few months earlier. There was one final, sad echo of those earlier endeavours when in December 1939 Rab found himself dispatched as the leader of the British delegation to what was to prove the last, somewhat forlorn, Council meeting of the League of Nations in Geneva. Before the Council was Finland's complaint against Russia for her attack (in November) upon her. There was clearly little that the League in its amputated state could hope to achieve; but at least it conducted its final act on the world stage with dignity. It announced that, by reason of her own actions, the USSR had 'placed herself outside the League of Nations' and proceeded to record its first-ever expulsion of a member state.

It may even have been the impression left on Rab by that poignant experience (he stayed in Geneva for a full week) that led him, on his return to London, into his one recorded strategic intervention of the war. Ever since September Churchill had been agitating in the War Cabinet for the mining of Norwegian territorial waters in order to prevent merchant ships sailing from Narvik with cargoes of iron-ore destined for Germany. The War Cabinet at this stage had taken no decision on Churchill's request but the First Lord of the Admiralty had been given permission to consult other Government Departments in order that plans might be laid for speedy and effective action if such should prove to be needed. It was, no doubt, as a result of these consultations that the Narvik enterprise – now, indeed, coupled with a far more ambitious scheme for the landing of British troops to occupy the iron-ore fields themselves – reached the ears of Rab. His reaction – delivered in a memo both to his ministerial chief, Halifax, and to the Permanent Under-Secretary at the Foreign Office, Sir Alexander Cadogan* was fierce and unequivocal. He opposed the venture on every ground: it was an abuse of international law, it would risk alienating the whole of Scandinavia from the Allied cause, it would incite Germany immediately to seize all the ore she wanted, and above all it was unfair on Finland, who would immediately risk becoming the victim of a pincer movement on the part of both the Germans and the Russians.

For Rab, it was an uncharacteristically impassioned outburst – committed to paper with the injunction attached to it at the end, 'If you agree, as I hope, destroy.'[3] The document was not destroyed and its main interest today probably arises from the light which it throws on the attitude with which Rab, as late as January 1940, was still regarding Churchill. For, to clinch his argument, the Under-Secretary at the Foreign Office, quite undaunted by his boldness in venturing into the, for him, unfamiliar territory of strategic decisions, did not shrink from concluding his memorandum with a pointed, if veiled, *ad hominem* attack:

> I dislike action for action's sake, but if we want activity let us help Finland to a greater extent. We have moral cover for such help and we should be acting in our best interests. This would be a better alternative to an expedition, which may have unforeseen results and may rank in history with Walcheren and the Dardanelles. However brilliant a mind may have conceived it, let us remember that Jellicoe and the War Cabinet resisted the same Narvik temptation last time.[4]

* Alexander George Montagu Cadogan (1884–1968). Minister Plenipotentiary at Peking 1933–5. Deputy Under-Secretary of State for Foreign Affairs 1936–7. Permanent Under-Secretary of State 1938–46. His surprisingly scathing private comments on the conduct of the war surfaced posthumously in *The Diaries of Sir Alexander Cadogan 1938–45*, ed. David Dilks (Cassell, 1971).

Eventually, though not until April, the 'brilliant mind' did get its way – if in rather different circumstances from those it had originally envisaged (the Germans had already occupied Narvik by the time the British arrived). The results were, as Rab had indicated, 'unforeseen'. There is perhaps no greater irony in the history of the Second World War than that the Cabinet Minister who stood most exposed to criticism over the disaster of the Norwegian Expedition of April–May 1940 should have risen to supreme power on the back of it. Yet that, although it can hardly have been one of the 'unforeseen' consequences that Rab had in mind, was precisely what occurred.

How much of a blow the fall of Chamberlain was to Rab he always took great pains to disguise.* Certainly at the time of Chamberlain's resignation – unlike, for example, 'Chips' Channon – he gave way to no loud lamentations, and the most eloquent surviving evidence of his attitude is a letter he wrote to Mrs Chamberlain, not after her husband's departure from No. 10 in May but rather after his death in November. There at least, however, he placed no inhibition on his feelings – opening his letter with the announcement, 'You can imagine how lonely and sad I felt in Parliament, and indeed in the whole political world, when I knew that Mr Chamberlain had gone.' In Party terms, too, he did not seek to conceal that he still felt himself a Chamberlain man rather than a Churchill one – 'I do not think that the party will ever be the same again. I looked upon him as the last leader of the organisation in the State which I joined very late in its life but which has been responsible for much of England's greatness.'[5] If it was an elegantly worded letter, it also bore all the appearance of being an honest one. There can be little doubt that even by the end of 1940 Rab still saw himself as belonging far more naturally to the pre-war Tory Party than to the wartime Party as it had been reshaped and restructured by Churchill.

Certainly, on 10 May 1940, when the transfer of power took place between Chamberlain and Churchill, Rab had every reason to feel apprehensive about his own fate. He was not, however, wholly taken aback by Chamberlain's humiliation in the Narvik debate, held in

* This disguise has to some extent been stripped away by the subsequent revelations of others. According to Sir John Colville, Rab was to be found with 'Chips' Channon on the evening of Friday 10 May in his room at the Foreign Office drinking the health in champagne of 'the King over the water' (meaning Chamberlain). He is also reported to have referred to Churchill as 'a half-breed American' and 'the greatest political adventurer of modern times'. John Colville, *The Fringes of Power* (Hodder & Stoughton, 1985), p. 122.

the Commons over two days between 7 and 8 May. On the morning the debate opened he had been visited in the Foreign Office by Lord Dunglass,* the Prime Minister's Parliamentary Private Secretary, with whom he had enjoyed a close personal association ever since Chamberlain had succeeded Baldwin in 1937. Any false sense of optimism that Rab may have felt about the prospects for Chamberlain's survival was soon shattered by his visitor:

> Alec, with his Scottish shrewdness, said he thought things would go badly for Neville. There was a very strong feeling in the country which was not reflected in the Whips' Office – and there would be difficulties with the Labour leaders. He told me there was probably a danger of a vote. Neville was talking of staying if the vote was more than 60 in his favour – but again Alec pointed out that this depended on the extent to which the Labour leaders were encouraged to enter the Government. He asked me to talk to Halifax and to persuade him to become Prime Minister.[6]

In fact, Chamberlain attained a majority of 81 – but, with 41 Tories and their allies voting against the Government and a further 60 abstaining, the outcome was lethal for him and for his Government. Rab's own feelings were expressed in a private memorandum he wrote just after the division figures had been announced:

> The final scene in the House was very distasteful. It reminded me of certain episodes in the history of Peel. The singing of 'Rule Britannia' by Harold Macmillan was much resented by Neville who rose looking old and white-haired, as he has become, and marched out realising, as he did, that he could not go on.[7]

Two days later, having learnt, in a message from its Party Conference at Bournemouth, that the Labour Party would not enter into a coalition headed by him, but that its leaders would serve in a National Government headed by someone else, Chamberlain resigned. On his advice, following Halifax's intimation that he felt his membership

* Later Lord Home of the Hirsel (1903–). As Viscount Dunglass, MP for South Lanark 1931–45 and for Lanark 1950–1. Parliamentary Private Secretary to Neville Chamberlain 1937–40. Succeeded father as 14th Earl of Home 1951. Secretary of State for Commonwealth Relations 1955–60. Secretary of State for Foreign Affairs 1960–3. Renounced earldom on becoming Prime Minister as Sir Alec Douglas-Home in October 1963. MP for Kinross and West Perthshire 1963–74. Leader of the Opposition 1964–5. Secretary of State for Foreign Affairs for second time 1970–4. Created life peer 1974.

of the Lords debarred him from the Premiership, Churchill was invited to the Palace and on Friday 10 May accepted the King's invitation to form a Government.

For Rab the next five days were ones of suspense – though, typically, even through a Whitsun weekend, he made it his business to be out and about in places where he would meet people and might even hear something about his own future. As he recorded in an intermittent diary he kept at the time:

> Sydney came up for the day, although it was Whit Monday. We dined at the Berkeley. I had a sort of instinct we ought to keep in touch. Hely-Hutchinson, Secretary of the 1922 Committee, came in and presently asked if he might join us. He said 'You must not underestimate the great reaction which has been caused among Conservative Members,* among whom you will find over three quarters who are ready to put Chamberlain back.'[8]

When, however, Rab returned to the Foreign Office on the morning of Tuesday 14 May, it was only to find the Foreign Secretary gloomily certain that the die had now been cast:

> I went into Halifax's room early on reaching the Office. He suddenly said 'It's all a great tragedy, isn't it?' I replied 'That is because you did not take the Premiership yourself.' He said 'You know my reasons, it's no use discussing that – but the gangsters will shortly be in complete control.'[9]

By 'the gangsters' Halifax apparently meant the Churchill entourage – such figures as Beaverbrook, Brendan Bracken† and Professor Lindemann (later Lord Cherwell).‡ They had always been looked at somewhat askance by the more 'respectable' elements of the Tory

* Caused by Hitler's invasion of Holland and Belgium on the night of 9–10 May – which had persuaded not only 'Chips' Channon that Chamberlain might, after all, be able to carry on. Robert Rhodes James (ed.), *Chips: The Diaries of Sir Henry Channon* (Weidenfeld & Nicolson, 1967), p. 249.

† First Viscount Bracken (1901–58). Conservative MP, North Paddington 1929–45. Parliamentary Private Secretary to Winston Churchill 1940–1. Minister of Information 1941–5. First Lord of the Admiralty 1945. MP, Bournemouth 1945–50, East Bournemouth and Christchurch 1950–1, when raised to the peerage as Viscount Bracken of Christchurch.

‡ First Viscount Cherwell (1886–1957). Personal Assistant to Winston Churchill 1940. Paymaster-General 1943–5 and 1951–3. Student of Christ Church, Oxford 1921–56. Created first Baron Cherwell 1941 and first Viscount Cherwell 1956.

Party; and for many of the more morally fastidious among them the sight of such people moving into even the ante-rooms of No. 10 was a much greater shock than the full-blown vision of Churchill himself sitting in state in the Cabinet Room.

It was to that Cabinet Room that Rab was eventually summoned on the morning of Wednesday 15 May. There he found the new Prime Minister, in his own description of the time, 'looking very flushed and with gleaming eyes holding the remains of a very wet cigar half bitten-through'.[10] There does not seem to have been much preamble. 'I wish you', said Winston Churchill, addressing the young Foreign Office Under-Secretary, 'to go on with your delicate manner of answering Parliamentary Questions without giving anything away.'[11] Although he had been given grounds for believing the previous evening – in messages from both Beaverbrook and Bracken – that he would be invited to continue, there seems little doubt that Rab was genuinely touched by this singular mark of magnanimity shown towards him (indeed, much later in his career, he was to refer to it as 'the biggest single compliment I have ever been paid in politics').[12]

The truth was that if any junior Minister might have expected to be marked down for victimisation, it was Rab: he and Churchill had, after all, been consistent political opponents from the days of the India Bill onwards. It was perhaps characteristic of the new Prime Minister that he should not have shirked making a reference to what he politely termed their 'disagreements' – only to seek to bury them in a personal compliment over his feeling of appreciation at having once been invited to Stanstead. (It was also, in its way, entirely typical of Rab that he should have replied, 'That was not very remarkable' – only to be crushed by the genial retort, 'No, but at least it showed goodwill.')* More directly to the point, however, was probably the final remark that Churchill made just as his visitor was reaching the door – 'Halifax asked for you. He seems to get on with you.'[13]

For the next seven months, in fact, the old partnership continued at the Foreign Office – with Rab taking on more and more of the burden of talking to foreign Ambassadors, both friendly and unfriendly ones. It was this particular duty of his which led to an incident in June 1940 that not only nearly catapulted him out of office but also left something of a cloud over his reputation at least

* See p. 64 n.

among those of his parliamentary colleagues who learned about it (usually at second- or third-hand).

From the beginning of the war one of the main indirect channels of communication between the British and German Governments had been through diplomats or businessmen belonging to neutral Sweden – one such, indeed, a businessman named Birger Dahleras, had played a very active part, supposedly on behalf of Marshal Goering, both in the days immediately before war broke out and during the first month of hostilities. On the second occasion his activities had been taken seriously enough for them to be reported to the War Cabinet by Halifax with the recommendation that, if they genuinely did represent a peace bid, then 'we should not absolutely shut the door'.[14] Nor was that by any means the only occasion on which the question of peace terms was broached, in however gingerly a fashion, by Halifax within the War Cabinet. On 1 November 1939 he had raised the topic again, reporting to his colleagues that a message had been passed through a Swedish intermediary to the German Government emphasising that it would be impossible for Britain even to contemplate holding any discussions with Germany 'unless Hitler had ceased to hold a position where he could influence the course of events'.[15] At first sight that might seem a response cautious enough to involve remarkably few risks – but its negative tone did not save it from incurring the wrath of Churchill, who, after the Cabinet meeting was over, took the unusual step of sending a private note to Halifax drawing attention to what he termed 'the great danger' of indulging in any such secret communications. Halifax does not, however, appear to have taken the warning to heart, for he was back at the same game even after Churchill became Prime Minister. On at least four occasions, as late as May 1940, he was still urging the course of a negotiated peace upon his colleagues – this time with, of all people, the Italian Ambassador in London as his intended intermediary.[16]

It is only against this background that the significance of a, no doubt, injudicious conversation that Rab held with the Swedish Minister in London, Björn Prytz, on 17 June 1940 can be properly assessed. In truth, Rab seems to have said no more than his departmental chief had been saying for months on end – though it was, of course, unfortunate that sentiments smacking more of defeatism than of defiance should have fallen even from the lips of a junior Minister on the very day France surrendered to Germany.

The circumstances of the conversation appear to have been these. Rab was returning from lunch – walking, as he often liked to do, across St James's Park – when he met Björn Prytz, a businessman-diplomat whom he had known for some time. Unwisely, if only because it meant that there would be no official record of the meeting, Rab invited him into the Foreign Office for an informal chat. Of what exactly was said there can be no certainty since the only evidence that survives is contained in a telegram Prytz sent that evening to his Foreign Ministry in Stockholm. The key passage in it read:

> Mr Butler's official attitude will for the present be that the war should continue, but he must be certain that no opportunity should be missed of compromise if reasonable conditions could be agreed, and no diehards would be allowed to stand in the way.
>
> He was called into Lord Halifax and came out with a message to me that common sense and not bravado would dictate the British Government's policy.
>
> Halifax had said that he felt such a message would be welcome to the Swedish Minister but it must not be taken to mean peace at any price.[17]

The text of that telegram did not, of course, instantly become public knowledge – indeed, it took twenty-five years for it to surface even in Sweden – but its contents very soon became known to a small group at the top of the British Government. The official explanation for that is that they heard about it through the British Minister in Stockholm, Victor Mallet,* who had got hold of a summary of Rab's alleged remarks to Prytz through the *News Chronicle* correspondent in the Swedish capital with good contacts in the Parliamentary Foreign Policy Committee.[18] But a far more likely explanation is that the British Government first heard of it through the usual security channels for monitoring and deciphering cables sent out by foreign Embassies in London. Certainly, within a week Churchill knew all about it – and the other diplomatic repercussions it had set off (including direct contacts between the Swedes and the Germans) – as the following magisterial rebuke delivered by the Prime Minister to Halifax made all too plain:

> It is quite clear to me from these telegrams and others that Butler held odd language to the Swedish Minister and certainly the Swede

* Sir Victor Mallet (1893–1969). Minister at Stockholm 1940–5. Ambassador to Madrid 1945–6, Rome 1947–53.

> derived a strong impression of defeatism. In these circumstances would it not be well to find out from Butler actually what he did say? I was strongly pressed in the House of Commons in the Secret Session to give assurances that the present Government and all its Members were resolved to fight on to the death, and I did so taking personal responsibility for the resolve of all. I saw a silly rumour in a telegram from Belgrade or Bucharest and how promptly you stamped upon it, but any suspicion of lukewarmness in Butler will certainly subject us all to further annoyance of this kind.[19]

If Rab was the Prime Minister's direct target on this occasion, then Halifax may well have recognised that he was under oblique attack. Certainly there was an unaccustomed note of firmness, almost of asperity, in the reply that the Foreign Secretary sent round to No. 10 one day later:

> I had been into the matter of Butler's conversation with the Swedish Minister with Butler before I got your letter last night. He has since given me a full note of what passed between him and the Swedish Minister, and I have discussed the matter fully with him. I am satisfied that there is no divergence of view, and that the explanation is partly to be found in the last paragraph but one of the telegram No. 534 Dipp of 23 June[20] that we sent to Sweden, after we had explored the matter further with the Swedish Minister here. I should be very sorry if you felt any doubt either about Butler's discretion or his complete loyalty to Government policy, of both of which I am completely satisfied.[21]

In a sense what Halifax did not say in that note was more revealing than what he actually wrote – he failed, for instance, to disclose to the Prime Minister that Rab had made a half-offer to resign (though a personal hand-written four-page letter retained only in the Foreign Office official archives, makes it clear that he realised he was at fault).

The full text of the letter a plainly embarrassed and highly defensive Rab wrote to his Foreign Office chief on 26 June ran as follows:

> *26 June 1941*
>
> Dear Secretary of State,
>
> Thank you for showing me the Prime Minister's letter on the subject of my interview with the Swedish Minister of 17 June.

I feel sure that Mr Prytz did not derive any 'impression of defeatism' and I know that he would be glad to give you his impression of the talk we had if you would care to send for him. Meanwhile his view, and I believe the true view, is included in No. 534 Dipp which I attach and which he and I thought had cleared up the matter.

It has been a source of great distress to the Swedish Minister and myself that this matter should have assumed the wrong significance which it has. I happened to meet him in the Park and he came into the office for only a few minutes; not being an arranged interview, I did not keep a record. You know that I send you records of all my talks and you know that I see most of the foreign ministers and transact office business with them. I am prepared for you to ascertain from any of them whether any 'lukewarmness' has been exhibited in my conversations. To suggest inquiring from them may seem odd, but the fact is that our relations are so friendly that this might be the most effective course.

In my public defence of most contentious public policy over the past ten years, and through perpetual heckling, I am not aware that I have trembled or been regarded as giving away a single wrong point. This instance of my private conversation can only be judged by the Swedish Minister since no one else was present. I do not recognise myself or my conversation in the impression given.

You may inquire why any conversation with a foreign representative took this line at all and why I was reported as saying that 'common sense and not bravado would dictate our policy'. In meeting me, the Swedish Minister has since agreed with me, that he opened the conversation by saying that there was more need than ever for successful diplomacy now that Great Britain was left alone to continue the struggle. We ran over the many efforts to improve our position in the international field, and Mr Prytz made it quite clear that it was in the interests of the neutrals to see an end to the war. I reminded him that if we were to negotiate, we must do so from strength, and that force must be met with force. From this he did not demur and he has since agreed with me that this account of our talk is correct.

It may be that I should have entertained no conversation with Mr Prytz on the subject of an ultimate settlement. But I am satisfied that I said nothing definite or specific that I would wish now to withdraw. I am usually cautious in following the leads of foreign representatives. I can see that in this case I should have been more cautious and I apologise.

I now place myself in your hands. It is essential in the work that I do that there should be absolute confidence between those whom I serve and myself. Had I not been ready to subscribe to the Prime Minister's courageous lead in the House of Commons, I should have felt bound to inform you and to leave the administration.

I feel that I have been placed in a wrong light but I absolutely understand the Prime Minister's inquiry.

Under the circumstances I await your and the Prime Minister's final opinion after you have read this letter and made any further inquiries.

Yours ever

R. A. BUTLER[22]

How indiscreet, not to say irresolute so far as the war was concerned, had Rab been? It was, no doubt, significant that the worst charge Churchill felt able to bring against him was one of 'lukewarmness' – and certainly there is nothing even in Prytz's summary of their conversation together that convicts him of anything more than that. On the other hand, to hold any form of conversation with a neutral diplomat embracing the questions of a negotiated peace on the very day France fell betrayed a certain insensitivity. The fairest judgment may be that if the whole incident illustrates anything, it is that even by June 1940 Rab had not entirely succeeded in shaking off the influence of the appeasement school in which he had been trained.

There were soon signs, however, that 'the gangsters' did not regard him as past redemption and were prepared to take the task of his re-education in hand. It was not long, for instance, before Lord Beaverbrook was inviting him to dine, though Rab's pleasure in the occasion was slightly diminished by the discovery that his only fellow-guests were the Soviet Ambassador, Ivan Maisky and his wife.[23] The methods of the new regime were, however, something of a shock to Rab. Of Beaverbrook he noted, 'he works any hour of the day or night and expects his secretaries to be at the end of a telephone whenever he wants them', adding ruefully, 'in this respect he is only more uncomfortable than the Prime Minister who only really gets going at 11 p.m. and rings any of us up for advice up to 2.30 in the morning'.[24]

With his belief in an ordered, structured lifestyle, it was perhaps as well for Rab that the summer recess of 1940 brought him some respite. His holiday was spent with the family at his father-in-law's country house, Gatcombe Park in Gloucestershire – 'the discovery of the summer' as he was to put it in a letter to his sister, Iris, in India.[25] Certainly Gatcombe must have seemed remote enough from the now year-old war – which may even have helped to explain Rab's sense of surprise at finding pieces of wire stretched taut between steel posts above the main roads on the way back, to say nothing of the fortifications, whether of stone or sandbags, at the entrance to every village.[26] The invasion threat was still considered imminent and, though the Battle of Britain had not yet started in earnest, the journey home brought Rab into his first direct contact with the German war machine.

On the last leg of their drive back to Essex, the family Wolseley, containing Rab, his wife, Sydney, and their two elder sons, found itself just outside Hertford in the middle of an air raid. It was Rab's second son, Adam, who first spotted, with great excitement, some silver gleams high up in the bright blue sky. Sure enough, there was soon the familiar wail of an air-raid siren – on this occasion, as Rab was wryly to put it, 'loosing itself from the very house which we were passing'. Pausing only momentarily to shut the sunshine roof, Rab drove resolutely on at least until the car with its human cargo was safely clear of a local railway-line. 'We then did a slightly undignified scramble from the car and grouped ourselves gracefully in a ditch.' Their reward was to see a Hurricane doing a 'victory roll' over a funeral pyre that had suddenly appeared on a hill opposite. For Rab, as much as for his eight-year-old son Adam, it appears to have been a moment of real drama – 'We heard the crack of batteries and the clump of bombs, then we decided to sally forth'.[27]

Once Hitler's air attack on Britain got seriously under way not all experiences of it were so exciting and exhilarating. Within a fortnight Rab's own town house (3 Smith Square, Westminster) was one of the first casualties, with most of its windows blown out and its doors blown in. Rab was reduced to going to stay with his father-in-law, Sam Courtauld, at his Mayfair home in North Audley Street, where the two of them slept in bunks in the cellar. From there he was very soon bombed out again, this time finding a somewhat more luxurious refuge in 'Chips' Channon's mansion at 5 Belgrave Square. Not that any of the same dislocation ever disturbed the even rhythm of life at Stanstead. There, as Rab was prepared to admit, the family's existence remained 'absolutely normal' – with only the continuing reduction in the number of men employed and the severe restrictions on central heating reflecting the fact that there was a war on at all.[28]

For Rab, though, unlike the rest of the family, the main focus of existence was his ministerial life in London. There, as very much a nomad by now (the bombing of the Carlton Club in October caused him particular distress), he was not subjected to the same domestic pressures that affected most of those who came to see him. He even began to take a certain pleasure in flaunting his own readiness to confront the blitz in face of his more timid Foreign Office visitors:

> Nearly all the Diplomatic Corps live in secluded comfort at Ascot, driving up in powerful American cars in the morning and asking for interviews immediately after lunch. When I feel wicked, I offer 5 p.m. which they always refuse and say they would like to come next day. An interview at 4 p.m. will always be over by 4.20.[29]

The main burden of the routine work at the Foreign Office seems during this period to have fallen increasingly on Rab. It was not merely that there were some things that Halifax refused point-blank to do – he would never, for example, if he could help it, meet either the Russian or the Japanese Ambassadors: he also, at least since the changeover of Prime Ministers, seems to have withdrawn more and more into his shell, finding the duty of regularly attending Cabinet meetings more than enough to exhaust his energies. ('Winston talked from 9.30 till 12, round and round and across. It is quite shattering to me, the love of talk some people have.')[30]

The truth, of course, was that the Prime Minister and the Foreign Secretary were never really compatible and it should not have come as a surprise when Churchill at the first suitable opening – a vacancy in the British Embassy in Washington, caused by the death of Lord Lothian – resolved to send his old rival to the other side of the Atlantic. Although he was not taken into Halifax's confidence till the deed was done, the move did not come as a surprise to Rab either – his famous political antennae had already begun to develop:

> I had an instinct that Halifax was going to Washington. What made me certain was when the PM said in the House, 'This is a job worthy of the very best in our land.'
>
> Halifax's manner had been uneasy and he had talked a great deal of duty during the last day or two and so I was convinced I was on the right track. Most of the work has to be done by instinct since there are so many masters to serve in a Coalition Government. I had come down to Stanstead on Friday night but was telephoned by the Permanent Under-Secretary [Sir Alexander

> Cadogan] who thought it would be tactful for me to come up on Saturday. I went in to see Halifax as usual and he said, 'It is very sad – I did not want to go a bit.' And then he told me that his wife had had a stormy ten minutes with Winston in which she had told him that he was making the biggest mistake of his life: he was getting rid of the one man who had been loyal and sensible and who would remain so and would always give Winston good advice. Winston listened gravely and then he said that he regarded the job in America as equivalent to one in the War Cabinet, that Halifax would retain his position in the War Cabinet and, if he came back, he could sit with them. Halifax agreed that this was all very nice but added: 'I am glad Dorothy said what she said, as it is what I felt.' Then he said, very whimsically, 'I think this is through a wish to get rid of all the gentlemen.' I told Halifax that I had said this would happen when he resigned himself to not becoming PM. I also said, 'You have always underestimated the strength of the friends you can rally in the House of Commons.'[31]

Rab's reaction was not, of course, entirely disinterested. The removal of Halifax from the Foreign Office inevitably meant that someone else, almost certainly from the Commons, would be put in charge. Rab's worst premonitions were fulfilled when he found himself being asked by Halifax whether he would like to serve under Anthony Eden:

> I said, 'No, I would not be very keen to, in any case – and certainly not be under him in the House of Commons, if I can help it.' He then broke off and said, 'I hope there will be something for you – it is all very unpleasant and I cannot bear to talk about it.'[32]

The last of 'the gentlemen' did not, however, prove a very formidable patron – and within two days Eden's appointment was announced as the new Foreign Secretary, with Rab continuing as his subordinate. The only consolation for Rab was to be found in *The Times* leader column, which cordially remarked, 'Members of the Commons and diplomatists of many countries will be glad that Mr R. A. Butler remains Under-Secretary of State for Foreign Affairs. He succeeded Lord Cranborne in 1938 and has done his work with great tact and imaginative talent.'[33]

Golden journalistic opinions, however, were one thing; political promotion, after what was now eight full years as an Under-

Secretary, was clearly something quite else – and Rab's position cannot have been made any easier by a flurry of Press speculation which broke early in the New Year that at last he was about to be awarded a Department of his own.[34] The original stories all suggested, prematurely as it turned out, that he would be appointed to the Board of Education; but within three weeks his name was also being floated for the Colonial Office – for whose 'contacts with the Free French and the Belgian colonies', ventured the Tory *Daily Telegraph*, 'Mr Butler's experience would be invaluable'.[35] But, whether they were inspired or not, nothing came of either of these suggestions, and Rab was left to settle down, as best he could, under his new Foreign Office chief for whom he had never had a particularly high regard. Probably the most humiliating task that he had to undertake was to send the new Secretary of State an outline of the duties he had been accustomed to perform under Halifax and to inquire whether it would be in order for him to continue with them. His memo came back with a graceful manuscript scribble at the top from Eden – 'Thank you for your most helpful note' – but to someone who had grown used to paddling his own canoe there was perhaps something faintly ominous about the sentence that followed, 'I hope you will regard me as available at all times if I can be of any help.'[36] (Not for nothing did Eden always have a reputation as a poor delegator.)

Fortunately for Rab, however, at least a temporary deliverance was at hand. In February Eden was dispatched on a special mission to the Middle and Near East – partly in order to weigh up in concert with the Commander-in-Chief of the Middle East, General Sir Archibald Wavell,* the pros and cons of British military support for Greece against what was increasingly looking like the certainty of a German invasion. The mission eventually had disastrous results, especially for Wavell's campaign in North Africa, but at least it lasted for nearly eight weeks. For all that time Rab was in sole political charge of the Foreign Office, even being expected to appear regularly at meetings of both the War Cabinet and the Defence Committee. His impression, perhaps not surprisingly, was that the Government was run at the top largely as a one-man show:

> The PM sits, looking very pink and large, in the middle of the table [*sic*], smoking an enormous cigar and, after asking all the

* First Earl Wavell (1883–1950). Commander-in-Chief Middle East 1939–41. Commander-in-Chief India 1941–3. Viceroy and Governor-General of India 1943–7.

Chiefs of Staff for their views on the war, proceeds to give his own appreciation of the situation in the midst of voluminous puffs. Attlee* sits next to him and nods his head like one of those animals in the nursery with wire necks and heads that nod up and down. The Service Ministers wait anxiously for an indication from the conductor's baton when they are to give tongue, which they do as efficient members of the orchestra.[37]

By now Rab had come – almost in spite of himself – to admire Churchill. He was particularly taken with the meetings of the Defence Committee:

More fascinating than the Cabinet has been the Defence Committee which meets in the depths of the Cabinet Offices at night. These are heavily shored up and inside they are almost exactly like a liner, with the corridors and shaded lights of a ship. At night, the PM wears a blue siren suit, with a zip-fastener up the front, and again smokes a cigar. He is usually at his best after dinner.

The room is surrounded by maps, which show the mountains and plains through which the German army is usually moving with remarkable rapidity. These meetings only the Chiefs of Staff attend. On the last occasion the PM used his invariable technique, which is violently to attack a Department from which he wants to get good results. Whether presiding over meetings on the Battle of the Atlantic, or in the Cabinet, or presiding over questions like the provision of shelters, the PM gets his effects by attack and only yields to counter-attack. Those who say his only strength is in making speeches are wrong. I do not think he is by nature an administrator but he certainly forces the issue on the administrators.[38]

With Halifax out of the way, there was also a growing readiness in the Churchill camp to overlook Rab's past associations – a process probably assisted by the fact that the new American Ambassador in London, John G. Winant (successor to the unlamented Joseph P. Kennedy) became very early on in his five-year term one of Rab's

* Clement Richard Attlee (1883–1967). Labour MP, Limehouse 1922–50, West Walthamstow 1950–5. Chancellor of the Duchy of Lancaster 1930–1. Postmaster-General 1931. Deputy Leader of the Opposition 1931–5. Leader of the Opposition 1935–40. Lord Privy Seal 1940–2. Deputy Prime Minister 1942–5. Prime Minister 1945–51. Leader of the Opposition 1951–5. Created 1st Earl Attlee 1955.

more earnest admirers. The formation of this friendship was a bonus dividend of Eden's two-month absence in the Middle East – normally a US Ambassador would have bypassed an Under-Secretary and gone straight to the Secretary of State. By good luck, however, it fell to Rab to make the first contacts with Winant (about whom he had originally written a slightly sniffy departmental minute)[39] and thereby to forge what was to be not only a close personal friendship but also, at times, a useful political link. Certainly, Winant seems to have recognised in Rab from the start exactly the type of figure destined to play a leading part in the restructuring of Britain after the war – and it was he, in fact, who first encouraged him to look for his next field of endeavour at the Board of Education, insisting at their first dinner together, 'That must be made the vantage point for bringing about changes in England.'[40]

10 *Boarded to Education*

Rab was appointed President of the Board of Education on 20 July 1941, though he had known about the move for at least the previous six weeks.[1] That was more than his predecessor, Herwald Ramsbotham, the Conservative MP for Lancaster, had done. He found himself unceremoniously removed to a peerage and the chairmanship of the Assistance Board.

Rab's appointment, however, was only part of a general reconstruction of the Government designed by Churchill to bring on younger men. The promotion in it which caught the headlines was not Rab's but that of Brendan Bracken, who found himself riskily elevated from being the Prime Minister's PPS to the until then luckless post (it had had three occupants in the previous two years) of Minister of Information. Brendan Bracken's new official position made, of course, very little difference to his power base – which had always rested on his rights of access within No. 10. There is, in fact, good reason to believe that he was responsible for Rab's own appointment: certainly, he had been busy promoting it throughout the previous six months and was probably the source of the original newspaper predictions that had surfaced in January. What, however, was wrong in the Press stories that appeared alongside the announcement of Rab's appointment was the repetition of the idea that he had previously refused other offers of full ministerial rank.[2] He had not: for the last six months he had been very anxious indeed to get out of the Foreign Office.

In part that was the product of his slightly complicated relationship with Eden – though the Foreign Secretary had done him proud by giving him a farewell dinner at the beginning of July, at which the only other guests were the Prime Minister, his wife and Lord Beaverbrook. One of Rab's difficulties, however, had always been his inability to take Eden wholly seriously. There is, for instance, a markedly ironic note to Rab's description of how, after a major debate on military aid to Greece in May (in which Eden had performed disastrously, he had accompanied the Foreign Secretary on what was clearly designed to be the progress of a conquering hero:

> I walked back afterwards with A.E. As usual, everybody in the street bowed and smiled. He walked without a hat, looking first to the right then to the left. I told him I was getting quite a public myself simply by walking about with him.[3]

Presumably Eden took that as a compliment, though whether it was intended as such is quite another question. But there was another reason anyway why Rab was relieved to leave the Foreign Office. His life there had degenerated more and more into one of routine drudgery. Indeed, the most striking aspect of surviving documentary accounts of his day-to-day activities is just how little the central issues of the war seem to have impinged upon him. Instead, the Under-Secretary's activities appear to have concentrated on peripheral matters – authorisation of priority air or sea passages for arriving or departing diplomats, negotiations for the repatriation of neutral seamen serving on impounded merchant ships, arguments over blocked gold reserves held in London banks, even attempts to solve the problems that clothing rationing was causing for grandees like the Spanish Ambassador (as commemorated in one of Rab's last memoranda to the Secretary of State):

> The Duke of Alba has evidently got into trouble with his hosier and would value a few extra coupons for socks which he has bought. I think it would be best to accede to this wish of the Duke's as he appears deeply engaged to his hosier. I should like at the same time a general ruling as to extra coupons for the Diplomatic Corps, since they talk of little else.[4]

It may be that there was an element of a slightly 'demob-happy' Under-Secretary about that particular minute – it was written in the same week that the Edens gave their farewell dinner party for Rab – but it reflects not unfairly the trivial tasks to which Rab had found himself relegated. Of course, Hitler's invasion of the Soviet Union on the night of Saturday 21 June might have been expected to give Rab's sphere of responsibility an entirely new dimension (especially as his most regular visitor and persistent petitioner throughout the first twenty-one months of the war had been the Soviet Ambassador in London, Ivan Maisky). But here again, once Russia had entered the war, the decisive change in relations between the British and Soviet Governments merely served to demonstrate just how subordinate the role of diplomacy becomes in wartime to the challenge of attaining victory. Maisky, who had been in and out of the Foreign Office at least once or twice a week ever since Rab first became Under-Secretary back in February 1938, reappeared in Rab's room on only one further occasion after his country had joined in the war – his new ambassadorial ports of call having changed virtually overnight to places like the Air Ministry, the Admiralty and the War Office.

The truth is, as Lord Grey had noted as a result of his experiences at the beginning of the First World War, that in wartime diplomacy is a thankless task. By the summer of 1941, Rab certainly thought himself well rid of it – and it was only voices wedded to the *ancien régime*, like *The Times* newspaper, that saw any need to dwell on the 'regret' that it was sure would be felt – 'and not only by foreign diplomatists in London' – at his move.[5] Elsewhere his promotion was received with satisfaction – and not least by his mother and father at the Master's Lodge in Pembroke College, Cambridge, to whom he had never made any secret of his reluctance to carry on at the Foreign Office once Eden was appointed in place of Halifax.[6] A certain myth has, admittedly, grown up – fostered to some degree in his later years by Rab himself[7] – that in offering him the Board of Education, at a moment of high crisis during the war, Churchill intended to insult him. The contemporary note that Rab made of his interview with the Prime Minister supplies, however, absolutely no support for that view (or, indeed, substantiation for such bits of national folklore as Churchill's famous alleged remark about 'wiping babies' bottoms'). The following is Rab's own account of his visit to Downing Street written within a week or two of its taking place:

> The PM saw me after his afternoon nap and was audibly purring like a great tiger. He said, 'You have been in the House for 15 years and it is time you were promoted.' I said I had only been there for 12 years but he waved this aside. He said, 'You have been in the Government for the best part of that time and I want you to go to the Board of Education. I think you can leave your mark there. It is true this will be outside the mainstream of the

war, but you will be independent. Besides,' he said with rising fervour, 'you *will* be in the war. You will move poor children from here to there' – and he lifted up imaginary children from one side of his writing pad to the other – 'and this will be very difficult.' Then he said, 'I am too old now to think you can improve people's natures.' He looked at me pityingly and said, 'I think everyone has to learn to defend themselves. I should not object if you could introduce a note of patriotism into the schools. Tell the children that Wolfe won Quebec.' I said I would like to influence the content of education but this was always difficult. Here he looked very earnest and said, 'Of course not by instruction or order but by suggestion.'

I said I had always looked forward to going to the Board of Education if I was given the chance. At this he looked ever so slightly surprised, which showed that he felt that in war a central job such as the one I am leaving is the most important. So he seemed genuinely pleased that I had shown such pleasure and seemed to think the whole appointment quite suitable. He said, 'Come to see me to discuss things, not details, but the broad lines.'[8]

It was Rab's disregard of this final bit of advice which nearly wrecked all his ambitions at the Board of Education. He had been appointed to the Board towards the end of the summer parliamentary session and, beyond a brief talk with James Chuter Ede,* the experienced Labour Party educationalist whom he found *in situ* as Parliamentary Secretary, and a not particularly encouraging meeting with the Archbishop of Canterbury† two days after he took over at Alexandra House in Kingsway, had not been able to achieve very much before Parliament rose for the summer recess on 7 August. There was no doubt, however, as to the height of his aspirations – indeed, in his original letter to Ede on the day after his appointment was announced, he had written specifically of 'the opportunity we have to give the educational system of the country a real helping hand'.[9] Nor had he shrunk from admitting to the Archbishop that his ambition was to secure the raising of the school leaving age, if

* James Chuter Ede (1882–1965). Labour MP, Mitcham 1923, South Shields 1929–31 and 1935–64. Parliamentary Under-Secretary Board (later Ministry) of Education 1940–5. Home Secretary 1945–51. Leader of the House of Commons 1951. Created life peer 1964.

† First Baron Lang of Lambeth (1864–1945). Bishop of Stepney 1901–8. Archbishop of York 1908–28. Archbishop of Canterbury 1928–42.

in two stages, to sixteen[10] – an objective not finally attained until 1973.

Both were perhaps early indications that Rab was in some danger of rushing his fences – and there was further confirmation of that when the new President of the Board, after barely three weeks in office, resolved to go ahead with a plan initiated by his predecessor to receive a full deputation of Anglican and Free Church leaders at the Board's headquarters on Friday 15 August. It did not turn out to be a wholly propitious occasion but, before describing it, it is probably necessary to explain why the role and influence of the Churches was so central to Rab's new responsibilities.

For almost a century, education had provided the chief arena in which the various religious denominations in England and Wales had exerted their political muscle. The reason for that went back well into the nineteenth century. Schooling had started off not as a State but a religious responsibility (it was not until 1870 that the Government intervened independently in the field at all). By then there was a whole network of schools run by the various religious denominations – with the Church of England very much to the fore, especially in rural areas, the Roman Catholics coming up rapidly particularly in the inner cities, and the Nonconformists beginning to falter in their efforts to maintain such fragile innovations as the Wesleyan schools. The W. E. Forster Education Act of 1870 marked the moment at which the State accepted its responsibility to run schools – if only to provide compulsory primary education for all. Yet in doing so the Gladstone Liberal Government of the day expressly stopped short of seeking to create a *tabula rasa*: the aim, as Forster explained it to the House of Commons, was 'to fill up the gaps' and in so doing, 'not to destroy the existing system in introducing a new one'.[11] The result, inevitably, was a typically British compromise – or, more bluntly, muddle – in which some parents could choose between secular and denominational education while others, mainly in rural villages, had no choice but to send their children to schools in which the dogmas of the Established Church formed a specific part of the curriculum. The seeds for the last great battle fought on behalf of the historical forces of Dissent in Britain had been sown.

So firmly were they planted that they defied the successive efforts of Governments of differing political complexions over the next seventy years to uproot them. The first major attempt came with the Balfour Education Act of 1902. With the Churches now finding it more and more of a struggle to meet the costs of their own schools, the Balfour Act was specifically designed to put a provision for their maintenance (including teachers' salaries) on to the local government rates. The consequence was not only the last great convulsion of the Nonconformist conscience in Britain, but also the formal sanctioning of what had come to be known as 'the dual system' in British education – whereby denominational schools run (though no longer wholly paid for) by the Churches lived cheek-by-jowl with schools both administered and supervised by the State through local school boards.

The balance was never, of course, an even one. The great strength of the Church schools lay in primary education – back in the nineteenth century they had set out merely to provide 'the three Rs' of reading, writing and arithmetic – and the increasing strain on their resources meant that they had been able to do little in the field of secondary education. Nor, at least in the case of the Anglicans, had they contrived to hold the line even at the point where it had been drawn by the Balfour Education Act of 1902. During the first forty years of the twentieth century the total number of Church of England schools had dwindled from 12,000 to 9,000. Since many of those surviving were small village schools (sometimes run by a single teacher), the proportion of the nation's children the Church was educating had fallen even more drastically – this declined from 40 to 20 per cent.

The Roman Catholics' position, admittedly, was different: the number of their schools had actually increased from the beginning of the century – from 1,000 to 1,200 – and they were now educating 8 per cent of the child population. But in one way the predicament of the two denominations was identical. In terms of modern facilities, the 1¼ million children in Church schools were getting a much worse deal than the 3 million in State schools – their buildings were older, their classrooms more antiquated, their amenities (all the way to schoolyards in place of recreational facilities) in every way inferior. The statistics, indeed, told their own story. On 'the black list' of school buildings compiled by the Board of Education just before the outbreak of war were only 2 per cent of council schools compared with 4½ per cent of Church of England schools and well over 6 per cent of Roman Catholic ones.

It was this fact, more than any other, which was to provide Rab with his lever for prising a settlement of the schools question out of the Churches. But in the very early days it is doubtful if he had entirely grasped the complexities of the issues with which he was faced – or indeed realised the danger of the 'sunken rocks' which

12 Neville Chamberlain with his Parliamentary Private Secretary, Alec Douglas-Home (then Lord Dunglass), carrying the Prime Minister's gas mask outside No. 10 on 3 September 1939, the day war was declared

13 Under-Secretary at the Foreign Office. Rab leaving Downing Street and walking towards St James's Park with Sir Alexander Cadogan and Lord Halifax in April 1940

14 President of the Board of Education at the time of the publication of the White Paper in July 1943

15 With Churchill at a Conservative Central Council meeting after the defeat in 1945. Anthony Eden is in the background behind them

still lurked beneath the seemingly placid surface of what had become a predominantly secular system of State education.*

Certainly, the amiability of his first encounter with the Anglican and Free Church leaders seems to have misled Rab into believing that a settlement of the religious question would be a good deal easier than it eventually turned out to be. That was, no doubt, partly because no Roman Catholics at all were included in the 33-strong deputation of Churchmen who waited upon the new President of the Board of Education on the afternoon of Friday 15 August 1941. Led by the two Church of England Archbishops, Canterbury and York, and including a cross-section of the leadership of British Nonconformity, it was still a pretty formidable example of the Church Militant in action.

The main purpose of the Free Churches and the Church of England in coming together in this way had been to lay before the Government the 'five points' (originally published in a joint letter to *The Times* the previous February) to which they attached particular importance in any future settlement of the schools question. The trouble, however, was that the 'five points' were now being put forward against the background of some provisional proposals of educational re-organisation issued earlier that summer by Rab's predecessor at the Board in a consultative document (largely shaped by officials of the National Union of Teachers) that came to be known as 'the Green Book'. Although the Archbishops and the Free Church leaders could not at that stage have been expected to realise it, the Green Book itself was soon to become a dead letter. There was a certain air of unreality, therefore, to the whole occasion – an air of unreality increased, if anything, by the exaggerated amity that the Church leaders brought to their presentation. Whether this atmosphere went to Rab's head or not, there is no doubt that he thought the interview 'successful' – being particularly pleased with his master-stroke in calling upon the Archbishop of Canterbury to wind up the meeting with a prayer. A more mordant view of this piece of inspiration was taken by James Chuter Ede, who recorded in his diary that night, 'The President took everyone by surprise by asking the Archbishop

* In his Diaries James Chuter Ede, Butler's Parliamentary Under-Secretary, claims that on the morning of the day on which the first deputation of Church leaders was received at Alexandra House, the President of the Board of Education was actually to be heard inquiring, 'What is an elementary school?' – prompting the sour comment on the part of the diarist, 'He has not yet grasped the difference between "elementary" and "secondary".' Ede Diaries, British Library, additional MS 59690, diary entry dated 15.8.1941.

of Canterbury to close the proceedings with a prayer. He was obviously taken aback by the suggestion, and mumbled a collect.'[12]

Nor was Chuter Ede, for his part, at all deceived as to the difficulties that lay ahead. Already nearly sixty, he was old enough to remember the high hopes with which H. A. L. Fisher had started out on the quest for a religious settlement while President of the Board of Education in the Lloyd George Government at the end of the First World War – and the speed with which those hopes had been dashed. He had also been a Labour MP at the time of the Ramsay MacDonald Government of 1929–31, and vividly recalled the three separate efforts which Sir Charles Trevelyan had then made to untangle the anomalies of the dual system, only to be ultimately defeated (and driven into resignation) by an unholy alliance between rabid sectarians and backwoods Tory peers. Not that Ede stood at all for a policy of *tranquilla non movere* – indeed, as someone who had been born a Nonconformist and started out as a teacher, he could claim himself to have been a victim of the injustices of the dual system. Although he had been a pupil in a Church of England school and had gone on to be one of its managers and chairman of the county authority that financed it, the one thing he could never have hoped to be (unless he changed his religion) was a teacher in it.

It was unfortunate that immediately after the Churches' deputation left his office in Kingsway, Rab should have gone off on holiday, for it meant that during the next two weeks he was deprived of the kind of cautious counsel that Ede (and, indeed, his Civil Servants) might have offered him. At what stage he resolved to write to Churchill and outline his plans for the future – including his hope of introducing a major Education Bill (along the lines of the 1902 measure) – can only be a matter for conjecture, although all the evidence points to it having been a decision taken in holiday isolation (a draft was shown to Chuter Ede within a day of Rab's return from holiday). The letter which Rab sent to the Prime Minister on Friday 12 September was a curious document to come from so practised a diplomatic hand.

It started off tactfully enough by reminding the Prime Minister of his offer to give Rab advice from time to time. But, even by its second sentence, it had changed gear with the not yet two-month-old Minister announcing, 'I should now like to give you my first impressions of the questions immediately before the Board': the trouble, of course, was that such questions were hardly likely to seem of pressing importance to a national leader who, in the autumn of 1941, still saw his role very much as that of an embattled warlord.

Worse, however, was to come – indeed most of the damage was probably done by the next paragraph, in which Rab ticked off what he saw as the main issues one by one:

> There is, first, the need for industrial and technical training and the linking up of schools closely with employment. Secondly, a settlement with the Churches about Church schools and religious instruction in schools. Both these questions are nationwide. Thirdly, there is the question of the public schools, which may easily raise widespread controversy.[13]

It was not surprising if the last two points at least seemed to Churchill simply an invitation to stir up a hornet's nest. Certainly the rejoinder that Rab received the very next day from No. 10 could hardly have been more crushing:

> It would be the greatest mistake to raise the 1902 controversy during the war, and I certainly cannot contemplate a new Education Bill. I think it would also be a great mistake to stir up the public schools question at the present time. No one can possibly tell what the financial and economic state of the country will be when the war is over. Your main task at present is to get the schools working as well as possible under all the difficulties of air attack, evacuation etc. If you can add to this industrial and technical training, enabling men not required for the Army to take their places promptly in munitions, industry or radio work, this would be most useful. We cannot have any party politics in war time, and both your second and third points raise these in a most acute and dangerous form. Meanwhile you have a good scope as an administrator.[14]

At face value this looked like a blanket veto on all the aspirations for reform that Rab (initially inspired by the American Ambassador John G. Winant) had brought to his new job – and, interestingly, it was in this sense that it was interpreted by Rab's experienced Permanent Secretary at the Department, Sir Maurice Holmes.* In what Rab was later to term a 'disappointingly compliant letter'[15] Holmes tried to do what he could to cheer his Minister up. After

* Maurice Gerald Homes (1885–1964). Deputy Secretary Board of Education 1931–7. Permanent Secretary 1937–45.

remarking, in a somewhat Panglossian spirit, 'I do not think we need be unduly cast down', Holmes warmed to his task of being a Job's comforter:

> There are, I feel, some advantages in our having more time than even your detailed programme contemplated for reaching the greatest common measure of agreement on the more contentious issues so that, from this point of view, the Prime Minister's frigid reception of your proposals has its brighter side.[16]

That 'brighter side' was certainly not apparent to Rab, who lost no time in proving that he was made of sterner stuff than his principal Civil Service adviser. He could not, of course, defy the Prime Minister's edict but he could seek to circumnavigate his way around it. For the next eighteen months that was precisely what he did.

It was a delicate operation – if only because it would have been fatal to let any of the various religious bodies know that the Prime Minister had, in effect, vetoed any comprehensive measure of educational reform until the war was safely over. That involved something of an ethical dilemma – as Rab recognised when, at the beginning of 1942, he inquired of that pillar of integrity, James Chuter Ede, whether he thought he 'was morally justified in pursuing negotiations without the PM's consent to a Bill' (fortunately, he was given a suitably robust answer).[17] During this limbo period Rab came to rely more and more on the Labour Party for whatever political support he had for introducing a major measure of educational reform. The three Ministers he had on his side in the War Cabinet were the three Labour representatives – Attlee, Bevin* and Greenwood† (it was Attlee, in fact, who persuaded him out of his initial idea, as outlined in his original letter to the Prime Minister, to go for a Joint Select Committee on the pattern of the legislative prologue to the India Bill of the 1930s). And it was, predominantly, Labour Members of Parliament who tended to show, at Question Time and elsewhere, an active concern for the future pattern and structure of British education. Certainly, Rab was telling nothing less than the truth when, in writing to Alec Dunglass, he readily

* Ernest Bevin (1881–1951). General Secretary Transport and General Workers' Union 1921–40. Labour MP, Central Walthamstow 1940–51. Minister of Labour and National Service 1940–5. Foreign Secretary 1945–51. Lord Privy Seal 1951.

† Arthur Greenwood (1880–1954). Labour MP, Nelson and Colne 1922–31, Wakefield 1932–54. Minister of Health 1929–31. Member of War Cabinet and Minister without Portfolio 1940–2. Lord Privy Seal 1945–7.

admitted, 'I find in Education that much of the drive towards a vaguely progressive future comes from Labour.'[18]

There was, of course, a reason for that – quite separate and distinct from any natural opposition to what were coming increasingly to look like discriminatory provisions in the Churches' sector of the educational system. The evacuation of children – at the beginning of September just before war broke out in 1939 – had come as a great shock to the rural middle class. As F. A. Iremonger, the biographer of William Temple,* put it nearly a decade later:

> Who were these boys and girls – half-fed, half-clothed, less than half-taught, complete strangers to the most elementary social discipline and the ordinary decencies of a civilised home? Only one answer was possible. They were the products of free institutions of which Britons are bidden to think with pride.[19]

Little wonder that there was a clamour, at least from the left, for a general overhaul of the nation's schools – an overhaul that would, ideally, given the common bonds that now united the entire population in the war effort, take in the fee-paying schools and weld them on to an improved and reconstructed national system. So far as the politicians of the left were concerned, the question of Church schools was very much of secondary importance, though the shrewder of them were probably wise enough to see that a settlement of the religious issue was a necessary precondition of any wider reform. The problem, in fact, was that the Church of England's defence of its position in primary education operated as an effective road-block to any wider restructuring of the whole system. To put the point in its simplest form, it was virtually impossible to raise the school leaving age (anyway to sixteen) unless the old Church categories of 'Infants' and 'Seniors' were changed at the same time. 'Secondary education for all' – which was Rab's declared objective throughout – meant, in effect, that the Church of England would have to withdraw from its direct participation in education not at the age of fourteen but at eleven.

It was because of this threatened sacrifice that the Church of England had always shrunk from any agitation calling for root-and-branch educational reorganisation. Here, however, Rab was to enjoy a stroke of luck. By the beginning of 1942 the Archbishop of

* William Temple (1881–1944). Bishop of Manchester 1921–9. Archbishop of York 1929–42. Archbishop of Canterbury 1942–4.

Canterbury for the past thirteen years, Cosmo Gordon Lang, was already seventy-seven years old and in January he announced his intention to retire. Rab had enjoyed reasonably cordial relations with him but had seen enough of his essentially Establishment cast of mind to doubt whether he would ever make an effective ally in any serious effort at educational reconstruction. In fact, at their last meeting together the previous November, the Archbishop had made Rab feel 'rather apprehensive' by raising the question of the future of the public schools and insisting that, as chairman of the governors of Charterhouse, he saw the issue as 'one of paramount importance'.[20] So it was probably with a measure of relief that Rab learned, on 20 January 1942, of the impending change at Canterbury: he may even have secretly shared his Permanent Secretary's (Sir Maurice Holmes's) view that the best aspect of it was that it offered 'a chance of getting the Church of England into play'.[21]

As things turned out, that ranked as a remarkably accurate forecast. For, though he was not Rab's own first choice, the man chosen by Churchill as Lang's successor was the socialist-inclined Archbishop of York, William Temple. He combined two singular distinctions in the world of education: he had been a public school headmaster (of Repton) at twenty-eight and President of the Workers' Educational Association for sixteen years, starting at the even earlier age of twenty-seven. If it would be an exaggeration to claim that he procured the religious settlement, which was the *sine qua non* of the 1944 Education Act, it is certainly true to say that it would not have happened without him. That was not because he entered into any private deal or secret arrangement with Rab; it was simply because he was a realist and recognised, at the crucial point, the force of the argument that Rab had to put to him – that the Church of England could continue to maintain its 'voluntary' sector only at the expense of those pupils who found themselves within it.

A great deal of ground, however, still had to be cleared before that decisive moment in the negotiations was reached. The subject, in fact, which preoccupied the Board in the early months of 1942 was not so much the religious settlement (the change of Canterbury meant that negotiations went into abeyance for the time being) as the almost equally vexed question of the future of the public schools. One reason why Rab had been so taken aback by Archbishop Lang's threat to sound a trumpet call on the issue was that he was already engaged in very secret and sensitive negotiations with the public schools' Governing Bodies Association. At least at the outset he does seem to have believed that he had a fighting chance of incorporating the fee-paying sector into an entirely restructured secondary educational system. Never a worshipper at the public school shrine, Rab was quite enough of a rationalist to see the advantages of ending 'the great divide' in British education, against which respected socialist academics like R. H. Tawney had inveighed for years. Nor, in the climate of the time, was that so remarkable. The cartoonist David Low's immortal creation, Colonel Blimp, had damaged the legend of the old school tie and there was widespread doubt, even in some Conservative quarters, as to whether such citadels of privilege could expect to survive in the post-war world. Such doubts, indeed, reached all the way to the Prime Minister himself – whose views appeared to have softened a good deal since he touched on the topic in his curt memo of the previous September.

On 4 February 1942 Churchill summoned Chuter Ede to No. 10 to offer him a move to the Ministry of War Transport where his departmental head would be in the House of Lords and where he would, therefore, have a fuller role to play in the House of Commons. Ede, greatly daring, asked permission to refuse the offer and, while waiting for Churchill to get through to Attlee on the telephone in order to tell him of this rebellious decision by his subordinate, was rewarded with a monologue by the Great Man of which, fortunately, he wrote a graphic account that evening:

> The PM was glad to know that the public schools were receiving our attention. He wanted 60–70 per cent of the places to be filled by bursaries – not by examination alone but on the recommendation of the counties and the great cities. We must reinforce the ruling-class – though he disliked the word 'class'. We must not choose by the mere accident of birth and wealth but by the accident – for it was equally accident – of ability. The great cities would be proud to search for able youths to send to Haileybury, to Harrow and to Eton.[22]

As a romantic vision of the future, it was not perhaps expressed in quite the form to be palatable to a Labour veteran whose own pre-parliamentary career had been spent as an elementary schoolteacher; but from the Leader of the Conservative Party it was still a remarkable enough utterance. Rab's own approach to the subject tended to be expressed in more modest terms – indeed he had warned Ede that the Conservative Party 'would be up in arms unless a boy could get into a public school on payment'.[23] Not that that necessarily represented his own position, which he had previously summarised with typical irreverence, 'For himself, he would not exclude a child because his parents could afford to pay but he would not admit a child who had fallen on his head while out hunting with the Quorn.'[24]

Nor was that all simply idle, amused speculation. Through all this time the Board of Education had been quietly working on a private document concerned with the likely future of the public schools, if they were to be left on their own. The document divided such schools into four categories – those whose future was almost certainly assured, those who had suffered a decline but were still believed to be in a healthy condition, those whose future was doubtful and those in danger of extinction. Interestingly, those in the third and fourth categories included schools as renowned as Harrow, Marlborough, Lancing, Tonbridge and Repton.[25] The fact that schools as famous as these were considered vulnerable may help to explain Rab's strategy. Very early on he passed a message to the Governing Bodies Association that, so far as participation in any future State scheme of secondary education was concerned, it would have to be a case of all public schools coming in or none. He was not prepared to accept a situation whereby the weaker brethren sought a blood transfusion and the stronger brothers continued to go their own independent way.

How far Rab's agnostic attitude towards the divine status of the public schools was known in the Tory Party it is impossible to judge – though he certainly made no secret of it. In fact, in writing to his eldest son, Richard's, housemaster at Eton in April 1943 he was to go out of his way to spell out his own sense of detachment by stating bluntly, 'I do not personally think that the whole of the public school system is necessarily the best form of education, particularly when there is too much worship of games and the herd spirit.'[26] Politically, however, at some point his nerve clearly failed him. Instead of conducting bilateral negotiations with the Governing Bodies Association – the way he was beginning to tackle the denominational problem – he chose the easy way out and plumped for an independent committee of inquiry. It is always, of course, a politician's natural inclination to kick for touch at a moment of difficulty. Earlier in the year there had been some ominous rumblings on the issue, notably from the conventionally minded Bishop of London,* who had been a public school headmaster for some eighteen years, and who now,

* Geoffrey Francis Fisher (1882–1972). Headmaster of Repton 1914–32. Bishop of Chester 1932–9. Bishop of London 1939–45. Archbishop of Canterbury 1945–61. Created life peer 1961.

significantly, found himself silenced by being made a member of the new committee of inquiry. Established under the chairmanship of a Scottish judge, Lord Fleming,* the committee – an unwieldy body of some eighteen very disparate individuals – was given the vaguest possible terms of reference: its purpose, Rab declared in the House of Commons on 16 June 1942, would be 'to investigate how the facilities of a boarding school education might be extended to those who desired to profit by them, irrespective of their means'.[27] Not surprisingly, the suspiciously anodyne nature of such a statement of aim immediately drew a tart rebuke from the *Manchester Guardian*. Expressing the hope that the committee would 'take a large and generous view of its duties', the voice of liberalism in the north went on to remark sharply that 'it would be disastrous if it confined itself to schemes for providing free places in boarding schools' – rounding off its comment with the magisterial pronouncement, 'The nation is ready for the daring and imaginative treatment of its problems.'[28]

On this particular issue anyway the Fleming Committee did not seem to be getting that kind of guidance from the centre – and, predictably, the committee laboured for two years before producing under its Scheme 'B' (Scheme 'A' dealt with Direct Grant grammar schools) the mouse of a recommendation that local education authorities could, if they so wished, offer a 25 per cent share of places, to be paid for out of ratepayers' money, at public schools willing to allocate bursaries in this way. The Fleming scheme, as it came to be called, thus depended on a two-way traffic: a local authority ready to make a heavy investment in individual pupils rather than in a collective facility like a school swimming-bath, and a headmaster or a governing body prepared to accept such 'guinea pigs' as part of the school's regular entry. Predictably enough, a modified version of the Fleming scheme (brought into existence only after Rab's own departure from the Board) soon foundered – with public school headmasters making only a token obeisance in its direction and local education authorities, in the period immediately after the war, becoming increasingly reluctant to favour a particularly bright child as against the general mass of run-of-the-mill pupils in

* David Pinkerton Fleming (1877–1944). Solicitor-General for Scotland 1922–3 and 1924–6. Conservative MP, Dumbarton 1924–6. Created a Scottish law lord on being raised to the bench in 1926. Rab was to write of him in his memoirs, 'I had been advised that Fleming was a distinguished Scottish judge who could be relied upon to provide impartiality; I had not been prepared for the limitations of his views or for the humourlessness with which he gave them rein.' *The Art of the Possible* (Hamish Hamilton, 1971), p. 119.

their care. If the experiment (which gradually petered out) is today recalled at all, it is probably only because it provided the raw material for a film that helped launch Sir Richard Attenborough on his post-war screen career.*

It has to be conceded that Rab's handling of the public schools question represented the one real failure in his general strategy for educational reconstruction. The time was ripe, the public mood was propitious, the opportunity was there. And yet he contrived to throw it all away. Why? The cynical answer would, no doubt, be that as an ex-public schoolboy himself, a parent who sent his own three sons to Eton, and an Essex MP who dutifully sat on the governing body of one of the county's own public schools, Felsted, he lacked enthusiasm for the task in hand. But as an explanation that is not entirely satisfactory. For one thing, as has been noted, Rab never really approved of birth exclusively providing the winning ticket in the national education lottery (if anything, indeed, he was in principle a 'meritocrat' – much more so than Churchill); and for another, he was quite enough of a central planner to realise just what the eventual impact of the withdrawal of the top 5 per cent of parents from a national structure of secondary education would be. He needed them to be involved, as he confessed in old age, if only to make sure, through their influence and articulacy, that standards in the State sector were kept high.

How, then, was it that in this particular area he should so resignedly have accepted failure? For what eventually transpired – a smattering of council-financed pupils totally overwhelmed by a vast array of traditional public schoolboys – certainly represented a sad comedown from the arrangement which Robert Birley, the headmaster of Charterhouse, had tentatively suggested to the Board of Education even before the Fleming Committee first met: a ratio of 50 per cent state-aided pupils and 50 per cent fee-paying ones, starting in Charterhouse's own preparatory school.[29] The best answer probably is that, like all politicians, Rab preferred to fight one battle at a time rather than have to wage war on two fronts simultaneously. There had been quite enough warning shots from the public school lobby – which, unfortunately, overlapped at virtually every angle with the Anglican Establishment – to persuade him that in tackling it head-on he might well imperil the gains he was seeking to make elsewhere. In withdrawing from the prospective

* *The Guinea Pig* by Warren Chetham-Strode. It was first produced as a play, at the Criterion Theatre, London, in 1946.

combat – and passing the buck to the Fleming Committee – he may not have made a particularly courageous decision; characteristically, however, he probably made a sensible one, at least in terms of his immediate objectives.

As it was, Rab soon found himself in trouble enough. Although a short Commons debate on the religious question, which Rab left Chuter Ede to handle, had passed off relatively satisfactorily towards the end of November 1941, a two-day Lords debate on the same subject in February 1942 provided a clear warning of the rapids that lay ahead. Initiated by Cosmo Gordon Lang, the outgoing Archbishop of Canterbury, the debate was, quite transparently, designed to put pressure on Rab to deliver on the 'five points' which the Anglican–Free Church deputation had presented to him a full six months earlier. Those points – covering such matters as a guaranteed place for Christian teaching in every school, the inclusion of an act of worship on every working schoolday and the removal of the requirement for religious instruction to have to come either at the beginning or the end of each day's timetable – were not in themselves especially difficult to accept (they were, in fact, all included ultimately in the 1944 Education Act). The trouble arose from the fact that, with one exception (an administrative matter of making religion a credit-worthy subject in teachers' training college exams) they all required legislation – and legislation was precisely what Churchill had ruled against. Rab was thus caught in a trap: if he was to preserve his own credibility as a negotiator, he could not afford to point to the real impediment that was holding things up; on the other hand, the longer he delayed, the more he risked alienating the good will (particularly of the Anglicans) which he knew he was eventually going to need.

There is some evidence that in the spring of 1942 Rab began to waver. Certainly, a Bill was drafted within the Board which would simply have sought to deliver the 'five points' to the Protestant leaders and, being relatively uncontroversial, might have stood a chance of getting past Churchill. It was Chuter Ede who had to pull his chief back from embracing this soft option. Rab found himself being sharply reminded that 'a Bill to deal with the religious problem only will deprive us of our chance of a general advance'. So agitated, indeed, was Ede that he even produced his own slogan for the Department – 'No settlement without a general advance remains our only chance of getting a general advance.'[30]

But how to get 'a general advance' – or, indeed, one that Churchill would accept? The one part of the preliminary agenda that Rab had not so far even attempted to clear concerned the Roman Catholics. His initial, somewhat remote, contacts with them had not been especially encouraging. One trouble was that they tended to be a much more heterogeneous force even than the Anglicans or the Nonconformists; and Rab never seems quite to have solved the problem of with whom it would be most profitable to conduct negotiations. The Archbishop of Westminster at the time was Cardinal Hinsley,* but he was already over seventy-five and suffering from failing health: in any event he showed singularly little enthusiasm to become involved. It was not until the summer of 1942 that Rab had anything approaching a proper talk with him.† The occasion, in June, was a lunch party given by the wife of the Lord President of the Council, Sir John Anderson‡ and, although Rab went to it with high hopes, they were by no means wholly fulfilled. The presence of the Spanish Ambassador as a fellow-guest inhibited any serious domestic conversation and the Cardinal himself, as Rab ruefully reported afterwards, had not exactly helped matters by announcing, in Anderson's hearing, that he regarded the Presidency of the Board of Education as the most important job in the Government, second only to the Prime Minister's.[31] Until then, according to Rab, the Lord President had done his conscientious best to be constructive but his efforts visibly flagged from that moment onwards. The most Rab was eventually able to come away with was a promise from the Cardinal-Archbishop that he would 'appoint people to meet us as negotiators'.[32]

Even so, it was not until September 1942 that the first formal deputation representing the Roman Catholic viewpoint was received at Alexandra House, Kingsway. It may be that the delay by this stage owed as much to design on Rab's part as to any procrastination on the part of the Cardinal-Archbishop. For, at least in retrospect, it appears to have been Rab's view that there never was any hope

* Arthur Hinsley (1865–1943). Apostolic Delegate in Africa 1930–4. Canon of St Peter's Rome 1934–5, Archbishop of Westminster 1935–44. Created Cardinal 1937.

† They had, in fact, met on neutral ground in November 1941, but their conversation then had centred almost entirely on the 'Green Book' issued by Rab's predecessor. The Cardinal strongly objected to it. Conservative Party Archives, Bodleian Library, Oxford. R. A. Butler's files on Education Bill, Box 2, interview note dated 7.11.1941.

‡ John Anderson (1882–1958). Permanent Under-Secretary, Home Office 1922–32. Governor of Bengal 1932–7. National MP, Scottish Universities 1938–50. Lord Privy Seal 1938–9. Home Secretary and Minister of Home Security 1939–40. Lord President of the Council 1940–3. Chancellor of the Exchequer 1943–5. Created 1st Viscount Waverley 1952.

of avoiding 'a head-on collision' with the Roman Catholic Church – and that, therefore, it was better to present its leaders with a virtual *fait accompli* rather than go through the unrealistic pretence of a negotiation.[33] If that was the strategy, it had certainly fallen conveniently into place by the autumn of 1942.

The breakthrough in negotiations with the Anglicans had occurred in mid-summer. William Temple, who had succeeded Cosmo Gordon Lang at Canterbury on 1 April, had made his first public intervention in the debate with a robust speech in defence of Church Schools – entitled 'Our Trust and our Task' – at the annual meeting of the Church of England's National Society on 3 June. Within the Board its general tone was not considered particularly helpful – though, to be fair to the Archbishop, he was reacting to what could plausibly be presented as a perceptible shift in the Board's own policy. The 'Green Book', which Rab had inherited from his predecessor and which had generally pleased the Anglicans, had now been replaced by the 'White Memorandum' which, particularly in its call for the ending of the 'single-school areas' in which the Church of England had hitherto enjoyed an educational monopoly, could be considered a great deal more injurious to Anglican interests. This new 'White Memorandum' had largely been the work of James Chuter Ede and its harsher provisions aimed at the smaller denominational village schools had never entirely commended themselves to Rab (who had any number of such schools in his own rural constituency). The Archbishop's speech, in any event, provided him with an opportunity of reopening the issue – an opportunity that he was able to take up very quickly as he already had a meeting scheduled with Temple and other representatives of the National Society (the Church of England's schools organisation) on 5 June.

In all subsequent accounts that he gave of the battle over the Education Bill Rab never wavered from portraying that meeting as the turning point in the whole struggle. Armed with the facts and figures, as incorporated in the Board's own 'black list' of condemned and sub-standard schools, Rab was able to make the Archbishop – and, to a lesser degree, his other colleagues – realise not only the dimension of the financial challenge the Church of England would face if it sought to maintain its school system unimpaired, but also the scale of the educational disadvantages it would be inflicting on the children within its care. If that had been all there was to the meeting, its impact would, at best, have been negative: it could hardly have qualified as productive.

But Rab had also taken the precaution of arriving at it equipped with what, after much reflection, he had convinced himself was the only possible solution to the problem. The key to it lay in its total absence of compulsion – it threw the burden of decision on to the Churches themselves. The offer of State assistance rested on a choice between two alternatives – a choice left to the recipients to make. If the managers or governors of a denominational school were able and willing to contribute 50 per cent of the necessary cost of required improvements or alterations to school buildings, then they could apply for 'aided' status – in which case the governors or managers would continue to appoint staff and organise religious instruction exactly as before. If, however, that 50 per cent contribution was considered too great a strain on limited resources, then the school could elect to become 'controlled' – which meant, in effect, that it was taken over by the relevant Local Education Authority, which would automatically acquire a majority on its board of managers. Even 'controlled' schools were, however, to be guaranteed religious instruction – though it would have to be conducted on the basis of a non-denominational 'agreed syllabus'. (Temple was later able to modify this by gaining access twice a week for denominational teachers, whether clergy or others, for those children whose parents desired it.)

Such were the bones of the settlement that by the autumn Rab and Temple had worked out between them – indeed well before the arrival of the first official Roman Catholic delegation at the Board's headquarters in Kingsway. The discussions between the two men had been highly confidential (Temple, initially, was apprehensive as to whether he could deliver the Church of England's agreement to such a scheme) but Rab had obtained his permission to outline its basic provisions to the Roman Catholic leaders and to the representatives of the Free Churches. In the case of the former the consequence, not unnaturally, was consternation. At the meeting on 15 September Rab found himself being roundly told that the proposed arrangement offered the Roman Catholic Church precisely nothing. The option of 'controlled' status was simply not open to those belonging to a faith which had always looked on its schools as an integral part of 'a worshipping community'; and, as for the 'aided' alternative, it would simply be prohibitive in cost if it was to be spread across a total of some 1,200 schools. This reaction does not seem to have come as a surprise to Rab;[34] so far as he was concerned, the battle-lines had been drawn exactly where he had anticipated.

Far more vital to him was the need to make sure that the Free Churches did not now withdraw their support from a *concordat* that might well seem a little too transparently tailormade to suit the body of Anglicanism. Three weeks later, the divines of English and Welsh Nonconformity came, in their turn, to the headquarters of the Board to learn what the Government had in mind. Fortunately Rab, as Chuter Ede noted, was on his very best form:

> The President said they were engaged on a task that must be completed in the interests of the children. It had daunted great men in the past but he hoped a better spirit now prevailed. He asked them to state their views but they said they wanted to hear what he had to say from his position of supreme responsibility.
>
> The President said the Board had made sallies and reconnaissances. They had published the Green Book and the White Memorandum. Casualties had been suffered but much valuable information had been gained and, as general-in-command, he was able to get a picture of the battlefield.
>
> With light touches he put the conference in very good humour and then laid down his two *desiderata*: first, schools should reach a reasonably high standard physically and educationally; secondly, recommendations which had been hanging about since 1926 must be completed and made nationwide within a reasonable time of the school leaving age being raised to 16.
>
> The Church of England had been rather surprised to find the earnestness with which he held those two *desiderata*.[35]

Whether the Church of England had really been 'surprised' or not, the Free Churches were, as Rab had intended, much relieved. He, naturally, gave rather more emphasis to the 'controlled' option than to the 'aided' one – but in so doing he was in no way being disingenuous: the best estimates of the Board at this stage were that only some 500 of the 9,000 Anglican schools would elect for the costly independence offered under the 50 per cent Exchequer scheme.[36] The fact that the total eventually turned out to be nearer 3,000 was foreseen neither by Butler nor by Temple – though the Church of England's ultimate insistence on putting 'aided' status as the first alternative and relegating the 'controlled' option to the second choice may have played some part in procuring that result.

In the autumn of 1942, however, Rab was certainly confident that he had cleared away enough of the difficulties to be in a position, for the second time, to contemplate legislation. This time, however, he did not make the mistake of dealing directly with Churchill: instead he launched a subtle campaign of persuasion aimed at rallying support from his Government colleagues. It was a campaign – strengthened by some useful editorial comments in the Press[37] – which at first seemed likely to be crowned with success. The objective, admittedly, was a limited one: not a Bill at the beginning of the session but rather a commitment in the King's Speech preparing the way for legislation by the summer of 1943. Throughout October that was certainly seen as a realistic enough prospect within the Board for there to be much drafting and re-drafting of the actual passage in the Gracious Speech to be submitted to No. 10. By Monday 26 October that process was complete – and a minute incorporating the proposed paragraph for inclusion in the King's Speech went across to the Cabinet Office. Nor was Rab simply attempting a shot in the dark. Since the middle of September he had been busy lobbying his colleagues and had ended up with a formidable array of support ranging from the Lord President of the Council, Sir John Anderson, through the Chancellor of the Exchequer, Sir Kingsley Wood,* to the Minister of Labour, Ernest Bevin.

It was all, however, to prove of no avail. For on the morning that Rab was due to make his final pitch before a meeting of Ministers, presided over by the Deputy Prime Minister, Attlee, *The Times* carried a letter written by the Cardinal-Archbishop of Westminster that effectively wrecked the whole enterprise. During the past few months Dr Hinsley had sometimes seemed to Rab an evasive quarry. Now the Cardinal's letter demonstrated that anyone who stalked him did so only at his own peril. It was a classic piece of political footwork – and for that reason alone deserves quotation at least in part:

> Sir,
> The air is full of discussion on reform of education. On this great question of the reconstruction of the national system of education there are three points which we Catholics desire should be kept in mind. (1) The freedom of consciences of all must be respected: Mr Roosevelt has made it clear that this is one of the four great

* Kingsley Wood (1881–1943). Unionist MP, Woolwich West 1918–43. Postmaster-General 1931–5. Minister of Health 1935–8. Secretary of State for Air 1938–40. Lord Privy Seal 1940. Chancellor of the Exchequer 1940–3. Rab had first broached the idea of an Education Bill with him on 9 September 1941 when they met together in the Chancellor's London Club, the Athenaeum, and was assured by Sir Kingsley Wood that 'he would like to back a measure of social reform' even in wartime. PRO, Ed. 136/215.

> liberties for which we are fighting. (2) Next we stoutly maintain that in the past we have proved our determination to promote the progress of education and, while we cling to our principles, we are confident that justice done to us will not obstruct the advancement we all desire in the future. (3) The Catholic body in this country comes mostly from the workers and from the poorer sections of the community. Therefore our Catholic parents have a special claim for fair play, especially from any and every party or group that professes to uphold the just claims of the workers and the rights of minorities . . . .[38]

Few arrows, particularly the last one, can ever have been more delicately aimed at the heart of a Coalition Government. For Churchill, the Archbishop's minatory words fulfilled all his original forebodings: there could, he resolved immediately, be no question of introducing an Education Bill that session – a message he is said to have delivered to Rab by having the Archbishop's letter cut out, stuck on a piece of cardboard and sent round to him with the message scribbled on it, 'There you are, fixed, old cock.'*[39]

What, accordingly, appeared in the King's Speech of 11 November 1942 was a single non-committal sentence remarking merely that 'conversations are taking place between My Ministers and others concerned with the provision and conduct of education in England and Wales with a view to reaching an understanding upon the improvements necessary' – a statement prompting Rab to remark bitterly within the sanctity of his Private Office that he assumed the phrase 'My Ministers' meant himself, Chuter Ede and no one else.[40] He refused, however, to be 'downcast' – even while faithfully reporting to Ede that it remained the Prime Minister's view that they would fail in the task of securing an inter-denominational understanding.[41] No doubt, he was partially buoyed up by his detection of a public mood which his now fully developed political antennae persuaded him even Churchill would not ultimately be able to withstand. Indeed, he had said as much to Ede in the week before disaster struck – claiming that the feeling outside Westminster in favour of educational reform was 'massive' and that he and his

* That at least was the version Rab always told in subsequent years. A contemporary note he made in November 1942 makes, however, no reference to this alleged incident at all. Instead Rab records Churchill ringing him up and asking, 'Have you read Cardinal Hinsley's letter? You are landing me in the biggest political row of the generation.' Conservative Party Archive, Bodleian Library, Oxford. R. A. Butler's files on Education Bill, Box 2, confidential minute dated 3.11.1942.

Under-Secretary could claim to have 'stirred the country by our various wanderings'.[42]

For the moment, however, there was nothing for it but to resume those 'wanderings' – and over the next few months Rab sentenced himself to a succession of 'sorties', primarily in search of a Roman Catholic dignitary with whom he could do business. On one occasion he drove out to Hertfordshire to talk to Archbishop Hinsley, already seriously ill with angina pectoris. On another he presented himself at Archbishop's House in Southwark only to be asked what he had come for. Much later on, he and Ede drove all the way up to Hexham to meet the northern Catholic Bishops assembled at Ushaw College, where they were rewarded with a good dinner but very little else. Not surprisingly, all these experiences left Rab with a feeling of frustration: he later wrote quite candidly of his 'error' in the way he handled the Roman Catholic Bishops and attributed it to his failure to discover 'one man of dignity and reliability with whom one can perpetually be in touch on a personal basis'.[43]

If that was an 'error', it almost certainly did not come about by accident – as Rab himself perceived by simultaneously noting, 'A hydra-headed organisation like the Church of Rome has been, I suppose, deliberately calculated to confuse and deceive the negotiator' (adding the, for him, uncharacteristically defiant rider: 'But I have not finished with them yet!')[44] It could, indeed, be argued that this limbo period, following the disappointment of all his hopes in the autumn of 1942, represented Rab's own 'finest hour'. With nothing really to do – and no part at all to play in the grand strategy of the war – it would have been the easiest thing in the world for him to cut his losses and search for some fresh field of endeavour. And, interestingly, at this stage just such a prospect was dangled before him. The impending retirement of the Marquess of Linlithgow as Viceroy of India meant that there was a prospective opening in New Delhi. There is no evidence that the notion of his possibly filling this vacancy himself had even occurred to Rab: indeed, his only correspondence on the subject, earlier in the year, had been with Sir Samuel Hoare (now exiled as the British Ambassador in Madrid) in which he discouraged his former India Office mentor from entertaining any aspirations to the post.[45]

Towards the end of November, however, Rab found himself visited by the ubiquitous Brendan Bracken, who claimed to have been authorised on behalf of the Prime Minister to inquire if Rab himself would have any interest in the position. Rab's answer, as rehearsed in later life, was that he simply asked for time to think about it – and that within a day or two Bracken came back to him with the intimation that Churchill had thought better of the half-offer and was proposing to appoint Field-Marshal Sir Archibald Wavell, already the British Commander-in-Chief in India.[46] Here, however, Rab did himself an injustice: for not only does there survive among his private papers a draft letter addressed to Brendan Bracken (though never apparently sent) refusing even to contemplate the project, if in tactful terms – 'I have always thought of a later destiny';[47] he also, without at all betraying that any private approach had been made to him, spoke candidly to his Parliamentary Under-Secretary of the impossibility of any person recognising (as he did) that there existed such a thing as 'a political class' in India accepting such a post while Churchill was still Prime Minister.[48] Of course, in retrospect, it became one of Rab's defence mechanisms to pretend that the Viceroyalty was the one office he had ever really hankered after;[49] and, for that reason, he may have tended to exaggerate the tussle of conscience he suffered at the time. The contemporary records, however, suggest that he endured no such thing – that he knew his duty lay with education and that he was not even tempted to diverge from the path of domestic social reform on which he had embarked fifteen months earlier.

There is no doubt, however, that at this period Rab did find his energies somewhat unfulfilled. Until the autumn of 1942 he was still living at 5 Belgrave Square in the sumptuous surroundings (yielding nothing to wartime austerity) afforded to him by his former Foreign Office PPS, 'Chips' Channon – though the two of them had parted professional company when Rab moved to the Board of Education in July 1941. He was maintaining his practice of returning to Stanstead at weekends, although more and more as a temporary visitor from London rather than as the father of a family and the head of a household. If he discovered any compensations for his thwarted reforming zeal at the Board of Education, they tended to lie more and more in peripheral matters. Through 'Chips' he had formed a friendship with the Duke and Duchess of Kent. The death of the Duke in an air crash in Scotland on 7 September 1942 thus meant more to him than to most politicians, at least one of whom resented the elaborate speech of condolence that Churchill insisted on delivering in the House of Commons.[50] Rab's own contacts with the Royal House had, in fact, by now become close enough for him to be recruited as a speech-writer for King George VI's 1942 wartime Christmas broadcast – a responsibility that he took with all the seriousness to be expected of the son of a former Indian pro-consul.

The shadow of the war, however, was soon to touch him even more directly. Against all the advice of the family, his younger brother, Jock, though in a 'reserved occupation' as an established Civil Servant in the Home Office, had insisted shortly after the outbreak of war on enlisting in the Royal Air Force. By the end of 1941 he had completed his training as a navigator and had joined an RAF bomber station as a Pilot Officer. On his first operational flight, the plane, through having ice on its wings, failed to take off and Jock was killed. For any family such a hapless accident would clearly have been an uncovenanted blow; but for the Butlers it was worse than that. Quite without any martial tradition of their own, the Butler family necessarily saw Jock's death as a proof of the sheer futility of war. For his part, Rab reacted stoically enough. He said nothing to anyone in his Private Office about the tragedy and simply took a day off to attend the funeral, which was held at Greenstead Green, Essex on 12 January 1943. Afterwards, he unbent sufficiently to confide in his Parliamentary Under-Secretary that an adjustment, on which he had insisted, in the normal Anglican funeral service – substituting a passage from Isaiah for the normal gloomy reading from the First Epistle to the Corinthians – had brought some comfort to his father, Sir Montagu Butler, whose own views on Church ritual had always been something less than conventional.[51] (Rab also behaved meticulously in pursuing the Air Ministry in order to ensure that his 29-year-old brother's widow received her full entitlement of an 'Active Service' pension – and, indeed, afterwards personally provided for the two children of the marriage, one born posthumously, in terms of their education.)

Though there was an eleven-year age gap between them, Rab had been almost a surrogate father to Jock while he was growing up and their parents were absent in India. He therefore felt his brother's death particularly keenly and work was plainly the only therapy for his loss. The difficulty, in face of Churchill's continuing veto on any education legislation, lay in deciding in what direction his efforts could most profitably be employed. Fortunately, help was here soon to be at hand. The *Observer* might have announced, rather prematurely, just before Christmas, 'The major Education Bill, which Mr R. A. Butler has in hand, is now taking its final shape'[52] – but what was true was that the lesson was gradually sinking into the Government Whips' Office that an Education Bill was in every way preferable to having to enact an equally complex, and far more expensive, measure based on the contents of the Beveridge Report.*

* The Beveridge Report on Social Insurance, the work of Sir William, later Lord, Beveridge (1879–1963) had been published early in December 1942.

(The Chancellor of the Exchequer, Sir Kingsley Wood, had already put the point vividly to Rab by bluntly remarking that he 'would far rather give money for education than throw it down the sink with Sir William Beveridge'.)[53] By the early spring of 1943 even Churchill had been forced to focus at least some part of his attention on the question of post-war reconstruction. No doubt, that was the reason why an invitation came to Rab to dine and spend the night at Chequers on Thursday 11 March.

When Rab arrived, having been driven down by Lord Cherwell, it became clear almost at once that what the Prime Minister had in mind was that the youngest, and intellectually brightest, of his departmental Ministers should perform the speech-writing service for him that he had given to the monarch the previous Christmas. He was, Churchill explained (confirming what Cherwell had already said to Rab in the car), contemplating a speech ranging over the whole area of the Home Front. Inevitably, a certain amount of declamation followed – though only after various distractions including two games of Corinthian bagatelle in which Rab was compelled to join. Towards the end of dinner, however, Churchill came to the matter of his speech and, before leading his guest into the Long Gallery to watch a film about Tsarist Russia, handed the whole text over to Rab so that he might have the opportunity of reading and revising it overnight. (Once the film was over, Churchill apparently changed his mind and, before going up to his bedroom, demanded the document back. He left Rab with only the four pages that concerned education, and instructions to talk to him about them in the morning.)

Rab dutifully discharged the task allotted to him and next morning, at a quarter to eleven, a somewhat later hour than he had anticipated, eventually found himself summoned to the Great Man's bedroom. His main contribution overnight had been to inject into the draft a passage about the place of religion in education – a theme that did not seem immediately to commend itself to Churchill, who proceeded to transform it into an oratorical flourish in praise of toleration. For Rab, however, the most significant aspect of their conversation was the intimation that the Prime Minister was still not really thinking of introducing any specific measures of reform until such time as Germany had been defeated – which he now thought would be 1944, leaving ample opportunity for the Government to announce a four-year plan covering such matters as agriculture and education on which it could then go to the country. With his own plans for educational legislation well advanced, this was not at all what Rab had hoped to hear so, disregarding Churchill's advice 'not to come out too much on education immediately', he boldly announced, not once but twice, 'I am drafting an Education Bill.' To this the only response was an essentially non-committal injunction to make sure that the plans were shown to the Prime Minister when they were ready – accompanied by the slightly condescending observation that he had no doubt they would be 'very interesting'.[54]

For Rab, however, that was enough – and having ensured, through the Private Secretaries' network, that there was nothing in the final draft of the Prime Minister's speech (eventually delivered as a Sunday evening broadcast on 21 March) to preclude further immediate progress on the educational front – the forty-year-old President of the Board of Education immediately began preparing a memorandum on the future structure of British education for submission to the Cabinet. In one sense, the long delay in getting even an amber light had probably been helpful to Rab. No longer bogged down in negotiations over the denominational question (though his vain quest to establish some common ground of understanding with the Roman Catholic hierarchy continued throughout 1943) he was now able to raise his eyes to the broader issues involved in restructuring the entire British educational system.

Certainly, the most striking aspect of the White Paper, eventually published on 16 July 1943 and entitled 'Educational Reconstruction', was how comparatively limited a part the discussion of the Church schools question played in it. The provision of nursery schools, the raising of the school leaving age immediately to fifteen and thereafter to sixteen without any form of exemptions, the opening of free secondary education to all, the proposal to introduce compulsory part-time education up to the age of eighteen for those already at work – all, not unnaturally, took pride of place even in the headlines over what the White Paper tactfully called 'the necessary amendment to the law to enable the schools provided by the voluntary bodies to play their part in the proposed developments'. Nor perhaps should that have been any occasion for surprise. Changing the status of the Church schools was never the main aim of Rab's plans – but it was a necessary precondition if his reforms were to be nationwide and effective. Except for one wobble, back in the spring of 1942 when he appears to have toyed with the notion of introducing a purely religious Bill, Rab himself had always understood that. The White Paper – starting off with its rousing quotation from Disraeli ('Upon the education of the people of this country the fate of this country depends') – represented the formal endorsement of that essentially Erastian view.

Not, of course, that all the ghosts from the past could be banished quite as easily as that. The debate on the White Paper, which took place in the House of Commons on 29 and 30 July, may have been a fairly low-key occasion (the House was due to rise for the summer recess the following week) but it was distinguished by a pair of eloquent speeches pleading the cause of Roman Catholic schools delivered by two MPs from Liverpool, one Conservative and one Labour; there was also some criticism, this time predominantly from a Welsh Nonconformist, that the White Paper had failed to follow the logic of its own argument in stopping short of demanding the abolition of the dual system altogether. For the most part, however, the atmosphere was much more peaceful than it had been on such occasions in the past – and Rab could claim some credit for that. He had set its tone with a homely analogy comparing the British educational system to a schoolboy's jacket which, having given wonderful service in the past, was now in danger of giving way to wear-and-tear.[55]

The debate in the Commons was almost immediately followed by one in the Lords, where the tone was slightly more alarming, if only because of an unexpected speech from William Temple demanding further concessions for the Anglican Church over and above those offered in the White Paper. In particular, the Archbishop wanted the building repair grants raised from 50 per cent to 75 per cent and some financial provision to be made for the building of new denominational schools in areas where 80 per cent of the local population signified a wish for them.[56] This was a highly dangerous development from Rab's point of view, since it held out the risk of the forging of an entirely new alliance between the Anglicans and the Roman Catholics, leaving the Free Churches resentful and isolated. Temple, however, seems eventually to have succeeded in convincing Rab that all he was trying to do was to draw the teeth of his own Anglo-Catholic critics;[57] certainly, he very soon made amends both by a highly constructive speech to his diocesan conference at Canterbury, in which he spoke of the White Paper as 'a glorious opportunity',[58] and by a letter to *The Times* in which he warned his fellow-Christians about the danger of their differences leading to the possible 'postponement or withdrawal of a measure so important to the welfare of the country'.[59] Given the skill that Cardinal Hinsley had previously displayed as a political tactician, it was, though, perhaps as well for Rab that his most formidable opponent should have died the previous March and that the papal announcement of his successor, Bishop Bernard Griffin of Birmingham, should not have been made until December 1943, by which time Temple was already safely back in line.

For the rest, the story (with one dramatic exception) was one of relatively plain sailing. The Education Bill was finally published on 15 December 1943 when it was given its formal First Reading in the Commons. It proved to depart in no significant detail from the blueprint outlined in the White Paper – thus vindicating Rab's chosen approach 'to test the temperature of the water before taking the plunge'.[60] It was given a remarkably placid Second Reading in a two-day debate held on 19 and 20 January 1944 and Rab, ably assisted by his Under-Secretary, Chuter Ede, soon got down to the task which in many ways he liked best – piloting a major and complicated piece of legislation through all the shoals and reefs of a parliamentary Committee Stage. His skill in doing so was widely acknowledged – which made the upset to the Bill's progress, when it finally came, all the more of a shock. On the evening of 28 March the Bill had reached the 82nd of its 111 clauses, one concerned with the salary scales of teachers.

A Conservative Member, Mrs Thelma Cazalet Keir, who had taken a prominent part in the Committee Stage and had only recently been narrowly defeated over a demand for an early vesting date for the raising of the school leaving age to sixteen, moved an amendment to the clause calling for the President of the Board, in approving teachers' salary scales, not to differentiate between men and women solely on the grounds of sex. Rab had rather the worst of the debate and made a slightly unhappy winding-up speech in which at moments he seemed deliberately to be picking a quarrel with the newly-founded Tory Reform Committee, whose brain-child the amendment was. But, having survived all other challenges to the Bill – the last one over the school leaving age by a majority of thirty-five – the Treasury Bench betrayed no perceptible signs of alarm when the vote was called at around 7.30 p.m.

No sooner, however, did the Tellers appear at the Bar of the House than it became clear that the National Government, for the first time in the war, had been defeated. True, the majority was as small as it could have been – 117 votes had been recorded for the amendment and 116 against – but it was, after all, Winston Churchill who coined the phrase, 'One is enough.' The result, therefore, caused consternation on the Treasury Bench – and, according to the *Daily Telegraph*, some shock amongst the Government's 'Young

Turk' Conservative critics. Rab himself refused to say anything beyond impatiently waving his hand when Arthur Greenwood, on behalf of the Opposition, somewhat unctuously announced that the vote did not mean 'any lack of confidence in the President of the Board of Education'. It was left to Anthony Eden, in his role as Leader of the House, to announce that 'the Government would make its viewpoint clear at the earliest possible moment'. Meanwhile Rab was reported to have 'slammed his documents into his despatch case, banged its lid and walked out'.[61]

The rumours at the time that he went straight to No. 10 and offered his resignation were, however, wide of the mark. What happened was that he went home – he was now living back in a repaired 3 Smith Square – to have dinner with his faithful PPS (who had both preceded and succeeded 'Chips' Channon), Wing-Commander Archibald James.* While still at the table, he was asked by the secretariat at No. 10 to go round and see the Prime Minister. He found Churchill in a thoroughly robust mood – 'He reminded me of the Battle of Dunbar and said that the Lord had delivered the enemy into his hands.' The very next day the Prime Minister proposed to go down to the House of Commons and insist that the original clause was restored to the Bill as a matter of confidence in the whole Government.[62]

In fact, for procedural reasons, that was not possible and Churchill the next day was able to announce only that the Government was putting down a confidence motion: he had to wait twenty-four hours 'to rub the rebels' noses in the mess they had created'.[63] If anything, the twenty-four-hour intermission gave Rab the opportunity of appreciating the level of support he enjoyed among even his non-Tory colleagues: Ernest Bevin announced roundly that he would leave the Government if Rab's position was in any way prejudiced,[64] and similar messages of support came from a number of Labour Ministers, including an intimation from Chuter Ede that he was perfectly ready to resign with him.[65] It was all, of course, quite unnecessary. On Thursday 30 March Churchill sat glowering in his place at the Despatch Box and, though he was deprived by a ruling from the Chair of delivering the elaborate Grand Remonstrance that he had prepared, had the satisfaction of seeing the 48-hour-old equal pay clause deleted from the Bill by a massive majority in a vote of

* Archibald William Henry James (1893–1980). Conservative MP, Wellingborough 1931–45. PPS to R. A. Butler at India Office and Ministry of Labour 1936–8, Board of Education 1942–4. Knighted 1945.

425–23 (the original clause was subsequently put back at the Report Stage).

In the aftermath of the episode Rab was inclined to blame no one but the Government Whips. And it did, indeed, seem extraordinary that on an issue upon which there had been many hints of trouble, they could muster no more than 116 Government supporters, or 56 fewer than they had been able to summon on the equally contentious school leaving age amendment of only a week earlier. But it remained an awkward episode for Rab – and even more for Churchill and the Coalition Government. As *The Economist* pointedly remarked on 8 April, 'The leadership of the war is not in question but for every one elector who, two months ago, suspected that the Government was ruthlessly obstructing reform, or who doubted whether Mr Churchill is the man to lead the country in peace as well as war, there must now be three or four.' And subsequent historians have probably been correct in detecting in the equal pay revolt – and the massive retaliation it called forth – one of the contributory factors to the astonishing Labour victory of the following year.

For the moment, however, all that was in the future; and Rab's Bill wound its way steadily towards the Statute Book. It was scarcely amended even by the House of Lords (the one major change, substituting the title 'Minister' for 'President', had been a Government concession offered in the Commons). Rab increasingly found himself wreathed in laurels. The Third Reading in the House of Commons on 11 and 12 May 1944 turned almost into an embarrassing *Festschrift*. By that time Rab had succeeded in buying off his most combative Roman Catholic opponents by offering favourable Government loans in order to finance the capital expenditure which would necessarily be incurred in bringing their schools up to standard. Even the new Archbishop of Westminster had had the grace to smile when, in moving the Second Reading back in January, Rab, glancing up to the distinguished strangers' gallery, had quoted the verse in the well-known hymn:

> Ye fearful saints, fresh courage take
> The clouds ye so much dread
> Are big with mercy, and shall break
> In blessings on your head.[66]

It seemed, however, at the time as if the blessings were primarily breaking over Rab's head. His fourth child, a daughter after three sons, had been born on 27 February 1944,* he had been elected in October 1943, while still not yet forty years old, an Honorary Fellow of his original Cambridge college, Pembroke (of which his father was Master), and more and more newspapers were beginning to speculate on his chances of being the ultimate successor to Churchill. Against all that background of achievement and promise, it may have seemed a trivial thing when an obscure Conservative back-bencher, Sir Edward Campbell, the MP for Bromley, suddenly remarked during the debate on the Third Reading of the Education Bill on 12 May 1945, 'We called the old Act, the Fisher Act. How are we going to remember this Bill? Shall we not call it the Butler Act?'[67] As the years rolled by, bringing their inevitable disappointments along with them, that particular claim to fame remained perhaps the single memorial of which Rab would always remain proudest.

* Sarah Theresa Butler. She married in 1969 the film producer, Anthony Price.

11 Remaking the Tory Party

Throughout the nearly four years he spent at the Department of Education, Rab led a second and (at the time) hidden political life. Within a week of his appointment as President of the Board of Education in July 1941, he acquired another, and by no means insignificant, political hat – that belonging to the head of the Party's chief policy-making committee.

A full year earlier Rab had been invited by the then chairman of the Conservative Party Organisation to undertake a programme of research into the currents of opinion in the country 'with a view eventually to adjusting the party's outlook to the radically different trends of thought that prevail at a time like this'.[1] In a summer that saw the fall of France, the evacuation from Dunkirk and the preparations in Britain for a German invasion, that necessarily seemed a somewhat peripheral and irrelevant task. And it was hardly a cause for surprise that Rab's involvement in it went little beyond a token suggestion that an 'intelligence centre' should be set up to invigilate BBC broadcasts to see to it that the Conservative Party's interests were not adversely affected by the type of message that 'the national instrument of broadcasting' delivered to the British people.[2]

By the early summer of 1941, however, the situation had changed sufficiently for there to be some hope of a viable future not just for the nation but for political parties, too. On 26 May 1941 Sir Robert Topping, the General Director of the Conservative Central Office, wrote to Rab inviting him to become chairman of a small committee that the Party organisation was proposing to establish. This would examine the whole question of the Tory attitude to post-war policy. Rab, given his background in the Conservative Central Education Committee of pre-war days, accepted with alacrity. On 24 July 1941 he was duly elected to take the chair of the Conservative Party's Post-War Problems Central Committee.

For understandable reasons – in a war that was, after all, being waged by a *National* Government – the news of his new role (in addition to that of being President of the Board of Education) attracted little Press publicity. There was a short paragraph – appropriately in that loyal Fleet Street supporter of the Tory Party, the *Daily Telegraph*[3] – announcing the formation of the new committee and giving some prominence to the name of Rab's deputy (a rising young KC and Member of Parliament named Major David Maxwell Fyfe);* but beyond that remarkably little. It was almost as if the Conservative Party managers, whose brain-child the new committee was, spotted well in advance the dangers of even appearing to 'put party before country'. The war had imposed a virtual moratorium on normal political activity: the three major Parties had submitted to, and sustained, an electoral truce so far as by-elections were concerned; they had, to some extent, dismantled their organisational apparatus in the country at large (the Conservative Party, for example, did not even hold an Annual Conference between 1937 and 1943); and, most important of all, they almost contended with each other in seeking to give the impression that all partisan differences had been sunk in a disinterested national search for the common good.

It was thus a bold, if shrewd, stroke of the Central Office's General Director to detect in long-term research a respectable substitute for day-to-day political activity. And the new committee was, in effect, filling a vacuum so far as any form of Conservative forward planning was concerned. Neville Chamberlain's jealously guarded Conservative Research Department had been closed down on the very eve of the outbreak of war; and, although it reopened for a few months during the days of 'the phoney war', its record had been the opposite of that of the Windmill Theatre. There was some evidence, too, that the Conservatives were losing the ideological battle elsewhere; while the Fabian Society might have gone underground and into uniform in such bodies as the Army Current Affairs Bureau and the Army Education Corps, those of a more conventional cast of mind tended to gravitate simply into the officers' messes of infantry regiments

* David Patrick Maxwell Fyfe (1900–67). Conservative MP, Liverpool, West Derby 1935–54. Solicitor-General 1942–5. Attorney-General 1945. Home Secretary 1951–4. Lord Chancellor 1954–62. Created 1st Viscount Kilmuir 1954, 1st Earl of Kilmuir 1962.

(with political results that the Conservative Party was to rue by 1945).

How much of that was apparent to Rab in 1941 can only be a matter of conjecture – but certainly he threw himself into his new role with a remarkable degree of energy and enthusiasm. The committee of which he was chairman initially included only two representatives from Westminster (Lord Cranborne and Henry Brooke)* in addition to himself and Maxwell Fyfe; but Rab had lost no time in sending out a circular letter to selected individuals, mainly of an academic background, whom he wished to see involved. The letter reveals enough of his essentially non-apparatchik's approach towards policy-making to be worth quoting at least in part:

> I have been made chairman of the Conservative Policy Central Committee and we are setting up a series of sub-committees on various aspects of national life. It will take a little time to constitute these sub-committees effectively. Meanwhile I am anxious to associate with them figures who, though in general sympathy with the party faith, are not of the machine. Thus I want to bring in new blood.[4]

Perhaps inevitably in wartime, the blood he finally attracted tended to be old rather than young. However, the new committee – as a result of Rab's venture in casting his net predominantly in university waters – was not short of distinguished names. Nor was it intended, at least by the man who recruited them, that such well-known historians as Arnold Toynbee, Keith Feiling and G. N. Clark should serve as mere window-dressing. By September 1941 eight sub-committees of the Post-War Problems Central Committee were already in being covering such disparate areas as agriculture, electoral reform, the constitution and finance and industry. Other topics were soon added – indeed, by the last period of activity in 1945, the PWPCC (as it came to be known) could claim to have some sixteen working parties, each with about a dozen members.

Its work, however, had its complications. The fact that so few MPs were involved predictably had the effect of raising hackles at Westminster; and more than one report hit the buffers when it

* Henry Brooke (1903–84). Conservative MP, West Lewisham 1938–45, Hampstead 1950–66. Financial Secretary to the Treasury 1954–7. Minister of Housing and Local Government 1957–61. Chief Secretary to the Treasury 1961–2. Home Secretary 1962–4. Created life peer 1964.

reached the terminus of the 1922 Committee. There was some sign, too, of the Party organisation becoming apprehensive when it saw the lusty growth of the child it had created. Certainly by the summer of 1943 there appears to have been some sort of collision between Rab and his original sponsors in the Central Office and the National Union of Conservative and Unionist Associations. Officially it was given out in July 1943 that Rab was withdrawing from the chairmanship of the PWPCC because of the pressure of work involved in the presentation of his Education Bill to Parliament; a private diary note Rab made at the time indicates that there was rather more to it than that. He had, he wrote, grown tired of 'the ratiocinations' of the parent committee – adding, unkindly, that they were 'likely to be a liability to any known party'; while, for its part, the Central Office was, or so he claimed to have discovered, 'tiring of the diplomatic manner in which they were always being saved from making major errors'.

The occasion for the break was a document on imperial policy which had come up from a sub-committee but which the Central Committee refused to approve – an embarrassment for Rab since he had personally encouraged its author, Sir Edward Grigg,* to produce it. Still, few bones appear to have been broken – even though it is possible to detect a note of bruised pride in Rab's own confession that had the Party managers 'not shown slight signs of losing their nerve at the progressive nature of my Education proposals, I believe they would have pressed me to remain as chairman'.[5]

It was all a bit of a storm in a teacup, since within a year – with his Education Bill safely through Parliament – Rab found himself back at the helm of the PWPCC. Undoubtedly the Conservative Party's effort to produce post-war plans lost some momentum through his absence – if only because his deputy and stand-in successor, David Maxwell Fyfe, proved to be a rather different sort of political animal. His interests, at least at that early stage of his career, lay far more in the crude business of devising Party propaganda than in the more sophisticated art of political policy-making – and the nature of the PWPCC's output changed radically as a consequence. It was not, however, a change that Rab had much trouble in reversing when he returned, since the propaganda element introduced into the committee's work had proved much more

* Edward William Mackay Grigg (1879–1955). National Liberal MP, Oldham 1922–5. Governor of Kenya 1925–31. Conservative MP, Altrincham 1933–45. Minister Resident in Middle East 1944–5. Created 1st Baron Altrincham 1945.

expensive than anyone had foreseen. The economic troubles of the committee's new regular publication, *Politics in Review*, to say nothing of the difficulties it was experiencing in selling its *Signpost* series of pamphlets, meant that its members turned back almost with relief to Rab's far more austere, academic approach towards the world of post-war reform.

But the PWPCC was not the only forum in which Rab found himself wrestling with the problems of the future. In November 1943 he was nominated by Churchill to sit on a rejuvenated Reconstruction Committee of the Cabinet presided over by Lord Woolton,* the newly appointed Minister of Reconstruction. Again, although he was rubbing shoulders with Ministers generally much senior to himself, it does not appear to have been a wholly happy experience. One of the reasons for that may well have lain in Rab's private conviction that the whole issue of the Beveridge Report had been badly mishandled by the Government – and in particular by its Conservative members[6] (that was not, however, anything he shouted from the housetops as he was, even by then, quite shrewd enough a Whitehall operator to realise that the adverse reaction to Beveridge on the Conservative back-benches had been the key which finally unlocked the gate for his own Education Bill). A more fundamental reservation was probably his own attitude to Woolton, whom he seems to have disliked virtually from the start.

Rab could certainly claim to have detected very early on the overweening ambition that formed a part of Woolton's make-up. A conversation they had together as early as September 1944 left Rab with the distinct impression that his senior Cabinet colleague already saw himself as Churchill's successor – a piece of self-revelation all the more breath-taking to him since Woolton was not yet even a member of the Conservative Party. No doubt, it was in part his sense of the lack of propriety in such an ambition that prompted Rab to take, for him, a most unusual course. One of the other things Woolton had said to him in that same conversation was that he did not feel the five Conservative members of his Reconstruction Committee were pulling their weight fully[7] (implying clearly that they should be pulling in a right-wing direction). Vastly irritated by this, Rab simply sat down and wrote a letter of rebuke to a figure whose own place in the Government was then considerably grander

* First Earl of Woolton (1883–1964). Minister of Food 1940–3. Minister of Reconstruction 1943–5. Lord President of the Council 1945 and 1951–2. Chancellor of the Duchy of Lancaster 1952–5. Chairman of Conservative and Unionist Central Office 1946–55.

16 Rab's first wife, Sydney Butler: 'She flew like an arrow'

17 The rising 'modern Conservative' in the garden of 3 Smith Square

18 'The Monty Butlers'. The family clan assembled at Pembroke College, Cambridge, to celebrate Monty and Ann's Golden Wedding in 1951. Back row: Richard Butler (with his sister, Sarah, in front), Major G. E. Portal, Sydney, Rab, Laurence Middleton, Jane Portal, Adam Butler (with his brother, James, in front). Seated front row: Rab's sister, Dorothy Middleton; his parents, Sir Montagu and Lady Butler; and his other sister, Iris Portal

than his own. Again, one section of the letter provides illuminating evidence of Rab's own attitude to the 'diehard' world:

> I could write at greater length, but it suffices to say that it would be wrong to say that the Conservative element [on the Reconstruction Committee] has not sufficiently influenced the social reconstruction of the country in a proper manner – that is to say, in the national interest and with a view to the trend of opinion at the present time. Of course, if non-co-operating Conservatives are wanted, they can be found at three-a-penny.[8]

That was not perhaps quite the tone – even in the political world – in which a 61-year-old expected to be addressed by a 41-year-old: it says something for Rab's strong feelings both about the original criticism, and its source, that he should have been prepared to commit such an act of temerity. Alas, no record of Woolton's reply survives; but it is not perhaps entirely a matter for astonishment that the Woolton/Rab relationship should eventually have turned out to be one of the more complex and difficult of post-war Tory politics.

By now, however, Rab was plainly growing in self-confidence all round. He had developed, largely as a result of his success with the Education Act, into a political figure just as much as a ministerial one. Indeed, as still very much a protégé of the Party organisation, it was he who was selected to preside over only the second full Annual Conference that the Conservatives held during the war years – at the Central Hall, Westminster, in March 1944. On that occasion he served as little more than a supporting player for the Prime Minister, whose own oration to the Party faithful was plainly seen as the main purpose of the exercise. But that he himself was in no sense in thraldom to Churchill was proved fairly early on in the following year. With the indications growing that the Coalition Government was finally undergoing internal strains which it could not hope indefinitely to withstand, the leading Conservative members of the national administration were summoned to the Cabinet Room of No. 10 to give their views as to when an election should be held. Most were eager to hold a general election as soon as possible after the now seemingly inevitable victory over Nazi Germany. Among the inner circle of Churchill's Party colleagues Rab alone spoke up on the side of caution and delay: for one thing, he felt that the Coalition still had useful reforming work which it could do; for another, he was quite sure that the Conservative Party, both in terms of its policies and its organisation, was in no fit state to risk an early encounter with the electorate. His intervention was not a popular one – it attracted from Lord Beaverbrook the baleful warning, 'Young man, if you speak to the Prime Minister like that, you will not be offered a job in the next Conservative government.'[9] But Rab at least had the subsequent consolation of knowing not only that he had been proved right but that others of his colleagues were prepared to recognise that fact.[10]

It was highly unlikely, however, that the reservations registered by a single Minister would deflect the Prime Minister and the rest of his Party colleagues from a course that had begun to appear both sensible and natural. Nor was the matter by any means entirely under their control: in an ideal world Churchill would have preferred to wait not only for victory over Germany but for the defeat of Japan as well – although the Labour Party, understandably sniffing a repeat of Lloyd George's 'khaki' election of 1918, was having none of that. The final argument thus came down to a slightly ironic one over the merits of a general election in July (favoured by the Conservative Party) or October (heavily backed by the Labour Party and the Liberals in, of course, complete ignorance that the Japanese war would be well over by then). Since the right to request a dissolution belonged to the Prime Minister, there was never much doubt as to the way the ultimate decision would go; and accordingly – helped, as he believed, by the Labour Party's formal refusal, emanating from its May 1945 Conference at Blackpool, to countenance a continuance in office until the end of the Japanese war – Churchill went to the Palace on 23 May 1945 to tender the resignation of a Government that had lasted, through bad times and good, for just over five years. His action was in essence a classical piece of British political pantomime; for within four hours he was back at the Palace, this time to kiss hands on his appointment as Prime Minister of a caretaker Government to hold office not only through Dissolution Day (17 June) but on to Election Day (5 July) and beyond that, given the need to collect and collate the Forces' vote, to the date the general election results would actually be declared (26 July).

In retrospect it is striking that no one seems to have thought of Churchill's new Government as a 'caretaker' administration at all: on virtually every side it was assumed that the Ministers who had now taken up their new posts would simply, once the votes had been counted, continue in office. Of no one was that more publicly obvious than Rab – who, having stolen most of the headlines by his promotion to succeed Ernest Bevin at the Ministry of Labour and National Service, found himself subjected to various solemn lectures from

Lobby correspondents as to how the real testing time for the genuine nature of his political aptitudes and administrative abilities had finally arrived.[11] Not that Rab himself could afford, at least officially, to appear at all cynical about it: indeed, the tone of his own letters, to those who wrote to him to congratulate him on his dramatic preferment, was almost equally grave and serious. Thus to the new Archbishop of Canterbury, Dr Geoffrey Fisher, whom he had known well in his Education days, he wrote somewhat sententiously:

> I cannot help thinking that this is the one move I could have made with honour. I do not think I should have liked to move anywhere else. I did not, of course, seek this, but it is such a great opportunity to serve in an important capacity on the home front, and I am very relieved that no alternative offer was made to me, since I should undoubtedly have had to refuse it.[12]

In the event, Rab spent hardly two months in his new Ministry, and at least three weeks of that time was exclusively devoted to electioneering. On the demobilisation policy already devised by Bevin he left just about as little an impact as he did on his predecessor personally – who, on the day Rab arrived to take over the Minister's office, called for his hat and promptly left the building.[13] The imprint he made on the Department was, in fact, almost as nebulous as that which he had made during his previous nine-month stint there during the pre-war reign of Ernest Brown.

This was hardly Rab's fault. No sooner had he arrived to take over his new responsibilities than he found himself distracted by the very need to fill the gap which he had warned Churchill about at the ministerial exchange of views in Downing Street earlier in the year. The fact was that the Conservatives did not have a collection of policies – let alone the raw material for a manifesto – to lay convincingly before the electorate. Rab's own prescription, given his provenance as a politician, was – not wholly surprisingly – to revert to the old Baldwin formula of 'Safety First'. Thus in his BBC Radio election broadcast, in marked contrast to the 'Gestapo' threat delivered by Churchill, he emphasised the theme that 'progress can best be achieved by the patient fitting of different points of view into an agreed plan, and not by throwing everything upside down'. In his own memoirs, published a quarter of a century later, he was honest enough to confess that he had been 'on a completely different wavelength from millions of voters . . . who wanted, or at least thought they wanted, a great deal turned upside down';[14] but in admitting that, he was in no sense intending to make an act of contrition towards his own Conservative colleagues. Significantly, of the letters he decided to keep as a memorial to the campaign, the vast majority united in blaming Churchill's conduct of the election as a prime reason for the humiliation of the Conservative Party.* None, however, can have offered him greater balm than the one he received, ten days after the results were announced, from the Conservative Party Chief Whip, James Stuart.† It opened, 'My dear Rab, I do not forget that you were against fighting when we did – however it is done, and with dire results.'[15]

The results, in fact, were a good deal more dire than even Rab can have anticipated. Three days after polling day he had written a strangely complacent letter to his old Cambridge friend, Patrick Devlin, who had come to assist him in his own campaign in Saffron Walden. In it there was absolutely no intimation that he felt in any danger – indeed, he boldly announced, 'The omens are favourable – we lost in about eight villages but led in the rest.'[16] As an estimate even of local electoral behaviour that was rather wide of the mark – for when the ballot boxes were opened three weeks later, the secret they yielded up was that Rab had had a very narrow squeak indeed. His 1935 majority of 10,066 was drastically reduced to 1,158 – and even that might well have disappeared entirely but for the intervention of a Liberal who, in losing his deposit, siphoned off 3,395 votes that might well have gone to the almost-successful Labour candidate, the wartime Mayor of Saffron Walden and long-time local Labour agent, Stanley Wilson.‡

Rab appears to have borne some scars from this campaign. His Labour opponent's shrewdest stroke was to saturate the constituency with portraits of himself in mayoral robes – and the injunction underneath 'Support the Mayor'. In writing an introduction to Stanley Wilson's autobiography, printed privately in 1971, Rab was wryly to recall that it was 'this picture which I dreaded most in the 1945 election campaign', adding that Stanley Wilson, whom he had

* This was also Rab's own view: 'I personally think that Churchill had an overpowering effect on the 1945 campaign . . . I thought the Gestapo speech a great mistake and it did cloud the whole election.' Conservative Party Archive, Bodleian Library, Oxford, Box 2006/02.

† James Stuart (1892–1971). Unionist MP, Moray and Nairn 1923–59. Government Chief Whip 1940–5. Secretary of State for Scotland 1951–7. Created 1st Viscount Stuart of Findhorn 1959.

‡ The figures were R. A. Butler (Con.) 16,950, S. S. Wilson (Lab.) 15,792, G. Edinger (Lib.) 3,395. Conservative majority 1,158.

crushingly defeated in 1931, had by the end of the war become 'not only popular but powerful' as a local figure.[17]

At least, however, Rab got back – which was more than could be said for nearly 150 of his defeated former colleagues in the old House. Not surprisingly, relief at his personal deliverance seems to have been the strongest reaction within the family – with his father writing to him from Pembroke College, Cambridge in notably philosophic mood:

> My dear Rab,
>
> I am so glad you are in and it is a personal triumph with the tide set so strongly the other way. I was prepared for a socialist majority and saw some advantage in it, on the domestic as opposed to the foreign front, but did not think it would be so sweeping . . . Be of good cheer. The wheel turns and will come full round.[18]

If Rab *was* despondent at the scale of the Tory Party's defeat, he certainly contrived to disguise it – indeed, Lord Devlin remembered him likening the Labour 1945 triumph to 'a bout of the measles' which the country would have to suffer but from which there was no doubt the British people would ultimately pull through.[19] Nor, unlike some of his colleagues, did Rab appear prostrated by the loss of office. He made a distinctly light-hearted speech from the Opposition front-bench on only the second full day of the first session of the new Parliament, two days after the defeat of Japan, likening the new Government to the Chamber of Horrors at Madame Tussauds.[20] The truth probably was that, after nearly thirteen years continuously in ministerial office, Rab was glad of the break – and of the opportunity it would afford him, at long last, to pursue something resembling a normal family life. During the war he had seen all too little of Stanstead, where there was now a one-year-old daughter, as well as three schoolboy sons, to divert him.

But, at the political level too, Rab must have realised something else. It was precisely the dimension of the Conservative defeat that offered him his chance of rebuilding the Tory Party – and adapting it and its policies to what he had always foreseen would be the totally changed conditions of the post-war world. The man who had insisted on the *nom de plume* 'A Modern Conservative' appearing on the cover of a political education pamphlet all those years ago now had a far greater opportunity than he can ever have anticipated in 1938 of putting his theories into practice. Like Peel, always his political hero, who had dragged the Conservative Party into the post-Reform Bill era a century earlier, Rab found himself facing the challenge of persuading his Party to face a future that was different almost in every respect from the climate in which it had flourished in the past.

In one way, at least, Rab was fortunate. The ten-year duration of the previous Parliament meant that even out of the rump of 213 Conservative and allied MPs elected in 1945, over a third (or 76) had never sat in the House of Commons before (the equivalent figure, 244, on the Labour side was, of course, much more immediately striking). Nevertheless, the average age of the new Conservative parliamentary Party was a gratifying forty-one years, four months – a full four years younger than the equivalent figure (forty-five years six months) on the Government side of the House.[21] Since so much has been made of the transformation that came over the Conservative Party in the House of Commons, with its vintage entry in the general election of 1950, it is perhaps worthy of note that at least the negative part of that process had started a full five years earlier. If a Party has to endure the ordeal of losing 173 seats, it does at least gain the benefit of clearing out a satisfactory amount of dead wood at a stroke.

The Conservatives could count themselves lucky, too, since most of their leading figures survived. Moreover, those who didn't, like Brendan Bracken and Harold Macmillan, soon found themselves back in the House as a result of early by-elections. In the far-off days of the immediate post-war world there was no such thing as a formal Shadow Cabinet with a rigid allocation of front-bench responsibilities: instead in the 1945–51 Conservative Party there were two parallel bodies, the Leader's 'Consultative Committee', to which admission was by Churchill's invitation only and which was supposed to assemble every Wednesday but tended to meet somewhat more haphazardly for periodic meals, and the committee of appointed chairmen of back-bench committees, sometimes known as the 'Business Committee', which assembled on a more regular weekly basis under Eden's leadership. The truth was that, at least at the beginning of the 1945 Parliament, the Opposition's organisation was somewhat chaotic, partly because of the unpredictable approach of Churchill himself: he would frequently leave a decision as to whether or not he would speak in a particular debate until the last possible moment, and saw nothing inconsiderate in deputing one of his colleagues to be on stand-by, ready to step into the breach if the spirit finally should not move him to intervene himself. Since Rab was still regarded by Churchill as a young man with his way to make in the world, this was a duty that he found himself fulfilling more times than he probably found altogether comfortable.

Still, this sort of experience (however nerve-racking it must have been at the time) did Rab's standing as a parliamentarian nothing but good. In the immediate aftermath of the election, his old patron and mentor, Stanley Baldwin, had written to him urging him to concentrate on the House of Commons and at all costs to avoid getting sucked into boardrooms in the City – explaining, characteristically, 'It does not look good if our people rush into these jobs which in practice are not open to our opponents.'[22] Rab did accept one directorship – that of the family firm, Courtaulds – but otherwise abided by Baldwin's advice, using the years of Opposition to turn himself into a thoroughly accomplished and adaptable parliamentary performer, capable of speaking on virtually any subject that came up (an investment, as we shall see, that eventually paid him an unlooked-for dividend).

Nevertheless it was, in a sense, outside the House that Rab's real reputation was built in the years between 1945 and 1951. The foundation for this was laid in an appointment made by Churchill in November 1945 that, strangely, at the time seems to have attracted no publicity at all. Perhaps, however, that was not so strange, after all – for when Churchill invited Rab to take charge of the Conservative Research Department, that once formidable organisation was to all intents and purposes moribund. Neville Chamberlain had held on to the chairmanship (the only office within the Party he did not voluntarily relinquish) until the moment of his death in November 1940; he had been succeeded (at least nominally) by his old friend and close Cabinet colleague, Sir Kingsley Wood; and, when Wood died in 1943, control at least of the accounts had passed to the Research Department's last active director, Sir Joseph Ball, who also assumed the title of acting chairman.

Just what a ghost ship he had been offered command of was proved almost as soon as Rab made his first investigations. One former staff member from the pre-war era, David Clarke,* had, admittedly, returned from war work at the beginning of 1945 but, having first been deflected into composing almost single-handed various drafts of the general election manifesto, he had immediately afterwards been given charge of the newly formed Parliamentary

* David Kenneth Clarke (1912–). Joined Conservative Research Department 1935, Director 1945–51. Director of Research, Administrative Staff College 1951–61. Director of Management Studies and Research Fellow, Bristol University 1961–7. Principal, Swinton Conservative College 1967–72.

Secretariat, devised to act as a servicing agency for the Opposition front-bench. The only other survivor from the pre-war Research Department staff was Henry Brooke, who, although he had lost his own seat at West Lewisham in July, was now planning to set out on a fresh career as leader of the Municipal Reform (or Conservative) group on the LCC. But, if there was no personnel, there were also no premises, funds or even records either. The last two elements had remained throughout the war under the care of Sir Joseph Ball – and, initially at least, he appears to have been in no hurry to release them from his custody (as an old Chamberlain loyalist his relations with Churchill had remained consistently distant). The notion of Rab taking over seems, however, to have appealed to him – in a way that an earlier rumour that Churchill's son-in-law, Duncan Sandys,* was to be the next nominated chairman clearly had not. Eventually, sufficient assurances were given to Ball that the reconstituted Conservative Research Department would have a truly independent identity for him to feel free to abandon his own stewardship of its surviving effects. All this, however, took time; and it was not until the autumn of 1946 that Rab felt able to write to Ball announcing that the Department was back in business and suggesting that it might be a convenient moment for the somewhat complex financial arrangements (deriving from investment income) that had been made with the Central Office during the period of wartime abeyance to be wound up.[23] To this Ball concurred and the maintenance of the Department from then on became (not always to the pleasure of Party Chairmen) a direct charge on the Central Office budget.

For the next eighteen years the Research Department was to provide the essential power base on which Rab's influence over the Party rested. The other policy-making roles he acquired all stemmed from his central responsibility for the Party's research organisation. In December 1945 he was appointed – and this time an official announcement surfaced in the Press[24] – chairman of the Advisory Committee on Policy and Political Education (the ACPPE). In this case the appointment was nominally made by the National Union (the body representing the voluntary work of the Party in the constituencies); but Rab was left a free hand so far as the committee's function was concerned and its membership. He took full advantage

* Duncan Sandys (1908–). Conservative MP, Norwood 1935–45, Streatham 1950–74. Minister of Works 1944–5. Minister of Supply 1951–4. Minister of Housing and Local Government 1954–7. Minister of Defence 1957–9. Minister of Aviation 1959–60. Secretary of State for Commonwealth Relations 1960–4. Created life peer 1974.

of it, aiming (as he openly put it) to attract 'the brighter people of the Party'.[25] It also gave him the lever for prising his way into the Central Office, which was persuaded in the same month to set up a political education unit, known as the Conservative Political Centre. Any doubt that this was also one of Rab's progeny was adequately disposed of by the news that its first Director was to be C. J. M. Alport, the *amanuensis* he had used for the original Conservative Education pamphlet 'A National Faith' back in 1938. Rab was also quite capable of being tough with the Chairman of the Party Organisation, under whose aegis the CPC formally came – asking for, and getting, an assurance that, as head of both the Conservative Research Department and the Advisory Committee on Policy and Political Education (to which the CPC was answerable), he would enjoy a direct line of access, not through the National Union, but straight to the Leader of the Party.[26] (Rab displayed a certain shrewdness in getting this matter clarified when he did, since later that summer the Party Chairman who had presided over the Conservatives' disastrous election defeat, Ralph Assheton, was to be replaced by Lord Woolton, with whom Rab's relationship was, predictably, to prove a good deal more difficult.)

If the Research Department and the Conservative Political Centre (coupled with the ACPPE) were the first two stakes that Rab drove into the ground to support his platform as the policy originator of the Party, the third – which came into being only in the autumn of 1946 – was to offer the greatest short-term value of all. The Conservative Party's first post-war Conference at Blackpool in October 1946 was a somewhat unhappy affair. The air, understandably, was loud with lamentations over the Party's electoral defeat and there were many demands that Conservatives needed to identify much more clearly than they had in the election precisely what they stood for. This was hardly music to Churchill's ears – whose basic position throughout the 1945–50 Parliament remained that policy-making was a dangerous business out of which advantage only normally accrued to one's political opponents, who were provided with targets to shoot at. The strength of feeling displayed by the Tory rank and file seems, however, to have persuaded him to relent, at least partially. Certainly, within a week or two, the Party Leader announced the formation of an 'Industrial Policy Committee' charged with the specific task of producing the first post-war statement of Tory policy in a particular area.

Given the weight of that responsibility, it was not perhaps surprising that Churchill took unusual precautions to make sure that the committee was an exceptionally heavyweight one. This was clearly no matter to be left to the Advisory Committee on Policy and Political Education or indeed (though it had already done some preliminary work in the same area) to the Conservative Research Department, now at last functioning, if not at full throttle, then at least on three or four cylinders. Instead, Churchill announced a membership consisting entirely of MPs – five front-benchers and four back-benchers. The former, indeed, could hardly have been more illustrious – since they comprised, as well as Rab himself, Harold Macmillan, David Maxwell Fyfe, Oliver Stanley* and Oliver Lyttelton.† Amid such a *galère* it was a striking tribute to the position Rab had already won for himself as philosopher-in-chief to the Party that he should have been named by Churchill as the chairman (Oliver Stanley, for example, at the time was clearly senior to him). It was also, no doubt, equally gratifying to Rab that David Clarke, director of the Research Department, rather than the head of the Parliamentary Secretariat (nominally responsible to Eden), should have been made responsible for the administrative chores of the committee – with all that that implied in terms of keeping not only the records of its deliberations but also in doing the necessary work to provide the raw material for its final report.

The committee, as things turned out, performed its task with both speed and efficiency: it was not only the rank and file who sensed the need for the Conservative Party to have some specific policy proposals to put forward – so also did many members of the Leader's own 'consultative committee' (including those whom Churchill had nominated to produce this particular report). There was nothing, however, hurried or casual about the way in which the committee went about its work: in contrast to the manner in which the future Conservative 'Charters' were produced, those responsible for this one actually went on tour throughout the length and breadth of the United Kingdom – meeting industrialists, businessmen and sometimes even trade unionists in nine separate provincial centres. There was never much doubt about what Rab wanted the final report to

* Oliver Stanley (1896–1950). Conservative MP, Westmorland 1924–45, Bristol West 1945–50. Minister of Transport 1933–4. Minister of Labour 1934–5. President, Board of Education 1935–7. President, Board of Trade 1937–40. Secretary of State for War 1940. Secretary of State for the Colonies 1942–5.

† Oliver Lyttelton (1893–1972). Conservative MP, Aldershot 1940–54. President, Board of Trade 1940–1. Minister of State and member of War Cabinet 1941–2. Minister of Production and member of War Cabinet 1942–5. President, Board of Trade 1945. Secretary of State for Colonies 1951–4. Created 1st Viscount Chandos 1954.

say: he was determined that the Conservative Party should come to terms with 'the mixed economy', that a future Conservative Government should not waste its energies on seeking to unscramble everything that a Labour administration had done and that, if that meant accepting public ownership in such areas as coal, rail transport and even the Bank of England, then so be it. Perhaps, however, more significant in the light of contemporary politics was the emphasis the eventual agreed document gave to the role of the State in planning the economy – down to, and including, an incendiary reference to 'wage-fixing machinery'. Above all, though, the aim of its authors was clearly to banish the damaging notion of the Conservative Party as the accomplices (if not the active originators) of policies that produced mass unemployment. For that reason alone, the *Industrial Charter* still probably stands today as the most memorable concession a free enterprise Party ever made to the spirit of Keynesian economics.

It has become slightly the fashion to deride the idealistic tone of the *Industrial Charter* – and certainly its recommendations, not least in the passages in the proposed 'Workers' Charter' in which it talked about the need to 'humanise not to nationalise industry' do have a musty, period flavour. But there is no question that Rab himself – with his background as the son-in-law of the chairman of the progressively minded firm of Courtaulds – attached particular importance to this kind of co-partnership view of industry. It is possible, indeed, to detect the influence of Sam Courtauld throughout the final report. Although a man who kept very firmly out of the public eye (he had been offered a peerage by Baldwin and had refused it in 1937),[27] he had never been shy of pressing his views on selected influential individuals. And his son-in-law, especially now that he was applying his attention to the world of industrial relations, plainly counted as one of those.[28]

The views, however, even of so illustrious an industrialist as the then chairman of Courtaulds were by no means guaranteed of gaining a sympathetic hearing from Winston Churchill. Once the draft of the *Industrial Charter* was completed and sent to Churchill in page proof on 21 April, the main question-mark hung over what the Party Leader's reaction to it would be. Here there remains a direct conflict of evidence. In his memoirs Harold Macmillan claims to have been 'surprised', once the document reached Churchill, 'at the attention he gave not merely, as one might expect, to the drafting but to the substance'.[29] Writing two years later, however, Rab himself offered a very different version of events. According to him, the Party

Leader's imprimatur had to be 'not so much obtained as divined'[30] – a divination that Rab felt able to make from the cordiality with which Churchill treated him at one of the periodic dinners, held in May, given for the Leader's consultative committee at the Savoy. That was, Rab always maintained, the only indication he had of the Leader's approval until he heard Churchill give his official blessing to the *Industrial Charter* at the Party Conference in the succeeding October.

The probability is that Rab's version is the more accurate of the two – certainly Reginald Maudling* was later to recall how at that Party Conference at Brighton in October 1947 Churchill requested him, as his speech-writer, to put into his speech 'five lines explaining what the Charter says'. When they were produced, the Party Leader read them slowly and then, somewhat disconcertingly, announced, 'But I don't agree with a word of this.' Fortunately, however, by then the document had been triumphantly passed by the Conference with only three dissentients and Maudling was able to reply, 'But, sir, this is what the conference adopted', leaving Churchill to take refuge in a discontented grunt, 'Oh well, leave it in.'[31]

What can, therefore, be confidently asserted is that the extraordinary success of the *Industrial Charter* – it ended up by virtually sealing the Party off from its pre-war past – owed little or nothing to any support given to it by Churchill. From its publication date on 11 May to his Party Conference speech on 4 October he had, in fact, nothing to say about it – and it was left to its authors (supported, it is only fair to say, by Eden) to fight their own corner even at the 1947 Party Conference. That, however, they contrived to do with some skill – putting the onus of 'rocking the boat' very firmly on the document's critics (they were, no doubt, also helped by the fact that the most vocal of these was a redoubtable right-winger, Sir Waldron Smithers, the arch-reactionary Tory MP for Orpington). Rab himself wound up the debate on the *Charter* – stealing all the limelight from Eden, who had delivered the platform speech in a debate that same day on the economy – but the decisive development had already taken place by the time Rab rose to his feet. Whether out of congenital caution or simple ineptitude, the resolution the National Union had selected as the proposal to be put before the Conference was a meaningless mish-mash of verbiage extending a welcome to the

* Reginald Maudling (1917–79). Conservative MP, Barnet 1950–79. Minister of Supply 1955–7. Paymaster-General 1957–9. President, Board of Trade 1959–61. Secretary of State for the Colonies 1961–2. Chancellor of the Exchequer 1962–4. Home Secretary 1970–2.

Charter merely as 'a basis for discussion'. The *Charter*'s supporters wanted to tie the Conference down much more firmly than that – and they had taken the precaution, towards the end of September, of submitting an amendment that would commit the Party to accepting the *Charter* as 'a clear statement of the general principles of Conservative economic policy'.

It was, admittedly, something of a transparent manœuvre: the man who moved the amendment was the young prospective candidate for Barnet, Reginald Maudling, who had actually been one of the three secretaries to the *Industrial Charter* working-party, while the man who summoned him to the microphone was none other than Harold Macmillan, who, while that year's president of the National Union, also happened to be one of the *Charter*'s principal authors. Although it was one of the more naked pieces of Conservative Conference stage-management, the trick worked: Maudling made a conciliatory speech, as if he were moving a mere drafting amendment; the original mover announced (by pre-arrangement) his readiness to accept it; and by the time Rab rose to speak all he really needed to do was to declare, 'I think it is important for this Conference to decide in favour of the *Charter* unequivocably.'[32] This the 3,000 representatives then duly did – throwing 'the anticipated attack from the Right,' as the *Daily Telegraph* noted, 'into a fiasco'.[33]

For Rab it was a significant symbolic victory over the Party's right wing, who throughout the summer had accused him of 'milk and water socialism'. He was always perfectly clear in his own mind what had been achieved – and he was to express it, quite unrepentantly, in his own autobiography, 'The Charter was first and foremost an assurance that, in the interests of efficiency, full employment and social security, modern Conservatism would maintain strong central guidance over the operation of the economy.'[34] Its central message could hardly be put more clearly than that – and the wonder perhaps remains that a Party dedicated to free enterprise should have swallowed it without gagging. Behind the scenes there had, in fact, been a hiccough or two but at least (like Churchill's reservations) the active unhappiness of, for instance, Lord Woolton,[35] had been satisfactorily hidden from public observation. So, too, had an embarrassing *contretemps* that arose at the last minute with Harold Macmillan. Scheduled to speak at a by-election in the week before the document's publication, he appears to have decided that it would do his career no harm if he became the first person to claim credit for its recommendations. He, therefore, composed a speech that effectively gave away not only the working party's lines of thought but in some cases the actual language to be discovered in the *Charter* itself. It says something for Rab's own competitive instinct, at least as displayed in his middle years, that he should have moved with great suppleness to make sure that this little foray was thwarted. Macmillan found his speech – submitted in the normal way to the Central Office for circulation to the Press – returned to him with sections of it blocked out and a polite note attached explaining:

> The Publicity Director feels, after comparing notes with Butler, that some of the language in your excellent speech at Jarrow rather coincides with that in the *Industrial Charter*. Press reports are being issued with slight modifications in language. Hope you will understand this is due to desire not to take gilt off gingerbread next week.[36]

It also, no doubt, speaks volumes for Macmillan's resilience that he should, within four days, have been writing to Rab expressing his gratitude for the way in which he had handled the whole industrial policy working party – 'Without you, it would have been quite impossible to have reached any conclusion at all.'[37] That was, however, only one of many tributes that Rab received at the time – others coming in equally appreciative terms from the rest of his colleagues on the committee, including Oliver Stanley, who may have caused Rab to smile wryly with his blunt announcement, 'If any credit comes out of this, it should all go to you.'[38]

The year 1947, in which Rab and Sydney, once the *Industrial Charter* had been published, enjoyed their first genuine holiday since the outbreak of war (a six-week tour of the United States), at first sight seemed to mark a new high-water mark for Rab.* His work outside the House was now securely based on the Research Department, to whose offices at 24 Old Queen Street he would walk from Smith Square virtually every morning, taking up residence in a large first-floor conference room with a battered mahogany table. His role overseeing the whole of the Party's research also gave him a far broader brief than that of his other colleagues in the top counsels of the Parliamentary Party. In the House of 1947 he ranged far and

* It did, however, end with one touch of sadness for the Butler family. On 1 December Sam Courtauld died at the age of seventy-one, leaving the bulk of his fortune to his only child, Rab's wife, Sydney. To Rab himself he bequeathed Gatcombe Park and the farm attached to it. This was not to prove an unmixed blessing – Rab finding it difficult to let it even at a rent of £300–£400 a year. For a period it became a 'rest home' for senior Courtauld executives.

wide – leading for the Opposition in debates on India, agriculture, foreign affairs, education and the Labour Government's Parliament Bill curtailing the delaying powers of the House of Lords. Not surprisingly, certain jealousies seem to have arisen and a reorganisation of the information, parliamentary and policy-making services of the Party in the autumn of 1948 may have been designed in some way to clip Rab's wings.

The restructuring originated with a minute from Churchill calling for closer co-ordination of the long- and short-term policy machinery. However, it perhaps reflected, rather more, some border incidents that had arisen on the always awkward frontier between policy formulation and party propaganda. Rab had already had a run-in or two with Woolton on the subject and as the various policy reports in succession to the *Industrial Charter* – starting with the *Agricultural Charter* in June 1948 – began to have a declining impact on the public, it was perhaps inevitable that matters should come to a head. The basic trouble was that Rab did not believe that Central Office was doing enough to push the Party's new 'modernist' image, while – for his part – Woolton plainly felt more at home inveighing against socialist controls or holding out the alluring prospect of more 'red meat' for every family in the land.

There was also, arguably, something of a geological flaw in the way in which, within the Party bureaucracy, related spheres of work had been separated. Thus, while the Research Department bore the responsibility for working out policy, the whole question of its presentation was a matter for the Publicity Department – and so far as MPs and Party activists were concerned, the Information Department – within Central Office. There was, in addition, another artificial 'divide' – or so it certainly seemed to some of Rab's colleagues on the front-bench – between the 'boffins' he kept in the backroom at 24 Old Queen Street and the young men (and women) in the Parliamentary Secretariat who would rush out of the same building to make a three-minute dash across to the House of Commons in order to service some back-bench parliamentary committee.*

* These latter, including such figures as Reginald Maudling, Iain Macleod and Enoch Powell (all later destined to be Cabinet Ministers), were often later referred to inaccurately as Rab's 'back-room boys'. They were in origin nothing of the sort – being recruited as members of the Parliamentary Secretariat, over whose staffing Rab initially had little or no control. Maudling, Macleod and Powell were originally brought into the Secretariat by David Clarke in the short period he ran the unit before moving over to the Research Department.

The fact, however, that a settlement of all these issues took months to reach suggests that it was not an easy process – and that Rab recognised in what was superficially an administrative rationalisation a hidden threat to his own independence vis-à-vis the Chairman of the Party. Certainly, the final memorandum distributed to the staff recording the eventual amalgamation, dated November 1948, bore all the signs of having been written in blood rather than ink – and there may have been an element of face-saving in the fact that it was signed by Rab alone:

> The Conservative Research Department will be a self-contained unit within the framework of the Party Headquarters and will thus be under the general administrative control of the Chairman of the Party Organisation. The Research Department in its various forms has always had a Chairman appointed by the Leader of the Party and responsible to him for matters affecting party policy, and I have been asked to continue in this capacity in the newly combined organisation.[39]

How much, if anything, had Rab really lost? He had, certainly, gained a larger empire since the transfer of the Central Office's Information and Library services to the Research Department – and the formal allocation to his control of the Parliamentary Secretariat – increased its size by a half. But the price he had to pay was, to him, a severe one – the need to bow the knee to the superior authority of the Chairman of the Party. In the event that probably did not much matter: as a senior parliamentarian, Rab was quite capable of protecting the independence of his own patch – and certainly nothing much seemed to change after the fusion took place. If anything was sacrificed, it was perhaps the amateur, almost Senior Common Room, ethos that had characterised both the Research Department and the Parliamentary Secretariat from their earliest post-war days. Not for nothing were the Maxwell Fyfe organisational reforms simultaneously being applied to the Party at large – and something of the shadow of the Organisation Man began to be felt from now on in 24 Old Queen Street and in the new extension it had acquired, as a result of its enlargement, at No. 34 as well.

The Maxwell Fyfe reforms also affected another aspect of Rab's extra-parliamentary work. To his regret, the Advisory Committee on Policy and Political Education, which he had headed since 1945, was wound up in 1949 and replaced by two separate committees, one on policy and the other on political education. Rab accepted the chair of the first but he lost the right of selection to it. It soon became a more unwieldy body than he had been used to (part of the fault here may have been his own, since the Party organisation men had become rather taken with his notion of 'the two-way movement of ideas' and wished to cast the communication net ever wider). In his national Party role Rab certainly suffered a net loss as a result of the changes introduced in the Conservative Party's consultative procedures in 1949. He no longer bore any responsibility for political education and, as he had launched that particular endeavour – first with the Conservative Political Circle in 1937 and then, after the war with the appointment of C. J. M. Alport as the first post-war director of the Conservative Political Centre – he was probably entitled to feel a little sore.

All things considered, it was natural enough that Rab should have considered a counter-attack. But its savagery, when it came, might well have given pause to those accustomed to think of him as 'a milk and water' figure. Early in March 1949 Rab sat down and wrote not so much an 'Open Letter' as a 'Grand Remonstrance' to the panjandrums of the Conservative Party, including the Chief Whip, his closest colleagues on the front-bench and (perhaps its prime target) the Chairman of the Party. The document was headed 'Conservative Party' and its general tone of undoubted grievance was such that it is worth quoting almost in full:

> In the war years we kept the illusion going that the Conservative Party was alive by issuing documents from the Post-War Problems Committee of which I was Chairman and David Maxwell Fyfe, Vice-Chairman. This was succeeded by the Advisory Committee on Policy and Political Education, which reports to the National Union. We built up a nationwide system of education discussion groups, bookshops and members – all run by the CPC.
>
> We have published endless pamphlets and booklets and, with the aid of my colleagues and the reorganised Research Department, have issued general reports, including the *Industrial* and *Agricultural Charters*. The Leader gave the strictest instructions that no detailed policy was to be published, hence the general form and conception of the *Charters*.
>
> I have, on repeated occasions, stated that I am not attempting to produce propaganda or simple factual statements on the party attitude. I have always been informed that this was the task of the Party Organisation . . . I have never been satisfied with the progress made.

> I must register my intense disappointment that the *Charters* have been followed up by inadequate publicising and propaganda. No concerted attempt has been made by the party to follow them up. As a result, it has become fashionable – and, indeed, an amiable pastime – to smile at the *Charters* . . .
>
> The *Charters* are attacked because they are too generalised. The Leader requested that they should be produced in 'general' language so as not to commit us to detail. The party, as a whole, has not explained them. Therefore, they wilt away. Such may be the fate of our future policy-making, unless this be backed by active publicising and propaganda.[40]

Rab's sense of timing had not deserted him – for a fresh argument had recently broken out within the Conservative Party over the need for a comprehensive policy statement embracing everything that the Party stood for. It had been sparked off, in part, by the Party's disappointing failure to win the North Hammersmith by-election on 24 February 1949 (where Labour's 1945 majority of 3,458 was vulnerably small) and also by a spontaneous correspondence that had surfaced at the same time in *The Times*, in which each and every doctrinal section of the Party successively touted its wares.[41] And Rab must have known that a meeting of the Conservative Party's Central Council was due to take place in London on 17 and 18 March. Churchill had said, long before, that he would be unable to attend, so the gathering might easily degenerate into a duel between himself and Woolton. Once the lesson of North Hammersmith had sunk in, this no longer appeared to be a confrontation that Woolton welcomed – and the Central Council meeting easily carried a motion (eagerly endorsed by Rab) that the Party 'would welcome a restatement of policy in simple, clearest terms'. Woolton, however, had clearly not finally hauled down the flag, since his winding-up speech to the conference included the warning:

> We should not be too impetuous about a policy. We really know what we are doing. It is no use coming out now with a policy and saying to the Socialists, 'This is the line we are going to the electors with – now you can tear it to pieces'. Let us employ our strategy with some sense. We shall win the next general election if we are prepared to win it.[42]

Whatever sneaking sympathy Churchill may have had with that line, he appears to have recognised that the battle was lost: indeed, on the eve of the National Union Council Meeting he had given a dinner for prospective candidates in which he virtually promised that, immediately after his return from a prospective visit to the United States, he would use the occasion of his first public speech to issue a policy statement himself. Churchill's colleagues had been lulled by that trick before (at the 1946 Party Conference he had converted a promise to issue a policy affirmation into a collection of Christian platitudes lacking only the statement that 'God is love'); and they were not to be had again. Although some of the steam went out of the demand for a restatement of Tory policy with the striking Tory gains made in the LCC elections of April 1949, behind the scenes the work quietly went on. Rab had, indeed, found a new ally in Eden who, although away ill, had been sufficiently shocked by the Party's failure to win North Hammersmith (and by a previous bad result for the Conservatives at Brigg) to write to Rab announcing:

> We cannot make any real dent upon these industrial centres except by a constructive alternative. That means the *Charter* and how to fulfil it . . . If we continue as we are now moving I cannot see that any majority we may win next year can be large enough to enable us to do our job – and a small majority would be a calamity.[43]

Braced by that sort of support, Rab pressed ahead with the preparation of a comprehensive document taking in all the various individual policy proposals the Party had made. But he was in for a rude shock. On 1 April the news was communicated to him that the first draft of such a statement would not be handled by the Research Department but rather by the Central Office which had delegated the task of draftsmanship to Quintin Hogg,* one of the remnants of the old Tory Reform Committee (the body that had defeated Rab in the Commons back in 1944 on Equal Pay). Rab's own reaction to the news is best perhaps expressed in the note he scribbled on the memo delivering him that message – 'I won't and can't interfere

* Lord Hailsham (1907–). As Quintin Hogg Conservative MP, Oxford City 1938–50. Succeeded father as 2nd Viscount Hailsham 1950. First Lord of the Admiralty 1956–7. Minister of Education 1957. Chairman of the Conservative Party and Lord President of the Council 1957–9. Minister for Science and Technology 1959–64. Renounced peerage as 2nd Viscount Hailsham 1963. Conservative MP, St Marylebone 1963–70. Created life peer as Baron Hailsham 1970. Lord Chancellor 1970–4 and 1979– .

now, but someone might discuss with Woolton who gives all our secret papers to *The Observer*'[44] (a reference to a story that had appeared that week boosting Woolton at the expense of Rab).

In the end, of course, Hogg's draft document came back to the Research Department, though not with entirely easy results. The Conservative Member for Oxford City (and the holder of a Prize Fellowship at All Souls) took a certain pride in his literary skills – and he did not take kindly to having his writing style adapted into a kind of committee prose. By the end of May (he had completed his draft by the 4th) Hogg was writing, as much in anger as in sorrow, to the Chairman of the Research Department:

> My poor Rab,
>
> Your friends are beyond human aid, and I am tempted to conclude that it is impossible to assist them. They may be tigers at policy; but the language in which they clothe their thoughts is, unfortunately, not the English tongue of our forefathers and, when they write in their queer pidgin-English jargon, they make no real effort to sustain a coherent or even intelligible argument.
>
> Your document is now as full of solecisms as a colander of holes, and as impregnated with bromides as a mothball with naphtha. I think it is past saving . . .[45]

Eventually, however, it *was* saved – with Hogg declaring, if not peace, then at least an armistice:

> My dear Rab,
>
> I shall undoubtedly go to Heaven. I have picked a painful and laborious way through the thickest of mixed metaphors and clichés once more. I congratulate you. The document is greatly improved.[46]

What, though, mattered a great deal more than the sensitivities of the author was the reaction of the Party Leader. Again, for a long time, all was dark – though an invitation to lunch at Chartwell in June was, no doubt, a propitious omen and by 16 July Rab felt confident enough to convey discreetly to the *Daily Telegraph* that Churchill's speech on the following Saturday at Wolverhampton would be 'a great one'.[47] Decoded, that meant that Rab had had his way – down to and including the advance Research Department drafting of the speech Churchill delivered that day (and, for that matter, of the speech made simultaneously by Harold Macmillan at a large fête at Stanstead and of the talk given that same Saturday on the BBC by Anthony Eden). All were designed to launch the Party's first post-war comprehensive policy statement, *The Right Road for Britain.* Since all the material in this had been derived from the *Charters*, Rab was – if not the 'onlie begetter' – then at least the principal one.

It was forgivable, perhaps, if he showed a certain paternal pride at that autumn's Party Conference at the Empress Hall in Earl's Court. The document, he boasted to the assembly of Tory Party representatives, had broken all records for any publication by a political Party: it had sold 2·2 million copies (of the full and the popular version) in the three months since it had been published.[48] To Rab's obvious gratification the cause of modern Conservatism was once again overwhelmingly approved. The most that his old opponent, Sir Waldron Smithers, could rally against it was eight votes – which, though a larger total than he had got behind him at the Party Conference in 1947, was still minimal. Yet the greatest indication of Rab's confidence was the gauntlet he threw down to the Labour Party in his own speech, calling on them to fight not on the Conservatives' past but on their own future policy – and to match it against that of the Opposition.[49] That was not a challenge that Rab, or anyone else, would have felt able to make in 1945.

'The New Model' Conservative Party – largely created by Rab – had, however, taken a certain risk in publishing what was, in effect, an electoral programme without knowing the election date; there was always the danger that by the time the election came, the various commitments and pledges made would look as if they were promising either too little or too much. In the event, it was the latter that proved to be the case. The economic crisis of July and August 1949, leading to Sir Stafford Cripps's dramatic announcement of the devaluation of the pound (from a parity rate of £4·03 to £2·80 with the dollar) on 18 September may, in a sense, have been encouraging news for the Conservative Party; it was not, however, particularly cheering tidings for Rab – for it meant the pressure was on again for the Party to give undertakings to cut social services, slash Government expenditure and rein in the Welfare State.[50] Fortunately from his point of view, and that of other Tory reformers, the time-scale did not leave much chance for anything in the way of a radical re-appraisal of the Tory programme. Four days before *The Right Road for Britain* was launched on 23 July, Attlee had summoned Labour Ministers to a council of war on the general election date; and although nothing was firmly decided at No. 10 on 19 July, a general consensus emerged that the election should be held early in 1950 – probably in February (the Prime Minister's own preferred date).[51] Conservative leaders did not, of course, know that at the time, though they do seem to have realised (despite an official announcement from No. 10 in October that there would be 'no dissolution this year') that politics had moved inexorably into a pre-election atmosphere.

One indication of this was Churchill's insistence that from now on he should be consulted in the minutest detail on anything that was going into the Party programme. David Clarke, as Director of the Research Department, was cast as the go-between. It was not a role that he found entirely easy, reporting to Rab on one occasion that the Leader's ideas 'will almost certainly give you a fit'.[52] Clarke was also somewhat unnerved on a later occasion to discover that Churchill was contemplating a justification of his 1945 'Gestapo' broadcast – defiantly rambling that all he needed to withdraw was the word 'Gestapo' and substitute instead 'NKVD' (the then title of the Russian secret police).[53] In that context, it was perhaps something of a miracle that the preparatory work on the Conservative manifesto went through with as little tension as it did – the first draft, written by David Clarke, being available to the Policy Committee by 1 December. It was circulated with a covering note from Rab – which sought perhaps to soften any shock to those who had been looking for a straight reprise of *The Right Road for Britain*:

> It will be noted that there are a good many 'try-outs' in possible policy, e.g. abolition of certain Ministries, cuts in food subsidies both on home-produced and imported food, reforms in the Health Service etc. These are all included for purposes of discussion. It will further be noted that certain detailed proposals of *The Right Road*, e.g. pensions increase, equal pay etc., are included subject to a caveat about the financial position.[54]

To some, including Reggie Maudling, the manifesto in its final form was a bit of a disappointment – if only because it represented a distinct back-track on the more radical policy positions the Party had publicly taken up just six months earlier. No one, however, wished to emphasise that. It was, no doubt, significant that when the document was published on 24 January 1950 it was found to be called – in an obvious echo of *The Right Road for Britain* – *This is the Road*. It was largely Rab's handiwork – an offer by Churchill to put the whole thing into his own prose having been skilfully deflected at a quadrilateral lunch the Party Leader, Eden, Bracken and Rab held at the very outset of the campaign.[55] Given his work over the previous five years, the *Sunday Times* certainly did Rab no less than justice when it announced half-way through the election that his was 'the shrewd, hardworking brain of modern Toryism'.[56]

Attlee had announced on 10 January that polling day would be 23 February, allowing in effect for a longer than usual six-week campaign. In his own constituency, Rab had few qualms: during the past five years he and his agent, B. T. Powell, had rebuilt the constituency organisation and the fact that he had recently celebrated twenty years as the division's MP can only have done his prospects good. He found himself, however, facing the same formidable Labour opponent as in 1945 and the opinion polls at least had made it clear that the election nationally was going to be a close-run thing. Strangely, or perhaps not so strangely, since it came under the control of Lord Woolton, Rab played very little part in the Party's national campaign – not even (as he had in 1945) delivering one of the Party's election broadcasts. In addition to a speech at Wembley in London, he made just a single foray into Norwich and Yarmouth to support Conservative candidates. Otherwise he devoted himself to cultivating his own constituency. The scare he had had in 1945 must have had something to do with that, but if he erred at all, it was probably on the side of caution. Certainly, when the figures for Saffron Walden were announced on Friday 24 February, Rab had every reason to feel pleased: he had more than quadrupled his former majority of 1,158 to 4,889, for while the Labour vote had held reasonably steady, his own had dramatically increased.* If nothing else, the voters in his own division appear to have responded to the highly personalised call he had made to them in his election address:

> The Rt. Hon. R. A. Butler has been our Member for over 20 years. We all know him. In those 20 years he has never spared himself on our behalf. His constituents of every shade of political opinion have learnt to turn to him in their troubles and he has never failed them. No Member has deserved better of those he represents. Mr Butler is a family man. He and Mrs Butler and their four children live among us. It is here he is happiest, in close association with our farming district.[57]

* The figures were R. A. Butler (Con.) 19,797, S. S. Wilson (Lab.) 14,908, O. Smedley (Lib.) 4,963. Conservative majority 4,889.

In subsequent years a number of tributes were to be paid to Rab's record as a constituency MP, even by hard-bitten visiting Fleet Street journalists – but it seems safe to assume that the 1950 election marked the moment at which he himself felt he had securely put his local roots down.

Elsewhere the election was a more frustrating affair for the Conservative Party. At first, especially in the light of the overnight results (which led Labour's general secretary rashly to predict a solid victory), it looked as if the Conservative challenge had been easily crushed: but as the returns from the more rural areas came in during the following day, it became apparent that the final result was going to be tantalisingly close. Eventually, when the last Scottish island constituencies had reported, it was clear that the Labour Government would have an overall majority of just seven, reduced to six when Manchester, Moss Side (where the election had been delayed by the death of the Conservative candidate) voted on 7 March.

The general public reaction tended to be that the Tories had done extremely well. Certainly, cutting a Labour majority of 146 to a bare six was no mean feat – especially given the fact that the Conservative Party had been unable to gain a single seat at any by-election from Labour during the lifetime of the 1945–50 Parliament. But to come so far and yet still not to win was undeniably a disappointment – though to Rab it may have been less so than to others since there is no indication, even in his private correspondence, that he ever expected an outright Conservative victory. He may also have felt – as Eden had intimated to him he did in his 1949 letter – that the worst disaster of all would have been for a Conservative Government to get elected without a working majority: for the predominant initial reaction was that the election result meant that Parliament would simply be paralysed.

In fact, the 1950–1 Labour Government showed that it is perfectly possible to retain control of affairs with the barest of parliamentary majorities. The second post-war Labour Government confounded the sceptics – and irritated its opponents – by contriving to stay in office for eighteen months. For Rab, as for other Conservatives, they became increasingly impatient months – but at least he did not make the mistake (as some other Tories did) of rounding on the Liberals as the architects of the nation's misfortunes. It was perfectly true, of course, that the 475 candidates the Liberal Party had put into the field in 1950 had not helped the anti-socialist cause; but Rab seems to have decided very early on that nothing was to be gained by denunciation or recrimination. Instead, he launched a much more sophisticated exercise to embrace the remnant of the Liberal Party (they attained only nine seats in 1950 while losing 319 deposits) and, who knows, possibly ultimately to smother them as well.

In this enterprise, which seems to have originated as early as April when some confidential Liberal executive minutes fell into Rab's hands and were promptly forwarded to Chartwell, Rab certainly had the personal backing of Churchill; indeed, during the summer of 1950 he briefly became something of a plenipotentiary for his Leader in negotiations with the formidable Lady Violet Bonham Carter. Lady Violet had been a friend of Churchill's since the days before the First World War when he served in the Cabinet of her father, Herbert Henry Asquith; but, for understandable tactical reasons, Churchill chose to leave the handling of what was obviously a delicate task of persuasion to Rab. The objective plainly was to arrange some form of pact to come into operation at the forthcoming election – and with that aim in view Rab in June drew up what he called an 'Overlap Prospectus of Principles'. This he forwarded to Churchill and later, with his permission, sent on to Lady Violet. The best indication that, for a time anyway, the negotiation was a serious one is perhaps revealed by an exchange of letters that took place between Lady Violet and Rab at the beginning of August. As a footnote to British political history, it is reproduced here almost in full, starting with a letter from Lady Violet:

1 August

My dear Rab,

Forgive my long delay in acknowledging the 'Overlap Prospectus' which you have kindly sent me. I assume it to be a kind of 'general' preamble to the more detailed statement of Conservative policy which you told me might be published sometime in July.

As we agreed at our first talk, there is no question of any joint endorsement of a common programme but only of a statement of general principles with which both parties might find themselves in general agreement.

I can speak only for myself, of course, but I should have thought the general principles enunciated there were, as far as they go, unexceptionable.

The only things I can imagine Liberals kicking at are the two references to Imperial Preference on p. 5 (two last lines), and p. 7 para 3 (three last lines), which may conjure up shades of the Ottawa Agreement in some Liberal breasts. (I suppose we must accept differences here though they are far less acute than in the past) . . .

But let me repeat once more that policy alone will not do the trick – particularly with the vital omission of Electoral Reform. The absence of any reference to it will, of course, hit every Liberal in the eye and they will draw the conclusion that the battle has been lost – and may even doubt whether it was ever seriously fought, inside the Conservative Party.

No approach whatever has been made by Lord W. [Woolton] to C. D. [Clement Davies, the Liberal leader] on seats to date. So we shall disperse, as I forecast, with nothing done or doing and the only advice I can honestly give to Liberals (who constantly ask for it) is to put up candidates how and where they like.

You did not in your covering note reply to my last letter, but may I take it that '*qui ne dit mot consent*' and that I should tell our people (1) that Electoral Reform is off the map, and (2) that on seats there appears to be nothing doing.

Ever Yours

VIOLET B.C.

P.S. I think I ought perhaps to have a word with Winston either on paper or by telephone before he goes to Strasbourg to sum up the present position.[58]

To this Rab replied with some alacrity two days later:

3 August 1950

My dear Violet,

Thanks very much for yours of 1st August. The whole international situation [a reference to the outbreak of the Korean War] has certainly postponed any statement of Conservative Policy, so I should hold the 'Overlap Prospectus' till after the summer. Meanwhile every one of your points will be carefully noted and I will do some re-thinking.

On Electoral Reform the battle was only too seriously engaged. I do not find that you have taken up my point, which I have tried to make once or twice, that if this issue were pressed you would get at the present time so resounding a negative answer as would do us all harm. That's why I am particularly anxious not to bring the matter to the front for the time being.

On seats, I am sorry that Woolton has done nothing. Frankly, this is news to me since I know both Winston and I had understood that he had it in hand. Since I have no *locus standi* in this department I must leave you to have a word with Winston, which I think would be beneficial.

Despite all our differences I enjoy corresponding with you and must again stress how much closer I think we have got despite the obvious setbacks.

Yours ever

R. A. BUTLER[59]

Two points perhaps stand out from that correspondence. First, that the whole idea was very much a Churchill/Butler initiative – with no great support for it in the Conservative Party Organisation (an impression reinforced by a subsequent letter from Lady Violet reporting that she had had tea with Churchill and that 'he was evidently displeased that Woolton had made no move and *I think* suspects, as I have always done, a lack of *bonne volonté* in this matter').[60] Secondly, and perhaps more important, it is clear that the two Parties were at cross-purposes from the beginning – what the Tories were offering, via Rab, was a kind of shared blanket of philosophic agreement while what the Liberals wanted, even through Lady Violet Bonham Carter, was the nuts and bolts of an electoral arrangement preferably based on PR but, if not, then on some sort of constituency carve-up.

In any event the parleying seems to have run into the ground, especially after a particularly robust Conservative Party Conference that autumn. (It remains, however, interesting that, when the general election came in October 1951, Lady Violet was one of only three Liberal candidates – and the other two were the result of local pacts in two-seat towns – not to have a Conservative opponent: she fought, and lost, Colne Valley in a straight fight with Labour despite Churchill's own quixotic gesture in going to speak there on her behalf.)

If news of this secret negotiation had leaked out at the time, would it have done Rab any harm? That is not an easy question to answer – certainly in the immediate aftermath of the 1950 general election the idea of a concerted anti-socialist front held its attractions (the Conservatives and Liberals between them had, after all, polled 1·85 million more votes than the Labour Party). But by the autumn of 1950 the Tory mood began to change and soon became notably more buoyant and aggressive.

That mood found its own eloquent expression in the Party Conference at Blackpool – the occasion for the first genuine assertion of grassroots rebellion during all the years of Tory Opposition. A somewhat pedestrian debate on housing policy, held on the penultimate day, provoked increasing signs of restiveness from the floor, with the representatives clamouring for some concrete target in terms of house-building to be included in the resolution before them. In vain did the chairman, a luckless female dignitary from the National Union, insist that such a move would be quite out of order. Uproar promptly ensued, from which she was only rescued by Lord Woolton stepping forward and announcing (with questionable justification, since the chair had obviously lost control of the Conference), 'This is magnificent. You want a figure of 300,000 put in. [Cries of 'Yes!'] Madam Chairman, I am sure that those of us on the platform here will be very glad indeed to have such a figure put in.'[61]

At least one of those sitting on the platform was not – as Rab was to make all too clear in his memoirs. Characterising the momentum which had built up behind the Conference demand as a 'wave of hysteria', he left little doubt that Woolton's 'beaming surrender' in reaction to it had represented a serious economic misjudgment (with consequences that were to haunt Rab between the years 1951 and 1955). On the actual occasion there was nothing, however, that Rab could do – beyond responding to Woolton's urgent whispered inquiry, '*Could* we build 300,000 houses?' with the academic's correction, 'The question is *should* we?'[62] (a philosophic point that was bound to sail safely over that populist politician's head). The incident throws, in fact, some light on Rab's own attitude to policy-making. Although he had always claimed to be in favour of 'the two-way movement of ideas', he had consistently taken pains to ensure that the agenda was, as it were, set from the centre: indeed, ever afterwards, he was to recall the 1950 Conference as an illustration of the dangers of permitting a vacuum to exist in an area where the Party Leadership should have put forward its own policy proposals. (It was not Rab's fault that such a vacuum existed: in the summer of 1950 he had wanted to come forward with a review of the Party's election programme, in the light of changed circumstances, but had been overruled by Churchill and Woolton.)[63]

As it was, however, the damage was done – and the best that Rab could do was to insist that Churchill, in his Leader's winding-up speech the next day, qualified the pledge by making it clear that it was applicable only 'in a time of peace'[64] (a reference to the rearmament programme necessitated by the outbreak of the Korean War). That was not, however, the passage in Churchill's speech that commanded the headlines. For the newspapers the story in it was his call for 'one more heave'[65] to oust the Labour Government – in itself an oblique indication that in the Leader's mind the time had passed for altering the rules of the game by seeking a common front with the Liberals. Indeed, though one further meeting was to take place that November,[66] Churchill himself virtually read the burial service over Rab's initiative by announcing in relation to the Liberals in that same speech (perhaps not wholly truthfully), 'No offer has been made by us to them.'[67]

At least, however, Rab emerged unscathed from the abortive negotiations. In fact, the year between the Party Conference of October 1950 and the general election of October 1951 saw, if anything, a perceptible increase in his prominence and influence within the higher councils of the Party. This was largely due to one of those unpredictable accidents of politics that no one can ever foresee. Throughout the Opposition years since 1945, the acknowledged third figure in the Conservative Party hierarchy had been that Prince Rupert of parliamentary debate, Oliver Stanley.[68] A younger son of the 17th Earl of Derby, he brought to the Opposition front-bench not only an unmatched lightness of touch but also a shrewd tactical brain.[69] From June 1950, however, Stanley had been mortally ill and on 10 December he died at the early age of fifty-four. There were, no doubt, others who aspired to the vacancy he had left in the ranks of the Conservative Party's high command; but unobtrusively, and certainly without any form of obvious exertion, Rab was soon filling his shoes. The proof could be found even in his parliamentary performances: in November it was he who was called upon to open the second day of the King's Speech debate, in April it was he who made the considered reply on behalf of the Opposition to Hugh Gaitskell's* first (and only) Budget, in July it was he who opened a Foreign Affairs debate specially called by the Conservatives in the light of the grave international situation occasioned by the nationalisation of Britain's oil assets in Iran and by the continuance of the Korean War. The personal investment that Rab, on Baldwin's advice, had made in mastering the art of being an all-round House of Commons performer had certainly paid its dividends.

Not that he necessarily found himself agreeing with the whole of his Party's parliamentary strategy. In March 1951, partly, no doubt, in response to a sudden upturn in their favour in the opinion polls, the Conservatives suddenly began to adopt much more aggressive

* Hugh Todd Naylor Gaitskell (1906–63). Labour MP, South Leeds 1945–63. Minister of Fuel and Power 1947–50. Minister of State for Economic Affairs 1950. Chancellor of the Exchequer 1950–1. Leader of the Opposition 1955–63.

tactics in order to bring the Labour Government down. Immortalised, at least in political folklore, by Robert Boothby's* speech at Banstead,[70] in which he spoke of the Opposition 'harrying' the life out of the Government, the new strategy rested on nothing more than the discovery by some Conservative back-benchers of the procedural fact that by putting down 'prayers' against ministerial orders – 'prayers' that could only normally be debated at the conclusion of the day's normal business – they could keep the House sitting till all hours. It was essentially a back-bench insurrection – born largely of frustration and irritation at the sight of the Labour Party still surviving in office after more than a year – and, predictably, it attracted no support at all from Rab. Indeed, quite the reverse, for by the beginning of April he found it necessary to write to Churchill:

> To have a division at any price is not necessarily a point of honour or of successful tactics. Some closer relation between the minds deciding upon a division and those who rally and mass the troops seems necessary and desirable. The Whips do their best and I think some of us could give them a little more help.[71]

By then, as it happened, the need for such advice had passed – since the Government had found an effective counter-measure to the 'prayer' device by simply moving the adjournment of the House at the end of each day's normal business (a piece of resourcefulness that almost certainly came as a relief to those in the Tory Party, like Rab himself, who did not see themselves cast by nature as 'parliamentary guerrillas'). One striking aspect of Rab's own standing as parliamentarian was, in fact, the good relations he tended to keep with his opponents – and this was especially true in the immediate post-war period when figures such as Chuter Ede and Ernest Bevin, who sat directly facing him on the Treasury front-bench, had only a few years earlier been among his most stalwart supporters in the Coalition Government.

But by the spring of 1951, after nearly six years in Government, the whole shape of that Treasury bench was starting to look a good deal less familiar. Stafford Cripps had resigned through ill-health in the autumn of 1950, dying just over a year later; and early in 1951 the same pattern was repeated in the case of Ernest Bevin, with

* Robert Boothby (1900–86). Conservative MP, East Aberdeenshire 1924–58. PPS to Winston Churchill as Chancellor of the Exchequer 1926–9. Knighted 1953. Created life peer 1958.

death in his case following within a matter of weeks after his departure from the Foreign Office in March 1951. Worse than that, from Attlee's point of view, the following month saw the resignation of two Cabinet Ministers – Aneurin Bevan and Harold Wilson – over the Labour Government's rearmament programme; and with the echoes of that dispute necessarily reverberating through the Parliamentary Party, the whole Attlee administration inevitably started to seem as if it was suffering from a death-wish.

The Labour Prime Minister, however, still held one card up his sleeve: the timing and grounds on which he would ask the King for a dissolution. In the event, though, the card was played not entirely voluntarily: King George VI was much exercised over leaving the country for a proposed tour of Australia and New Zealand at a time of domestic political uncertainty[72] and Attlee, a loyal monarchist to the last, resolved to put the Sovereign's mind at rest by allowing a general election to take place before he was due to depart. (In fact the King never did go on his tour and, indeed, underwent a lung operation five days after the pre-arranged formal request for a dissolution was made by Attlee at the Palace.)

None of this, however, was known, or even suspected, by the Conservative Party of the time. Throughout the summer of 1951 it went on with the normal preparations for its Annual Conference due to be held at Scarborough from 10 to 12 October. In these preparations Rab played his usual leading part – being determined that this time there should be a proper policy statement to put before Conference in order to prevent any recurrence of the untoward happenings of the previous year at Blackpool. The document was forwarded to Churchill on holiday, given his somewhat grudging assent and finally approved by the Shadow Cabinet at a meeting held at the Leader's London home in Hyde Park Gate at the end of the first week of September: it was already at the printers when on 19 September the official Government announcement came that Parliament was to be dissolved on 5 October and an election held on 25 October. In a sense *Britain Strong and Free*, as the policy statement had been entitled from the moment of its very first draft, had always been seen as a dual-purpose document – devised either for the benefit of the Party Conference or for the edification of the electorate at large; but that the first alternative was the one the majority of those who worked on it saw as the more likely is perhaps conclusively revealed by the fact that its original author, David Clarke, actually left the Research Department three weeks before the election was announced. His successor as director, Michael

Fraser,* whose career was to straddle nearly three decades of Tory politics, could certainly thus claim to have had a baptism of fire.

But, then, that was also true of *Britain Strong and Free* itself. Stopped twice in the presses – firstly, to take account of the election and, secondly, to include a passage on a pledge that had been somewhat rashly given about the introduction of an excess profits levy[73] – its eventual launching was also overshadowed by Churchill's decision to produce what was, in effect, a rival personal manifesto of his own. Published on 28 September and described simply as 'The Manifesto', this Churchillian flourish turned out to be a 3,000-word document bearing the imprint throughout of the Party Leader's own prose style: like an election address, it even bore his signature – a perhaps unnecessary precaution, given the oratorical tone in which its proposals (drawn, it is only fair to say, from the original document) tended to be presented throughout. Rab's reaction to it is nowhere recorded – but it was perhaps in character that, just five days later, he should stoically have gone through with holding a Press conference of his own to launch what had been intended as the keynote document for the whole Conservative campaign – the 10,000-word policy statement entitled *Britain Strong and Free.*

Just occasionally, however, the role of the suffering servant can offer its rewards. Whether from a feeling of sympathy for Rab – or simply out of gratitude for a second Tory news story – the Press tended to treat *Britain Strong and Free* as the authentic Conservative campaign document. Certainly, in presenting it to the newspapers, Rab did himself no harm. Possibly the tribute that pleased him most was the one which appeared the following day in the *Daily Mail* – which, having conceded that he was 'not a glamorous political personality' went on to adjudicate that 'thoughtful and sober in dress and speech, he is a symbol of the new Conservatism which has arisen from the ashes of the 1945 election'.[74]

In reality, of course, Rab was more than that – he was the architect behind the rebuilding of the Tory Party's entire post-war fortunes. In the eyes of posterity at least, the ultimate 1951 Conservative victory was as much his achievement as Churchill's. It was he, after all, who had cut the Party afloat from its 1930s' unemployment moorings; it was he who had brought it to accept the concept of the Welfare State; it was he, perhaps above all, who had made sure

* Lord Fraser of Kilmorack (1915–). Joined Conservative Research Department 1946. Head of Home Affairs Section 1950–1. Joint Director 1950–9. Director 1959–64. Chairman 1970–4. Deputy Chairman Conservative Party Organisation 1964–75. Knighted 1962. Created life peer 1974.

19 Three Cambridge generations: Sir Montagu Butler, Rab and his son, Richard, on the day the last took his degree in June 1952

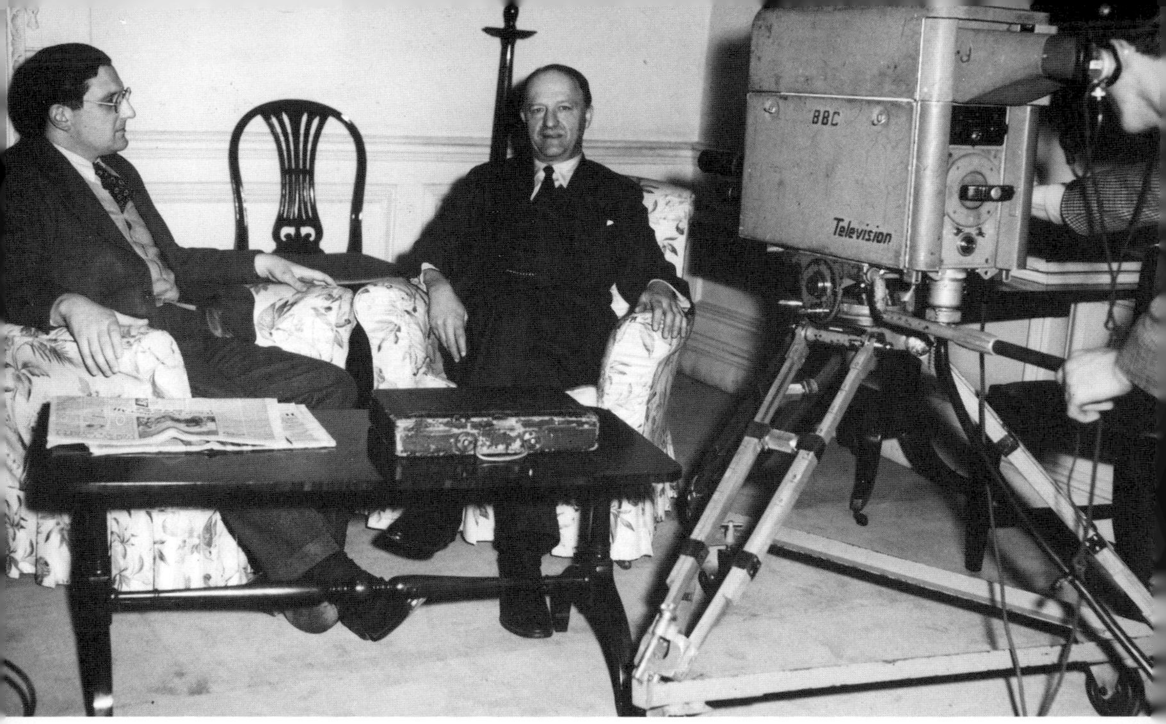

20 The Chancellor facing the cameras in the very early days of television. The interviewer seated in the other armchair is William Clark, later Sir Anthony Eden's Press Secretary at No. 10

21 Members of the Cabinet listening to Churchill's last Conference speech in October 1954. From left: Florence Horsbrugh, Peter Thorneycroft, Harold Macmillan, Walter Monckton, Earl Alexander of Tunis, Rab, David Maxwell Fyfe

that, if the voice of the Tory turtles was still heard in the land, they were henceforth regarded as mere historical curiosities. All that was no mean achievement, but there was something else besides: the bloodline of new talent in the Conservative Party was by now almost exclusively traceable back to Rab. If ever a politician appeared to have the next decade at his feet, it was the still youngish man of forty-eight who, on 26 October 1951, became not only the freshly re-elected Conservative Member for Saffron Walden* but also the new Prime Minister's adventurous choice as Chancellor of the Exchequer.

* The figures were R. A. Butler (Con.) 20,564, R. Groves (Lab.) 15,245, O. Smedley (Lib.) 3,774. Conservative majority 5,319.

12 *High Noon at the Treasury*

The Conservatives won the October 1951 general election with an overall majority of seventeen – which, though a more slender margin than any of the polls had forecast, was still quite enough to restore Winston Churchill to Downing Street. After an exile from Government of more than six years, the new Prime Minister moved with quite exceptional speed to form the first post-war Tory administration. There was no question of waiting for Attlee to vacate No. 10; instead, on the very evening he accepted the King's Commission, Churchill started summoning his leading colleagues to his London home at 28 Hyde Park Gate.

One of his first callers was Rab, only just back from the declaration of his own poll in Saffron Walden. Some years later, employing possibly a little artist's licence, he was to produce his own word picture of the visit:

> Winston was lying in bed puffing a large cigar, most of the ash of which had fallen on the counterpane. He said, 'You'd probably like to see a list.' He then handed me an enormous list, typed in great letters, and opposite 'Chancellor of the Exchequer' was the name 'R. A. Butler'. So I said, 'This is very surprising – I hadn't expected this. I had very much looked forward to *a* job but . . .' And he replied, 'Anthony and I think it had better be with you.'[1]

How really surprised, though, was Rab? Certainly, he always maintained that the Chancellorship would not have been his if Oliver Stanley had lived[2] – and that, at least, there is no reason to question. But Stanley had been dead for over nine months and, although Rab had not succeeded him as chairman of the back-bench Conservative

Finance Committee (a post which had gone to Oliver Lyttelton), he had, as has already been noticed, assumed his mantle as the third figure of the Party in the Commons in virtually every other respect. It seems almost inconceivable, therefore, that it would not have occurred to someone of Rab's own sensitive political antennae that, if the Conservatives succeeded in forming a Government, he would have a claim to the Treasury. Some evidence survives to suggest that was the case.[3]

It was by no means, however, a cut-and-dried decision, even if at the end it was taken very rapidly. The man generally tipped by the newspapers to become Chancellor had been Oliver Lyttelton – partly, no doubt, because of his chairmanship of the Finance Committee but also perhaps because of his greater maturity (at fifty-eight he was ten years older than Rab and possessed a much wider experience of business, if not of politics). As things turned out, though, Lyttelton's business background counted against him, for in the City he had something of a reputation for being 'a gambler and market operator';[4] he had also failed to shine in mounting the Conservative Opposition's case against Hugh Gaitskell's one-and-only Finance Bill the previous summer – and another factor in Rab's favour was undoubtedly Churchill's confidence in his ability to 'handle the Commons stuff'.[5]

But Lyttelton, if the word of a not entirely disinterested witness can be believed, was not Rab's only rival. Writing over four years later, Woolton was to recall in a private diary, which he kept intermittently between 1951 and 1955, how he himself had been urged to take the job. According to this version – composed, admittedly, just as Woolton was leaving the Cabinet – he had been asked by Churchill 'whether I would go to the Commons and become Chancellor of the Exchequer if he made the necessary law, and I had refused because I knew it would be so unpopular in the House of Commons to bring a peer in to fill a recognised House of Commons job, and so we fell back on Butler'.[6]

The last phrase may well be the give-away – for there is nothing elsewhere to suggest that Woolton (as opposed to Anthony Eden) was ever involved in that kind of relationship with Churchill when it came to consultation over Cabinet appointments. If further evidence of Woolton's malice, at least as directed towards Rab, is required, it can be found in the inherently improbable claim retrospectively advanced in that same diary entry, 'When Churchill was forming his last Government, I begged him to choose Macmillan and not Butler.'[7]

Certainly, these machinations – if they ever took place – never reached Rab's, or anyone else's, ears. Indeed, so crisp and clean was the change-over from one Chancellor to another that Hugh Gaitskell was to write, with wry admiration, in his *Diary* of how he learned of Rab's appointment as his successor even before he had left his own constituency in Leeds for London on the morrow of polling day.[8] The formal announcement of the first eight members of the Cabinet came on Saturday 27 October, as did their swearing-in at Buckingham Palace; and Rab, as easily the youngest among them, had little reason to complain at his place – number five in the 'pecking order' – even if it did rank him below two peers, Woolton and Salisbury, and also, more surprisingly, beneath not just Anthony Eden but another Commons colleague, the new Home Secretary, Sir David Maxwell Fyfe. (Interestingly, Harold Macmillan's name at this stage did not surface in the list at all; and, when it finally did the following week, it was as the third most junior member of a Cabinet of sixteen.)

The impetus that had gone into the selection of the Cabinet continued right through to the haste with which its earliest members took up their departmental duties. Rab went to the Treasury for the first time as Chancellor on the morning of Monday 29 October – although, having learnt perhaps from his encounter with Ernie Bevin in 1945, he sent a message to his predecessor that he had no wish to hustle him out and, tactfully, took up residence in the Permanent Secretary's room rather than the Chancellor's. It was a mark of consideration by which Gaitskell was much touched – and the two of them did, in fact, meet for an amiable ten-minute conversation in the Chancellor's room that Monday. If it was envisaged by Rab as little more than a courtesy call, it turned out to pay a rather more substantial political dividend than that. At some stage in their conversation Rab apparently dropped a hint that the new Prime Minister was contemplating the appointment of 'some senior and much older man in the background to take charge of economic affairs': this proved quite sufficient to raise all Gaitskell's protective Treasury hackles, and the new Chancellor found himself the target of a lecture by his predecessor on the theme of how no self-respecting politician in charge of the Exchequer could possibly be expected to tolerate such an arrangement.[9] Whether Rab's resolve needed to be stiffened can only be a matter of conjecture; but the threat of an 'overlord' for the Treasury – just as there were 'overlords' for other departments such as Transport and Fuel and Power – subsequently failed to materialise (although Churchill was widely believed to have had his last wartime Chancellor, Sir John Anderson, firmly in mind for such a post).

Elsewhere, however, Rab had less luck in resisting some of Churchill's more eccentric dispositions. At his original interview at Hyde Park Gate he had been told by the new Prime Minister not to worry about his lack of professional economic credentials as 'I am going to appoint the best economist since Jesus Christ to help you.'[10] This mystic figure turned out to be a rather elderly and pedantic Conservative MP, Sir Arthur Salter,* who, having previously been an Independent Burgess for Oxford University, had returned to the 1951 House of Commons by winning for the Conservatives the Lancashire seat of Ormskirk. At the age of seventy Salter was given the grand title of Minister of State for Economic Affairs and, if he had carried more political clout, could conceivably have transmogrified into just the kind of 'senior background figure' whom Churchill initially had had in mind. Fortunately, though, from Rab's point of view, Salter proved to be totally ineffective, particularly in the House of Commons; and after thirteen months, having written a succession of memos in green ink to the Chancellor from the isolation of his own eyrie in Great George Street, was moved to another non-job as Minister of Materials. When he departed from the Treasury in November 1952, he did, though, write Rab a most cordial letter which – while not minimising the policy disagreements they had had – assured him of how much he had 'enjoyed' his work:[11] typically, Rab reciprocated by characterising him in his memoirs as 'a nice man'.[12] If he had been otherwise, this bizarre dual-harness arrangement would, no doubt, not have survived, even for thirteen months. As it was, Salter was never more than a minor, and sometimes risible, irritant to the new Chancellor as he embarked upon what turned out to be a four-year-stint at the Treasury. If the episode left any scars, they were perhaps to be seen in the firmness with which Rab thereafter always insisted that every member of the Treasury team should be his own hand-picked nominee.†

A far more serious challenge to Rab's authority was posed by Churchill's eventual success in prevailing on another Oxford figure,

* James Arthur Salter (1881–1975). Independent MP for Oxford University 1937–50. Chancellor of the Duchy of Lancaster 1945. Conservative MP, Ormskirk 1951–3. Minister of State for Economic Affairs 1951–2. Minister of Materials 1952–3. Created 1st Baron Salter 1953.

† They were a distinguished bunch, starting off with John Boyd-Carpenter as Financial Secretary in 1951, who was succeeded in 1954 by Henry Brooke. When Salter departed in 1952, Reginald Maudling became Economic Secretary to the Treasury (a new post), being succeeded, in his turn, by Sir Edward Boyle in 1955.

this time the physicist, Lord Cherwell, to join his new Cabinet as Paymaster-General. 'The Prof.' had, of course, been a long-time associate of the new Prime Minister, going back to pre-war rearmament days; and, given that his function had always been to provide a one-man, all-purpose brains trust for his patron, it was not only the Opposition who wondered whether he was not to be the new Chancellor in fact while Rab held the office only in name. This suspicion was, if anything, reinforced when Cherwell in November not only became an additional member of the seven-man Ministerial Advisory Committee appointed to supervise the Treasury but actually moved into the Chancellor's traditional private apartments above No. 11 Downing Street (official accommodation that Rab had refused because he and his wife preferred to stay in their London home at 3 Smith Square less than a mile away).

Initially it was hardly surprising if Rab appeared, not least to the Civil Service, as one of the most circumscribed Chancellors in history. If he succeeded, as he did, in repulsing all the threats to his independence and autonomy it was largely because of the alliance he immediately formed with the Treasury mandarins. The Permanent Secretary to the Treasury (and, significantly, also Head of the Home Civil Service) when he took office, and throughout the whole period of his tenure, was the legendary, somewhat austere, figure of Sir Edward Bridges.* The son of the former Poet Laureate, Robert Bridges, and Churchill's wartime Secretary to the Cabinet, he – like Rab – was a man without any economic qualifications. He was, though, the Oxbridge mandarin *par excellence* and, as such, could be counted upon to repel any barbarian marauders at the gate. Nor, as a generalist, did he seek to hold any undisputed sway over the Chancellor in his charge: he was quite content to leave expert advice to his subordinates – to such people as Sir Edwin Plowden† (the chief of the economic planning staff) and William Armstrong‡ (the Chancellor's Principal Private Secretary) upon whom Rab came to rely more and more. Many of the then senior Treasury officers had

* Edward Bridges (1892–1969). HM Treasury 1919–38. Secretary to the Cabinet 1938–46. Permanent Secretary, Treasury and Head of Home Civil Service 1946–56. Created 1st Baron Bridges 1957.

† Edwin Noel Plowden (1907–). Chief Planning Officer and Chairman of Economic Planning Board, Treasury 1947–53. Chairman Atomic Energy Authority 1954–9. Created life peer 1959.

‡ William Armstrong (1915–80). Principal Private Secretary, Treasury, to Sir Stafford Cripps, Hugh Gaitskell and R. A. Butler 1949–53. Permanent Secretary to the Treasury 1962–8. Permanent Secretary, Civil Service Dept and Head of Home Civil Service 1968–74. Created life peer 1975.

been admirers, if not actual acolytes, of Hugh Gaitskell and Sir Stafford Cripps. However, they appear to have suffered no great strain in transferring their allegiance to the new Conservative Chancellor – who, after all, was never ashamed of maintaining that he saw the task of the State as one of 'regulating the economy'.[13] From the moment he accepted a lunch invitation to the Athenaeum with Bridges and Armstrong on his first day at the Treasury, Rab had thus armoured himself with a formidable shield against what, even in those days, could have developed into a serious doctrinal assault from the cruder exponents of the 'free market economy'.

Conveniently, however, for Rab the nation's financial position in October 1951 was sufficiently grave for there to be no possibility of that particular philosophical battle seeming to have any immediate relevance. The Conservatives had inherited from the previous Labour Government a balance-of-payments deficit of some £700 million – and in the early 1950s (as, indeed, in the late 1960s) a balance-of-payments equilibrium was the golden calf before which the whole nation was required to fall down and worship. Rab, indeed, was to carry away from that first lunch at the Athenaeum the shocked memory of a remark about 'blood draining from the system and a collapse greater than had been foretold in 1931'.[14] No doubt predictably, his message to the first meeting of the new Conservative Cabinet the following day was distinctly sombre in tone.[15]

It was Churchill, however, who called for action. Rab found himself deputed to preside over a group of Ministers with whom he should discuss his proposals for remedying the economic situation – and which would be expected to produce its recommendations by the next Cabinet meeting. Meanwhile Churchill also directed that a note written by Sir Edward Bridges outlining Britain's parlous economic condition – which Rab had handed round the Cabinet – must be sent immediately to the Leader of the Opposition, who 'should at once be made aware of the financial position as it had been known to the Government when they first took office'.[16] It is the tendency, of course, of every incoming Government to exaggerate the gruesomeness of its inheritance – and the 1951 one proved no exception. To be fair to it, though, its initial alarmism about the threat to the reserves seems to have been wholly genuine. Brought up in a world where the stability of sterling was regarded as only slightly less of a sacred trust than the security of the Crown Jewels, the men who sat around the Cabinet table in the autumn of 1951 simply had no grasp of such future black arts as the manipulation of interest rates to bring 'hot' money pouring across the foreign exchanges. Instead, the only available defence against another dreaded devaluation, to follow in the wake of Sir Stafford Cripps's notorious one of 1949, appeared to be a severe policy of retrenchment, particularly in terms of cutting Britain's import bill.

Rab set himself the task at once – as he told the House of Commons on the second day of the Debate on the Address[17] – of trying to save some £350 million a year out of Britain's overseas expenditure. This was to be achieved largely by cuts in the imports of unrationed foodstuffs and raw materials, although the psychological impact was probably most severely felt in the Chancellor's simultaneous announcement that he was immediately cutting the foreign travel allowance from £100 to £50. The biggest shock of all, however, at least for traditionalists, was the increase of Bank Rate from 2 to 2½ per cent – the first time it had been moved since 1939. (Rab himself had originally wanted to raise it even further – as he was to do in his first Budget, to 4 per cent – but had been dissuaded by the conventionally cautious Governor of the Bank of England, C. F. Cobbold.)

The first few months at the Treasury were undoubtedly dispiriting ones for Rab, if only because the patient did not initially betray much sign of responding to the treatment he had prescribed. Having announced his first programme of surgery in November, Rab was back in the House of Commons proposing more of the same at the end of January: this time he was seeking cuts of a further £150 million, and the foreign travel allowance was cut in half again, on this occasion to a meagre £25.[18] His colleagues, led by Woolton, proved particularly obdurate in face of his recommendations for cuts in rationed foodstuffs – and Rab, even when he had secured the agreement of the Minister of Food, was finally denied permission to reduce even the sweet ration from 6oz to 4oz a week.*[19] Equally implacable opposition came from Harold Macmillan, the Minister of Housing, in face of any proposal that seemed to threaten the housing drive; and Rab sustained his first serious Cabinet defeat over his proposal to cut the import bill for soft-wood timber.[20] The truth, of course, was that the 300,000-a-year housing target – carried amid scenes of ecstatic enthusiasm at the 1950 Party Conference – was a wonderful breast-plate for any spending Minister to have at

* The sweet ration was to be abolished on 4 February 1953. The end of all rationing came in 1954.

his disposal; and Macmillan knew just when to buckle it on in any Cabinet dispute.

Certainly, by the end of January 1952, the outlook to Rab still seemed fairly grim – and, to his credit, he made no effort to hide his fears or to disguise his apprehensions. On the same day as he announced his further package of cuts in the House of Commons, he delivered a rather remarkable ministerial broadcast on the radio. It represented, no doubt, his effort – as he constantly told the Cabinet he wished to do – 'to bring home to the public the gravity of the situation'[21]; and in those terms, by the skilful deployment of homely metaphors and analogies, it was pretty well done. But, as an indicator of Rab's own morale, the passage that revealed most was perhaps one that he used right at the beginning of his broadcast, 'We really are up against it. Our life-blood is draining away, and we have got to stop it.'[22] Consciously or not, it was, of course, an echo of the phrase about 'blood draining from the system' that had so startled Rab when he originally heard it at his lunch with the two Treasury Civil Servants on his first day in office; but that he should be repeating it again now – after three months of his own stewardship of the economy – was a vivid sign of his own mood of despondency.

That mood may well explain why over the next few weeks he was tempted by a quite uncharacteristic gamble. For some time the Bank of England had been working on a scheme – as the insiders' formula had it – 'to take the strain off the reserves and put it on the rate of exchange'. The brain-child of one of the Bank's executive directors, Sir George Bolton, this represented an attractively simple device to enable Britain at one bound to break free of its post-war trap in terms of dollar and gold reserve problems. There were two basic elements to the plan – first, a 'floating' rather than a 'fixed' rate of exchange for the pound, and, secondly, the opening of some, though by no means all, sterling holdings to a convertible status with the dollar. In the fullness of time both strands of the proposed policy were to come to pass – though not, as things worked out, in the synchronised form in which they were first put forward. In the climate of the early 1950s, however, there was no doubt that they had about them all the shock of the new. As if in recognition of that, the scheme, which had supporters in the Treasury (though not in its economic section) as well as at the Bank, even went under a daringly modern code-name: it was known as 'Operation Robot' – though, disappointingly, the derivation of the second word owed more to the initials of the three most prominent officials who backed it than to any automatic association with the 'Dr Who' world of the future.

At what stage, and in what manner, the package was sold to Rab as the one sure path to economic salvation has never been established. Certainly, 'Operation Robot' had powerful allies on the fringes of the Government – one of them, Brendan Bracken, was already writing to Beaverbrook in mid-January announcing, 'He [Butler] is, I think, converted to the policy of freeing the pound.'[23] Put like that, of course, the strategy was hard to resist, especially by those who had just fought two elections on the slogan 'Set the people free.' But, in truth, the emotive reflection of *Fidelio* behind 'Operation Robot' was always misleading: under the precautionary provisions of the scheme the major part of the sterling area's London balances were to be blocked, as were 90 per cent of the balances held by those who were neither in the sterling nor the dollar areas. Virtually the only people whose pounds were to be 'set free' were those lucky enough to be dollar-area residents.

Initially, however, Rab appears to have been carried away by the superficial simplicity of the plan as a way of escape from the nightmare of always having to live with the possibility that the reserves might run out. Although he said nothing about the proposed panacea to a meeting of Commonwealth Finance Ministers held in London in January, he did get them to agree to convertibility as a major aim of sterling area policy. Significantly, he also announced, in his economic policy statement in the House of 29 January, that Budget Day would be brought forward to the earliest possible date – not the then usual first or second Tuesday in April but the first Tuesday in March, which happened in 1952 to fall on the 4th.

The first indication that everything was not running quite smoothly came some four weeks later when the new Leader of the House of Commons, Harry Crookshank,* made a surprise Business Statement, just ten days before the Budget was due. He informed the House that, 'for various reasons', the Budget would not, after all, be presented on the scheduled date but one week later, on 11 March.[24] For some reason, unprecedented though such an announcement was, it aroused few suspicions – but then 'Operation Robot' had been from the beginning a closely guarded secret and few outside the corridors and alcoves of Whitehall and Threadneedle Street even guessed at what was being contemplated.

* Harry Frederick Comfort Crookshank (1893–1961). Conservative MP, Gainsborough 1924–56. Secretary for Mines 1935–9. Financial Secretary to the Treasury 1939–43. Postmaster-General 1943–5. Minister of Health 1951–2. Leader of the House of Commons 1951–5. Lord Privy Seal 1952–5. Created 1st Viscount Crookshank 1956.

From the Government's point of view, that was just as well – for by mid-February the policy which Rab had embraced was provoking one of the biggest Cabinet convulsions of post-war politics. Rab had originally hoped to obtain his colleagues' swift consent to a proposal that, in his view, embodied an idea whose time had come; and at the start – perhaps because even Cabinet Ministers' minds were concentrated more on the death and funeral of King George VI, who had died on 6 February, and the launching of a new reign under a 25-year-old Queen – the omens looked propitious enough. In particular, the Prime Minister, while perhaps not fully understanding the issues involved, gave every sign of being sympathetic (the theme of 'freedom' had an obvious appeal for him), while Rab's former rival for the Treasury, Oliver Lyttelton, now helpfully emerged as his most stalwart ally. Rab, however, also faced a formidable foe in the person of Lord Cherwell – and a slightly less powerful critic in the shape of his own Minister of State, Sir Arthur Salter. Once again, though, it was Woolton who pulled the rug out from underneath Rab by taking the lead in insisting that, since the issue affected the country's relations with foreign powers, it could not possibly be decided without referring the whole matter to Anthony Eden, the Foreign Secretary (inconveniently away at that time attending a NATO meeting in Lisbon). Two high-powered Treasury and Foreign Office emissaries were sent out to see him there in mid-February and, after some hesitation, Eden sent back a hand-written letter to Churchill suggesting that the whole question required much deeper thought than had yet been given to it. For the advocates of Robot, that was really the end (at least for the proposal in its original form). The notion that it should provide the adventure element in Rab's first Budget was formally buried at two Cabinets held on Thursday 28 and Friday 29 February – and for Rab and his Budget team in the Treasury it became a case of going back to the drawing board, thereby accounting for the week's delay in the Budget's presentation.[25]

It is difficult to establish just how mortified Rab was by this failure. Certainly, he does not appear to have pressed his case with any great fire or conviction – resting content with preserving for posterity a note passed to him some time in February at a Cabinet meeting by Oliver Lyttelton, 'This goes ill. The water looks cold to some of them. They prefer a genteel bankruptcy, *force majeure* being the plea. Micawber Salter.'[26] That could be said to argue an attitude of detached amusement rather than any sense of powerful indignation; and Rab was candid enough to confess in his own memoirs that one of the things that had given him pause was a note of warning he had received from his admired veteran Government colleague, Lord Swinton,* pointing out that the Robot plan could not be expected to work unless and until the countries of the Commonwealth put their own economic houses in order.[27] Nor does he seem to have returned to the fight with any greater determination when the matter once again came before a meeting of Ministers in June, shrewdly recognising the superior forces ranged against him, and seeming more or less ready to let it lapse.[28] There could, of course, have been another reason for that. By the middle of the year Britain's gold and dollar reserves had not sunk to anything like the level that the Bank of England had been alarmedly forecasting (they stood at $1,685 million rather than the predicted $1,300 million) and Rab may well have felt that his original remedies were beginning to do the trick. If he did sense that, he could certainly claim to have been vindicated: by the end of 1952 those same reserves had risen to $1,864 million.

Yet to claim that Rab was bounced into his original support of the Robot project would probably be putting things too strongly. Interestingly, when he had a brush with Churchill that August over a disobliging newspaper column written by A. J. Cummings of the *News Chronicle* – suggesting that he had lost all battles in Cabinet to Cherwell and that he had not even been allowed to produce the Budget that he had wanted to the previous spring[29] – it was to Robot that Rab immediately jogged back (though Cummings himself, through ignorance, had not mentioned it). Rab's relations with his official neighbour at No. 10 were later to become so good that the incident is illuminating of the initial tensions that existed between them. Churchill appears to have been particularly incensed by the implied suggestion that he had not loyally supported his Chancellor – and went out of his way, in a conversation with Sir Edward Bridges held on the day on which the article appeared, to insist that 'no Chancellor has ever had such support as Rab has had'.[30] However, Rab himself seems to have remained unconvinced by this claim – and in two letters drafted for (though not necessarily sent to) the

* Philip Cunliffe-Lister (1884–1972). Conservative MP, Hendon, 1918–35. President of the Board of Trade 1922–3, 1924–9 and 1931. Secretary of State for the Colonies 1931–5. Secretary of State for Air 1935–9. Cabinet Minister Resident in West Africa 1942–4. Minister of Civil Aviation 1944–5. Chancellor of the Duchy of Lancaster and Minister of Materials 1951–2. Secretary of State for Commonwealth Relations 1952–5. Created 1st Viscount Swinton 1935, 1st Earl of Swinton 1955.

Prime Minister could not resist referring to the Robot episode. In the second of them, obviously composed with considerable care, the Chancellor expressed, if in temperate terms, what was plainly an abiding sense of grievance:

> We have, so far as I know, had only one difference of opinion, on a very intricate matter. My view was that if we did not take the plunge early into the freedom of the price mechanism – even in the external field – we should go without the benefits of full planning and of the full discipline of the Rate. I further felt that nothing could control the vast spreading leaking sterling area but the Rate.
>
> As against my original recommendation there were ranged very powerful arguments, which prevailed. I still regret that decision, since I believe our policy lies between two stools and that we as a team – and I latterly – have lost *élan*. Looking to the future, however, we have endless opportunities to regain spirit and dash as well as the construction of prosperity.[31]

The chances are, since it survives only in manuscript, that, even in its exceedingly moderate form, this letter was never sent. The only real challenge posed to the Chancellor was the Prime Minister's threat to call for an inquiry within the Treasury into how the alleged 'leak' to Cummings had come about in the first place: typically, Bridges eventually advised Rab to write simply saying, 'You don't really see on what an inquiry could be based and how it could be carried out.'[32] But, if only as a matter of injured pride, it is fairly clear that Rab, even by as late as August, still retained some passing resentments against all that had occurred. By then he could, however, afford not to advertise them for, at least in the judgment of the political world, he now counted as an outstanding success.

His first Budget in March had inevitably, without Robot, been restricted in scope (the most Rab had been able to do was to lower tax thresholds and raise the allowances): but the proof of his political suppleness lay in the way in which he had managed to present his proposals as interesting and novel ones. 'Restriction and austerity', he had boldly declared towards the end of his speech, 'are not enough. We want a system that offers us both more realism and more hope'[33] – and in saying that he had shrewdly judged the prevailing anti-controls mood of the country. Personally he also had the undoubted satisfaction of knowing that the major change he was proposing – the slashing of food subsidies by £160 million to enable the distribution of 'goodies' elsewhere – was one calculated to provide the maximum possible embarrassment to his arch-critic, Lord Woolton, who had rashly stated in a Conservative election broadcast that there was 'not a word of truth' in the Labour charge that 'Tories would cut the food subsidies'.[34] (This particular item in Rab's Budget actually drove Woolton to submit a rather half-hearted letter of resignation to the Prime Minister, though it was brushed aside with a typically grandiloquent reply from Churchill, 'Pray dismiss from your mind any idea of resigning from the Government because of mischievous debating points made by those who have brought the British community into deadly economic and financial peril.')[35]

Quite apart, though, from the Woolton incident, Rab, by midsummer, was riding the crest of a wave. The favourable Press reception given to his first Budget – *The Times* had actually called it 'a triumph'[36] – seemed to have taken root not just with the domestic electorate but with the international financial community: the drain on the reserves stopped almost as suddenly as it had begun and by the autumn Britain found herself back in a balance-of-payments surplus. Nor was Rab without personal achievements of his own. In June he collected, within three weeks of each other, honorary DCLs from both Oxford and Cambridge; in July he became the first leading politician to have a current affairs programme devoted to him on British television (being the guest on the first-ever edition of the BBC's 'Press Conference');[37] while in September he actually took charge of the Government for the first time, chairing the Cabinet in the absence abroad of both Churchill and Eden.[38]

This last was, in its way, a highly significant sign of his political progress: when Churchill and Eden had each been away at the beginning of the year three successive Cabinet meetings had been presided over by the Leader of the House of Commons, Harry Crookshank. Now Crookshank, a decade older than Rab, sat well down the table while the Chancellor of the Exchequer occupied the seat at the centre with his back to the fireplace. Nor was Rab's new prominence hidden from the public. The newspapers were duly informed that he was in charge (as the Lobby briefing seems to have had it) 'of Cabinet affairs' and it was also widely noticed that he would be combining his own eventual one-week holiday at Antibes with a day visit to Winston Churchill, then staying in Lord Beaverbrook's villa at Cap d'Ail.[39]

When Rab returned from his holiday, it was to face the challenge of delivering two major speeches. The first was at the annual Lord

Mayor's dinner to bankers and merchants at the Mansion House, where he gave a progress report on the state of the economy after nearly a year of Tory rule: if his tone was by no means boastful – he claimed no more than that the country had gained 'an invaluable breathing space'[40] – it was at least very different from the sombre warning he had felt it necessary to deliver on the radio at the beginning of the year. Two days later he was in Scarborough facing the far larger 3,000-strong audience of the Tory Conference. Again his theme was similar – something had been achieved but there was still much, much more to do, 'We have got to keep up the pressure, we cannot relax.'[41] It seemed, however, to be exactly what his audience wanted to hear – and he was accorded the greatest ovation of the Conference. Moreover, in an unusual unanimity, the political correspondents of both the *Sunday Times* and the *Observer* agreed that he had been the star of the show, with each claiming to detect a change in his personality. Gone, the readers of both papers were assured, was the placid, pale academic of yesteryear; in his place stood a formidable politician who spoke with warmth and passion and who at the same time contrived to give the tough impression of someone who had lived and wrestled with a chronic problem to which he now at last had the answer.[42]

Yet if the sun shone on his public career, the latter part of 1952 was to cast two shadows over Rab's private life. The first Friday in November saw the death from a sudden heart attack of his father in Cambridge – Sir Monty had retired some four years earlier from the Mastership of Pembroke but had taken up residence in a flat in the town with Rab's mother: they had only the previous autumn celebrated their golden wedding. Sir Monty had also during the summer of 1952 been to see his grandson, Richard, take his degree in the Senate House (representing the fifth successive generation of Butlers to do so, as he proudly noted in a letter to his son).[43] Rab's affection had always probably been greater for his mother than for his father; but Sir Monty's death (albeit at the age of seventy-nine) nevertheless represented the sharp snapping of a powerful link with the past.

The other family shadow that autumn seemed at first sight a good deal more trivial, though eventually it was to cast an even heavier cloud over the family. Rab's wife Sydney started to complain of pains in her jaw and preliminary dental investigations failed to establish any obvious cause. It was, at the outset, no more than a private worry, although Rab did confide his concern about it to at least one of his Essex neighbours.[44] For the time being, however,

Sydney was able to carry on life perfectly normally – she had always been a woman of strong determination and saw no reason to allow pain to disrupt what had become a fairly regular pattern of social and political entertaining. A highly efficient, if sometimes slightly intimidating, hostess, she had long devoted herself to promoting Rab's career by giving some of the best dinner parties in London; and that December she surpassed even her own standards by holding an enormous reception, for all the representatives attending a Commonwealth economic conference, in the State Rooms at No. 11 Downing Street. (It was the second piece of grand entertaining held at No. 11 that year – the first having been the wedding reception that Sydney gave the previous July to celebrate the marriage of their eldest son, Richard, to Susan Walker at St Margaret's, Westminster.)

By the end of 1952, the Butler family had become, in effect, an established part of the British social and political furniture. The three boys, Richard, Adam and James, had been much photographed setting out to hear their father's first Budget speech, and Sydney herself had overcome her natural reserve to give a number of newspaper interviews on the life of a Chancellor's wife. At Christmas the family was to be in the public eye again, with front-page pictures of Rab and his wife and their two younger children – James (sixteen) and Sarah (eight) – enjoying the opening performance of the Bertram Mills circus. But the fiercest spotlight necessarily played on Rab himself. Aged only fifty, inevitably he was seen as the coming man of Tory politics and at the end of December enjoyed the singular distinction of being chosen by two columnists – in, respectively, left- and right-wing newspapers – as their 'politician of the year'.[45] Perhaps, though, even more gratifying – given the troubles earlier in the year – was a telegram (presumably in reply to a Christmas card) that arrived at Stanstead on New Year's Eve. Sent from Whitehall it bore the simple message, 'Thank you both so much, every good wish from us' and was signed 'Winston'.[46]

In any political sense, therefore, 1953 could hardly have opened more promisingly. Rab's sole real ill-wisher in the Government, Woolton, had been out of action since collapsing with a perforated appendix at the Conservative Party Conference the previous October, and there is some indication that Rab was behind the various background moves to get him permanently replaced as Party Chairman (the name floated as his potential successor – that of the back-bench Conservative MP, Malcolm McCorquodale – certainly belonged to someone very much aligned with Rab's own wing of the Party). That particular ploy may not have prospered, mainly because of the resistance of Anthony Eden; but, after a joint trip made with Rab to Washington in February, he, too, fell ill and was removed from the scene for a period of six months. Rab consequently became not so much the number three figure on the Commons front-bench as the number two.

It was also, as he must have realised, bound to be his year of economic opportunity. Britain was continuing to benefit from the dramatic turn in the terms of trade in her favour (brought about largely by the ending of the Korean War) and, having subjected the country to its period of retrenchment, Rab was now, with even the balance of payments looking healthy, able to distribute the rewards of virtue. In 1953, unlike in 1952, he chose to deliver his Budget late – selecting the day (Tuesday 14 April) that Parliament returned from its Easter recess. No doubt the choice of date was made to give him the maximum room for manœuvre – and Rab took full advantage of it. He launched off with a statement that was perhaps the least modest he had yet made:

> When I opened my first Budget some 13 months ago I began, as is customary, with a review of the previous year. The account I gave was as objective as I could make it and was inevitably a bleak one, a story of mounting deficits overseas and of inflation at home. The difference today is very striking.[47]

That introduction provided the background for the first post-war Budget to introduce no new taxes or raise the ones that already existed. Rab's expansionist proposals included sixpence off all rates of income tax, a quarter reduction at every level of purchase tax and the promised abolition in the following January of the highly unpopular Excess Profits Levy (imprudently insisted upon by Churchill as a pledge in the 1951 Conservative election manifesto). There were some rumblings on the Conservative back-benches that Rab might have gone even further in the direction of stimulating the economy; but, by and large, Conservative supporters were content simply to count their blessings – of which, by many Tory workers in the constituencies, the Chancellor's own guiding hand at the Treasury was seen as the chief one.[48]

Certainly, Rab's second Budget did nothing to diminish his standing with the Party – indeed, it markedly increased it. Within the Treasury, too, it was regarded as 'a peach' – as admirably ripened politically as it was economically.[49] Among Rab's own Cabinet colleagues it was noted, however, that it marked the end of a running fight that had lasted virtually as long as the Conservative Government:[50] from now on, having put his shirt on economic expansion, he would hardly be able to resist the demands of the Minister of Housing, Harold Macmillan, for an ever-increasing share of the nation's resources in order to attain the target of 300,000 new houses a year. On 31 December 1953 Macmillan – with a wholly characteristic flurry of publicity – was able to announce that that target had, in fact, been reached.

For the time being, however, Macmillan was recognised by no one as an ultimate rival to Rab. The *Sunday Times* might have observed the previous autumn that it was 'reassuring to many Conservatives to see two such able men standing in the wings able to take the lead when necessary'[51] – but the two personalities it had in mind were Eden and Rab. Not unnaturally, the public promulgation of such a rivalry for the eventual Leadership – usually expressed in the form of Eden certainly being ahead but Rab not being far behind – did nothing to ease the always somewhat prickly relationship between two figures whose sharply contrasting ministerial careers reached far back into pre-war politics. As the promotion of Rab's cause rolled on, it was probably just as well for Eden that he could claim to be honourably disqualified from any competitive struggle by reason of undergoing serious surgery, first in London and then in Boston.

What Eden can hardly, however, have been expected to regard with anything but alarm was Churchill's own stroke towards the end of June just as he himself was beginning to recuperate in America from his third major operation. It was the kind of dramatic development in politics for which no one is ever prepared. Churchill, admittedly, was seventy-eight but such was his indomitable image that sudden failing powers, or even any intimations of mortality, had somehow never been associated with him. If anything, indeed, he had appeared to the public to draw new strength from the Coronation of the young Queen on 2 June: it seemed not only right but wholly appropriate that a man who had first been elected to Parliament in the reign of Queen Victoria should now be presiding over the dawn of 'a new Elizabethan Age'. Certainly, Rab appears to have had absolutely no inkling of the blow that was about to fall. Not only had he been lunching alone with Churchill, going through a welter of Cabinet business (ranging from the impending Television White Paper through the imminent Bermuda conference with Eisenhower and the French to the private affairs of Princess Margaret) the day before the Prime Minister's stroke occurred:[52] he had also been present at the State Dinner for the Italian Prime Minister, De Gasperi, on 23 June when Churchill first sensed the loss of the use of his left arm. Rab did not observe then that anything untoward had occurred; all he claimed to have noticed was that the Prime Minister 'could barely speak when I said good night'[53] – but that, of course, could have been put down to the lateness of the hour and the lavishness of the hospitality. In any case, whatever doubts Rab may have felt even on that score seem to have been satisfactorily laid to rest by the Prime Minister's loyal PPS (and son-in-law), Christopher Soames,* who asked him on his return to the House of Commons that same evening whether he and his wife had noticed 'how tired WSC was'.[54]

The next morning, however, when Churchill gallantly insisted on taking a Cabinet, receiving his colleagues while already sitting down, was a different story – with 'some of us', according to Rab, 'noticing that much was wrong'.[55] In his memoirs, published nearly twenty years later, Rab contrived to leave the impression that the first real confirmation he had of the seriousness of the Prime Minister's condition came when he arrived at Chartwell on Friday 26 June (having been summoned from a nursing home in Norfolk where he was visiting his dying mother)† to be handed a letter written one day previously by the Prime Minister's Joint Principal Private Secretary, John Colville, explaining everything that had occurred.[56] That does not, however, seem to have been a strictly accurate record. For, according to the diary notes Rab wrote at the time, he had more advance warning than that. On the evening of Thursday 25 June he and Sydney gave a music party at No. 11 Downing Street; in the course of it, his niece, Jane Portal,‡ who for the past two years had been working as a secretary at No. 10 and was a great favourite of the Prime Minister's, took him out into the garden and, without giving any secrets away, told him enough to convey that 'things were

* Arthur Christopher John Soames (1920–). Conservative MP, Bedford, 1950–66. PPS to the Prime Minister 1952–5. Secretary of State for War 1958–60. Minister of Agriculture, Fisheries and Food 1960–4. Ambassador to Paris 1968–72. Vice-President of the European Commission 1973–8. Created life peer 1978. Lord President of the Council 1979–81.

† Lady (Ann) Butler died on 23 July at the age of seventy-seven and was buried in Greenstead Green Churchyard next to her husband. Rab cancelled all his engagements to attend her funeral, held on 28 July.

‡ Jane Gillian Portal (1929–), the daughter of Rab's sister, Iris. She left No. 10 in 1955 to marry Gavin Welby. In 1975, having obtained a divorce, she married the merchant banker, and later chairman of the Callaghan Labour Government's Price Commission, Charles Williams. He was created a life peer in 1985.

not good'. Furthermore, again according to Rab's contemporary record, the next morning, even before he left for Norfolk to see his mother, the Prime Minister's other PPS, David Pitblado, called on him at the Treasury to tell him 'how things were'. He was swiftly followed by Lord Salisbury, who announced that 'he had been asked to go to Bermuda' in place of the Prime Minister.[57]

Rab cannot, therefore, have been wholly unprepared when at his mother's bedside in Hunstanton he received an urgent phone call requiring his presence at Chartwell. Without the use of his official car he took a train to London on a blazingly hot day – with, as he describes in his memoirs, 'a blinding headache'[58] – eventually reaching Chartwell in the evening. There he found the Churchill family assembled – and, significantly, the battle-plans already prepared. The old warrior might have been felled but his relations and official retainers were not yet ready to give up the ghost. The letter he found waiting for him from Colville, although giving a reasonably candid explanation of all that had occurred (and adding the rider that the Prime Minister 'himself has little hope of recovery'), made it clear that he was expected to 'keep the whole matter strictly private for the time being'.[59] There is some doubt, indeed, whether on that day Rab was even allowed to talk to the Prime Minister at least by himself – though later (perhaps telescoping two visits) he was to recall 'sitting at dinner whilst Winston with his good arm carried to his lips a beaker of brandy'.[60] The reasons anyway for the iron security curtain were soon apparent enough. On Sunday 28 June, having resolved to stay in London throughout the weekend as a result of what he had seen and heard at Chartwell, Rab received at his home in Smith Square an outline draft of future Government arrangements – the composition of which had become almost the main preoccupation of those within the family circle who were determined, in the immediate aftermath of the Prime Minister's stroke, not to bow to the seemingly inevitable.

It was accompanied by a private note from his niece, Jane Portal, now acting almost more as a go-between than as a secretary at Chartwell. Since hers was in some ways a more revealing document than the proposed announcement of Government dispositions, it is perhaps worth quoting first:

> Dearest Rab, *27 June 1953*
>
> We spoke about this. If you like to make any alterations you think fit and send it back via No. 10 we will forward it to London to your office to be typed for you to sign on Monday.
>
> He is definitely weaker physically and fell down today. In fact

he cannot really walk at all and his swallowing is bad. However, he is very cheerful and his courage is remarkable – he seems completely detached in a funny sort of way.

Jock [Colville] told me that the PM and everybody were most impressed yesterday by your gentlemanly behaviour. I hope you like the arrangement; I am sure that, even if it may seem unsatisfactory at the moment, it is in your own interest.[61]

The last sentence, of course, was a reference to the guidelines that the Churchill entourage had laid down for the immediate running of the Government. From Rab's point of view, they were, in fact, far from satisfactory since – although it fell to him to shoulder the burden – he was armed with virtually no authority. Nevertheless, after first informing his colleagues in the Cabinet of the proposed dispositions, he loyally offered the following Business Statement to the House of Commons on the afternoon of Monday 29 June:

The House will have learnt with regret that the Prime Minister has been ordered to take a complete rest and that the Bermuda conference has been postponed with the concurrence of the United States and French Governments.

The Prime Minister will keep in close touch with events but he will not be able to resume his full duties for at least a month. During this time he will have the assistance of the Lord President of the Council [Salisbury] though the Minister of State [Selwyn Lloyd]* will continue to be responsible for the day-to-day conduct of Foreign Office business.

The Leader of the House, the Lord Privy Seal [Crookshank] and I will share the responsibility for making any Statements or answering any Questions in this House on matters of general Government policy.[62]

It hardly sounded like a ringing mandate for a man who was, in effect, being required to take charge of the entire Government machine – but that had been the least of Rab's problems. A far more urgent one originally was just what – and how much of the truth – the public should be told of the real nature of the Prime Minister's

* John Selwyn Brooke Lloyd (1904–78). Conservative MP, Wirral 1945–76. Minister of State, Foreign Office 1951–4. Minister of Supply 1954–5. Minister of Defence 1955. Secretary of State for Foreign Affairs 1955–60. Chancellor of the Exchequer 1960–2. Leader of the House of Commons 1963–4. Speaker 1971–6. Created life peer 1976.

condition. Here Churchill's doctors, Lord Moran and Sir Russell Brain, seem to have wanted to be reasonably honest, preparing a medical bulletin which specifically referred to 'a disturbance of the cerebral circulation' and consequent 'attacks of giddiness'.[63] At some stage, though, their original draft communiqué was heavily tampered with – and the first bulletin put out for public consumption on the afternoon of Saturday 27 June was so anodyne as to be virtually meaningless:

> The Prime Minister has had no respite for a long time from his very arduous duties and is in need of a complete rest. We have therefore advised him to abandon his journey to Bermuda and to lighten his duties for at least a month.[64]

When full evidence of what had gone on came to light, through the release of Government documents under the thirty-year rule in January 1984, the finger of suspicion naturally pointed at Rab himself. The charge, however, seems to be an unjust one: the manuscript alterations are, for example, certainly not in his handwriting[65] – they were, in fact, made by the pen of Sir John Colville; and what appears to have happened is that the Prime Minister's own staff (guided throughout the course of Churchill's illness by the Secretary of the Cabinet, Sir Norman Brook)* took a number of soundings, particularly from friendly Press proprietors,† as to what would be the minimum that could be said without arousing public suspicions.[66] In the light of that advice the alterations were introduced, considerably toning down the original draft bulletin that the two doctors had prepared; thus the most that Rab can be accused of is of going along with a medical report that he, of all people (especially in the light of the letter from his niece), knew to be telling rather less than the truth.

On the other hand, he was hardly in a position to stand out against it. Not only had he been carefully deprived of any formal authority as the acting head of Government; he was also simultaneously the target of an establishment manœuvre designed to ensure that, even if the worst happened, it would not be he who succeeded to the

* Norman Craven Brook (1902–67). Secretary of the Cabinet 1947–62. Joint Secretary of the Treasury and Head of the Home Civil Service 1956–62. Created 1st Baron Normanbrook 1963.

† Brendan Bracken, by then Viscount Bracken, Lord Beaverbrook and Lord Camrose, the chairman of the *Daily Telegraph*, all visited Chartwell before the final medical bulletin was issued.

actual Premiership. At first, the Prime Minister's family and staff do indeed appear to have despaired of a full recovery, or of one sufficient to allow Churchill to return even temporarily to No. 10. That posed them with a problem. Was it right, was it fair, that Anthony Eden, Churchill's heir apparent for the last dozen years, should lose out on his chance of the succession simply because he happened to be unavailable through illness at the precise moment that a vacancy might occur? To some in Churchill's circle (perhaps with memories going back to pre-war appeasement days), that seemd quite enough of an injustice for a contingency plan to be needed – and, accordingly, one was worked out. In the earliest days of Churchill's illness an approach was made to Sir Alan Lascelles, the Private Secretary at the Palace, suggesting that in the event of Churchill not being able to carry on, the Queen should send not for Rab but instead appoint Lord Salisbury as interim Prime Minister until Eden was well enough to return to duty and assume the succession that was rightly his.[67] It was, in many ways, an extraordinary constitutional proposal – and there is no proof that the Palace would ever have been ready to go along with it. What, however, there is proof of is that Rab, even while he was shouldering the whole burden of Government, knew all about it. 'At the time,' he was to recall in his retirement,

> I was forbidden to mention it – forbidden. But, yes, it is fundamentally true. I kept quiet at the time because I felt there was something to do with the Crown being involved, in the very early days of the young Queen's accession. The point was that I was the only person who was active, fit and running everything – and I think they felt they should protect Anthony.[68]

Not all Tory MPs, though, would have endorsed that feeling. In fact, Rab soon came under some back-bench pressure to exert himself – advice that he may have preferred to the more predictable pleas of his Cabinet colleagues not to overdo it. He was to preside over sixteen successive Cabinet meetings between 29 June and 18 August and the wonder perhaps is that he should have remained content with a mere chairman's role. If he had actively pushed for the Prime Ministership, could he have got it? Interestingly, in the view of Churchill's oldest friend, Lord Cherwell, as transmitted many years later to Rab, if he had demanded the title in addition to doing the work, he could not have been refused.[69] No doubt, his knowledge of the Salisbury 'plot' inhibited Rab to some extent; but he was, after all, in 1953 at the height not only of his powers but of his reputation – and he certainly did not lack for active supporters both in the Commons and the country. The obvious attraction for them in Rab becoming Prime Minister, almost, as it were, overnight, was that it would solve what was increasingly coming to be seen as 'the Churchill retirement problem' – and there were many in the party who doubted (rightly, as things turned out) Eden's capacity to do that. A typical plea at the time addressed to Rab came from a highly respectable back-bench Brigadier of eighteen years' standing in the Commons, who happened to be a connection of Rab's through the Courtauld family. Starting with the instruction 'Tear this note up' (an order that Rab evidently resolved to disobey) it went on:

> Anthony Eden is one of the most delightful chaps you could find and it is impossible not to feel some affection for him but, fit or unfit, he is *not* the right Prime Minister for Great Britain 1953/4. Things have always fallen his way, at least up to his recent illness, but he has never really scored a six off his own bat. I used to think that you were brilliant and sound but no leader: now, however, like a lot of others, I have changed my mind. I, therefore, come to the point of this note.
>
> You are in charge for the time being and you will, no doubt, feel that, out of loyalty to Anthony and the Old Man, you must stick to your own financial line and only branch off it as needs be. It is my opinion that, as things are now, the needs of the country come before personal loyalties. I (and countless other people) would like to hear you make one or two great speeches – the speeches of a leader and not of a Chancellor. I daresay you may have already lined up the interests of the country in your own mind but I feel sufficiently strongly about it to write you this note.[70]

Alas, it was not merely the injunction to destroy the letter that Rab chose to ignore: he also disregarded the advice. With the exception of one major excursion into foreign affairs in the Commons*[71] he used his period in charge of the Government to deliver no great speeches, sounding national trumpet calls or otherwise. Instead, he concentrated on the smooth running of the administrative machine – something he did extremely efficiently but which was hardly likely to arouse any popular clamour for him to take over the reins of leadership. A

* Not apparently a great success. 'Rab's big speech this week on Foreign Affairs was not up to his usual standard, and in fact was considered "a flop".' *Chips: The Diary of Sir Henry Channon*, p. 478. Diary entry dated 26 July 1953.

valid comparison can perhaps be made with Harold Macmillan. If he had found himself in Rab's position – in fact he was in hospital that July undergoing a gall-bladder operation – would he not have played a very different hand? The easy answer, of course, is (as was often said subsequently) that Rab, in contrast to Macmillan, simply lacked 'the killer instinct'. A more perceptive formulation of roughly the same point may well be that Rab had never had a fighter's training and, therefore, never quite knew, even when the opportunity presented itself, how to deliver the knock-out blow.

One thing he knew, however, was how to run a Government[72] – and, whatever he may have lost, he certainly gained golden opinions for himself as a result of his virtual three-month stewardship of No. 10 (Churchill came back briefly for two Cabinet meetings in August but then took off for Balmoral and the South of France,* returning only just in time for the Conservative Party Conference at Margate, where Eden also made his first public reappearance after an even longer six-month absence). As a result of the return of both *prima donnas*, the 1953 Conference was, from Rab's point of view, something of an anti-climax, at least when compared with the previous year. Indeed, his chief memory of the occasion seems to have lain in the moment when Churchill, having triumphantly carried off the Leader's speech, about which there had been much foreboding, immediately summoned him to the Conference hall green-room and – with the injunction, 'You have been doing too much' – peremptorily ordered him to take a week's holiday.[73]

Rab did so, but there was no question of going away. The condition of his wife's jaw had shown no improvement and by now the infection had spread to her face. Discreetly, Rab had started making inquiries among his medical friends – and by November Sydney was in Westminster Hospital having what was described as 'an operation to deal with a mouth infection'.[74] At this stage it was not something that Rab wished to discuss publicly – but, once the announcement had appeared in *The Times*, there was inevitably sympathetic comment. One letter that appears to have particularly touched him – especially perhaps in the light of the rumoured constitutional events of the previous summer – came from the Queen's Private Secretary,

* Rab visited Churchill in the south of France, who was staying in Lord Beaverbrook's villa at Cap d'Ail once again. One member of the Prime Minister's staff retains a vivid memory of the two of them painting together at their easels alongside each other, looking out over the Mediterranean. Rab's pursuit of painting as a hobby, providing a common bond with Churchill, dated from his period as Chancellor.

which, having dealt with another matter, went on, 'Her Majesty hopes sincerely, as I do, that all goes well with your wife.'[75]

At first that did, indeed, seem to be the case – with the surgeon, who went on to explain that he was waiving his fee in the light of Rab's great services to education, writing to insist that 'the successful issue is ours already'.[76] (Later Sydney was to complain of his always being 'too anxious to reassure me'.)[77] But, in fact, there was really no progress and Sydney continued to have a running sore on the right side of her jaw, which she would mop with a handkerchief or hide with a scarf. Originally she had been planning to join Rab on his trip to the Commonwealth Finance Ministers' Conference held in Australia at the beginning of 1954. It soon became clear that this was not a practicable proposition. Sydney remained at home at Stanstead trying to persuade herself that she was getting better, while Rab flew half-way across the world as leader of a powerful British delegation to a conference on which a lot of hopes had been pinned. In the event, as is the way of such gatherings, it failed to fulfil expectations or, indeed, to justify all the careful groundwork that had gone into it – one Australian newspaper dismissed it as 'a damp squib'.[78] Yet of Rab's own personal success – not least in selling the story of Britain's 'recovery' to the Australian public – there was no doubt at all. He was helped by the fact that on the day the conference opened his appointment was announced as a Companion of Honour; and *The Times* was not alone in remarking that 'there was special point in the opening of the Sydney conference being chosen as the occasion for the honour'.[79] In fact the timing was purely fortuitous, being the result of a simple mistake by a Private Secretary in No. 10, who had overlooked Churchill's instruction for Rab's name to be included in the New Year's Honours List.[80] At least, however, 'the clerical error'[81] – to which Churchill confessed in a phone call to Stanstead on 7 January – appears to have amused Sydney (no bad thing, since the rest of her news was rather gloomy). 'Food', she reported to her husband, was 'still a bore – so I certainly could not have travelled with you'; even worse, her surgeon had said, 'he can't improve my appearance and only possibly prevent my mouth from slipping right all the time'. Small wonder that she also announced, 'It is all very depressing.'[82]

There was not much cheer elsewhere either – for when Rab got back from Australia, it was only to jolt the House of Commons with the use of the dreaded word 'recession' in making his report on what the conference had achieved in terms of Britain's immediate trading prospects.[83] The use of the term 'recession' was probably a little over-dramatic (certainly Rab was promptly rebuked by a Labour MP who told him sharply to watch his language);[84] but there was a general feeling that, in economic terms, things were unlikely to go as well for the Government in 1954 as they had in 1952 and 1953. Wages – after a surprisingly successful period of voluntary restraint – were beginning to rise sharply and there had been some inflationary settlements during the previous two months. Over one of them, initially reached in No. 10 with the railwaymen just before Christmas, Rab had not even been consulted – and it is probable that he did not altogether disagree with *The Economist*'s characterisation of it as the new Government's 'Munich'.[85]

That specific criticism – and maybe the analogy was not one calculated to appeal to Rab – appeared, though, in an article that otherwise was to do him a good deal of personal damage. It was not that it was composed in any unfriendly spirit;* it was simply that it was one of those rare pieces of political journalism to employ a conceit that really takes off. Headed (slightly mysteriously) 'Mr Butskell's Dilemma', it very soon spelt out what it meant:

> Mr Butskell is already a well-known figure in dinner table conversations in both Westminster and Whitehall and the time has come to introduce him to a wider audience. He is a composite of the present Chancellor and the previous one . . . Whenever there is a tendency to excess Conservatism within the Conservative Party – such as a clamour for too much imperial preference, for a wild dash to convertibility, or even for a little more unemployment to teach the workers a lesson – Mr Butskell speaks up for the cause of moderation from the Government side of the House; when there is a clamour for even graver irresponsibilities from the Labour benches, Mr Butskell has hitherto spoken up from the other.[86]

As a flight of fancy it had just enough truth in it to cause the maximum mischief – and the enemies of both Rab and Hugh Gaitskell were not slow to exploit the gift they had been delivered. Which of the two the catch-phrase, 'Butskellism' – soon taken up by cartoonists of both left and right – harmed more it is difficult to say (though it may well have been Rab, since Gaitskell, less than two years later,

* Although written anonymously, like all articles in *The Economist*, its author was Norman Macrae.

did at least become Leader of his Party).* The trouble, of course, was that the whole notion had not been plucked out of thin air: Gaitskell had always been suspected by some in his own party of being 'a closet Conservative', while Rab, as has been noticed, was no stranger to the charge of being 'a milk and water socialist'. But, in truth, all they really shared was a common allegiance to Keynesian economics and demand management of the economy – although even there, as Rab was to write in his memoirs, 'We spoke with different accents and with a differing emphasis.'[87] They certainly tended to take rather greater care to do so in the months following the publication of *The Economist* article.

Not that Rab's third Budget, which he presented on 6 April 1954, gave much opportunity for any clash on ideology. It was, in a phrase he used in his own speech, very much 'a carry on' Budget,[88] while Gaitskell described it in reply as 'a tiny, insignificant Budget'[89] (Woolton was even ruder in characterising it as 'the dullest thing that anybody ever created').[90] The only real changes it introduced were the invention of a new 'investment allowance' to replace the old 'initial allowance' for companies investing in new plant, premises or machinery, an adjustment in favour of cinemas in Entertainment Tax, a slight easing of the repayment rules over post-war credits and a concession to family businesses over Estate Duty putting inherited private company assets on the same tax basis as agricultural land. Whatever it was, it was hardly an electioneering Budget – and that may even have been part of the strategy that lay behind it: for reasons that remain obscure Woolton seems to have thought that it would be a good idea to stop the Opposition from thinking 'there was going to be an election in October'.[91]

But, in fact, it was not just the standstill Budget that made such a prospect unlikely. An even heftier obstacle lay in the whole question-mark hanging over the Party Leadership. Originally, before his stroke, Churchill's great reprieve had seemed to come with the death of Stalin in March 1953 – leading him to believe, and to some extent persuade his colleagues, that only he could now co-ordinate a positive response from the West to the new Soviet leadership under

* This did not, however, prevent his posthumous biographer, Philip M. Williams, from devoting six pages to an attempt at demolishing 'The Butskellite Myth': a forlorn endeavour since half-way through he offered the most potent symbol of Butskellism of all – the fact that Gaitskell's sister was married to Rab's PPS, Hubert Ashton. Williams adds the intriguing detail that it was through Ashton that nearly all negotiations between Chancellor and 'shadow' Chancellor were conducted. *Hugh Gaitskell*, p. 314.

Malenkov: hence the importance that he had personally attached to the thwarted Bermuda conference. But even after the postponement of that three-power Western gathering – it eventually took place in a much less dramatic form in December 1953 – Churchill had lost none of his peace-making ardour, as Rab was to discover when he dined with him alone in March 1954.

True, the Prime Minister prefaced his *tête à tête* observations by intimating that he felt like 'an aeroplane at the end of its flight, in the twilight with the petrol running out, in search of a safe landing'; but that that was simply camouflage was soon revealed by the vehemence with which he went on to insist on his continuing interest in 'high-level talks with the Russians' and his determination to do something about controlling 'the future of the A-bomb'.* Once these two objectives had been achieved, Rab was given to understand, he would be more than willing to retire to Hyde Park Gate – though, slightly ominously, Churchill did not seem to be envisaging an election until 1955 or even March 1956 – 'he would not wish the Tory Party to be accused of running away from a depression'. Meanwhile, he was sure the great thing for the Chancellor to try to do was to settle the question of MPs' salaries on which 'much would turn – if they were promised a rise in the *next* Parliament, they would all wish the *next* Parliament to come as soon as possible'.[92] As a political survey from the mountain tops of international relations to the back alleys of parliamentary business, it was clearly a masterly performance; and Rab appears to have been left, quite rightly, with the impression that the Old Warrior was going to be difficult to shift.

That, of course, was worse news for Eden than it was for Rab, though of the two of them it was Rab who came nearer to resigning through impatience and frustration during the summer of 1954. That, however, had nothing to do with the succession and was entirely a matter of Rab's increasing obsession with the topic Churchill had craftily raised with him, that of MPs' salaries. In 1954 the parliamentary salary stood at £1,000 a year – and to Labour MPs, in particular, it was a perpetual struggle to survive (let alone to bring up a family) at that level of remuneration. In May, therefore, following a Select Committee Report, the House of Commons held two debates on what was tactfully called 'Members' Expenses'; at the end of the second one, the House voted, on a free vote, emphatically in favour of increasing 'the Parliamentary allowance' (the name under which

* The British Government announced it was making an H-bomb in February 1955.

an MP's salary went in those days) by £500 to £1,500 p.a.[93] It was not the solution Rab had officially endorsed (though it may have been the one he secretly favoured): on the floor of the House he had advocated a £500 expense allowance to be justified against actual expenditure. Unfortunately, though, during the course of the debate he had given a virtual guarantee that the Government would, in this matter, accept the guidance of the House – 'There is certainly no desire in our procedure to do other than take the will of the House. That is what we want to do.'[94] They were words which were to return to haunt him through most of that summer.

It was not that Rab changed his mind; it was simply that he proved quite unable to carry his Cabinet colleagues with him. On 5 June he formally gave it as his view at Cabinet that the Government 'would gain in the long run by putting into effect without further question the decision of the majority of the House in favour of a direct salary increase';[95] but with the exception of Churchill (who, as we have seen, may have been playing his own game) he could not raise a single supporter in the Cabinet Room. It had been the same at previous meetings: Rab was clearly indignant at the position he had been put in and may even have threatened resignation. Certainly, that would seem the most plausible explanation of a handwritten note he received that week from the Lord Chancellor:

4 VI 54

My Dear Rab,

You may well think this letter is awful cheek, but I will risk it. For I left the Cabinet meeting on Wednesday evening with the feeling that you were puzzled and unhappy, and I wanted very much to help you. Since then I have given much thought to your position and have read again every word of your speech. And, in the result, I am wholly convinced – as convinced as ever I have been in the course of many years dealing with other people's troubles – that no one could, with any semblance of justice, charge you with lack of good faith, or with any departure from the paths of strictest rectitude, if you did not introduce or support a flat increase of salary for MPs. I beg you not to let that thought worry you any more.

Your very sincere friend

GAVIN SIMONDS*

* Gavin Turnbull Simonds (1881–1971). Lord Chancellor 1951–4. Lord of Appeal in Ordinary 1954–62. Created 1st Viscount Simonds 1954.

The Lord Chancellor's letter was a generous gesture, and with Rab at least it seems to have done the trick. With a rather bad grace – he was particularly disdainful of the role of the 1922 Committee ('The partridges of the 1922 Committee are split up and indeed have started to "pair" with a view to breeding further ideas')[96] – he eventually went along with the compromise settlement of making available to MPs a 'sessional allowance' of £2 a day (amounting, at most, to an income of £288 a year): it may well, however, have been significant that the ultimate announcement was made to the Commons not by Rab but by the Prime Minister himself.[97]

Nor was that the only occasion during the summer of 1954 that Rab's colleagues seem to have taken a certain relish in cutting him down to size. He was in trouble again in Cabinet in July – though this time it was Churchill's fault rather than his own. Bilateral talks had taken place in Washington towards the end of June between, on the one side, the Prime Minister and the Foreign Secretary and, on the other, the President and the Secretary of State. During the return journey on the *Queen Mary* Churchill seems to have been seized with the notion that it would be a good idea if he sent a personal message to the Soviet Foreign Minister, Molotov, suggesting a visit to Moscow. A draft telegram making such a proposal was submitted to Rab, as acting Head of Government, from the ship and, having read it, he simply made arrangements for it to be forwarded to the Kremlin via the Soviet Embassy in London. At the first Cabinet meeting after Churchill's return, however, considerable anger was expressed as to why the telegram had not been referred to the Cabinet for its approval. The revolt was almost certainly directed primarily at the Prime Minister; but, as one Cabinet Minister after another weighed in with increasingly indignant protests, Rab necessarily became the ricochet victim. He was left, in fact, very much on the penitent's stool – rather lamely explaining that the Prime Minister's message had reached him over the weekend while he was in Norfolk and that not only had it been addressed to him personally but that there had been nothing in the accompanying explanatory telegram 'to suggest that the views of the Cabinet were being invited'.[98]

The storm, however, refused to blow itself out – and for some time there was even a danger that it would lead to resignations.[99] On 23 July Rab did his best to dampen the whole affair down by making a full act of contrition, as the Cabinet Minutes make clear:

> *The Chancellor of the Exchequer* said that, when he had received the draft of the proposed message, he had understood that it had been sent to him for his personal comments only. It would have been possible, though very difficult, for him to have contacted the Cabinet at that stage, and he must accept personal responsibility for having decided not to do so.[100]

Mercifully, however, the very next day the situation eased – and the Cabinet crisis ended – with the receipt of a message from the Kremlin, not taking up Churchill's offer but proposing instead a collective European security conference.

Probably Rab had made a mistake in not bringing the matter to the attention of the Cabinet, but that does not quite explain the ruthlessness with which the issue was pursued, notably by Woolton, Salisbury and Crookshank. What does, however, go some way to account for it is the open restiveness that was now starting to break out in the Cabinet over Churchill's position – and on this occasion it was Rab's bad luck to be delivered as the whipping-boy to the Prime Minister's most prominent critics. Moreover, his own position on Churchill's future seems, at this stage, to have been a shade ambivalent. He certainly saw more of the Prime Minister (and had been doing so for some time) than any other member of the Cabinet; his relationship with him was, of course, a good deal easier than that of Eden, who was coming increasingly to feel like a *dauphin* who was never going to be allowed to mount the throne. Rab became, in effect, that August very much the intermediary between the two of them – breaking the news to Eden that Churchill had no intention of going[101] and actually 'vetting' the Prime Minister's eventual letter to his aspirant successor in which he formally served notice that he intended to carry on.[102] It may not have been a heroic role; but it was a useful one – not least in terms of preventing an explosion that could have split the party asunder and precipitated an early election.

The most revealing document to survive from what was plainly an unusually tense holiday month for the Government is Rab's own letter to Churchill written following a visit to Chartwell on 13 August. (After the visit Churchill had sent him what he termed the 'final edition' of his elaborately rehearsed letter to Eden, warning him that he proposed to carry on as Prime Minister.)

22 Two Chancellors of the Exchequer: Rab with his predecessor at the Treasury, Hugh Gaitskell, and the Chairman of the LCC, Norman Prichard

23 The Emergency Budget of October 1955. Rab leaves his home at 3 Smith Square to go to the Commons

24 Rab returning to Smith Square on 10 January 1957, the day Harold Macmillan became Prime Minister

18 August 1954

Personal

Dear Prime Minister,

I value your confidence in asking me to look at your second epistle to Anthony. Since last summer, at the time of your severe illness, we have all accepted that Anthony is to be your successor. I have therefore a loyalty to him which you realise that I must be careful not to abuse.

Up till my visit to you last Friday I thought you would hand over to your successor this autumn, leaving him time to mobilise his forces, his programme and public opinion.

You have now thought over the situation and have introduced a new argument which you fortify with your experience, namely that you distrust the outlook for 'fag end' successor governments. This is an important argument; and no doubt in order to give it full force your second draft omits detailed description of the type of reconstituted government which you envisage and leaves this, as well as the detailed time-table of the change-over, until you have talked to Anthony. I think this is right . . .

My instinct about the election is that the party will do better if it appears normally to have gone on and done its job rather than that an abnormal summer date for an appeal should have been chosen. The summer is favourable to Labour outdoor speakers, as the Chairman of the party must know, and historically less favourable to the Conservatives. So I am glad to see that you keep the election date open in your letter . . .

To sum up, therefore, I think the party may suffer from an early election. This is my first reaction and I shall, of course, consider further. I realise that, if no election is decided upon, the question of a successor government will be more likely to remain open. You yourself leave open the detailed arguments for the change-over. I quite accept that we might have a successor government if the date for the election be postponed.

How we shall resolve all of this I don't yet see, but you may be sure that I shall from now on expend a fund of understanding on your arguments and shall evaluate at its priceless worth the boon of your strength and experience in handling world events.

R. A. BUTLER[103]

Whatever other message might have been concealed between the lines, the last paragraph made it perfectly clear that Rab was, in effect, acquiescing in Churchill's decision to carry on – even if it was not the one he had originally been expecting. Despite his protestations in the first paragraph, the question can, therefore, legitimately be asked whether his own interests did not lie in the Prime Minister 'playing it long'. No one can know whether or not that was a factor in Rab's mind – though it may be relevant here to note that in his later years he was always quite ready to assert, 'Winston doubted that Anthony was adapted to be Prime Minister' (adding, mischievously, sometimes, 'You know, in his last months, he often made funny little advances to me).'[104]

Certainly, Rab soon spotted that as a result of there being no imminent hand-over at No. 10, there might be a change in his own position. He fully supported Churchill's offer to Eden of 'command of the Home Front'* – but clearly only on the understanding that he would succeed Eden at the Foreign Office. Frustratingly, though, from Rab's point of view, Eden – after a certain amount of agonising – elected to stay at the Foreign Office; and Rab was, therefore, forced to go that September to Washington for the annual meeting of the World Bank and the International Monetary Fund (remarkably, the first such international gathering he had attended in his three years as Chancellor).

He went with no very light heart. His wife, Sydney's, condition had deteriorated throughout the summer – something that Rab did not seek to conceal from Vincent Massey, the Governor-General of Canada, to whom his second son, Adam, was serving as ADC, and whom he planned to visit on his way back from Washington. To Massey he had already written, in August, saying that 'I am in the prey of one of the greatest enemies of mankind' – and warning him that there might have to be 'last minute adjustments' to his visit.[105] In his memoirs Rab was to maintain that it was not until just before he left for America that he finally learned – as a result of a second operation carried out on his wife in Westminster Hospital in mid-September – that Sydney had cancer.[106] His suspicions, though, must have been aroused before then: as early as June he had made an inquiry of Lord Cherwell as to whether there was not cause for alarm in the fact that Sydney was receiving radium treatment – and, although the answer he got was a considerate one, it certainly cannot have laid all Rab's fears to rest.[107] Perhaps the truth was that it was only when he got to Washington that the full shock sank in. Certainly,

* Robert Rhodes James, *Anthony Eden* (Weidenfeld & Nicolson, 1986), pp.385, 387.

it was while he was staying at the British Embassy there that he received a letter from Sydney which, in its brusque, courageous way, effectively ruled out any further possibilities of pretence or self-deception:

> You worry me far more than I worry about myself. You will have to accept the fact that, whatever happens, I shall never really be strong again. I shall want to continue with some of my social life and art committees but I shall cut out a lot. I must reserve my energies for the things I enjoy and want to do. Don't try and decide for me and never worry about my being lonely. It is going to be a big change and luckily it has come, and is coming, quite gradually. We did not plan my growing old ahead of you like this, but we can make something useful of it, I am sure.[108]

In fact, though, even in saying that much, Sydney was letting Rab down gently. Before she went into hospital for her second operation she had typed out a letter (addressed, slightly curiously, to Rab *or* any of their three sons) disposing of all her personal effects and even going into such domestic detail as recommending specific money gifts for the servants at Stanstead. There seems little doubt that she had come to realise that she was not going to live for long well before Rab himself did.

One of the troubles, of course, was that in the mid-1950s cancer was still an unmentionable subject – and, gruesome though Sydney's illness rapidly became, Rab seems to have been extremely guarded in saying anything about it, even to his closest political associates. In following this reticent course, he was doing no more than obeying orders – having been told, quite firmly, that he was to say 'to outsiders' that the sepsis was 'showing signs of yielding and may be healed'[109] (by now, in fact, through surgery, Sydney had two holes on the side of her jaw, which made it difficult for her both to talk and to eat). Inevitably, the pain and distress took their toll and Sydney's instructions to Rab, now normally delivered in writing, became increasingly peremptory. Of her stoicism there could be no doubt; but it also says much for Rab's own courage that he lived with a private tragedy for nearly two months without giving anything away in public. Indeed, immediately after his return from the United States and Canada, he scored a marked success at the Conservative Conference at Blackpool by urging the youth of the Party to 'invest in success' and boldly (and, as it turned out, roughly accurately) predicting the doubling of the standard of living in Britain over the next twenty-five years.[110]

There was an additional problem in that Sydney, though born a Unitarian, began in the last months of her life to grope for consolation in the more spiritual side of religion – and Rab, despite being a dutiful Anglican who served as churchwarden at his local village church in Essex, was able to be of very little support or help in her quest for a genuine certainty. Through the good offices of her cousin-by-marriage (and Essex neighbour) Mollie Courtauld,* she was, however, put in touch with the local Anglican bishop, Dr Faulkner Allison of Chelmsford, who became a regular visitor to Stanstead, bringing her much comfort. (It was Mollie Courtauld also who took on the burden of preparing the family for what was to happen, writing, for instance, 'the best and sweetest letter' to Adam, in Ottawa, who had been advised by his father not to come home for fear of alarming his mother.)

Sydney's last appearance in public was at the Guildhall banquet given by the new Lord Mayor on 9 November. Mercifully for Rab, some of the tension was then to go out of politics, with all eyes being set on Churchill's eightieth birthday celebrations, which reached their culmination in a meeting of both Houses of Parliament held in Westminster Hall on 30 November. A few days before that, Rab had, however, confessed to at least one person just what the situation was. At a reception at No. 10 he had taken Lady Violet Bonham Carter on one side and admitted that there was 'really no hope'[111] – something, it seems, he must already have let Churchill himself know since, just before his eightieth birthday, the Prime Minister sent a most graceful hand-written letter to Sydney congratulating her on 'the fortitude with which you have borne your most cruel affliction'.[112]

Just how 'cruel' that 'affliction' was found its most eloquent expression in a seemingly peripheral correspondence Rab had at the time with the BBC. He had been asked to deliver the Christmas 1954 'Wireless for the Blind' appeal on both the Home and Light programmes of the BBC. He had accepted in principle but then, on discovering that it meant broadcasting 'live' from London on Christmas Day, withdrew his acceptance on the ground that 'it would

* Mollie, Lady Butler (1907–). Born Mollie Montgomerie, she married Sydney's cousin, August Courtauld, in 1932. During the years following Sydney's death, she and Rab became increasingly close – her first husband was suffering at the time from a mortal illness. Mollie Courtauld and Rab were married, after August Courtauld's death, in October 1959.

disturb my wife very much if I left her for a considerable period on that day'. The BBC and St Dunstan's eventually rallied and suggested that the appeal could, after all, be transmitted from Stanstead. Even then, however, Rab was determined that none of the advance arrangements should be allowed to disturb Sydney's normal routine: the final report from Rab's constituency secretary who was coping with the BBC engineers, sent to the Treasury on 1 December, speaks volumes for the stress the household must have been enduring. The BBC engineers had been instructed that they should aim at arriving to test their equipment before the broadcast not before 3 o'clock. 'We finally made it with ten minutes' grace as Mrs Butler only left the Hall [for her drive] at about 2.50 p.m.'[113]

By the following weekend (4–5 December) Rab himself had hauled down the flag. He remained at Stanstead, cancelling all his political engagements, and was at his wife's bedside when she finally died on his own fifty-second birthday, Thursday 9 December. She was buried on Monday 13 December, in the same churchyard as Rab's parents; a memorial service, attended by the Prime Minister and his wife together with virtually every other member of the Cabinet, was held a week later at St Margaret's, Westminster. *The Times* had already published an exceptionally vivid obituary, 'She was dark, slight, short, vital. Her eyes sparkled, lighting up her whole face. She had a certainty of movement which made her stand out in any company. But her essential quality was that of aim. She flew like an arrow.'[114]

The exact extent of Sydney's influence on Rab's political career – and, even more, the implications of its abrupt withdrawal when he seemed within striking distance of becoming Prime Minister – was inevitably to become a topic of argument among both his friends and his enemies. One thing, though, can be safely asserted. In the immediate aftermath of her premature death – Sydney had died at the relatively early age of fifty-two – Rab suddenly began to look oddly vulnerable. Of course, that might have happened in any event: the much-trailed reconstruction of the Government had occurred in mid-October 1954 and, as a result of it, Harold Macmillan had made his first crucial move on the political chequerboard by being promoted to the Ministry of Defence (within the course of the next fifteen months he was to make two further significant jumps, first to the Foreign Office and then to the Treasury). Rab's own fortunes, by contrast, were probably too tightly involved with the *ancien régime* for him to notice what was going on, as it were, behind his back – though, to his credit, he was to start being a good deal firmer on the subject of Churchill's retirement (taking a particularly tough line at a painful ministerial discussion, held, in Churchill's presence, just three days before Christmas).[115]

Probably, however, nothing much else would have mattered if he had managed to keep his reputation intact as the most successful Chancellor of post-war politics. But in 1955 it was precisely this claim that began to come under question. The troubles started in February when, to steady the pound and cut back on domestic consumption, Rab was forced both to raise Bank Rate (to 4½ per cent) and restore hire purchase restrictions. This bad economic news came at an awkward moment for the Party since the Central Office had just launched a poster campaign all over the country under the slogan 'Conservative freedom works' – and Rab's statement in the Commons offered a heaven-sent opportunity for the Labour Party to reply 'Oh no, it doesn't.'[116] The first impact of the Chancellor's announcement was thus to plunge his own supporters into despondency and provoke a mood of jubilation on the Opposition benches. Second thoughts, however, appear to have done something to temper the Conservatives' depression – if only because a more cheerful notion appears to have taken hold that, if the Chancellor reined back in February, he might have all the more opportunity to produce a carrot or two in April on the eve of what many already suspected would be a May general election.[117]

Whether that was the design or not, it was, in effect, the way things worked out. Rab's fourth Budget, delivered to the House on 19 April, after Churchill's retirement and when the date of the election was already known, did have something of the flavour about it of being an electoral aperitif. It took sixpence off income tax, raised personal allowances, cut back purchase tax on Lancashire textiles – while still leaving the Chancellor with a prospective £150 million budget surplus. Undoubtedly, as in 1953, there were Conservative back-benchers who would have liked the Chancellor to go further – indeed, this time members of the Government, too;[118] but the subsequent history of the year was to demonstrate that the far wiser course for Rab would have been to produce an April Budget every bit as austere as his February statement. As Hugh Massingham, the *Observer*'s political correspondent, noted with some foresight, 'The Chancellor may believe that the terms of trade will turn in our favour but he cannot possibly have any real proof.'[119]

For the time being, however, Rab's fourth Budget bore all the marks of being at least a political success. The Chancellor commended it to the country in a well-received broadcast – according to one old Cambridge friend, 'the best you have ever done';[120] and, as the election campaign was already effectively under way, its characteristic conciliatory tone ('I want you to feel the same sense of spirit and mission as I do, and to march forward boldly, and with faith')[121] was, no doubt, all the more valuable to the Conservatives. During the 1955 election Rab was probably the biggest asset the Government had – the symbol of continuity, as it were, between the past and the future. Churchill had finally departed from No. 10 on 5 April – sacrificing even his guaranteed trumpet voluntary from the Press as Fleet Street was undergoing its first-ever national newspaper strike. After some wobbling, Eden, who on Churchill's recommendation to the Queen had succeeded him the next day, made it known that he was calling an election for 26 May, the announcement coming just four days before Rab presented his Budget. With a new Prime Minister, a new Foreign Secretary (Macmillan) and even a new unknown Minister of Defence (Selwyn Lloyd), it was hardly surprising if Rab looked to the public like the one reassuring element of stability in an otherwise transformed administration.

Certainly, in his own constituency of Saffron Walden he had no difficulty at all, winning the best victory in a three-cornered contest he had yet enjoyed.* He had also played a prominent part in the national campaign – speaking widely across the country, taking part with the new Prime Minister and three other of his Cabinet colleagues in a somewhat staged TV press conference with ten newspaper editors and finally winding up the Conservatives' election broadcasts by delivering the Party's final appeal to the electors on the radio (Eden simultaneously addressing what in those days was a rather smaller audience on television). It must, therefore, have been all the greater shock to find that the new Prime Minister wanted him to leave the Treasury. The first effort to persuade him to do so – and to take on the Leadership of the House – originated, according to Rab's own account, 'in the summer'. Indeed, it had been inspired earlier even than that, as Woolton was to record that he had told Eden to 'get rid of Butler' on his very first day at No. 10 – receiving the gratifying reply 'You are so wise.'[122]

It is hard to think of any motive that can have prompted Eden to be so determined to make this particular change, except perhaps

* The figures were R. A. Butler (Con.) 20,671, H. N. Horne (Lab.) 14,253, Miss H. G. Green (Lib.) 3,209. Conservative majority 6,418.

simple jealousy. He knew, of course, to quote the words of the *Sunday Times*, that Rab was universally regarded as 'the architect of the new Conservatism in the domestic field' (perhaps even more woundingly, the paper had gone on to add the comment, 'Sir Anthony's absorption in foreign affairs has not permitted a close study of domestic problems').[123] It is, therefore, just comprehensible that, flushed with the rewards both of office and of electoral victory (the Conservatives had won the election with a majority of sixty), the new Prime Minister should have resolved that, if ever he was to leave his imprint on his own administration, the one important change he must make was at the Exchequer. It took him, however, a long time to bring it off – and, when he did, it was in the worst possible circumstances.

Rab himself – without giving away that he was under any pressure – was to write in his memoirs, 'If I had been less scrupulous about the economy I would have retired in May';[124] and certainly if he had done so, it would have been much better for his own Treasury reputation, and probably better for the standing of the Government as a whole. Instead, however, he dug his heels in – even if, when Eden formally made the request to him at Chequers in the autumn, he pleaded only for delay. At that point his attitude was understandable enough: he had just returned from the meeting of the IMF, held that year in Istanbul, and, by his firm discouragement of fresh rumours about the 'floating' of the pound and his strong pledge to the world's bankers to introduce further deflationary measures at home, had done a good deal to beat back the new wave of speculation against sterling which (unstopped by some essentially hortatory measures announced in July)[125] had developed over the holiday weeks into a renewed and alarming drain on Britain's gold and dollar reserves. But if Rab's initial resistance to the Prime Minister's desire for a quick change was understandable enough, it became a good deal less so a week or two later. For by then Rab had been defeated in the Cabinet on his recommendation to introduce an autumn package straight away, of which the main part was designed to be the abolition of the bread subsidy. Commenting on this failure, Rab himself was to write some weeks afterwards, 'I could not get my way and, no doubt, should have resigned.'[126] In his entire career, that was the only time he was to commit such a confession to paper.

In the event, however, Rab (perhaps characteristically) resolved to soldier on. His reward was the most critical reception he had ever received in all his years as Chancellor at that October's Conservative

Party Conference, held at Bournemouth, and also to be made to endure a succession of inspired Press leaks suggesting that his time was up at the Treasury and that it was only his own obstinacy that was holding up a Government reshuffle. Worse than that, he had to wait until the day after the House of Commons returned in October from its long summer recess to announce his package of remedial measures designed to restore confidence in the pound. It was not Rab's happiest period* and, significantly, it was during the fortnight between the ending of the Tory Conference and the return of Parliament that he rashly employed an image that was to hang around his neck for a long time to come. Speaking at the annual dinner of the Royal Society of St George on 18 October, after referring to the need for more strenuous economic efforts in the future, he suddenly conjured up the phrase, 'We must not drop back into easy evenings with port wine and over-ripe pheasant.'[127] In political terms it was an undoubted gaffe – if only because pheasant and port wine were quite remote from the diet or experience of the vast majority of the population. Rab was predictably taken to task by the most astringent columnist of the day – Cassandra of the *Daily Mirror* – who roundly accused him of having 'dropped his silver spoon upon the polished floor'.[128] It was a justifiable attack – made perhaps all the more hurtful to Rab as only just ten months earlier the same columnist had selected him as his 'Man of the Year'.

By late October 1955, however, those palmy 1954 days of popularity looked far distant. Rab had had, in one way or another, a pretty miserable time ever since the election – and he would hardly have been much cheered to learn that, even before he had to face the House of Commons on 26 October, his job had already been offered elsewhere by the Prime Minister.[129] He would have been even less amused if he had known of the terms the prospective recipient was laying down for taking it: that he must be the 'undisputed head of the Home Front', that his position in the Government must 'be not inferior' to that of the outgoing Chancellor and that the latter must on no account be 'appointed Deputy Prime Minister'.[130] The name of this tough negotiator was Harold Macmillan.

Against that background of intrigue by Eden, it really did not matter what kind of show Rab put up in the Commons when he

* The one cheerful feature in it was the marriage on Saturday 23 October at St Martin-in-the-Fields of his second son, Adam, to Felicity Molesworth-St Aubyn. Some dazzling photographs appeared in the popular newspapers.

finally came to face his critics. In fact, he made a perfectly respectable stab at defending his policy. He was, for instance, particularly trenchant in rounding on those in his Party who urged that the whole answer was to be found in cutting Government expenditure:

> Do those who say that government expenditure could be drastically reduced propose a reversal of policy in education, or a cut in the cost of pensions? Or are we to hold up work on the roads? Perhaps I can answer by saying that in each of these spheres we have to do all we can to meet imperative needs – in the case of education, of a rising school population, in the case of the old, of an increased number of retired persons, and in the case of the roads, with a programme which I cannot increase but which is already insufficient to deal with the needs of the country.[131]

It was brave, unrepentant stuff – fully deserving the plaudits of at least the *Daily Telegraph*, which wrote the next day of the Chancellor having been 'in excellent form, confident, resolute, good-humoured' (even if it did, in all honesty, add that his own performance had been overshadowed by that of Attlee in reply who, somewhat surprisingly, was reported to have 'sparkled and scintillated').[132] There were private notes, too – among them one from Rab's former Treasury colleague and now Minister of Supply, Reginald Maudling, declaring, 'Magnificently spoken and just right, your best ever', and another from the Deputy Governor of the Bank of England slightly less ecstatically commenting, 'Your mien and voice stood the test admirably.'[133]

The content of the Budget did not, however, go down so well – and that was hardly surprising, since it included an increase of a fifth in purchase tax at all levels, the raising of profits tax from 22·5 to 27·5 per cent and a sharp cutback on local authority building. (Remarkably, however, the extension of purchase tax to 'kitchen, tableware and other household goods' – which eventually got the whole package labelled 'the pots and pans Budget' – did not at first seem to attract all that much outrage.) Yet that may well have been because it was on Rab himself – and his whole record as Chancellor – that Hugh Gaitskell chose the next day to heap all the Opposition's indignation.

Even today Gaitskell's speech reads as a very powerful piece of invective – all the more surprising considering the source whence it came.* It badly shook Rab[134] – partly because of Gaitskell's talk of 'honour' and the straight accusation he made of the country having been deliberately deceived at the time of the election. When Rab tried to object, he was ruthlessly crushed:[135] he got his own back, however, when the Opposition rashly followed up its success in the original Budget debate with a subsequent censure motion of its own, in which Rab made a highly effective debating speech in response to a poor one by Herbert Morrison. He was particularly successful in playing on the then imminent Leadership struggle in the Labour Party – commenting tartly to 'the third man' in the contest, Aneurin Bevan,† that, after Gaitskell's performance the previous week, he would 'no longer need to stoop to conquer' (and being delighted to receive an emphatic nod of assent by way of reply).[136]

There could be no argument, however, that on balance the Commons inquest on what had gone wrong with the economy *had* damaged Rab. Indeed, it was suggested at the time that Gaitskell had deliberately set out to destroy him, if only to prove his credentials as a potential giant killer who could slay even a Chancellor.[137] In fact, however, Rab's future, as has been noted, was already settled before the debate opened – and, if charges of hypocrisy or deceit were to be flung about, they should perhaps have been aimed at the Prime Minister who wound up the censure debate by announcing, 'In all his work my Right Hon. Friend, the Chancellor of the Exchequer, will continue to have my full support.'[138]

Rab had been without that for the previous five weeks at least – and when he made a final vicarious appeal for its return a few weeks later, it was only to have his emissary firmly snubbed. As Rab was to record in a note he made just after leaving the Treasury, 'Some noble efforts made by Sir Edward Bridges to postpone the change till I had provided more evident results met with anger and a definite decision that he [the Prime Minister] had made up his mind'.[139] One

* When Rab was first appointed Chancellor in October 1951 the then Tory MP, Robert Boothby, is supposed to have said, 'Why that's Gaitskell all over again, but from Cambridge' – thus anticipating the invention of 'Butskellism' by at least two years. Rab himself was always to believe that the savagery of Gaitskell's onslaught upon him on this occasion (their relations later revived but were never quite the same again) was to be explained in terms of the Shadow Chancellor being in a bitter mood, having come from a Memorial Service held earlier that day for his Opposition front-bench colleague, Hector McNeil, who had died at the comparatively early age of fifty-five.

† Aneurin Bevan (1897–1960). Labour MP, Ebbw Vale 1929–60. Minister of Health 1945–51. Minister of Labour 1951. Deputy Leader of Labour Party 1959–60.

difficulty on Rab's side is that he never quite seems to have done the same. Eden may well have been exaggerating when he reportedly told Macmillan, back in September, that Rab 'seemed rather to like the idea' of a move[140] – but Rab's own mood does appear to have wavered. He himself was to admit as much in the same diary note he wrote just after leaving the Treasury. 'I was taken with the idea of a wider and freer job when first asked but stated that I must finish the Budget and carry out my promise at Istanbul. The PM agreed to this. Where things have gone wrong is that the Press publicity, which was to have made clear my staying on to do the job, has rather veered the other way . . .'[141]

That was putting the matter mildly. Rab's last weeks at the Treasury were, in fact, overshadowed by a perpetual succession of newspaper stories predicting, with varying degrees of accuracy, the long-rumoured Cabinet reshuffle but all suggesting that he was about to become Leader of the House in order to make way for Harold Macmillan. How much of this Press campaign was the result of a deliberate effort to put pressure upon him – and how much of it was simply the product of what the *Observer*'s political correspondent sharply called the Prime Minister's 'mania for asking people their advice'[142] – can only be a subject for speculation; but, whatever its cause, the consequence was humiliation for Rab.

Why, though, did the reconstruction of the Government – which was not announced till 20 December – take so long? There is one clue in Macmillan's own memoirs, in the passage where he wrote that 'I could not agree that he [Rab] should be Deputy Prime Minister' – the job description most of the advance newspaper stories had prescribed – adding that, 'After a further exchange of letters . . . I withdrew my objections as to a point which had arisen as to Butler presiding over the Cabinet in the Prime Minister's absence, since this had been the practice since the beginning of Eden's administration.'[143] In fact, of course, it had been the practice ever since September 1952, in the very first year of the Churchill Government; but that there should have been any dispute about it at all remains a revealing indication of just how the power balance had changed – and Rab's position had receded – under the new Leadership.

One other Press announcement surfaced in the wake of the Cabinet changes. It said simply that 'the Prime Minister and Lady Eden have invited Mr Butler and his two younger children to spend Christmas with them at Chequers'.[144] It was, no doubt, a kindly gesture – but it is difficult not to wonder just how festive the whole atmosphere proved to be.

13 *Leader in Limbo*

Even before he left the Treasury Rab had been warned – by a friend of Macmillan's rather than his own – that he was committing 'sheer political suicide'.[1] Nor was that necessarily an exaggeration. Rab's agreement, however reluctant, to give up what is always, in effect, the second position in the Government was puzzling enough; his acquiescence in being succeeded in it by the man who was rapidly emerging as his main rival was an even greater cause for perplexity. Rab could not, though, possibly have been expected to know of all the manœuvres that had gone on behind the scenes – of which Macmillan's confession to Woolton that 'he saw no reason why if he was going to take over all the troubles of the Treasury, he should be ruled out of the succession for the Premiership in order to ease in Butler'[2] – was perhaps the most startling. (That contemporary remark is a far cry from Macmillan's unctuous denial in his own memoirs that in accepting the Chancellorship he was 'actuated by some degree of personal rivalry with Butler'.)[3]

Rab himself, however, having survived his Christmas at Chequers, seems to have accepted his new job as Leader of the House with comparative equanimity. He was officially gazetted not even as Lord President of the Council (the post held by Lord Salisbury, who kept his precedence over him in the Cabinet 'pecking order') but in the lesser office of Lord Privy Seal; he was, however, permitted to take with him to his grand new official quarters in the boardroom at the old Treasury – which Clarissa Eden* promptly wrote to tell him she was sure he would make 'both hospitable and charming'[4] – two

* Clarissa Eden (later the Countess of Avon), who was a niece of Winston Churchill, had married Anthony Eden in 1952, following the dissolution of his first marriage in 1950.

high-flyers in the Civil Service, Burke Trend* and Ian Bancroft.† No doubt confident of their ability to establish a bridgehead, Rab left in the second week of the New Year for a fortnight's holiday on Cap Ferat, staying at the Villa Mauresque which Somerset Maugham (a fellow Companion of Honour) had generously offered to loan him the previous summer.

The weather throughout the two weeks he spent there was bad but in political terms, with the reshuffle over, there should not have been a cloud in the sky. It soon, however, emerged that there was. On the Sunday that Rab left with his daughter, Sarah, for his fortnight's holiday – the first proper one he had had in two years – the *Observer* carried a front-page headline; 'Eden-Must-Go Move Grows',[5] while a more popular newspaper, the *People*, declared bluntly, 'Sir Anthony Eden is now all set to retire. He is to be succeeded by Mr Butler. The only decision left to be made is the date of the change-over.'[6]

Such was the origin of, or at least the occasion for, Rab's most famous equivocal remark ever. In a phrase that went round the world, he described Eden as 'the best Prime Minister we have'. In fact, it was not a comment he volunteered but one he had foisted on him. At Heathrow Airport, after the flurry caused by the newspaper headlines of that morning, Rab found himself accosted by a reporter from the Press Association who proceeded to put a succession of questions to him. The last one simply asked for his assent to the proposition that Sir Anthony is 'the best Prime Minister we have' – something that Rab hurriedly, if unwisely, gave. In truth, however, Rab could hardly complain: for it was he who, earlier in that same interview, had offered the possibly even more damaging statement, 'My determination is to support the Prime Minister in all his difficulties.'[7]

Rab, of course, had no reason to feel particularly warm to Eden. The final frenzied atmosphere attending the announcement of the Cabinet reshuffle on 20 December had fulfilled everyone's worst forebodings. Rab himself had taken a certain amused pleasure in remarking to anyone within earshot, 'I have been very calm':[8] that

* Burke St John Trend (1914–). Office of the Lord Privy Seal 1955–6. Deputy Secretary of the Cabinet 1956–9. Head of the Treasury 1959–62. Secretary of the Cabinet 1963–73. Created life peer 1974.

† Ian Powell Bancroft (1922–). Private Secretary to Chancellor of the Exchequer 1953–5. Lord Privy Seal 1955–7. Cabinet Office 1957–9. Then in various Departments until being appointed Permanent Secretary of the Civil Service Department and Head of the Home Civil Service in 1977. Created life peer on premature retirement in 1981.

was certainly more than could be said for a number of his colleagues, including the Prime Minister, who, in face of an incipient revolt from all the peers in the Government, led by Lord Salisbury, retired to bed half-way through the day. From this vantage-point he eventually managed, by throwing the hereditary Landed Interest an additional job or two, to buy off a grandees' rebellion, which had at one stage threatened to lead to a wholesale boycott of his Government by members of the House of Lords.

That, though, was only the comic opera side of Eden's essentially frail, nervous grasp on the arts of political leadership. A far more devastating indictment of his lack of self-confidence lay in the two entirely different stories that he had separately told to Rab and Macmillan as to the implications of the dispositions that he was making. The contrast here posed a problem for the new Downing Street Press spokesman, William Clark,* who – facing the challenge of preparing 'guidance' for the Lobby – was candidly to confess, 'It was devilishly delicate because it had to satisfy Rab that he was being promoted to virtual Deputy Prime Minister, while reassuring Macmillan that nothing of the sort was happening.'[9] Typically, the first person to spot that the Prime Minister's personal insecurities might prove to be politically fatal was, according to Clark, Macmillan himself: a diary the No. 10 Press Secretary kept at the time recorded the new Chancellor as remarking chillingly, as early as 5 January 1956, that it would be 'interesting to see whether Anthony can stay in the saddle'.[10]

For his part, Rab, initially, seems to have entertained no such apprehensions. If anything he tended, publicly at least, to try to prop the new Prime Minister up, if sometimes in a slightly patronising way:[11] the difference perhaps was that, while Macmillan was nearly three years older than Eden, Rab was almost six years younger – and, therefore, found himself subject to no equivalent temptation to hurry events along. None the less the twelve months he served under Eden, after leaving the Treasury, can hardly have rated as anything but a frustrating period for Rab. In the first place, as Henry Fairlie the political columnist of the *Spectator* (a paper traditionally friendly to Rab) brutally noted, he had not really been given a proper job to do:

* William Donaldson Clark (1916–85). Diplomatic correspondent of the *Observer* 1950–5. Public Relations Adviser to the Prime Minister September 1955–November 1956. Director of Information for the World Bank 1968–73. Vice-President for External Relations 1974–80.

> Mr Butler has been removed to a post which I do not believe exists. There is a great myth in British politics about non-departmental, supervising, wide-ranging Ministers. (The myth is usually spread by the woolly-minded who want to find a spot for a woolly-minded friend.)[12]

That may have been putting things a bit harshly; and it was hardly surprising that Rab should have promptly received a note from Edward Boyle,* his former protégé at the Treasury, urging him to pay absolutely no attention to Fairlie at all.[13] But the dilemma implicit in Rab's new role could not be disposed of quite as easily as that.

On his behalf, his new position in the Government was faithfully presented to the Press (and, therefore, indirectly to the public) as consisting in essence of three separate threads. These derived from his parliamentary responsibilities as Leader of the House, his longer-term philosophic duties as chairman of both the Research Department and the Party's advisory committee on policy, and (a fresh assignment) his internal communications function in taking over the direction of the Liaison Committee charged with the task of linking the Party organisation to the Cabinet and the Government. *The Economist*, in particular (throughout 1956 a stalwart friend and ally of Rab's), put the best face it could on this curious tripod arrangement by announcing that 'much of his work will lie unseen in the twilight field where government and party merge'.[14] Of course, in political – or at least publicity – terms, that was just the trouble. Try as he might (and did) to prevent it, so far as public visibility was concerned, Rab's star faded once he left the Treasury.

That was true even in the House of Commons. Although he rose each Thursday to answer Business Questions – and always deputised for the Prime Minister at Question Time (on the first occasion, on 26 January, having to suffer the indignity of giving the House a job description of his own duties)[15] – Rab took part in only two parliamentary debates between January and July 1956. The first of these was almost certainly not of his own choosing. In the light of

* Edward Charles Gurney Boyle (1923–81). Conservative MP, Handsworth, Birmingham 1950–70. Economic Secretary to Treasury 1955–6. Under-Secretary, Ministry of Education 1957–9. Financial Secretary to Treasury 1959–62. Minister of Education 1962–4. Vice-Chancellor Leeds University 1970–81. Created life peer 1970.

the Timothy Evans case* the Government felt compelled to allow the veteran abolitionist, Sydney Silverman,† to bring the issue of capital punishment once more before the House of Commons. It appears to have been a decision taken with some reluctance: Silverman was a most persuasive advocate and he had already carried the House of Commons once (in 1948) in favour of a trial five-year suspension of capital punishment. Nor was the Government's anxiety as to the likely outcome diminished by the fact that the Home Secretary, Major Gwilym Lloyd George,‡ was a rather stolid parliamentary performer, who had already alienated liberal opinion by refusing to reprieve Ruth Ellis in 1955. If only to defuse a potentially dangerous controversy (the Conservative Party in the constituencies stayed totally undisturbed by the Ellis or Evans cases and remained staunchly in favour of hanging), Rab found himself put up to reply to the debate – and, it was hoped, carry a Government motion which would leave open the possibility of a reform of the law of murder while preserving the principle of the ultimate sanction untouched.

Given the atmosphere of the time, in which informed and enlightened opinion was moving decisively in favour of abolition, it was probably an impossible task. Certainly, from Rab's point of view, it was an unenviable one, hardly made any more alluring by the widespread newspaper suspicion that the choice of Rab to wind up the debate amounted to a deliberate 'fix' by the Government in order to tempt its more liberal-minded supporters into its own lobby.[16] To the surprise of his admirers, however, Rab refused to go in for any half-measures. He delivered a robust defence of hanging, offering some hefty hostages to fortune along the way, including a firm statement that 'no innocent man has been hanged within living memory';§[17] perhaps even more enraging at the time to abolitionists was the view he chose to give that 'life imprisonment is infinitely more cruel than capital punishment itself'.[18] In his entire

* After the conviction of John Christie for murder at the Old Bailey in 1953, a considerable controversy had arisen over whether Timothy Evans, who lived in the same house, had not in 1950 been wrongly hanged for the murder of his wife.

† Samuel Sydney Silverman (1895–1968). Labour MP, Nelson and Colne 1935–68.

‡ Gwilym Lloyd George (1896–1967). Liberal MP, Pembrokeshire 1922–4 and 1929–50, Liberal-Conservative MP, Newcastle upon Tyne North 1951–7. Minister of Fuel and Power 1942–5. Minister of Food 1951–4. Home Secretary and Minister for Welsh Affairs 1954–7. Created 1st Viscount Tenby 1957.

§ Timothy Evans was posthumously granted a free pardon by the Queen on the advice of one of Rab's eventual successors as Home Secretary, Roy Jenkins, on 18 October 1966.

speech there was only one hint of a saving grace, his intimation towards the end (in a classic echo of a well-known Cambridge formula)[19] that 'the position is not at present ripe for amendment to the law to abolish the death penalty'.[20]

Even as a get-out clause this *coda*, however, availed him little. The *Spectator* wrote derisively of 'Mr Butler's fantasies'[21] while even *The Economist* pointedly withheld any praise from his performance; nor did Rab succeed in carrying the day in the House of Commons. The Silverman amendment was passed by a majority of 31 (with over 40 Conservatives voting for abolition) while Rab's own Government motion was defeated by the even larger margin of 46. Worse than that, Rab had stirred up some trouble for himself and the Government by announcing at the beginning of his speech, 'When we have a free vote, we naturally expect to base our actions, if perhaps after mature, further deliberation, on the decision of the House.'[22] Fortunately for him, however, he was not on this occasion left quite as exposed as he had been, nearly two years earlier, on the question of MPs' pay: at the conclusion of the capital punishment debate the Prime Minister, in reply to a question from the former Labour Home Secretary, James Chuter Ede, gave an assurance of much the same kind: at least, therefore, this time the ministerial embarrassment was collective rather than individual.

The capital punishment controversy dogged the Government throughout the spring and summer of 1956, with Rab, as Leader of the House, behaving honourably by providing time for all the stages of the eventual Silverman Bill while, understandably, refusing to make it part of the Government's own legislative programme. This denial of official support did not, however, prevent the Bill from prevailing: it was eventually carried in the Commons on its Third Reading on 28 June by a majority of 19, only to be struck down two weeks later in the House of Lords at Second Reading by a far more decisive majority of 143 (thus preparing the way for Rab's own successful handling of the compromise Homicide Bill once he became Home Secretary in 1957).

The most striking aspect of the original Bill's passage through the Commons was, however, that Rab, having played the star part in the initial debate on the principle of the issue, took no further role in its progress on the floor of the House whatsoever. It may, of course, be that this was simply the result of pique at the experience of seeing his own advice disregarded. The alternative explanation, that he felt some sense of discomfort at finding himself isolated from all his most natural supporters within the Tory Party, should not, though, automatically be discounted. Significantly, his own favoured successor nine years later as MP for Saffron Walden was to be Peter Kirk,* the man who, through all the threats and pressures from both constituency parties and the Whips' Office, kept the Conservative abolitionists together during all the stages of the Silverman Bill.

Presumably it came as a relief to Rab that his only other front-bench speech in the first half of 1956 opened up no such internal Party stresses. He was in avuncular mood when he commended the Government White Paper on technical education to the House in June – recalling that 'parity of esteem' had been one of the phrases in his own White Paper of 1944 and resolutely rejecting the idea that 'there should be any difference in social status between the technician and the man of arts'.[23] It may not have been quite the equivalent of the take-over bid that the Labour Party was to launch for the leadership of 'the white heat of the technological revolution' some seven years later; but they were still bold words for a Tory of the 1950s. The White Paper, in fact, proposed the establishment of eight new Colleges of Advanced Technology – all of which were later, in the era of the Robbins report, to be promoted to the status of universities. The newspapers of June 1956 duly reflected this new emphasis given to technology as being very much Rab's own personal achievement – an impression, it has to be said, that he did nothing to minimise with his somewhat unusual throw-away line delivered from the Despatch Box, 'Nothing that the Chancellor of the Exchequer will say will contradict this decision.'[24]

It was not, though, wholly surprising if by mid-1956 Rab had formed the view that it was high time he was given credit for something that was happening – and, as the Minister who, since the departure of Lord Swinton from the Government with Eden's take-over in April 1955, regularly met the Lobby, he was, at least theoretically, in a position to achieve that. His difficulty, however, was that the flow of criticism directed at the Government since the very beginning of 1956 had been unremitting – and that most of the attacks were directed at areas which were known to be no part of his direct responsibilities. The principal source of criticism – oddly, given the Prime Minister's long experience in this field – lay in foreign affairs, particularly over the Middle East. The summary removal of General Glubb from command of the Arab Legion by King Hussein at the beginning of March 1956 had been a body-blow

* Peter Michael Kirk (1928–77). Conservative MP, Gravesend 1955–64, Saffron Walden 1965–77. Leader Conservative Delegation to European Parliament 1973–7. Knighted 1976.

to Britain's prestige in the region; and Sir Anthony Eden's ineffective performance in a debate in the Commons arising out of the humiliation had done nothing to soften it (with *The Economist* going so far as to announce, 'In the Jordan debate Sir Anthony was bowled middle stump by Mr Gaitskell and on his own favoured wicket of foreign affairs).'[25] Worse than that, a general mood of apprehension was gradually building up over Eden himself: in particular, his very personal policy of negotiating a voluntary withdrawal of British troops from the Canal Zone in Egypt – the agreement to do so had been signed as long ago as 27 July 1954 – was widely felt to be liable to blow up in his face. It had been Eden's view all along that only by a new Treaty, involving the evacuation of the base, could Britain hope to win 'the lasting gratitude and friendship of the Egyptian Government and people';[26] with the last troops due to leave in June, it now seemed far more likely that all the withdrawal was likely to achieve was an even more militant mood of anti-British nationalism on the part of Colonel Nasser and his new regime in Egypt. Here Rab was in some genuine personal difficulty, since he had never been an enthusiast for the evacuation strategy that Eden, as Foreign Secretary, had virtually railroaded through Churchill's Cabinet.[27] He had thought it rash and reckless from the beginning but now, whatever his original reservations, it was the policy he had to defend.

Fortunately, for Rab, however, he was not required to do that in many public places (what he said in private to the Lobby – a source of growing irritation to Eden – was, of course, a different matter). Excluded from any role in the affairs of the Foreign Office, which anyway were largely controlled from No. 10, and no longer exercising any dominion over economic policy, where Macmillan had just won the battle against bread (and milk) subsidies which Rab had lost six months earlier, he was beginning to look increasingly like a marginal figure. He still appeared, of course, on ceremonial occasions, attending, for instance, all the official receptions given for Bulganin and Khrushchev on their April visit to Britain. He was also gradually assuming the mantle of the Government's ambassador to the arts: as President, since 1951, of the Royal Society of Literature he inaugurated both the National Book League's National Book Sale Week of March 1956 and the International PEN conference held in London in July 1956 (he also in May was to be found taking the lead in launching the appeal for a new women's college at Cambridge to be called New Hall). But what he did not seem to be doing was playing any very active part in politics – a phenomenon that led not only the *Spectator* in the spring to remark unkindly that he was 'a horse ready to be put out to grass'[28] but, even more damagingly, provoked the *Daily Mail* to speculate four months later that he might well be 'on his way to the House of Lords'.[29] This latter rumour Rab moved swiftly to crush, denying it in terms on the floor of the House of Commons on the same day as it appeared;[30] but the mere fact that it should have been given currency in a Conservative newspaper demonstrated just how far his position had slipped since the days when he had been seen as the only visible alternative leader to Eden himself.

There was a personal, as well as a political, reason for all this. Having endured his four years at the Treasury with apparently the constitution of an ox, Rab in the summer of 1956 became far from well. Officially it was given out that he was suffering from hay fever – a malady which had affected him off and on since his boyhood days; but that there was something more seriously wrong than that was attested to by those who had seen him fall down and faint. With the typical unkindness of politics, there were even suggestions that he was drinking too much. The true position seems, however, to have been that he had contracted a virus affecting his inner ear that led to him losing his sense of balance. Eventually on 12 July, just before he was due to deliver his third Commons speech of the year on the hardy perennial of MPs' pay, it was announced that he had been ordered home to rest – and he was not to reappear at Westminster until the end of the month.

The dates have some significance – for they meant that Rab missed the origins of the whole series of international events that were to dominate British politics for the rest of 1956 and which, eventually, in January 1957, were to blow Sir Anthony Eden out of office. Even in retrospect their abrupt arrival banishes any suspicion of their having been foreseen – still less prepared for – by the British Government. It was, of course, common knowledge that all was not going well with Britain's Middle East policy: the Baghdad Pact, the one proud achievement of Harold Macmillan's Foreign Secretaryship, had virtually collapsed, the new Foreign Secretary, Selwyn Lloyd (according to Eden's own Press spokesman), had been 'fooled in Cairo and stoned in Bahrein',[31] while the US Secretary of State, John Foster Dulles, long before Suez, had made clear his own personal antagonism to any lingering imperial echoes still implicit in Britain's Middle East policy as represented in its attitudes towards such countries as Jordan and Iraq.

In June, or even in July, no one, however, could possibly have forecast the pattern of the classic Shakespearian tragedy (in A. C.

Bradley's sense of pressures conspiring to trap a flawed character) that was to come. The events themselves, indeed, seemed to be treated initially almost as isolated incidents. The newspapers faithfully recorded on 14 June that the last remnants of the British garrison had left the Canal zone – thereby withdrawing a British military presence from Egypt for the first time since 1882; just ten days later they similarly registered the fact that Colonel Nasser, having seized power from General Neguib, had been overwhelmingly elected President of Egypt. One month to the day after that they reported that both Britain and the United States had withdrawn their promised financial assistance to the construction of the Aswan High Dam. Just three days later – though by no means universally as the lead story – the British Press also carried the news that President Nasser was proposing to nationalise the Anglo-French Suez Canal Company. Even the Sunday paper columnists on 5 August apparently saw nothing to distract them from their normal routine of giving their regular end-of-session assessments.

Thursday 2 August, the last day of the parliamentary session, admittedly, saw a Suez debate taking place on the floor of the Commons – with the Labour Opposition displaying, if anything, an even greater outrage at the action Nasser had taken than the spokesmen for the Government. To *The Times* at least that was a reassuring sign – and it was not alone in bracketing the threat to international order posed by Nasser's action with the domestic challenge represented by BMC workers in Birmingham striking against redundancies.[32] Of course, the newspapers did not know what was happening behind closed doors and, if they had, they might have taken a rather different tone. The best available evidence suggests that the die may well have been cast on the evening of Thursday 26 July. Eden had been entertaining King Faisal of Iraq to dinner at No. 10 Downing Street when, towards the end of the evening, a Private Secretary brought him the news that Nasser had seized the Suez Canal and forcibly taken over all the assets of its controlling company. The Prime Minister's Iraqi guests soon tactfully departed, and a meeting then took place in the Cabinet Room of the various Ministers who had been attending the dinner together with the three Chiefs of Staff of the Armed Services, the French Ambassador and the Chargé d'Affaires at the US Embassy. Various contradictory accounts survive of this bizarre gathering – in vain apparently did a Downing Street Private Secretary keep putting in front of the Prime Minister a reminder that by no means all of those present were bound by the Privy Councillors' secrecy oath – but the best authenticated statement to emerge remains the Prime Minister's own impassioned outburst that Nasser could not be allowed 'to have his hand on our windpipe'.[33] Once that remark was delivered, the question in the minds of those who heard it was no longer the advisability of military action but rather the best means by which it could be pursued. (Mountbatten's own later claim that, as acting Chief of the Defence Staff, he had announced that the British Government's objective could be achieved in a matter of three days is not, in fact, borne out by any other contemporary record, including his own.)[34]

The following morning, Friday 27 July, an almost full meeting of the Cabinet took place – although still without Rab, recuperating at his home at Stanstead. Once again the military options were considered, if now with a little more realism than on the previous night. The main outcome of this meeting, however, was a decision to set up a special 'Egypt Committee' – the rough equivalent of what nearly thirty years later, during the Falklands conflict, was openly called a 'War Cabinet'. It was originally constituted with six members: the Prime Minister (Eden), the Chancellor (Macmillan), the Lord President of the Council (Salisbury), the Foreign Secretary (Selwyn Lloyd), the Commonwealth Secretary (Home) and the Defence Secretary (Monckton).* Rab was not present when this decision was taken; it is hard, however, to accept that it was solely for that reason that the number two figure in the Commons was excluded from membership of what was plainly to be for the next few weeks or months easily the most important sub-committee of the Cabinet. For one reason or another, even at this early stage of the crisis, Rab seems to have qualified for membership of the company which Eden was later patronisingly to call 'the weak sisters'. At least, the Prime Minister's ultimate condemnation – that some of these 'weak sisters' were subsequently to be found among 'those who were toughest at the outset of the journey' – could not conceivably be said to apply to him.[35]

What, though, was Rab's precise part in the events that led up to Britain's greatest post-war humiliation? It was a subject on which he always tended to be evasive – and certainly the private written records that he preserved from the period are singularly unilluminating. In a sense, of course, he was a prisoner of his own published

* Walter Turner Monckton (1891–1965). Conservative MP, Bristol West 1951–7. Solicitor-General 1945. Minister of Labour and National Service 1951–5. Minister of Defence 1955–6. Paymaster-General 1956–7. Created 1st Viscount Monckton of Brenchley 1957.

statements. For motives that remain obscure, he committed himself during the crucial months to two extremely injudicious public pronouncements: first, his rousing announcement to the Tory faithful at the Llandudno Party Conference in October, 'I have served under five Prime Ministers in different times . . . and I have never known the qualities of courage, integrity and flair more clearly represented than in our present Prime Minister',[36] and secondly, and even more unwisely, his astonishing assertion to the House of Commons on 13 November 1956, when all was over, that he had never wavered in his support for the Suez policy and, indeed, had been proud to be a member of 'a united Government and a united Party'.[37]

Neither of those statements carried much conviction even at the time they were delivered – it was, in fact, common political gossip that Rab had played some part in dragging the Government back from the brink of military action both at the beginning of August and again after the failure of the Suez Canal Users Association Conference held in London in September. It is important, however, not to over-emphasise the divergence of view that existed within the Cabinet. There was never any question of Rab (or even Walter Monckton, who played a much more openly critical role – moving, at his own request, from the Ministry of Defence to the Paymaster-Generalship in October, one week before the invasion) wishing simply to acquiesce in Nasser's action as a *fait accompli*: the disagreement was over means and not ends – and ultimately centred on a scheme, floated by Macmillan as early as 7 August, to rely on the prospect of Israel attacking Egypt to provide Britain with its best potential *casus belli*.[38] By contrast, Rab's aim all along was the more limited one of trying to save the Canal for international use – and (though he never seems to have opposed the use of force formally) that meant he was disposed to give a far greater weight to the provisions of international law, and in particular the enforceability of treaties, than were some of his more hot-headed colleagues.[39]

He was not, however, as has been noticed, at all in the confidence of the Prime Minister – or, indeed, involved in the inner counsels of the Egypt Committee (though he did subsequently take to turning up at some of its meetings)*; this remained particularly true during the climax of the crisis. In fact, there is some evidence that he was deliberately kept remote from the decision-making process. Thus,

* Rab attended an early meeting of the Egypt Committee on 30 July, the day of his return to London. He also, in the absence of Eden and Lord Salisbury, chaired a meeting of the committee held on 8 October. Robert Rhodes James, *Anthony Eden* (Weidenfeld & Nicolson, 1986), pp. 469, 524.

during the third week in October, when Eden and Selwyn Lloyd flew to Paris to concert invasion plans with the French, Rab found himself first on a Conservative Party tour in Scotland and then enrolled as the Minister in attendance on the Queen as she opened the new Calder Hall nuclear power station in Cumbria. It certainly looked as if someone had taken a decision that he was safer out of the way – the more so, as at Calder Hall he was merely deputising for Lord Salisbury, who at this stage was now reported to be the one member of the Cabinet to enjoy the Prime Minister's total confidence.[40]

Yet Rab's seniority in the Government meant that it was very difficult for him afterwards to claim that he was somehow removed from the policy the rest of his colleagues were pursuing. Admittedly, there were signs that he regarded the whole Suez episode as a tiresome distraction – not least because that autumn he had at last begun to rebuild his political reputation: in October he had been elected Rector of Glasgow University, handily defeating the former Labour Prime Minister Lord Attlee, and he had also enjoyed a considerable personal success at the Conservative Party Conference at Llandudno, delivering three separate speeches (including a very well-received address to the Conservative Political Centre), entirely wiping out the memory of his unhappy experience the previous year.[41] It would hardly have been surprising therefore, given his belief in the power of reason in human affairs, if Rab, especially after the eventual reference of the dispute to the United Nations, had simply come to the conclusion that no enterprise so irrational as an invasion of Egypt could possibly take place. Certainly, that was the impression that he contrived to give to the more agitated of his back-bench or junior ministerial colleagues who risked raising their sense of alarm with him. One such, even thirty years later, could still recall accosting him in the Athenaeum and boldly advancing four separate reasons why any Suez military adventure could not possibly succeed – only to be greeted 'with a poker face and a series of unintelligible noises'.[42] The truth probably was that, having – as he believed – held back Eden, Salisbury and Macmillan from precipitate military action in both August and September, Rab had convinced himself that he could do the same, if need be, in October.

It did not take long, however, for him to be disabused. Rab returned to London from Calder Hall in time to attend a Cabinet meeting held on Thursday 18 October. The Prime Minister and the Foreign Secretary had just flown back from Paris, where they had had talks with the French Prime Minister, Guy Mollet, and the

French Foreign Minister, Christian Pineau. Rab was to paint a vivid word picture in his memoirs of how, having had his arm gripped by Selwyn Lloyd in the Cabinet ante-room, he was subjected to an alarmed rundown on all that had occurred by a plainly badly rattled British Foreign Secretary. According to this same account, before he could give Lloyd any comfort or reassurance, Rab was summoned by Eden to join him alone in the Cabinet Room. There the Prime Minister repeated to Rab the gist of what he had already been told:

> He confirmed that it was suggested with Mollet and Pineau that in the event of war between Israel and Egypt we should go in with the French to separate the combatants and occupy the Canal. I asked whether a war between Israel and Jordan was not more likely. He replied that in such an event we should have to keep our word to defend Jordan against attack: the French had therefore been asked to make this clear to Israel. I was impressed by the audacity of thinking behind this plan but concerned about the public reaction. I wondered whether an agreement with the French and the Israelis, designed to free the Suez Canal and eventually to internationalise it, would not meet our objective, but the Prime Minister indicated that things were now moving in the direction he had described, and in all the circumstances I said I would stand by him.[43]

If there was a single moment when Rab crossed his own Suez Rubicon, this was clearly it – an impression reinforced by Selwyn Lloyd's recollection of the subsequent Cabinet meeting:

> Eventually it was accepted by Butler and the rest of the Cabinet that we and the French should intervene to protect the Canal, if Israel moved against Egypt. The feeling was that, although we should continue to seek a negotiated settlement, it was possible, or indeed probable, that the issue would be brought to a head as the result of a military action by Israel against Egypt.[44]

Two questions necessarily arise. Why did Rab finally capitulate to a plan that, for all his reference to its 'audacity', can hardly have come as a shock to him since, as has been seen, it had been first floated by Macmillan as long ago as 7 August? And, secondly, in going along with it, how much did he know, or even suspect, of its essentially collusive nature?

The second question can be more easily answered than the first.

On 18 October the secret synchronising arrangements with the Israelis had not yet been made – Selwyn Lloyd was not to visit the villa at Sèvres, where he met Ben-Gurion and Moshe Dayan, until Monday 22 October and the so-called 'Secret Treaty' was not to be signed until Wednesday 24 October when a senior Foreign Office official, Sir Patrick Dean,* made a second trip, this time to tie up loose ends with both the French and the Israelis and, finally, to sign a document carefully called merely 'a record of discussion'. Rab can, therefore, be acquitted on the count of having knowingly condoned collusion – he was always, in fact, to maintain that he knew nothing of the arrangements entered into at Sèvres until well after they had been made.[45]

The far more difficult question, though, is why Rab consented to the scheme, even as a contingency plan. It embodied, after all, everything that he had resisted over the past two-and-a-half months. 'In the modern world', he had insisted more than once over the previous weeks, 'you simply can't drop bombs out of a clear blue sky';[46] and yet here he was supporting what was essentially a pre-emptive strike against Nasser, and thereby throwing away the one card on whose importance he had insisted throughout, the security of Britain's position under international law. Rab was also – or at least should have been – quite worldly-wise enough to know what the likely transatlantic reaction to an invasion based essentially on a pretext would be, especially in a US presidential election year. Of course, there was nothing enthusiastic about the statement, 'in all the circumstances I said I would stand by him' – but the Chancellor of two or three years earlier would surely have summoned up the courage to give quite different, and more unwelcome, advice. Why, therefore, it has to be asked, did Rab – once he knew what was being contemplated – not at least try and stop the invasion by threatening resignation?

There is, inevitably, always the argument that more can be done to temper a policy from within than by denouncing it from without – and in his latter years this tended to be the position that Rab took up over Suez. He was also not above giving the impression that he sensed from the beginning that the whole thing would end in fiasco and that, therefore, someone would need to be in place to pick up the pieces. Neither point, however, reflected much awareness of the standing he enjoyed with his admirers – and, if there was one

* Patrick Henry Dean (1908–). Deputy Under-Secretary of State, Foreign Office 1956–60. Permanent UK Representative to the United Nations 1960–4. Ambassador in Washington 1965–9.

particularly painful moment for Rab during the whole Suez episode, it must have come when he learned that his own most faithful political follower, Edward Boyle, was quite determined to resign from the Government in protest against the action which had been taken.

For Rab himself, though, there was clearly no going back after the Cabinet meeting of 18 October, or at least after the two further meetings held on 24 and 25 October when the earlier contingency decisions were, in effect, formulated and ratified. He had cast his lot in with an enterprise in which he did not believe and he now faced the prospect of living with the consequences. Mercifully on the human, as opposed to the political or economic, level, they turned out to be neither lacerating nor long-lasting.* The Israeli attack on Egypt went in on 29 October, a British-French ultimatum calling on the combatants to withdraw ten miles from each side of the Canal was delivered to both Israel and Egypt (who rejected it) the very next day and on 31 October the bombing of Egyptian airfields began. Airborne landings followed on 5 November, a sea-borne invasion on 6 November and on that very same day at midnight the order for a general cease-fire was given.

The real drama, in fact, had taken place not in the streets of Port Said nor on the banks of the Canal, but at the UN in New York and on the transatlantic telephone between the White House and Downing Street. Even before the British and French troops landed, the General Assembly of the United Nations had carried a resolution demanding an instant cease-fire – a demand that President Eisenhower, facing re-election on the following Tuesday, was to follow up in even more peremptory terms through the American Ambassador in London. The day before the British and French parachute landings, there was even genuine doubt as to whether there was any need for them to take place. On Sunday 4 November a report reached London that the Israelis, having attained most of their objectives, were about to stop fighting: it was pounced on by Rab who, during an unusual Sunday Cabinet meeting, insisted on being told why, if hostilities had ceased, an invasion was still necessary to stop them. This question, as he proudly recorded fifteen years later, 'seemed to nonplus the Prime Minister' – who was driven into

* A White Paper, published after the operation was over, gave an estimate of 650 Egyptian dead in Port Said and 100 in Port Fuad, where the French had attacked: Sir Edwin Herbert, *Report on Damage and Casualties in Port Said* (Cmnd 47). The total of British servicemen who lost their lives was 16 while the French forces suffered 10 fatal casualties.

announcing that 'he must go upstairs and consider his position'.*[47] Unfortunately, the report proved a false one, and Eden was reprieved – if only for forty-eight hours. For on 6 November Macmillan had to inform the Cabinet that Britain had lost $270 million in reserves in the first few days of November and that there was no hope of staunching this haemorrhage until a cease-fire had been announced and a guarantee given of readiness to withdraw from the Canal. If it was a bitter pill for most members of the Cabinet to swallow, it must have felt like balm to Rab. Indeed, that evening he was reported as having sat on the front-bench 'smiling broadly' – and had earlier astonished the House by announcing that he would not 'hesitate to convey' the various arguments made by the Leader of the Opposition to the Prime Minister.[48]

The ultimate vindication, as events turned out, had thus been Rab's – but it had certainly been bought at a price. Reginald Maudling, at the time Minister of Supply (and a long-time personal admirer), was to comment in his *Memoirs* that Rab had given 'the impression that he was lifting his skirt to avoid the dirt',[49] while even Sir Anthony Eden's Downing Street Press Secretary, William Clark – whose resignation was announced, alongside Edward Boyle's, once the fighting was over – could not resist the exclamation in his diary, 'The way Rab has turned and trimmed!'[50] And, in truth, his had been a slightly convoluted course. On 31 October, the day the bombings had begun, Rab, deputising for the Prime Minister, had delivered a speech bitterly critical of the Americans to the Guild of British Newspaper Editors: driving back in the car he had confided in Clark that he was still sure that Eden was 'mistaken to ignore the UN' – drawing on his head the deserved rebuke that it was equally dangerous 'to be so anti-American'.[51] Nor did Rab exactly commend himself to Clark by writing him a letter once the crisis was over, saying:

> You know, I think, that I understand – and admire – the reasons which led you to take the course which you did . . . The last few weeks have been neither pleasurable nor – at any rate in a personal sense – profitable. But I felt I was able, and equipped, to do certain things; and the salvage operation has gone ahead pretty well; perhaps rather better than the literal one in the Canal . . . For obvious reasons I have marked this letter personal: I know you will understand.[52]

* This account of what happened in the presence of the full Cabinet is challenged by Robert Rhodes James. *Anthony Eden*, p.567.

The 'salvage operation', of course, was a reference to the legacy of Suez – which it soon fell to Rab to discharge. Maybe, as has been indicated, he had suspected all along that this would happen; but he could hardly have counted on the speed with which it came about. Eden, who had already fallen ill once during the crisis (being secretly admitted to University College Hospital, where he was visiting his wife, during the first weekend of October) suffered a further bout of high fever in the middle of November. On Monday 18 November a dramatic midnight communiqué from No. 10 announced that 'the Prime Minister is suffering from the effects of severe overstrain' – and intimated that he had finally accepted the advice of his doctors of 'the need of release from work as soon as possible'. Nothing was said in the official communiqué as to who would run the Government in the Prime Minister's absence; but the Press guidance from Downing Street was that 'Mr Butler will be in effective charge of affairs so long as Sir Anthony is absent'.[53] Rab, therefore, found himself poised to step into the place that he had always half-foreseen.

It was not an easy inheritance. In the role, as some newspapers unkindly pointed out, of 'the understudy', Rab suddenly discovered himself cast to take over the starring part in a production for which the notices had been dreadful and the box office returns even worse. Nor, so far as the Tory Party was concerned, was his performance likely to carry any great conviction. Whatever credit he might have attracted as a result of his bewildering, belated defence of the Government's Suez policy in the Commons on 13 November 1956 had been dissipated the very next night when, in the supposed privacy of a Commons dining-room, he had rashly blurted out all that had gone on (not leaving out the threat to sterling) to some twenty right-wing MPs who were members of the so-called Progress Trust. 'Wherever I moved in the weeks that followed,' Rab was to write in his own memoirs, 'I felt the party knives sticking into my innocent back.'[54]

In the immediate crisis, however, there was no time for self-pity. The American Administration, following a series of three increasingly peremptory telephone calls from Eisenhower to Eden on the day after the cease-fire was announced, ending up with the President firmly turning down the idea of a three-power meeting in Washington, had simply refused to have any further direct dealings with the British Prime Minister. Moreover, it was becoming increasingly clear that neither Britain nor France was to be allowed to rescue anything from the wreckage of their ill-fated adventure.

Following a resolution successfully carried through the United

Nations by Lester Pearson, the Canadian Foreign Minister, a UN Emergency Force was to take over the claimed Anglo-French 'peace-keeping' role in and around the Canal: there was no question of either British or French troops being allowed to participate. Nor were the two 'aggressor' nations to be permitted any part in clearing the Canal, deliberately blocked by Nasser in the aftermath of the invasion: that was a job to be left to countries, like Sweden, Norway and Yugoslavia, whose hands were clean. The message, in fact, was stern and unrelenting: the British and French Governments must withdraw their forces unconditionally from Egypt – and there was to be no bargaining even over such matters as salving pride or saving face.

It was Rab's misfortune that he should have taken over the responsibility for running the Government at precisely the moment when the true punitive nature of those terms – in effect imposed by the United States – was just beginning to sink into the collective consciousness of the Conservative Party. The first reactions were predictable enough: a wave of anti-American sentiment swept through the Party in the Commons and, with over 100 signatures on the Order Paper accusing the US Administration of 'gravely endangering the Atlantic Alliance', was threatening to get out of hand. It was against this background – not exactly helped by the Prime Minister's simultaneous announcement that he was proposing to spend the next two or three weeks convalescing at Ian Fleming's house, Goldeneye, in the West Indies – that Rab decided that he had no alternative but to spell out the new facts of international life to the Government's supporters in the Commons.

He did it in the first instance from the Despatch Box. It was a low-key performance; but it amounted to a tacit recognition – the first to come from the British Government – that from now on there was no further purpose in British troops remaining in Egypt:

> We are witnessing an attempt by the United Nations to organise an effective intervention in an area which has long threatened the peace of the world. This intervention has been made possible by Franco-British action. If this United Nations intervention succeeds, a precedent will have been set which will give mankind hope for the future.[55]

They were carefully chosen words but their import cannot have deceived anyone. British forces were going to be evacuated from Port Said – indeed, Rab had simultaneously announced, as an earnest of the British Government's intention, a readiness immediately to withdraw one infantry battalion. That day – Thursday 22 November – the Conservative Party came as near to mutiny as it had done at any time during the whole Suez imbroglio. Not that Rab, and the realistic view he represented, were entirely without support. One of the very few letters he kept from the Suez period came from the Secretary of State for Air, Nigel Birch* – who, extraordinarily, given his responsibilities, had never even been made a member of the Cabinet's Egypt Committee. Written the same day as Rab delivered his Commons statement, it ran as follows:

> I am sorry I missed your meeting yesterday afternoon. Until I was told by the Minister of Defence I had not realised the nearness of the crisis in the party. As you know, I always wanted to play the Suez hand long and expressed my views about the actual drop on Port Said very strongly in Cabinet. I may be out of date – one is always faced with a *fait accompli* as a Minister outside the Cabinet – but it does seem to me essential now to cut our losses and go along with UNO. To sit at Port Said with a UN force and a blocked canal in front of you, and the threat of oil sanctions behind you, seems a high price to pay for the smiles of the Suez Group. They are not the only people in the party whose feelings can be outraged.[56]

There was probably not a word in that with which Rab disagreed – though in public at least he was inhibited from using phrases like 'cut our losses'. As his Commons statement showed, he still felt under a compulsion to maintain the pretence that some good anyway had come out of the Suez operation – if only by summoning the United Nations Organisation to its peace-keeping responsibilities. So far as the right wing of the Conservative Party was concerned, that was not, however, an easy case to sell; and it was perhaps understandable that when Rab went that same evening to address the angry ranks of the 1922 Committee – never his favourite audience – he should have felt it only prudent to be accompanied by the Chancellor, Harold Macmillan.

From the perspective of his own ultimate Leadership prospects, this joint appearance turned out to be a highly expensive mistake. Rab spoke first – briefly, sombrely and somewhat flatly (even if

* Nigel Chetwode Birch (1906–81). Conservative MP Flintshire 1945–50, West Flint 1950–70. Minister of Works 1954–5. Secretary of State for Air 1955–7. Economic Secretary to the Treasury 1957–8. Created life peer as Lord Rhyl 1970.

25 Rab with Anthony Eden before the latter became Prime Minister. One of Rab's difficulties was 'his inability to take Eden wholly seriously'

26 At Chequers with Harold Macmillan. Peter Thorneycroft, restored to the Cabinet after his resignation as Chancellor, is behind them

27 The installation ceremony at the University of Glasgow on 21 February 1958. 'It was, of course, a lamentable scene'

he was rewarded with a scribbled note from the chairman, John Morrison, 'Well done. If I may humbly say so, I think the general feeling is okay now – from both ends!')[57] Macmillan, by contrast, turned in a veritable political organ voluntary lasting thirty-five minutes – pulling out every stop and striking every majestic chord in his well-practised repertoire, including a *tremolo* on his own advancing years. According to Enoch Powell who, as a back-bench Conservative MP, was present, 'One of the most horrible things that I remember in politics was seeing the two of them at that 1922 Committee Meeting – seeing the way in which Harold Macmillan, with all the skill of the old actor manager, succeeded in false-footing Rab. The sheer devilry of it verged upon the disgusting.'[58] His, however, was a minority view. In the version in the *Manchester Guardian* the following morning, it was Macmillan who was reported to have been 'particularly effective' – and that was said to have been conceded even by 'the more moderate Tories'.[59] So far as admiration from that quarter was concerned, Rab may well have compounded his original error in consenting to joint billing with the Chancellor: the strategy, worked out in advance, apparently was that Rab should direct his appeal to the right of the Party while Macmillan 'concentrated on the Centre and the Left' (thereby, as the *Sunday Times* shrewdly noticed, 'dissociating himself from the Right.')[60]

At least the two of them, against all the odds, had succeeded in keeping the Party together – 'I held the Tory Party for the weekend, it was all I intended to do' – Macmillan was to comment of his own performance afterwards:[61] it was probably an unduly modest assessment both of aspiration and achievement – for what he had really done that evening was to lay down his marker for the succession, whenever that might occur. Rab, on the other hand, as the Martha of the administration, faced the task of having to deal with all the chores of Government. Most of them, of course, still consisted of dealing with the aftermath of the Suez fiasco – and here Rab, at least in one respect, was lucky. One of his old friends from his own days as Chancellor was the US Secretary of the Treasury, George Humphrey. According to his own account, he had scarcely taken over the reins of Government in No. 10 before he was rung up by Humphrey from his home in Georgia. 'Rab,' the Treasury Secretary told him, 'the President cannot help you unless you conform to the United Nations resolution about withdrawal. If you do that, we will help you to save the pound.'[62] Characterising the statement as 'blackmail', Rab none the less did nothing to resist. With not much help from Goldeneye, where Eden was not even on the telephone, arrangements were set in train for a complete evacuation of the British Expeditionary Force from Port Said. The last troops, in fact, left on 23 December – and by then the Government was at least back on speaking terms with the US Administration, most directly through Rab's own channel of communication with Humphrey (Eisenhower had pointedly refused even to receive Selwyn Lloyd while he was still fighting Britain's forlorn battle at the UN debates in November).

There has been some suggestion, notably in a hostile biography of Eden published well after his death,[63] that one of the implicit conditions attached to a normal resumption of Anglo-American relations was that the British Government should find a new Prime Minister – and not one tainted, as Eisenhower apparently believed Eden to be, with the deceit practised upon him over Suez. The evidence for this thesis would seem to consist of some excitable comments passed on to the White House by the then US Ambassador in London, Winthrop Aldrich, and also in some notably conspiratorial correspondence between Brendan Bracken and Lord Beaverbrook (neither of them notably reliable witnesses). Certainly, there is nothing in Rab's own records of the crisis to support any such contention : in fact, rather the reverse since, even after Eden's return from Goldeneye, Rab was to receive a pressing invitation from George Humphrey to spend a few days with him and his wife in Georgia – 'We would plan it any moment that it might be possible for you to come.'[64] What seems to have occurred is that Macmillan, for motives of his own, tried very hard to get to see Eisenhower – and that this plea (made behind both Eden's and Rab's back) was passed on by the US Ambassador in London to the White House.[65] Naturally, the request was refused; but that cannot help seeming a frail foundation on which to build a theory of the US Administration being unwilling to talk to the British Government until its leadership was changed.

Eden returned from Jamaica – looking remarkably bronzed, in contrast to the pallid Rab, who met him at Heathrow – on 14 December 1956. To the airport reporters he appeared full of self-confidence,* but that does not seem to have survived the embarrassment with which he was received by his Cabinet colleagues. The more

* The Press statement he delivered at the airport had, however, been composed for him – over his own objections – by a triumvirate consisting of Rab, Salisbury and Selwyn Lloyd. Their insistence that the Prime Minister could use only words that they had approved hardly suggested a position of much residual political strength. Rhodes James, *Anthony Eden*, pp.590–1.

lurid accounts of the time even have him confronting a deputation (of which Rab was supposed to have been a member) requiring him to resign, at least by the spring, on the very day he got back into Downing Street.[66] Nothing as dramatic as that took place – if only because Eden, having announced his intention of carrying on from the airport, stayed only overnight at Downing Street for a medical examination before driving to Chequers where, the next day, he received separately Lord Salisbury at lunch and Rab at dinner. His Press and parliamentary reception must, though, have given the Prime Minister pause: it was bad enough that a left-wing weekly should have carried the headline on the day of his return 'Prime Minister visits Britain';[67] worse, from the political point of view, was his embarrassingly cool welcome in the House of Commons on 17 December, when only one Tory MP forlornly rose to his feet to cheer.[68] But, because of the Christmas recess, the Prime Minister at least was delivered a breathing space. Certainly Rab – reassured, no doubt, by *The Economist*'s judgment ('If Sir Anthony were to lay down the Premiership tomorrow, there is really no doubt that the Queen would be constitutionally bound to send for Mr Butler')[69] – seems to have had absolutely no premonition of the subtle political *bouleversement* that was to take place in the New Year. His engagement diary reveals, in fact, that most of his time over the next fortnight was spent shooting.

He had, it is true, been summoned to lunch at Chequers on 27 December – but he had not been invited alone. He had gone in the company of five other senior Cabinet Ministers – and, significantly, it was not Rab but the Lord Chancellor, Kilmuir, who was asked to stay behind afterwards for a private tête-à-tête. To Kilmuir Eden seems to have conveyed something of his doubts over how far he could legitimately hope to be anything more in the future than a 'Prime Minister at half-cock . . . unable to give a lead over the grave questions that faced us'.[70] Kilmuir, however, appears to have done his best to steady his chief's nerve – but it was still a pretty cheerless Cabinet that Eden presided over on Thursday 3 January 1957.

There was worse news, however, to come. Sir Horace Evans, his official medical adviser, had become sufficiently alarmed by Eden's condition – the fevers had returned and so had insomnia – to insist on calling in a second and a third opinion. The advice from all three doctors, delivered on 7 January, was unanimous: if the Prime Minister wished to live, he must lay down his burden. At first Eden fought against the verdict – insisting that both Lord Salisbury and the Earl of Scarbrough, Lord Chamberlain of the Queen's Household, personally cross-examine Evans as to the real validity of his professional judgment. This appeal to the opinions of lay assessors did, however, no good; and Salisbury had the uncongenial task of informing the man with whom he had resigned in 1938 that there was now no alternative to a second resignation. The question of how far Salisbury based his case on political as well as strictly medical grounds must remain unresolved – but at least the proprieties were publicly observed. On the night Eden resigned, the medical bulletin accompanying the news could hardly have been more emphatic or more trenchant:

> The Prime Minister's health gives cause for anxiety. In spite of the improvement which followed his rest before Christmas, there has been a recurrence of abdominal symptoms. This gives us much concern because of the serious operations in 1953 and some subsequent attacks of fever. In our opinion his health will no longer enable him to sustain the heavy burdens inseparable from the office of Prime Minister.[71]

Afterwards Rab was, to some extent, to reproach himself for not noticing what was going on. Even while acting as head of the Government in No. 10, he had, he subsequently wrote, been 'aware that frequent talks and reunions took place in the study at No. 11'.[72] But there was, of course, very little that he could do about that (even if he did wryly notice that those whom Macmillan saw most often were also later those who were most loftily elevated). But, in fact, Macmillan had not sought to disguise his feeling that the Prime Minister was 'done for'. He had been a particular opponent (as was Rab to a lesser degree) of the decision to go to Goldeneye and had predicted, only just inaccurately, that, if Eden went there, he would never come back, at least as Prime Minister.[73] The Chancellor had also warned Rab, on the day after Eden's return, that a number of the younger members of the Cabinet thought he could not possibly continue – a view at the time that Rab rejected, preferring the considered assessments of the Chief Whip and the Chairman of the Party, who both thought that the Prime Minister should at least be able to get through until the summer recess.

To be fair to Rab, he does appear to have modified this view early in the New Year, when he seems to have been made aware of the kind of reactions that MPs were getting in the constituencies – 'They found it impossible to answer the question in the pubs as to why we did not go further down the Canal.'[74] That, as Rab realised, was hardly good news for him: for if the decision to launch the Suez Expedition was plainly Eden's, the responsibility for winding it up was equally clearly seen as belonging to Rab. If there was going to have to be one scapegoat, was it not perhaps fairer that there should be two? The question may never have been put in those specific terms – but it is hard to believe that it did not lie behind the strong elements of resistance to Rab, particularly prevalent, for instance, in the old right-wing Suez Group. It was, of course, a manifest injustice: everything Rab had done between 20 November and 14 December had had the full approval of the Cabinet, the eager endorsement of Macmillan and at least the reluctant acquiescence (by cable) of Eden. No inside stories in politics, however, are ever a match for public images – and in the popular mind, just as Eden was the man who sent the troops in, so Rab was the man who brought them out.

It had, in its own way, been a considerable achievement, as Rab in his later years was quite ready to point out, 'I got the troops out, I restored the pound and, through my friendship with George Humphrey, I re-established the Alliance.'[75] All of those things, in fact, were true but they were not somehow feats of glory – or at least they did not seem so in January 1957. There is no concrete evidence that Rab had anything to do with persuading Eden to resign (though, interestingly, the Prime Minister's doctor, Sir Horace Evans, who was also Rab's, did write him a slightly ambiguous letter after Macmillan had become Prime Minister expressing his gratitude for 'your help and guidance over my difficult problems with AE' – and adding, slightly mysteriously, 'Here we have made, I have no doubt, the right decision.')[76] Taken at face-value, that does perhaps raise just a doubt as to how far Eden's decision to go on the grounds of ill-health was a purely voluntary one: any notion, however, that Rab had anything more to do with it, over and above receiving rather more advance notice of the announcement than most of his colleagues, must remain purely speculative – the more so as the direct political pressure on Eden seems to have come from quite a different quarter. As Rab was belatedly to discover, a secret meeting of four Cabinet Ministers had taken place on the very day the public drama of Eden's resignation began to unfold – and all four of these had been Macmillan's supporters rather than his own.[77] This cabal may not have had any assurance of victory; but they do seem to have grasped the fact that, if Eden could be persuaded to go promptly, they would be playing the next Leadership match on the ground, and at the time, of their own choosing. Rab, by contrast, never appears to have made an equivalent political tactical appreciation – thus guaranteeing, ultimately, that personal bitterness was added to the shock of political defeat. The best that could be said was that it was all over fairly speedily – so speedily, in fact, that Rab was later to make this one of his principal grounds of suspicion.

Undeniably, events moved fast. On Tuesday 8 January 1957 it was announced that the Prime Minister would be paying a visit to Sandringham to resume the practice of a weekly audience with the Queen. The next day (Sir Anthony having stayed the night at Sandringham), it was rather mysteriously given out that a visit to her dressmaker necessitated the Queen's own return to London. It was only a holding cover-story, for just after six that same evening – Wednesday 9 January – the Prime Minister's car drove into the forecourt of Buckingham Palace. Half-an-hour later when he got back into it to be driven away, Sir Anthony Eden was the Queen's First Minister no more. The Sovereign could, of course, have accepted her Prime Minister's resignation at Sandringham; but that, as it were, was the routine part of the business. A much more delicate matter was the operation of the succession – which, in the most awkward circumstances possible, it now fell to the young Queen to resolve by use of the Royal Prerogative.

The original expectation appears to have been that Eden's successor would be summoned to the Palace that same evening – a prospect that caused some alarm to the Macmillan supporters, who suspected, rightly, that any purely automatic summons could only favour Rab.[78] They had already won the first round, therefore, when it was intimated that there would be no further announcement that night and that the Queen, following the precedent of the hand-over from Churchill to Eden in April 1955, would wait till the next day to ask a new Prime Minister to form a Government. If that was reassuring news for Macmillan, it was not yet alarming tidings for Rab: indeed, his mood remained one of quiet confidence – quiet because he took himself home to a family supper in Smith Square, confident because during the course of the meal he filled his sister's heart with foreboding by asking, 'What shall I say in my broadcast to the nation tomorrow?'[79]

Macmillan, meanwhile, put on much more of a showman's exhibition. Leaving his home, No. 11 Downing Street, at around half-past eight he proceeded, with his wife and his daughter, to parade down Whitehall on foot pursued by photographers and journalists. Turning into Whitehall Court he was heard to inquire, 'Which is Lord Woolton's flat?' – a piece of knowledge that might have been assumed to be already available to him: having established its whereabouts on the top floor, and having also ensured that everyone knew where he was going, he entered the flat, remaining closeted with the former Chairman of the Conservative Party for the next three hours.[80] He did not return to 11 Downing Street until half-past eleven.

It may, of course, be that by then Macmillan had gathered rather better intelligence of the events of the coming day than had Rab. Eden's last Cabinet – held at five o'clock on the evening of Wednesday 9 January – had ended, after the withdrawal of the Prime Minister, accompanied by both Rab and Macmillan, with each of its remaining fourteen members being asked individually in an ante-room by Lord Salisbury and the Lord Chancellor for their views on the succession. It is traditionally claimed that this early version of a TV 'exit poll' disclosed a massive majority for Macmillan; and certainly only three possible votes for Rab have ever been identified.* If that was the case, the news would almost certainly have seeped out to Macmillan that evening: no bandwagon is ever more popular than that of a prospective Prime Minister.

The rest was simply ritual. Whether Eden, who was certainly asked, gave any specific recommendation as to his successor is still a matter of some dispute; but certainly the next morning, Thursday 10 January, the Queen was visited by both Lord Salisbury (who presumably presented his colleagues' views rather than his own personal ones) and Sir Winston Churchill (who apparently advised for Macmillan, on the grounds that he was 'more decisive').[81] Some time around noon the phone rang in No. 11 Downing Street, and the Chancellor was asked whether he could be at the Palace at two o'clock. A message of a more depressing kind went via Ted Heath (the Chief Whip)† to Rab; that lunchtime he was to be found strolling solitarily along the Embankment – helpfully explaining to a curious cameraman, 'I'm taking a walk – the best thing to do in the circumstances.'[82]

Undoubtedly, the shock to Rab was all the greater, since that

* These Rab believed to have been those of Walter Monckton, Patrick Buchan-Hepburn and James Stuart – all of whom left the Cabinet when Macmillan formed his new Government.

† Edward Richard George Heath (1916–). Conservative MP, Bexley 1950–74, Bexley, Sidcup 1974– . Government Chief Whip 1955–9. Minister of Labour 1959–60. Lord Privy Seal attached to the Foreign Office 1960–3. Secretary of State for Industry, Trade and Regional Development 1963–4. Leader of the Opposition 1965–70. Prime Minister 1970–4. Leader of the Opposition for second time, until defeated by Margaret Thatcher as Conservative Leader, 1974–5.

morning virtually every newspaper had predicted that it would be he who would be called to the Palace – and even *The Times*, which shrewdly stopped short of making any factual forecast, nevertheless gave his cause a warm editorial endorsement. It was, of course, the old story. Rab had strength everywhere – except where he most needed it, amid what Reginald Maudling was later to call 'the blue blood and thunder group' of the Tory Party.[83]

An avalanche of letters descended upon Rab in his disappointment – messages of sympathy (and outrage) coming from doctors, clergymen, diplomats, teachers, lawyers and the like: very few, since the nature of politics is to be on the winning side, seem to have been sent by active politicians, least of all Conservative ones.* Perhaps the nearest approach to filling that gap was one that belatedly arrived from the Bahamas. It did not beat about the bush, beginning, 'I am sorry you have been deprived of your Estate' – and going on to make two points of political substance:

1) If the House of Commons had been given the opportunity to decide the leadership, your selection was certain.
2) If the constituencies had been consulted, the result would have been in your favour – and very emphatically so.[84]

Both points were probably disputable – but the writer could at least claim to be a pioneer, forestalling, for example, Iain Macleod† and his thesis about the 'magic circle' in the *Spectator* by a matter of some seven years.[85] Maybe, however, that was not a cause for any great astonishment. The man who wrote the letter was a natural-born journalist who, while never a great admirer of Rab's, certainly had an eye for the character of Tory politics. His name was Max Aitken, 1st Baron Beaverbrook – and he, at least, would have known what Rab was driving at when, in the aftermath of defeat, he privately identified as one of the main factors for his failure 'the "ambience" and connections of the present incumbent of the post at Number 10'.[86]

* Rab did, however, receive a very touching letter from Clarissa Eden which, without being explicit, managed to convey the impression that the choice made by the Palace owed nothing to any recommendation offered by the outgoing Prime Minister.

† Iain Norman Macleod (1913–70). Conservative MP Enfield West 1950–70. Minister of Health 1952–5. Minister of Labour 1955–9. Secretary of State for the Colonies 1959–61. Chairman of the Conservative Party and Leader of the Commons 1961–3. Editor, *Spectator* 1963–5. Chancellor of the Exchequer 1970.

14 *The Years of Pooh-Bah*

In Rab's own view his treatment at the hands of the *magnificos* of the Tory Party in January 1957 was 'definitely unfair'.[1] Indeed, the very evening Harold Macmillan took over at No. 10, Rab poured out his bitterness so overflowingly to a Lobby correspondent that, out of protective feelings of friendship, the journalist concerned simply tore up his notes and wrote no story at all.[2] For once in his life, too, Rab's traditional reverence for the Crown wavered: the Queen was referred to throughout the day as 'our beloved Monarch', and the tone of voice, even on the telephone, left no room for doubt that the term was being employed sardonically.[3]

Rab deserves all the more credit, therefore, for the impression he created in public of being the good loser. He saw Macmillan twice on the day of the latter's accession to power – once in the afternoon and once in the evening; and, although the two successive visits do not appear to have raised any journalistic suspicions, they probably should have done. For the fact was that, having been disappointed in his primary ambition, Rab on that same day found himself blocked off even on his secondary one – his wish to become Foreign Secretary. With that gloss on the truth which sometimes characterises autobiographies, Macmillan was to write in his own memoirs, 'It was, therefore, a great relief to me when Butler chose the post of Home Secretary.'[4] But he had done no such thing: instead, as he wrote in his memoirs, he had pressed and urged his claims to the Foreign Secretaryship – only to have them rejected by Macmillan, sternly upholding Selwyn Lloyd's right to continue in office on the revealing ground that 'one head on a charger should be enough'.[5]

Rab was, nevertheless, the one indispensable element in the new Government's formation: it must remain a cause for some perplexity that even on his first day in office Macmillan was able to deflect his former rival's aspirations as easily as he did. His success in doing so was to set a pattern in the relationship between the two men which was to endure throughout Macmillan's Premiership; the story of the next seven years might well have been rather different if at the very outset Rab had exploited the strength of his position and refused to take 'No' for an answer. But, cast as he was by nature and upbringing in the role of the public servant, Rab was unwilling to do that: he permitted his mask of stoicism to slip in public only once. Asked, after his return to 3 Smith Square from his evening visit to No. 10 on 10 January 1957, whether he would be a member of the new Cabinet he replied somewhat bleakly (and perhaps in Macmillan's eyes none too helpfully), 'If my services are of value, they will be at the Prime Minister's disposal. There is a big difference between public life and private life. In public life one has to do one's duty. I would certainly not desert the ship at a time like this.'[6]

Predictably, having given his hand away like that, Rab found himself gazetted on the morning of Monday 14 January not to the job he coveted but to the dual posts of Home Secretary and Leader of the House of Commons, while retaining his sinecure office of Lord Privy Seal. True, his new incarnation represented an improvement on his position under Eden, for at least he now had a great Department of State behind him (it was typical of Rab that, almost from the first day of his appointment, he should have taken to referring to himself in public as 'Her Majesty's principal Secretary of State' – something which, though historically accurate, was of doubtful contemporary relevance). His place in the Cabinet 'pecking order', in any event, had not changed: formally he remained the number three figure in the Government, with Lord Salisbury, as Lord President of the Council, continuing to take precedence over him.

There were, in fact, relatively few changes in Macmillan's first Cabinet. Gwilym Lloyd George, already well past the age of sixty, had to leave the Home Office in order to make room for Rab, and Walter Monckton, Patrick Buchan-Hepburn and James Stuart (perhaps suspected to have been Rab's supporters in the poll of Ministers organised by Kilmuir and Salisbury) all departed from the Cabinet to the House of Lords. For the rest, it was more a question of musical chairs – with Peter Thorneycroft,* previously at the Board

* George Edward Peter Thorneycroft (1909–). Conservative MP Stafford 1938–45, Monmouth 1945–66. President of the Board of Trade 1951–7. Chancellor of the Exchequer 1957–8. Minister of Aviation 1960–2. Minister of Defence 1962–4. Chairman of the Conservative Party 1975–81. Created life peer 1967.

of Trade, taking Macmillan's own former place at the Treasury, thereby facilitating various consequential moves on the Cabinet chequerboard, of which the arrival of Lord Hailsham, formerly First Lord of the Admiralty, within the Cabinet Room, as Minister of Education, was perhaps the most significant.

It was necessarily, though, the change in the Leadership (of both the Government and the Party) which overshadowed everything else. This central change had, of course, been brought about by a unilateral exercise of the Royal Prerogative – something which immediately caused the Labour Party to serve notice on the Palace that any effort to repeat such old-fashioned constitutional usage in the event of a Labour Government coming to office would prove quite unacceptable. The Tories, however, were made of more pliable stuff – and saw nothing incongruous in going through the motions of *electing* a leader in the wake of the monarch having already *selected* one for them. As in April 1955, and, indeed, before that in October 1940 (when Churchill succeeded to the Party Leadership in the wake of Chamberlain's resignation just before his death), this required a ratifying 'Party meeting' attended by MPs, peers and Party workers. The date chosen for the formal laying of hands on Macmillan was Tuesday 22 January, conveniently the morning of the day on which Parliament was due to re-assemble. For Rab this represented the grisly epilogue to a drama from which he could have been forgiven for feeling he had already suffered enough: but, in the best public school tradition, the proprieties required that the vanquished should be seen raising aloft the hand of the victor. Accordingly, Rab was enrolled to second the nomination – Lord Salisbury was the proposer – of Harold Macmillan as Leader of the Conservative and Unionist Party. This ceremonial occasion took place in Church House, Westminster and the slightly heavy 1930s' ecclesiastical architecture may well have seemed to possess a certain appositeness for Rab: he brought his own speech off, though, with some aplomb – even managing to include in it one poignant personal shaft ('I find it particularly appropriate to support this motion when I think of the *effort* and *sacrifice* which must be involved for every citizen of the country if we are to surmount our current difficulties');[7] deliberate or not, such a double-edged sentiment seems to have sailed safely over the heads of most of his audience, who gave him an ovation rivalled only by that which greeted the ultimate arrival of the conquering hero himself, who plainly knew what was expected of *him* ('I certainly could not have accepted my task without the help Mr Butler has given me in true loyalty and partnership').[8]

There is no doubt, in fact, that by his external sporting demeanour Rab had won golden opinions for himself. A complete stranger, much later to become a Conservative MP, even wrote to tell him, 'If my three boys grow up with a fraction of your courage, I shall be well content',[9] while the Prime Minister's own PPS sent him a note the same day declaring, 'I only hope that if I were ever placed in a remotely similar position, I would act with the same dignity and composure'.[10] An identical chorus of approbation was reflected in the newspapers – with the *Sunday Express*, owned by Lord Beaverbrook, going out of its way to assure the man who had become Home Secretary, but who might have hoped to be Prime Minister, that he now stood 'higher in the estimation of the British people than ever he has done before'.[11]

No doubt, such fulsome tributes offered some comfort; but Rab, after his private grief of only just over two years earlier, knew that the best therapy was work. Here, in a sense, he was fortunate. In taking over the Home Office, he had to assume responsibility – almost, as it were, overnight – for the Government's Homicide Bill, then wending its somewhat unhappy way through the House of Commons. On only the second day after Parliament returned from the Christmas Recess Rab was to be found on the floor of the House presiding from the front-bench over the continuous process of its Committee Stage. Wisely he took no very active personal part in that day's discussion – the Bill (a compromise measure resulting from the clash between Lords and Commons over the abolition of capital punishment during the previous session) was even more of a legal minefield than a political one; and Rab was lucky in having as one of his two junior Ministers the lawyer and Conservative MP, J. E. S. Simon,* whom he had brought in with him (along with Pat Hornsby-Smith)† to produce a clean sweep from his predecessor's regime at the Home Office. Such a contentious piece of legislation was not, however, something from which a Secretary of State could conceivably duck out of all political responsibility; and, both during the subsequent debates on its Committee Stage and, a fortnight

* Jocelyn Edward Salis Simon (1911–). Conservative MP Middlesbrough West 1951–62. Jt Parliamentary Under-Secretary, Home Office 1957–8. Financial Secretary, Treasury 1958–9. Solicitor-General 1959–62. President, Probate, Divorce and Admiralty Division of High Court 1962–71. Created life peer 1971.

† Margaret Patricia Hornsby-Smith (1914–85). Conservative MP, Chislehurst 1950–66 and 1970–4. Parliamentary Under-Secretary, Ministry of Health 1951–7. Jt Parliamentary Under-Secretary, Home Office 1957–9. Jt Parliamentary Under-Secretary, Ministry of Pensions and National Insurance 1959–61. Created life peer 1974.

later, when the Bill came up for Third Reading, Rab boldly led from the Treasury Bench. It should have been an experience from which he had absolutely nothing to gain; but even during the Bill's Committee Stage his interventions had already extracted from the new acerbic political commentator of the *Spectator*, Taper (the early pseudonym of Bernard Levin) the remarkable compliment that his handling of it had 'markedly increased his political stature'.[12] Certainly, Rab – who, as many newspapers speculated, cannot have had much relish for the task in hand (if only because it would ultimately leave him with the responsibility of signing death warrants for the five categories of capital murder retained) – effortlessly carried the Bill's Third Reading by a good majority in a vote of 217–131, a far cry from the abolitionist majorities of the previous session.

The suspicion, at least in liberal circles, was that Rab himself was a secret abolitionist. But there was scant sign of this in the various speeches he made on the floor of the House – indeed, Taper was probably much nearer the mark in paying tribute to 'the moderation of his arguments and the care with which he has marshalled them'.[13] The truth was that Rab found himself back in his element, doing the thing he always liked best – taking a controversial, complicated Bill through the Commons as persuasively and conciliatorily as anyone could. It is conceivable, of course, that Rab foresaw all along that, having introduced so many anomalies over the application of the death penalty, there was simply no way that hanging could continue indefinitely; revealingly, he was to confess in his own memoirs that 'by the end of my time at the Home Office I began to see that the system could not go on'[14] – but by then, as at least one right-wing journalist was later unkindly to point out, he had already been responsible for sending more condemned prisoners to the gallows than any other post-war Home Secretary.[15]

Deciding on whether to grant reprieves was not, however, a duty upon which Rab ever embarked lightly: from the first hanging that he sanctioned in July 1957 to the last one for which he was constitutionally responsible, that of James Hanratty in April 1962, he took this particularly grim aspect of his office with extreme seriousness, frequently removing himself from all other departmental responsibilities for two days or more while he read all the relevant legal and medical papers and consulted with the trial judge and, if necessary, the Lord Chief Justice and the Lord Chancellor as well. The first occasion on which he had to deliberate on a reprieve was probably the worst, if only because no execution had taken place in

Britain for nineteen months. It says something for the relationship that Rab had already established with his own Home Office Ministers that on the night he had to make the decision he received a letter from both his Under-Secretaries saying they hoped he would 'feel that you can rely on our strenuous support whatever the outcome and that it may be some comfort that you command so fully our affectionate admiration'.[16] On this occasion, unlike a previous one only a month earlier, when he had been prepared to recommend a reprieve but had been forestalled by a last-minute judgment of the Court of Criminal Appeal, Rab decided that 'the law must take its course'. The decision did not spare him from some severe journalistic criticism but, perhaps because it coincided with the end of the parliamentary session, it did not provoke any major political storm.

In fact, by the end of the 1956–7 parliamentary session Rab had some reason to congratulate himself. In political, and indeed personal, terms it may not have started too auspiciously; but a sure indication of his skill as a parliamentarian was the ease with which virtually all political commentators had by the end of July slipped back into their normal practice of saluting the Government's achievement in getting through its legislative programme (it was almost as if it suited everyone to pretend that Suez had never happened). There had, of course, been some hiccoughs along the way – of which, in retrospect, possibly the least noteworthy was the resignation of Lord Salisbury at the end of March from the Cabinet in protest against the release of Archbishop Makarios from exile in the Seychelles. In the absence of the Prime Minister at the Bermuda Conference with President Eisenhower (the long-delayed reward for British co-operation in the military evacuation from Suez) it had fallen to Rab to handle the initial resignation rumblings from the familiar quarter of Hatfield House. He appears to have faced the challenge with equanimity: certainly, by the time the Prime Minister returned to London on 27 March the die seems to have been cast. True to form, in his own memoirs, Macmillan tends to neglect Rab's own role in containing what at the time was undoubtedly seen as the most formidable challenge possible to the new Government's survival. As events turned out, it was nothing of the sort: the fifth Marquess, perhaps deluded by the fame of his grandfather, Queen Victoria's last Prime Minister, had made the mistake of inhaling his own family's legend. When he finally departed, after a monotonous litany of resignation threats, he vanished from the British political scene almost as though he had never been.

His departure, at least, though, meant one bonus for Rab. With 'the Most Honourable, the Marquess of Salisbury' summarily removed from the official Cabinet List – and with no candidate from the House of Lords of sufficient eminence to replace him – Rab automatically moved up to the number two position not just in the Commons but in the entire Government. The promotion in protocol terms may not have signified much; but, for once, Cross-Bencher of the *Sunday Express* was probably astute in detecting a minor sense of vindication on the part of the Commoner who only eleven weeks earlier had had the ultimate blackball put on his hopes of the Premiership by the Nobleman who had now effectively snuffed out his own political career.[17] There was no bitterness, though, on Salisbury's side, who wrote to Rab thanking him for his 'most admirable patience'.[18]

Rab was also beginning by now to derive considerable satisfaction from administering his own Department. In many ways the Home Office was the ideal job for him: he rejoiced in its history, its extraordinary variety of responsibilities, even its quaintly old-fashioned customs (coal fires in Ministers' rooms were still part of the everyday routine of the Home Office even as late as the mid-1960s). It was, though, characteristic of Rab that very early on he should have spotted one aspect of the Department's work where there was a real requirement for a new broom. Prisons and penal reform had not occupied a very high priority with any of his immediate predecessors: the Prisons Department had, in fact, tended to be the Cinderella domain of the Office. Almost from the moment he arrived Rab resolved to change all that. Taking as his text Churchill's own dictum delivered as Home Secretary fifty years earlier – 'The mood and temper of the public with regard to the treatment of crime and criminals is one of the unfailing tests of the civilisation of any country' – he used an Opposition Supply Day debate in the House of Commons, within two months of taking office, to outline his own plans for a wide-ranging scheme of penal reform.[19] In the climate of the 1950s his was a refreshingly novel approach and his speech – with its emphasis on the need for more research into the causes of crime, the provision of after-care services and the essential requirement for an entire new prison-building programme through which offenders could be treated according to their needs rather than their deserts – made a considerable impression. Of course, nothing was going to change overnight; it took, in fact, two further years for the Home Office to come up with a comprehensive White Paper, 'Penal Policy in a Changing Society',[20] which, having been through at least four drafts before it reached its finished version, came in Rab's eyes to rank almost on a par with his Education White Paper of 1943.

His initial Commons speech served notice that he was proposing to set his own imprint on what had always been a distinctly conventional, and in some senses reactionary, Government Department. There was another equally decisive (if quieter) sign of that, when it was announced at the beginning of June 1957 that the formidable and renowned Home Office Permanent Under-Secretary, Sir Frank Newsam,* who had guided the footsteps of Rab's four immediate predecessors, would be retiring by the end of September. Sir Frank, at sixty-three, was in fact already well past the normal Civil Service retirement age of sixty; but such was the force of his personality that, while Home Secretaries had come and gone, it had somehow come to be assumed that he would simply go on for ever. That, however, was not an assumption that Rab was prepared to share; and, having secured for the most celebrated mandarin of his day a GCB in the 1957 Birthday Honours, he speedily eased him out of the Department which he had dominated for so long. As his successor he personally selected the Secretary of the Home Department at the Scottish Office, the equally able but far less flamboyant figure of Sir Charles Cunningham,† who was also to serve four Home Secretaries before his own retirement some nine years later. To the outside world it may have looked like one of those routine Civil Service transitions (normally commemorated in three or four lines on the Court Page of *The Times*); but in the corridors of Whitehall, and in the clubs of St James's, its significance was not missed. There it meant only one thing: the new Home Secretary, in contrast to his immediate predecessors, meant to be master of his own Department.

For Rab, given his seniority in the Government, there was perhaps more difficulty in achieving that than there might have been for some of his less exalted Cabinet colleagues. It was not simply that he found himself wafted off on purely ceremonial missions from time to time – as he was, for example, at the beginning of March 1957 to attend the independence celebrations of Ghana (the first former British African colony, previously known as the Gold Coast, to reach self-governing status). After the departure of Lord Salis-

* Frank Aubrey Newsam (1893–1964). Permanent Under-Secretary of State at the Home Office 1948–57. He served in the Home Office for a total of thirty-seven years.

† Charles Craik Cunningham (1906–). Secretary, Home Department of the Scottish Office 1948–57. Permanent Under-Secretary of State at the Home Office 1957–66.

bury, he also bore a specially heavy burden in chairing Cabinet committees – to say nothing of deputising for the Prime Minister during his various absences abroad.

The first of these, as has been noticed, involved the preliminaries to the resignation of Lord Salisbury from the Government. The second, remarkably, was to be similar, since it left Rab 'holding the baby' (his own characteristic phrase) in the aftermath of the resignation of the entire Treasury ministerial team at the beginning of 1958. No one perhaps had benefited more from Macmillan's accession than the man who had succeeded the new Prime Minister at the Treasury, Peter Thorneycroft. Accordingly, it cannot but seem extraordinary that, within a year of taking office as Chancellor, he should have embarked on a collision course with his benefactor that ended not only with his own resignation but also that of his two Treasury junior ministerial colleagues. The occasion for the conflict – a mere £50 million in the official Expenditure Estimates – was, no doubt, misleading: the Chancellor, rightly or wrongly, had staked his position on there being no increase at all over the total of Government expenditure of the previous year. And when he could not get his way on what for him, and perhaps even more profoundly for his two Treasury colleagues, Nigel Birch and Enoch Powell,* was an issue of principle, he insisted on resigning.

The timing of this protest demonstration within the Government could hardly have been more inconvenient. In those days the Press was not perhaps as alert to Cabinet disagreements as it was subsequently to become. So when, on 7 January 1958, the official announcement surfaced of the collective Treasury team's resignations, it came as the *Daily Mail* put it 'out of the blue'[21] (the *Mail* was at least more fortunate than *The Times* which, in its leader column only the day before, had congratulated the Prime Minister on 'coolly and firmly backing a courageous Chancellor').[22] The political difficulty, however, was that the next day Macmillan was due to leave for a long-scheduled Commonwealth tour planned to last for six weeks. A Prime Minister with less of a showman's instinct might well have cancelled, or at least postponed, his trip: Macmillan, laying the foundations of his later reputation for 'unflappability', did nothing of the kind. Instead, with a cheery wave to his assembled Cabinet colleagues at Heathrow, and a somewhat cavalier statement to the Press about settling up 'little local difficulties' before turning

* John Enoch Powell (1912–). Conservative MP, Wolverhampton South-West 1950–74, Ulster Unionist MP, South Down 1974– . Financial Secretary to Treasury 1957–8. Minister of Health 1960–3.

'to the wider vision of the Commonwealth', he simply flew off to the first stop of his tour, New Delhi, exactly as originally planned.

At least before leaving he had found a replacement for his Chancellor, the Minister of Agriculture Derick Heathcoat Amory,* and made the necessary other consequent Cabinet changes (as well as filling the two other vacancies at the Treasury). But the subsequent junior ministerial promotions were left for Rab to handle: one immediate vacancy, since his own former junior Minister, J. E. S. Simon, had been elevated to be Financial Secretary to the Treasury in place of Enoch Powell, was clearly of crucial importance to him. For it he chose another lawyer, David Renton,† at that time serving as Parliamentary Under-Secretary at the Ministry of Power. Renton was to stay with him for the next five years – until, indeed, the end of his own term at the Home Office – and was to exercise a decisive influence (not always in tune with Rab's own progressive inclinations) over departmental policy, especially on social questions like Commonwealth immigration and homosexual law reform.

For the moment, however, the least of Rab's preoccupations was the future policy thrust of his own Department. When he told a reporter, perhaps rashly, that he had been left 'to hold the baby,'[23] he was telling nothing less than the truth. In the first place, there was the report of the Bank Rate Tribunal, set up in the autumn to investigate Harold Wilson's‡ allegations that there had been a serious leak anticipating Peter Thorneycroft's decision to raise Bank Rate by 2 per cent in the previous September. In retrospect, the whole affair was to seem something of a mare's nest, but at the time it was taken extremely seriously, not least by the newspapers. It fell to Rab to introduce the Government motion in the Commons welcoming the Tribunal's report, which found no substantiation for any of Wilson's charges; and it was a task to which he brought an unfamiliar tone of acerbity, mounting a particularly scornful denunciation of the Opposition's resort to 'the political weapon of the smear'.[24] It was

* Derick Heathcoat Amory (1899–1981). Conservative MP Tiverton, 1945–60. Minister of Agriculture, Fisheries and Food 1954–8. Chancellor of the Exchequer 1958–60. UK High Commissioner to Canada 1961–3. Created 1st Viscount Amory 1960.

† David Lockhart-Mure Renton (1908–). Conservative MP Huntingdonshire 1945–79. Jt Parliamentary Under-Secretary, Home Office 1958–61, Minister of State 1961–2. Knighted 1964 and created life peer 1979.

‡ James Harold Wilson (1916–). Labour MP, Ormskirk 1945–50, Huyton 1950–83. President of the Board of Trade 1947–51. Elected Leader of the Labour Party 1963. Prime Minister 1964–70 and 1974–6. Leader of the Opposition, for second time, 1970–4. Made Knight of the Garter 1976 and created life peer 1983.

a speech which did him nothing but good with the Government's own supporters; indeed, in an astonishing turnabout from the events of almost exactly a year before, Rab, throughout the six weeks that the Prime Minister was away, was to bask in a general climate of Party approval.

Partly, no doubt, it was the result of the unsuspected taste for the limelight that he displayed: the Prime Minister had hardly left the country before Rab was receiving by turns, on successive days, the gossip columnists of the *Daily Mail* and the *Daily Express*; the following weekend he was to be seen launching a new current affairs series on Independent Television with a twenty-minute interview with Robin Day. Finally he successfully trumped interest even in Thorneycroft's resignation speech by announcing, on the eve of Parliament's return from the Christmas Recess, his decision to allow eleven Hungarian stowaways, who had arrived on a British liner a fortnight earlier, to remain in the country despite an initial Home Office ruling that they should be deported back to Brazil. None of these much-publicised interventions came about purely through chance; at a time of jagged nerves within the Party Rab was quite enough of an experienced political hand to recognise the value of diversionary tactics – and he, no doubt, shrewdly calculated that the best way to destroy the impact of the collective Treasury walk-out was to distract attention from it. However, what he may not have foreseen was the sudden surge of popularity all this activity would bring him personally. Such had been his high-definition performance as Macmillan's stand-in that even the newspapers seem to have been struck with wonder and awe. The best, if scarcely the most tactful, theory to explain Rab's extraordinary display of drive and energy was probably advanced by the *Scotsman*: he had clearly, its political correspondent wrote, found himself 'rejuvenated' by the Prime Minister's absence.[25]

Yet the two former rivals had, in effect, settled down to a perfectly adequate professional relationship. There was, it is true, very little warmth between them – they were, after all, cast in very different moulds. A letter Rab wrote at around this time to his old Cabinet colleague, Patrick Buchan-Hepburn (by 1957, as Lord Hailes, serving as the first and last Governor of the ill-fated West Indies Federation) reveals something of the detached but wary attitude that he had learnt to adopt towards the man who had walked off with what he had hoped to be his own inheritance:

My description of the Prime Minister as being the Restoration

> Monarch of modern times is, I think, just. He has the characteristic of working extremely hard and conscientiously at his problems and then spending infinite time without apparent fatigue in the Smoking Room, talking to his critics or friends, as the case may be. He has an infinite capacity for elasticity which might tire his friends, if they did not realise that he is ruthless in his determination to carry the disaffected along with him at all costs. This would not lead to great cosiness, were it not for the urbanity which accompanies his manner.[26]

However carefully balanced, that is not an assessment in which it is possible to detect any real affection – but perhaps to expect such a quality would in any event be naïve. It was not so much that Rab and Macmillan rubbed each other up the wrong way: it was simply that – fearful perhaps of what might happen if they came into too close contact – they both, at least initially, took some pains to keep their distance. The nearest they came in the early days to a frontal collision was when Rab appears to have formed a suspicion that he was in danger of losing his traditional policy-making function within the Party. That produced a fairly abrupt minute ('As you know, I have had certain responsibility for this area since 1945 under your two predecessors and was responsible for the policy statements which were not unattended by a meed of success');[27] Macmillan, however, was not to be deflected and by the end of 1957 a new body had been established called the Steering Committee, specifically charged with the preparation of the election manifesto (Macmillan was chairman and Rab deputy chairman.)[28] Undoubtedly it did a very efficient job with the 1959 manifesto, *The Next Five Years*, but Rab, despite having two strong allies in Macleod and Maudling among its membership of six, started off being suspicious of it.

For the most part, however, restraint, even formality, on both sides led to a remarkable absence of friction. When the Prime Minister returned, for example, from his Commonwealth Tour on 14 February he found awaiting him a model *aide-mémoire* from Rab explaining all that had gone on since his departure:[29] this was to become a regular practice of Rab's on each occasion on which he stood in for Macmillan – although, interestingly, it does not seem to have been a procedure he followed with either Eden or Churchill, both of whom, no doubt, preferred the intimacy of conversation to the relative remoteness of typed sheets of paper.

The Prime Minister's return in mid-February – just in time to catch the bad news of the Rochdale by-election, where the Tories not only lost the seat but suffered the further indignity of coming third to the Liberals – meant that Rab's own six-week reign in Downing Street was at an end. It had been, according to Rab's own calculations, the ninth time he had taken charge of a Government during a Prime Minister's absence; but somehow, Rochdale notwithstanding, it had been easily the most rewarding. He had faced a challenge in holding the Party together and he had sailed through it – though he was privately to note, with characteristic candour, that 'his [Macmillan's] going away made the Thorneycroft issue easier to handle because the Conservative Party is essentially loyal and they felt that no division should be allowed in his absence'.[30] More than that, however, he had, for the first time, fully enjoyed the trappings of being even an acting Prime Minister. He had entertained in No. 10, giving an official dinner party for Prince Souvanna Fouma, the Prime Minister of Laos, he had been summoned to Sandringham to stay with the Queen, he had even become involved in foreign policy, lunching at the Soviet Embassy and summoning Selwyn Lloyd home from Ankara to advise him on the latest round of East–West exchanges. If an energetic six weeks, it had also been a fulfilling one.

Rab could certainly, therefore, be forgiven if, anxious to avoid any feeling of anti-climax, he had eagerly looked forward to his next major public engagement away from Westminster. On Friday 21 February he was scheduled to deliver his Rectorial Address to the students of Glasgow University (he had been elected Rector sixteen months earlier but the installation ceremony had been twice postponed). He had taken some trouble with the speech – but, alas, hardly a word of it was heard. In the version given by one contemporary account:

> As Mr Butler entered the hall, he was welcomed by a jazz band, the bangs of exploding squibs, shouting and singing. And he got a warning. Many of the students seated on the floor of the hall held opened umbrellas above their heads.
>
> The first missiles began to fly. A tomato hit him square in the back. A flour bomb hit him full in the face.
>
> The barrage of missiles and noise continued throughout the ceremony and during Mr Butler's speech. Often he stood silent, waiting a rare chance to make himself heard.
>
> Finally the platform party stood and bravely sang 'God Save the Queen'. As they departed, fire extinguishers and water showered all over them.[31]

It was, of course, a lamentable scene – and Rab, no doubt, fully deserved the tributes that various newspapers paid to him for the calm he had displayed in trying circumstances. But soon there began to be an undertow of criticism, particularly within the Conservative Party – fuelled in part by the absurd pictures of Rab that went round the world, covered in flour and drenched in fire extinguisher foam, but provoked also by some curiously ill-judged comments, making light of the whole episode, that he chose to make afterwards. Somehow the announcement, 'I understand youth. I have children of my own and I like to feel I haven't lost touch',[32] was not quite what the Tory Party expected to hear; nor was Rab's cause helped by the fact that that very same day he was due to reply by written answer to a Commons question about young offenders. The intimation that his main concern was to see that the courts were provided with 'the information they need in determining treatment' may have been judged by the *Manchester Guardian* to be 'welcome but not very clear';[33] elsewhere, among the critics of Rab's penal policies within the Conservative Party, it was judged to be all too clear – and pitifully soft and inadequate.

How much damage the whole Glasgow episode did to Rab's long-term prospects within the Conservative Party it is hard even now to judge. But, given that pictures are far more emotive than words, and that the image they presented immortalised the Right's impression of him as a well-meaning but ineffective reformer being satisfactorily brought up sharp against the social effects of his own policies, it was probably not minimal. Nor did Rab privately show the sang-froid he had, perhaps unwisely, displayed in the immediate aftermath. When in January 1959 word reached him of a proposal that Harold Macmillan should stand as his successor at Glasgow he strongly advised him against accepting the nomination, 'You would certainly be less embarrassed if you feel you need not take it on.'[34] There could scarcely have been a more revealing, if also a more altruistic, piece of advice – and Macmillan, not surprisingly, took it.*

Throughout the summer of 1958 Rab's main apprehensions centred on that year's Conservative Party Conference. The previous October, for the first time since the war, he had not been present – undergoing a hernia operation during the Conference period which, while certainly no diplomatic illness, had at least relieved him from

* Lord Hailsham eventually drew the short straw and was elected as Rab's successor as Rector of Glasgow University.

attending an occasion which was plainly intended as Macmillan's coronation (though, in fact, it worked out rather differently with Hailsham, the new Tory Party Chairman, effectively stealing the show with a rabble-rousing address, provoked by his duty of handing over the bell to the next National Union chairman on the Saturday morning). At least, however, in 1957 Rab would have had few established policies to defend: now he did – in particular on crime and punishment. The 4,000 representatives were not, of course, to know that he had already, during the course of the summer, effectively set his hand to the reforming plough, sending letters to both the Chancellor of the Exchequer and the Prime Minister, which served notice that he would be making demands on the Government's expenditure programme in relation to his plans for a wholesale prison rebuilding scheme. His letter, in particular, to the Prime Minister was unusually tough – and for that reason is worth quoting in full:

27 June 1958

Dear Harold,

Since you asked me to take on the Home Office 18 months ago, I have found the work most congenial and rewarding. In its quaint and graceful traditions, and the variety of its problems, the Home Office is unique among Government Departments. But all is not steeped in history; and the longer I remain here, the more it is borne in upon me that the main part of my duty consists in taking what steps I can to carry out long overdue reforms in our penal system.

I would go further and say that I shall be unable to fulfil my mission here unless I find it possible to press forward a comprehensive plan of penal reform. As you know, I am as conscious as you or any of our colleagues of the need to lighten the burden on the country's economy, and I have no intention of embarrassing the Chancellor by making unreasonable demands on the Exchequer. At the same time I am convinced that I must leave behind some permanent record of my period of office here or I shall feel not only that I have been disloyal to myself, but also that I have failed in my duty to you and the Government which you lead.

Of course it is perfectly possible to hold all this up, through over-conscientiousness turning into obstruction, but I am convinced from my life's service to reform and public policy that to open up a few windows on the future cannot but help our Government.

Yours ever

RAB[35]

The Prime Minister was quite sophisticated enough a politician to know when he had to bend to the reforming ardour of a senior colleague – and he promptly sent back a personal minute, tinged with a vein of cynicism, intimating full support for his Home Secretary's plans:

> I am all for it. No doubt it will cost money, but I do not suppose the money will be spent very quickly. I take it, it will mostly be building new prisons, but they will take some time, especially if the Ministry of Works have anything to do with the plans.[36]

Rallying support, however, from the Prime Minister was one thing. Enlisting the enthusiasm of the Party for what was basically an unpopular cause was quite another – and here Rab was in some real difficulty. The backlash against the whole question of taking a serious approach to crime meant, as he explained to his new Permanent Secretary, Sir Charles Cunningham, that he had had to postpone any idea of publishing the Home Office's White Paper on Penal Reform that autumn – adding eloquently, 'I am to answer 28 bloodthirsty resolutions at the Conservative Party Conference at Blackpool. With the greatest difficulty we have chosen one out of the 28 which is at least moderate. On this I can make a reasonably calming speech.'[37]

And, in the event, Rab contrived to do just that – resting his case in the need to review the causes of crime if only to discover more effective means of combating it,[38] and in the judgment of *The Economist* delivering a speech of 'great skill and courage'.[39] In fact, somewhat to his surprise, he found himself in greater trouble in a debate on Commonwealth immigration* – where his plea to the Party to show itself 'worthy of its old traditions' went totally disregarded (a resolution demanding that 'the immigration laws of this country should be revised' was carried 'by a substantial majority').[40] In parliamentary terms, however, that was a problem for the future: a far more immediate challenge to Rab was the need to make some official Government response to the Wolfenden Report on Homosexual Offences and Prostitution,[41] which had been published a full year earlier. Here his instincts, initially, were to act on both parts of the Report: indeed, he specifically asked his new Parliamentary

* Proposals to limit immigration from the West Indies had first surfaced during the lifetime of the 1951–5 Churchill Government but had been turned down by the Cabinet. A subsequent dramatic increase in immigrants from the Indian subcontinent had brought the question back on to the political agenda.

Under-Secretary, David Renton, when he appointed him, whether he would be willing to help with carrying a Bill, covering both prostitutes and homosexuals, through the Commons. However, Renton replied that, though he would be happy to assist with legislation over the second part of the Report on prostitution, his conscience would not allow him to do so with the first part on homosexuals – and Rab soon discovered that this was a reaction very much on the plumb line of the Tory Party.[42] When, therefore, he finally came to open a general Commons debate on the Committee's entire Report, fairly early in the 1958–9 session, he made it plain that, though the Government would be legislating to clear women off the streets, it had no proposals for clearing homosexuals out of the nation's prisons. Although thoroughly lucid, it was not one of Rab's most convincing Commons performances, but at least he did not seek to disguise the principal obstacle that prevented him from going further, 'I do not think we have yet with us a general sense of opinion which would regard it as right to alter the criminal law in the sense suggested by the Committee.'[43]

The same inhibition did not apply to changing (and indeed strengthening) the criminal law in so far as it affected solicitation by women. In fact, the popular clamour here was all for getting 'common prostitutes' out of sight and, therefore, presumably out of mind – and the Government, bowing to pressure from the Church, the police and local councils in areas as different as Stepney and Kensington, whistled through its Street Offences Act in little more than six months. The only substantial objections to the measure came from women's organisations who, rightly, detected some discrepancy in the treatment of the prostitute who persisted in soliciting going to prison while her customer, who might well have taken the lead by accosting her in the first place, got away scot-free. Somewhat to his chagrin, Rab was even asked to resign from the Association of Moral and Social Hygiene – the high-minded Victorian rescue organisation founded some eighty years earlier by his great-aunt, the penal reformer Josephine Butler; and he also had to endure an upbraiding from a formidable feminist deputation of protest, representing twenty separate organisations, which he bravely received in person at the Home Office.[44]

All in all, it was probably just as well for Rab's general liberal reputation that the passage of the Street Offences Bill through the Commons should have coincided almost exactly with the progress of another measure for which he could claim at least indirect paternity. In his early months at the Home Office a clumsily drafted

Private Member's Bill had come up on a Friday afternoon seeking to loosen the bonds of literary censorship:[45] Rab, to the surprise of those used to the Home Office's obscurantist ways, had directed that the Department should not oppose the Bill but instead had authorised one of his junior Ministers to suggest that it should be passed to a Select Committee so that it could be put into a more workable form.[46] Within a year, the Select Committee had finished its work – and the obligation was plainly now on Rab to respond on behalf of the Government to a much more careful measure with whose general objectives he almost certainly sympathised. Without endorsing it fully (he still had some reservations over wording), in effect he pledged the Government's support;[47] and the Obscene Publications Bill, sponsored by Roy Jenkins,* made its eventual way on to the Statute Book, receiving the Royal Assent a fortnight after the Street Offences Bill.

Admittedly, there were those who saw this as a triumph of political expediency rather than a manifestation of any Home Office liberalising spirit: at an early stage in the eventual Bill's incubation, the veteran libertarian campaigner, Sir Alan Herbert,† had threatened to intervene in a crucial by-election then pending at Harrow East, unless the Government gave some positive indication that it was prepared to move towards reform of the censorship laws. But at least it can be said that the Labour MP who steered the measure safely into harbour took a more charitable view. Writing to Rab, at the beginning of the Summer Recess, Jenkins not only thanked him for his 'great help' with the Bill; he also expressed his own view that the whole effort 'would have been unavailing had you not been basically sympathetic'.[48] It was a striking tribute to come from an Opposition back-bencher to a Government Minister – not least on the eve of what most people now assumed was a certain autumn general election.

It had, of course, been a Parliament of mixed fortunes for Rab; unlike the House of Commons of 1951–5 when his reputation had grown steadily, this one had begun by witnessing a definite erosion in his political position. His stock had probably reached its lowest point when in January 1957 he was superseded in the succession

* Roy Harris Jenkins (1920–). Labour MP, Central Southwark 1948–50, Stechford, Birmingham 1950–76, SDP MP, Hillhead, Glasgow 1982– . Minister of Aviation 1964–5. Home Secretary 1965–7. Chancellor of the Exchequer 1967–70. Home Secretary 1974–6. President European Commission 1977–81.

† Alan Patrick Herbert (1890–1971). Author, barrister and journalist. Independent MP for Oxford University 1935–50.

stakes by Harold Macmillan. But, since Macmillan took over from Eden, he had, oddly, enjoyed something of an Indian summer. Certainly, as he looked back on the rehabilitation of his reputation since 1957, Rab was entitled to feel a certain quiet satisfaction: the Prime Minister was, after all, nearly nine years older than he was and even if, as the opinion polls were starting to suggest, the Conservatives did manage to bring off a third successive electoral victory he would still be only sixty-one when Macmillan reached the age of seventy.

To his colleagues, indeed, there was a whole new confidence about Rab – demonstrated by the firmness with which he insisted, over the Prime Minister's opposition, on including in the Tory manifesto a clear commitment to blow some of the Victorian cobwebs out of British life. True, the actual policy declaration – 'We shall revise some of our social laws, for example those relating to betting and gambling and to clubs and licensing, which are at present full of anomalies and lead to abuse and corruption' – did not go as far as the more progressive outriders of the new Toryism would have liked;[49] but it still represented something of a *coup* for Rab, as he was not above making clear in his own memoirs.[50] Strengthened by the approbation which was gradually greeting his Home Office work – his White Paper on Penal Reform had finally been published to a chorus of liberal approval in February 1959 – he had regained a good deal of his zest for political life. Certainly, a slightly surprising letter that he received from a former Vice-Chancellor of Cambridge (Rab had just been appointed High Steward of the University) sounding him out as to whether he would be interested in taking on the headship of either of a couple of Cambridge colleges that were about to become vacant got remarkably short shrift:[51] for the moment, retirement to academia had no part in his plans.

There could, of course, have been another, and more personal, reason for that. Latterly Rab had been subjected to a good deal of curiosity in the newspapers as to whether or not he intended to marry again – and the *Daily Express*, in particular, had wheeled forward several potential brides on his behalf. None of William Hickey's guesses could claim, however, to have been especially well-informed; and, from Rab's point of view, since his mind had been effectively made up for a number of years, they were probably more amusing than irritating. Yet until March 1959 he had not been able to contemplate any change in his widower's status, since the only person he wished to marry was already married herself. As Essex neighbours and members of the same family clan, Rab and

Mollie Courtauld were able to see a good deal of each other, and had been doing so ever since Sydney's death at the end of 1954. (It had been Sydney's wish that Rab should eventually marry Mollie.)[52] But until the death in March 1959 of Mollie's husband, the Arctic explorer, August Courtauld, who had been incurably ill for almost a decade, that had not been a practicable proposition. Now, at last, it was. The new spring in Rab's stride throughout the summer of 1959 may well have told as much about his personal life as his political one.

Neither Rab nor Mollie, after all their years of patient waiting, had any wish to rush their marriage – and its date became a matter of some delicacy. Here the general election came to their rescue. What more propitious time to make a new start to both their lives than immediately after an election campaign – a campaign, moreover, that might bring about a radical change in Rab's own public career? As with most personal decisions of this kind, there may well never have been any single clearcut moment when it was actually made: but it is at least evident that it pre-dated the general election results, since the Archbishop of Canterbury's Registrar, to whom Rab had applied for a Special Licence, replied to Rab, telling him everything was in order, on the day after polling (thereby proving that Rab's own initial approach must have been made well before voting took place).[53]

Perhaps not surprisingly, given the personal background, Rab's own participation in the Conservatives' national campaign was a good deal less dominant than it had been in 1955. He took part in two of the five Tory television election broadcasts – but in neither case in any starring role: the last two weeks of the campaign he spent principally in his own constituency, predicting (over-cautiously as events turned out) that the whole election would have 'a close finish'.[54] In fact, Rab comfortably increased his own majority,* as did the Conservatives in the nation at large, putting up their 1955 overall majority of 60 to 100. Properly, though, the result was widely recognised as Macmillan's own personal triumph – he had delivered a startlingly effective final solo election broadcast – rather than the Conservative Party's.

Inevitably, once the election was over, there was speculation that Rab would move his job – and most of it centred on his prospects of taking over the Foreign Office (a change that *The Economist* had

* The figures were R. A. Butler (Con.) 20,955, Rev. H. N. Horne (Lab.) 14,173, D. J. Ridley (Lib.) 4,245. Conservative majority 6,782.

been demanding for some time).[55] Curiously, Rab seems to have had much less appetite for the post than he had had in 1957:[56] it may, of course, be that since then he had noted that all Harold Macmillan's interest was in foreign affairs and thus had shrewdly decided that, for so long as he remained Prime Minister, the job would have little more than errand-boy status. Macmillan, in any event, did offer him a new job – though one that would only add a third hat to the two that he already wore as Home Secretary and Leader of the House of Commons. On 9 October, at an interview in No. 10, Rab found himself also urged to take on, in succession to Lord Hailsham (who was promptly, and mysteriously, released to the non-executive office of Minister for Science), the post of Chairman of the Conservative Party. Perhaps unwisely, he accepted – for while his new elevation delighted his friends, it was doubtful if in reality there was much substance to it. The job of Chairman of the Conservative Party is, undoubtedly, an important one in the run-up period to any election: it is of minimal significance in the wake of a victory in which a Conservative Government has been returned to office.

Rab's failure to spot this meant that the years of Pooh-Bah had begun. That did not, however, stop the less perceptive journalistic commentators from reading a quite unwarranted meaning into his new promotion, with even *The Economist* pursuing a ludicrous analogy with Mr Khrushchev's rise to power through 'control of the party machine'.[57] In any event there were bound to be difficulties in combining the essentially cheer-leading job of Chairman of the Party with the traditionally non-partisan role of Leader of the House – though it is only fair to add that Rab overcame these with rather more subtlety than his successor, Iain Macleod. However, the Chairmanship of the Party was not a job in which he ever really felt at home – complaining plaintively in his retirement, 'Going to rallies at the weekend in distant parts of England and having to make speeches about how wonderful the Government was I found very hard and difficult – and not at all rewarding.'[58]

Probably, if Rab's mind had not been on other things, he might have had the sense to reject Macmillan's offer. But, understandably, in the immediate aftermath of the election all his attention was concentrated on his forthcoming wedding. Its logistics soon posed a problem. It had been both Mollie's and Rab's hope that the wedding could take place very quietly. An unforeseen leak in two local Essex papers immediately put paid to that – and within a week of the election even *The Times* was to be found reporting on its Bill page, 'Mr Butler to Marry Again' (even if it did its best to preserve decorum by adding, 'An official announcement will be made in due course').[59] The only secret Mollie and Rab were left with was the date (21 October) and whereabouts of the ceremony; and even on this Rab finally felt it prudent to dampen the competitive instinct of the Press by attempting to enlist their co-operation. Two days before the wedding, the following private letter went out to every national newspaper editor:

19 October 1959

I am writing to let you know the details of my wedding arrangements so that you can make such plans to cover it as you may wish.

At the same time may I appeal to you to instruct your representatives to observe due restraint on this occasion? The attentions of the Press during this weekend have been most exhausting for Mrs Courtauld and myself. I have no complaints; all the Press representatives were charming and polite but we must both have a rest from them from now on. I am sure that I can rely on your kindness to see that your representatives will not pursue Mrs Courtauld or me between now and the ceremony; you will understand that I shall be too preoccupied to talk to them at all on Wednesday.

I shall be most grateful if our wishes can be met and hope that the enclosed details will be helpful to you.[60]

The letter appears to have done the trick. The venue for the service had been carefully chosen – it was the fourteenth-century church in the village of Ashwell, near Baldock, in Hertfordshire (which happened to be where Mollie's eldest daughter, Perina, lived) and even though there was an evident air of anticipation and excitement in the village, it appears to have been due more to a jungle drum emanating from the local butcher's than any beating of the bushes provoked by Fleet Street.[61] Although some villagers eventually crowded into the Church, it was very much a domestic occasion – with the six children of the bride and the four of the bridegroom making up the family part of the congregation. Rab's best man was his former PPS, Sir Hubert Ashton (the MP for Chelmsford), and Mollie was given away by her eldest son Christopher (then a theological student at Westcott House, Cambridge). The service was conducted by the Bishop of Chelmsford, Dr Faulkner Allison, who, in the course of his address, took the somewhat unusual step of declaring, 'No wedding I have ever had the privilege of officiating at has ever given me such genuine joy as this one.'[62] The photographers behaved themselves and kept to the north door of the church, though a rather striking picture – taken at the reception, which was held at Mollie's daughter's home – of the bride and bridegroom surrounded by their children and grand-children did appear exclusively in that week's *Saffron Walden Weekly News*.

Rab, of course, was overwhelmed with congratulations – the mass of letters he received being headed by a personal, hand-written one from the Queen, to whom he had had to write (as used to be the rule for Cabinet Ministers) asking her permission to be out of the country: Rab and Mollie spent their honeymoon in Rome, an experience marred only by the attentions of the *paparazzi* who pursued them throughout most of their sight-seeing expeditions. Conscientious to a fault, Rab insisted on returning to London within the week so that he could be in his place on the Treasury Bench on the day the new Parliament opened. He was rewarded by seeing the Queen's Speech give priority to his Betting and Gaming Bill, one of the proposals he had fought to get into the manifesto and which was eventually to lead to the opening of betting shops (in place of the operation of illegal bookies' runners) in virtually every high street in the land.

But if Rab had hoped he could concentrate his attention on patiently negotiating the new Bill's passage through the Commons, he was soon disabused. There is a tendency in British politics when Governments come back with large electoral majorities for things to start going wrong almost at once – and the autumn of 1959 proved no exception. No sooner had the House of Commons opened its new session than the rumblings of discontent began, with Rab becoming the object of most of his own Party's criticism. He had not, of course, been helped by a distinctly injudicious speech delivered by the new Lord Chief Justice, Lord Parker,* in Canada at the beginning of September: in it Lord Parker had attacked both the Homicide Act and the more recent Street Offences Act in a peculiarly uninhibited way, while also, for good measure, lending his support to all the calls for the return of corporal punishment as a judicial sanction.[63] Rab had much resented the Lord Chief Justice's speech at the time, and, indeed, had written a memo of protest about it to the Lord Chancellor in which he took particular exception to the allegation

* Hubert Lister Parker (1900–72). Lord Chief Justice of England 1958–71. He was generally considered less reactionary than his predecessor, Lord Goddard, but to Rab it may well have appeared a distinction without a difference.

that he had gone in for 'an indiscriminate commuting of death sentences' (in fact, of the nineteen capital sentences Rab had had to consider by the summer of 1959 he had commuted only eight).[64] That had not stopped the Lord Chief Justice returning to the charge – at least on the question of corporal punishment – when he addressed a subsequent meeting of the Magistrates' Association in London in October.[65] It was wholly predictable that, when Rab rose to his feet to answer Home Office questions for the first time in the new Parliament, he should have been subjected to a sustained assault from the troops behind him.[66] Had he no confidence in the Lord Chief Justice's judgment, was he not fearful of being so much out of tune with public opinion, was not the proper policy for his Department to 'whack the thugs'? It was, as the parliamentary correspondent of the *Guardian* put it, 'a depressing episode' – a clear indication that in the new Parliament 'the flogging lobby would not be content to play it mild'.[67] As Rab was to learn to his cost in the months ahead, that was by no means an inaccurate prognosis.

It was, however, the kind of attack for which Rab was braced. Another onslaught upon him in the early days of the new Parliament he can hardly have anticipated. It all came about through a decision – unilaterally made by the Commissioner of Metropolitan Police – to settle a civil action brought against one of his officers for assault and false imprisonment by an out-of-court payment of £300 plus the plaintiff's costs. The case, known as *Garratt* v. *Eastmond*, enjoyed a brief political notoriety – if only because there seemed to both sides of the House of Commons to be an important principle at stake: if public money was to be spent to buy protection from litigation, but without any admission of liability, were not the police, in fact, being shielded from the consequences of their actions? (P C Eastmond, the police officer involved, had not, it emerged, even been disciplined.) Confronted by what he perhaps regarded as a tornado in a tea-cup, Rab, for once, behaved somewhat insensitively. Initially he stood his ground simply on the Commissioner's decision, explaining that his own powers were in no way concerned with the internal disciplinary procedures of the Metropolitan Police.[68] It was an uncharacteristic piece of political misjudgment – and it soon got Rab into considerable trouble not merely with the Labour Opposition, who promptly put down a censure motion upon him, but also with a paper that was normally sympathetic, *The Times*, which savaged him in three successive leading articles.[69] By the time the censure debate took place, Rab had clearly recognised the danger signals and, to some degree, took the wind out of his critics' sails by

28 Rab, the widower, with his son, James, and his daughter, Sarah, in the garden at Stanstead

29 Mollie Courtauld on the day of her marriage to Rab on 21 October 1959

30 Rab and Mollie at the St Ermin's Hotel, Westminster, on the eve of the day he failed, for the second time, to become Prime Minister

31 Rab arriving with Mollie at 1 Carlton Gardens for a dinner with his predecessor as Foreign Secretary, Sir Alec Douglas-Home

offering an independent inquiry into the whole relationship between police and public, which would also take into account such matters as the organisation of police forces, recruitment and discipline.[70] In the House of Commons, it was a ploy that worked, with the Labour Party withdrawing its censure motion; with the Press, it was rather less successful – even the *Daily Telegraph* accused Rab of reaching 'for a pair of field glasses to see the horizon' instead of 'taking a microscope to a single case'.[71] For once – though the promised inquiry eventually became the 1960–2 Royal Commission on the Police – it did, indeed, look even to his friends, as if Rab had been more than a mite flat-footed.

All politicians, of course, have their ups and downs, but in the political trade when a run of bad luck begins, it tends to go on. That was certainly true of Rab towards the end of 1959. No sooner had he put the Eastmond affair behind him than he was hit by another controversy – this time very much of his own construction. When he first became Home Secretary in 1957, he had inherited from his predecessor an awkward imbroglio over phone-tapping: transcripts of phone calls made between a gang leader and a member of the Bar, named Patrick Marrinan, had been passed, with the Home Office's authority, to the chairman of the Bar Council and, via him, to the Benchers of Marrinan's Inn, who proceeded to conduct an investigation into his professional conduct. The incident provoked a storm, and Rab was fortunate in being able to make it clear in the end that all the relevant decisions had been taken by his predecessor, Lord Tenby, rather than by himself (Tenby was later pointedly criticised in a painstaking report made to Parliament by three Privy Councillors on the whole episode).

So if anyone should have been aware just what an incendiary issue telephone interception was, it ought to have been Rab. And yet in December 1959 he appeared, even to his Conservative colleagues in the Commons, to have made exactly the same blunder as Lord Tenby: faced with a request from the General Medical Council to make available to it the transcript of a telephone call, the police in Reading had gone to the Home Office for advice as to whether it should be released. At least Rab took counsel from the Lord Chancellor and the law officers before authorising the handing over of the transcript – but it still remains puzzling that he should have failed to recognise how similar the case was bound to seem to the one, involving another disciplinary professional body, that had got his predecessor into so much trouble more than two years earlier. He would certainly have saved himself a lot of embarrassment if he had, for he became the quarry of exactly the same parliamentary hue and cry. In a Conservative newspaper he was said, indeed, to have had to endure 'the most uncomfortable half-hour of his political career' while replying to questions on why he had authorised the transfer of the substance of a telephone conversation to a body outside the public service.[72] Though he fared somewhat better when facing his second censure debate within a month,[73] there can be little doubt that Rab had been guilty of, at best, a striking failure of imagination. What turned the scales with him – and persuaded him that this was not a case of interception at all – was the fact that all the Reading police had done was to listen in on an extension made available to them by one party to the conversation. To Rab, with his scholar's clarity of mind, that was not phone tapping. Alas, the British public and Press did not find it easy to make such a fine distinction – and even *Hansard* took their side: the censure debate, which took place on the evening before the House rose for the Christmas Recess, was described in both the index and the text of the Official Report as being on the subject of 'Telephone Tapping'.

Had Rab lost his touch? Revealingly, the one newspaper to pose the question[74] hastily backed away from it (as if in sheer horror at what it had done): Rab's relations with the Press – based, as they were, on the weekly Lobby conference which he still regularly took – were always a great source of strength to him. A shrewder criticism was probably that he was simply attempting to do too much. Significantly, when an elderly Conservative peer said so in the House of Lords,[75] the Press collectively felt that it was something that would not be ignored: the speech got quite a lot of play in the newspapers – and there was some sign that the spirited defence the Lord Chancellor offered of Rab ('My right honourable friend is one of the ablest and most hard-working people I have ever met in my life')[76] did not carry conviction. Rab's workload was certainly exceptionally heavy: in addition to trying to run possibly the most mine-strewn of all Departments of State, he was responsible for the Government's entire legislative programme – on top of which, despite the invaluable help he was given by his Deputy Chairman, Sir Toby Low,* he was now expected to give at least two mornings a week (to say nothing of his weekend wanderings) to the task of keeping the Party outside Parliament happy. But if the burden seemed formidable enough at normal times, it became positively

* Toby Austin Richard Low (1914–). Conservative MP, Blackpool North 1945–62. Deputy Chairman, Conservative Party Organisation 1959–63. Created 1st Baron Aldington 1962.

oppressive during those periods when Rab was expected to run the entire Government as well. No doubt, Rab's own answer would have been that it was much simpler to have one person 'running everything';* significantly, he never seems to have complained as more and more responsibilities were piled upon him – and, indeed, seems positively to have enjoyed the periods when the Prime Minister was away.

There was a substantial one of those at the beginning of 1960 when, on 6 January, Macmillan went on his 'wind of change' African tour (a companion piece to his Commonwealth tour of two years earlier). Once again, Rab was left in charge of the Government – by now there was a regular routine by which, on the day before he left, the Prime Minister would send Rab a minute asking him to be good enough to act for him in his absence and the Home Secretary would reply that he would be 'very honoured' to undertake such a duty. On this occasion the Prime Minister was to be away, again, for six weeks – and if, unlike the Commonwealth tour of 1958, there was no great Cabinet crisis to confront, Rab nevertheless did find himself handling a piece of Royal business of some constitutional delicacy.

It was not something of which he appears to have had any advance warning – suggesting perhaps that the liaison between No. 10 and the Home Office was not as close as it might have been. The Queen had been at Sandringham over Christmas and it was not until three days before Rab's first 1960 audience with her as acting Prime Minister that he appears to have been alerted to what was in the wind. Put briefly, what was at issue was the Queen's desire to incorporate her husband's adopted surname of Mountbatten not into the title of the Royal House but into the family name by which her descendants would ultimately be known. The matter seemed to Rab of quite sufficient sensitivity for him to telegraph almost at once to the Prime Minister, who had just arrived in Johannesburg:

> I have this weekend apprehended what was on foot at the Palace. The Lord Chancellor rang me in Gloucestershire on Saturday afternoon and from the parables I was able to understand that a change of name was envisaged for the children.
>
> I spoke with David [Kilmuir] and Alec Home on Monday and today the situation was made clear by a talk with the Queen. I was also much helped by reading for the first time the background

* Rab's own quote when both Churchill and Eden were ill in 1953: see p.199.

> papers of 1952, including Prince Philip's memorandum. Of all this Winston had told me, as a senior member of the Cabinet at the time, absolutely nothing.
>
> My talk with the Queen on this subject was rightly short and followed on usual routine reports on Cyprus, Kenya etc. Nevertheless the talk completely cleared my mind. She clearly indicated that the 1952 decisions [that the Royal Family should continue to be known as the House and Family of Windsor and that the Queen's descendants should bear the surname of Windsor] had been reached, and that she accepted them, but she did not indicate that she accepted them in spirit. She stressed that Prince Philip did not know of the present decision, on which she absolutely set her heart.[77]

It was not, of course, at that stage, as Rab's letter went on to make clear, a 'decision' at all. For what the Palace secretariat wanted was for the Queen to make the change 'on advice' – and that meant that the Cabinet would have to accept the constitutional responsibility for it. Hence, no doubt, the speed with which Rab got in touch with the Prime Minister – and a suggestion to him that he should make his own views known to the Cabinet. It was a suggestion that Macmillan does not appear to have taken up; and when the Cabinet met on Tuesday 2 February it was left to Rab and Kilmuir to try to steer the matter through.

It did not prove to be an altogether easy task – those around the Cabinet table were, of course, aware that the real pressure for the change emanated from Lord Mountbatten (who in 1952 had tried, and failed, to get the name of the Royal House itself changed to that of Mountbatten *tout seul*).[78] By the afternoon of 2 February Rab was, however, able to send the Prime Minister, now in Cape Town, the following telegram:

> The Cabinet had a long discussion this morning about the proposed declaration by the Queen. The Lord Chancellor explained all the background and the considerations which have led him to believe that the Queen's wishes should be met. Several of our colleagues expressed serious regret that this step had to be taken but, while recognising the dangers of criticism and unpopularity, particularly attached to the husband, none felt that the Queen's wishes should be refused.[79]

It may be safely assumed that that same evening Rab reported the decision in a rather different spirit to the Queen herself. Certainly, he was subsequently to inform Macmillan that the Queen had expressed 'her special gratitude' to the Prime Minister and wanted him to know that the decision had taken 'a great load off her mind'.[80] The 'gratitude', as has been indicated, might more properly be thought of as belonging to Rab – the more so as he personally seems to have had no great enthusiasm for the enterprise. (He would probably have had even less had he realised at the time that the change would not just apply to the Queen's distant descendants but would actually be commemorated on Princess Anne's marriage certificate in November 1973 – but then neither he nor any other member of the Cabinet had reckoned with the fast footwork of Mountbatten.)

To claim that so arcane a question monopolised Rab's attention while the Prime Minister was away would, no doubt, be misleading (though he did see the Queen on three successive Tuesdays) – but at least it illustrates the kind of unforeseen responsibilities that the Prime Minister's absence thrust upon him. A more down-to-earth matter was the hovering threat of a national railway strike, scheduled to start on Sunday 15 February, one day before Macmillan was due to return. Here the official position, as transmitted to the Press, was that the three rail unions were merely in dispute with the British Transport Commission, and that the Government was in no way involved. However, Rab had recognised from the outset that sooner or later there would probably have to be a Government intervention – and his main concern was to time it so that it would have the maximum impact. In the event, he resolved to leave it until almost the last moment, waiting until the night of 11 February to summon Sir Brian Robertson, the chairman of the British Transport Commission, to his room in the House of Commons. There is some indication that at that meeting, which was attended also by the Minister of Labour, Edward Heath, Rab personally hammered out the statements that each of them made the next day.[81] At the meeting Robertson was armed with authority from the Cabinet (encouraged by the Prime Minister) to go for a deal of 4 per cent; by the following evening it had become plain, however, that the price of averting the strike would be a 5 per cent pay increase across the board – an agreement that Rab reluctantly sanctioned but which, to his relief, was 'taken fairly calmly' by the country.[82] This was one question at least that he was not able to refer to Macmillan, who was already sailing home on the *Cape Town Castle*.

When the Prime Minister eventually returned on 16 February, at least the trains were running – though, even before that, Macmillan was commenting in his private journal, 'Butler has obviously been managing very well.'[83] There began, indeed, to be some sign of a thaw in their previously somewhat snowbound relationship – with Rab recording how, after the memorial service held for Edwina, Countess Mountbatten in Westminster Abbey on 7 March (she had died suddenly in Borneo in February) the Prime Minister had asked whether he might come home for a talk with Rab in Smith Square. The occasion seems to have been a modest success, as Rab was to make clear in a note he wrote two days later:

> It is nice to feel that there is confidence and that, under his very determined and worldly exterior, he conceals considerable anxiety. He has been feeling the weight of the decisions on Africa, and the difficulties of handling the team, and has, in fact, been taking some of the difficulties too seriously. The answer really is that a conversation enables him to get the problems off his chest. It is interesting, as Winston used to prove to us, how much problems are resolved by long and unrushed conversations.[84]

Not that conversations with everyone helped in the same way. That same day Rab recorded his growing sense of exasperation at going round the country, wearing his Party Chairman's hat, and listening to nothing but 'the very strong feelings of a huge section of the party in favour of birching and flogging'.[85] Fortunately, he had taken the precaution the previous autumn of referring the whole question of corporal punishment to the Home Office's own Advisory Council on Treatment of Offenders – and this became the breastplate that he tended to wear increasingly in face of the clamour for the return of the birch, if not the 'cat'. He even buckled it on when surrounded by angry policemen at a conference of the Association of Chief Police Officers in May – still, however, unrepentantly declaring, 'I am not convinced that the re-introduction of corporal punishment would have the effect for which its advocates hope.'[86]

Rab's main preoccupation, though, throughout the spring of 1960 was his own Betting and Gaming Bill. It had had a difficult time in Committee – debates which Rab had delegated to his new Under-Secretary at the Home Office, Dennis Vosper* (who had replaced

* Dennis Forwood Vosper (1916–68). Conservative MP, Runcorn 1950–64. Minister of Health 1957. Under-Secretary, Home Office 1959–60. Minister of State 1960–1. Secretary, Department of Technical Co-operation 1961–3. Created life peer as Baron Runcorn 1964.

Pat Hornsby-Smith the previous October). As Home Secretary, however, Rab took the lead on the Report Stage in the Commons and succeeded in steering what was in those days a fairly controversial Bill towards its Third Reading on 11 May.[87] But by then he had had at least one out-of-town academic outing – and a rather more successful one than his excursion to Glasgow two years previously. On 4 May – two days before the wedding of Princess Margaret to Antony Armstrong-Jones, which he attended, in Westminster Abbey – he was installed as Chancellor of Sheffield University, in succession to Lord Halifax. It may not have been quite the same thing as being elected Chancellor of Oxford, an endeavour in which Macmillan had already succeeded: but it remained for many years an association of which Rab was very proud, resigning it only in 1978, well after he had acquired a second university chancellorship at Essex.

Rab had hoped that Pandit Nehru, the Prime Minister of India, would be one of his first honorary degree holders – but the exigencies of the Commonwealth Conference held in London during the first two weeks of May made that impossible. As Secretary of State for the Home Department, Rab necessarily played only a peripheral, ceremonial part in this gathering, although, conscious of his family's connections with India, he did give a formal Government lunch for Nehru at No. 11 Downing Street (specially borrowed from the Chancellor for the occasion). Even that demonstration of interest in the Commonwealth can hardly have prepared him for the astonishing proposition the Prime Minister made to him some six weeks later. Rab had already been told at the beginning of June that Macmillan was contemplating moving Selwyn Lloyd to the Treasury in place of Heathcoat Amory (who was determined to retire from the Government) and replacing Lloyd at the Foreign Office with Lord Home, then Secretary of State for Commonwealth Relations. (Macmillan alleges in his memoirs that Rab 'had no desire either to return to the Foreign Office or to take on the Treasury'[88] but that, as has been noticed, is not necessarily conclusive.)* In any event, Macmillan displayed no great sensitivity in suggesting to Rab that he might like to succeed Home at the Commonwealth Relations Office. Revealingly or not, Rab makes no reference at all to this initiative of the Prime Minister's in his own autobiography – although he retained

* Contradictory evidence in fact exists in a manuscript note Rab made at the time, 'The PM never wished me to have the FO and said it would be like Herbert Morrison. I did not agree with this diagnosis but accepted it.' Butler Papers, Trinity College, Cambridge, G36, MS note headed 'Confidential' and dated 'August 1960'.

among his papers the draft of a minute, evidently written over a weekend at Stanstead, formally refusing the offer.[89] It is hard to believe that Rab took it seriously – although, interestingly, a letter does survive, written to him by his new PPS, James Ramsden* (who had succeeded Richard Sharples† the previous autumn), arguing that there might, after all, be something to be said for it. This letter does not, however, seem to have persuaded Rab, perhaps because earlier on Ramsden had not made any secret of his belief that the proper move for Rab should be to the FO.[90] Certainly, it is hard to think of a more hurtful insult to a man who had, after all, been Chancellor of the Exchequer, when Home was a mere Minister of State at the Scottish Office, than to invite him to step into the shoes of a former junior colleague now about to be elevated (as a peer) to the Foreign Office. None the less, as we shall see, Macmillan had at least succeeded in sowing a seed that was eventually to grow into a full ministerial plant just two years later.

For the moment, however, all Rab's ministerial attention was on the Home Office. With his Betting and Gaming Bill through, he did not have a great deal to worry about in terms of legislation. However, he was required at the end of June to defend the Government's decision not to take action on the first half of the Wolfenden Report concerned with homosexual offences under the law. Once again Rab played a totally straight bat, neither standing out against the need for reform of the law nor denying its desirability – but still insisting that the moment was not ripe for this particular change.[91] His reward, after one of his most persuasive, balanced performances at the Despatch Box, lay in seeing a Private Member's motion that had also been cogently and eloquently argued defeated by the surprisingly decisive majority of 114 in a vote of 213–99 (with only 22 Conservative MPs voting in favour, and no fewer than 173 against).

On another front, however, Rab was coming under increasing pressure. As if the demand for the return of corporal punishment was not enough, a potent lobby was building up within the Conservative Party in favour of introducing tighter immigration controls, another Home Office responsibility. One convert to the cause was

* James Edward Ramsden (1923–). Conservative MP, Harrogate 1954–74. PPS to Home Secretary 1959–60. Under-Secretary and Financial Secretary, War Office 1960–3. Secretary of State for War 1963–4.

† Richard Christopher Sharples (1916–73). Conservative MP, Sutton and Cheam 1954–72. He succeeded Hubert Ashton as PPS to Rab when he went to the Home Office in 1957. He relinquished the post on becoming an Assistant Government Whip in 1959, and subsequently was knighted and appointed Governor and Commander-in-Chief of Bermuda, where he was murdered in 1973.

Rab's own Home Office Under-Secretary, David Renton. For the moment, however, he made his pleas in vain – not least because the Government, especially after Edward Heath's appointment to assist Lord Home at the Foreign Office, was planning its application to join the European Economic Community. Any action that would necessarily be seen as discriminating further against the Commonwealth was considered, and not only by Rab, as likely to be unduly provocative.

Such was the skill of Tory managers in those days that the topic was even kept off that year's Conservative Party Conference agenda (and its leading advocate, Sir Cyril Osborne, the Tory MP for Louth, was reduced to standing outside the Conference hall morosely handing out leaflets).[92] Almost exactly a year after the Party's great election victory, the Conference at Scarborough in effect turned into something of a love-feast. For once, Rab did not even have to face the inevitable law-and-order debate (leaving it to his deputy, Dennis Vosper); instead, he intervened only at the end of the Friday afternoon to deliver an unexceptionable homily as Chairman of the Party. Even so, there were some danger signs for Rab: the *Sunday Times*, for example, wrote of him as the Party's 'father figure' while simultaneously referring to Iain Macleod as 'the only man with the personal strength and courage to lead the party' into the future.[93] It was an ominous sign that, in the wake of the third successive general election victory, the generation game had started to be played in Tory politics.

It was also, though no one (including Rab) seems to have recognised it at the time, a premonition of a shift at the top which was to happen just a year later. Iain Macleod had always been very much Rab's protégé – and yet, in the course of 1961, largely because of his courageous battle against the right wing of the Conservative Party over African policy, gradually he began to emerge as the new standard-bearer of the younger, more liberal elements among Tory MPs.[94] It was a process to which Rab himself, unwittingly, gave some assistance. Despite the opinion polls, which continued to show him as the candidate most favoured to succeed Macmillan,[95] 1961 was not a very good year for him. To begin with, in parliamentary terms, it started with the death of the veteran Labour peer, Viscount Stansgate,* within a fortnight of the new session opening. No one,

* William Wedgwood Benn (1877–1960). Liberal MP, St George's, Tower Hamlets 1906–18, Leith 1918–27. Labour MP North Aberdeen 1928–31, Manchester, Gorton 1937–42. Secretary of State for India 1929–31, Secretary of State for Air 1945–6. Created 1st Viscount Stansgate 1941.

of course, could possibly have foreseen at that stage what the consequences of this would turn out to be; but it immediately plunged Rab, in his capacity as Leader of the House of Commons, into the role of seeming to defend the indefensible. Other MP sons of peers previously – including Lord Hailsham in 1950 – had struggled hard against being automatically dispatched to the Upper House; but none had ever fought a more skilful or resourceful campaign than the heir to the Stansgate viscountcy, the young Labour MP, Anthony Wedgwood Benn. Rab started off pacifically enough, quickly agreeing that Benn's petition submitting that 'he is and should remain' a member of the House of Commons should be referred to the Committee of Privileges.* The troubles began for Rab when the Committee reported some four months later, and it was discovered that only his own casting vote (as Leader of the House he had voted on no other issue before the Privileges Committee) had defeated a proposal to introduce a special Bill to solve the dilemma of 'the reluctant peer' as Benn came to be known. When the Committee of Privileges report was debated by the House on Thursday 13 April, Rab had a particularly rough time defending his position; although the whips were put on, a total of twenty-two Tory MPs voted against the Government in a variety of divisions.[96] The blow was made all the worse for the Leader of the House as only two days before no fewer than sixty-nine Conservative MPs had staged a rebellion against him, in his separate role of Home Secretary, by backing an amendment to his Criminal Justice Bill demanding the return of flogging.[97] To Rab the second revolt was almost certainly more hurtful than the earlier one – if only because the MPs who rejected his advice on the peerage question were drawn predominantly from the ranks of his own former young admirers. They could hardly, however, be blamed for their demonstration: they had, after all, given their allegiance to Rab on the understanding that he, above all, stood for liberal reform – and yet here he was upholding one of the most anachronistic aspects of traditional feudal discrimination. To be fair to Rab, he did not take long to spot the internal contradiction in his position. A fortnight later he was to be heard on the floor of the House disclosing that the Government

* Anthony Wedgwood Benn, the signature at that time with which he still signed his name, wrote Rab a most fulsome hand-written note expressing 'thanks for all your kindness'. The letter makes it clear that the decision to refer the matter to the Committee of Privileges was a result of a deal between the Leader of the House and the determined Bristol ex-MP. Butler Papers, G35, letter beginning 'Dear Home Secretary' and dated 24.11.1960.

would be ready to set up a Joint Select Committee of both Houses to consider, among other matters, 'certain anomalies in our constitution' including 'the question of the surrender of peerages'.[98] Just two and a quarter years later that Committee's report – and the subsequent legislation it produced – would enable not only the notional Lord Stansgate to return to the House of Commons but the Lords Home and Hailsham as well.

That was by no means the only blunder Rab made that summer. He had, indeed, a rather disagreeable time of it – starting off with being roundly abused over his opposition to corporal punishment at the annual Conservative Women's Conference held that year at the Central Hall Westminster.[99] After this came his final reluctant acquiescence to the need to bring in immigration legislation (hardly a decision most happily expressed in his announcement to a Conservative teachers' conference that it would not be based 'on colour prejudice alone').[100] Finally he suffered a genuine banana skin incident during his Whitsun holiday, spent with his wife in Spain. Here what appears to have happened is that Rab, who had, after all, been away for some time from the world of diplomacy, simply fell into a trap. Invited on his first Sunday in Madrid to dine with the Spanish Foreign Minister, he found himself expected to make an after-dinner speech. He did it off the cuff from a few scribbled notes made on the back of a menu card. The Spaniards, however, plainly believing that a gift had been delivered into their hands, promptly put out through their Ministry of Information an account of his remarks. In the era of Franco, they turned out to be mildly embarrassing to the British Government, since Rab was reported to have called for 'a closer association between Spain and the West' and even seems to have implied that Spain should join NATO.[101] It is difficult to know how much damage the incident really did – either diplomatically to the British Government or personally to Rab – but certainly Macmillan was able to confide, with a certain melancholy satisfaction, to his private journal, 'Poor Rab has been unlucky, caught by an old trick . . . The Press – especially the "popular" Press is very excited here . . . It is really very tiresome and very silly.'[102]

Elsewhere, though, Rab did have his public successes. He got both his Criminal Justice Bill (thwarting a much-rumoured Lords revolt on flogging) and his Licensing Bill (extending the hours that pubs could open) safely through Parliament. He also continued to handle the House of Commons reasonably successfully, even if it had developed into one of its fractious moods by the winter of 1961 (particularly over Africa) prompting Rab to send out a circular to Government Ministers, urging them to be more attentive to their duties both in the Smoking Room and in their formal relationship with back-bench committees.[103] From his base at the Central Office, he had acquired the habit of issuing what were virtual encyclicals to Conservative constituency chairmen, for some reason sent out to coincide with the great festivals of the Church.[104] So the last thing he can have expected when Parliament rose for the summer recess was that, before it returned in the autumn, he would have been stripped of two of his hats and left with just one.

What prompted Macmillan – on the very eve of the 1961 Conservative Party Conference at Brighton – apparently to go out of his way publicly to humiliate Rab puzzled not only political journalists but perplexed a substantial segment of the Conservative faithful as well. Of course, the Prime Minister may have been offended by Rab's reluctance to fall in with his Commonwealth Office plans for him over a year earlier. But, even if that was so, the vengeance he took cannot help seeming excessive – not least because, just before Parliament rose, he had sent Rab a message thanking him for a report on morale within the Party and remarking that 'considering all the difficulties, it is really quite good'.[105] The truth, though, probably was that, by the end of September when the decisions, in so far as they affected Rab, seem finally to have been taken, Macmillan found himself under increasing pressure. The tension between the Commonwealth Secretary, Duncan Sandys (who had taken the job in lieu of Rab in 1960) and his brave but intense Colonial Secretary, Iain Macleod, was no longer tolerable. The first priority for Macmillan, therefore, was to resolve it; and if the only way to do that was by placating Macleod for his banishment from the Colonial Office – at the expense of Rab – then that, alas, was a regrettable necessity.

The course by which Macmillan sought to reach this objective was, however, distinctly devious. The first intimation which Rab had that anything untoward might be afoot came when he briefly broke his summer holiday on the Isle of Mull (where he had just bought a house) to spend a weekend shooting at Swinton in Yorkshire. Macmillan had been there just before him and it was from the Principal of the Swinton Conservative College, Reginald Northam (an old Cambridge acquaintance of Rab's), that he first discovered what was in the Prime Minister's mind. Macmillan, he learned, had discussed with Northam 'the desirability of my giving up the party chairmanship'. Strangely, however, the same topic does not seem to have been mentioned by the Prime Minister to their mutual host, the Earl of Swinton, who strongly urged on Rab that he must hold on to the Party Chairmanship and Leadership of the House, whatever eventually happened about the Home Office. Thoroughly bewildered, Rab returned to resume his holiday on the Isle of Mull.

Not surprisingly, when he got back to London on 12 September, he found that the Prime Minister was anxious to see him. They met first when they lunched together at Admiralty House (to which Macmillan had recently moved to allow a wholesale building reconstruction to take place in Downing Street). The occasion does not appear to have been a particularly happy one, if only because the Prime Minister started ruminating on the mistake he thought he had made 'in piling so many offices upon me'. There were, Macmillan argued, bound to be 'certain frictions between my Home Office views and record and the party's wishes to see flogging reintroduced; he also said, quite explicitly, that he thought it a pity to combine the Leadership of the House with the chairmanship of the party – a job for which he wanted someone with more fire than I had recently shown.' Had he, Rab finally found himself being asked, 'ever thought of a peerage'?[106]

It says something, no doubt, for Rab's reluctance to fulfil the role of the sacrificial victim – to say nothing of Macmillan's determination to play the part of the great manipulator – that two further lunches between them should have had to take place before the Prime Minister was able to announce his new Cabinet dispositions on 9 October, the very day that the Tory representatives were gathering at Brighton. After the second of these two lunches Rab drafted an anguished letter – poignantly, as events were ultimately to work out – destined to be sent to Lord Home. In it he explained, with as much surprise as pain, all that had gone on:

> I was finally informed by Harold that I was to give up being both Chairman of the party and Leader of the House in favour of Iain Macleod. I was told that I was too old and had anyway done the House for six years. I am not against giving up the Chairmanship and, within reason, not against a change in the House.
>
> I could have dug my heels in and refused to give up the Commons, where I have so much support. But I have accepted all without saying anything, and it is Harold's wish. But I now face singularly unpleasant resolutions at the party conference shorn of two plumes and retaining only the Home Office,

which is the one hot potato. I shall, therefore, need your help as a friend.[107]

In fact, Rab turned out to need no such thing. By one of the ironies of politics, he enjoyed that year probably his greatest triumph ever at a Conservative Party Conference, bewitching the audience and becalming the normally indignant debate on crime and punishment with a display of supreme political artistry. He managed to persuade the Conference to reject the substantive motion, calling for an extension of the death penalty and the restoration of corporal punishment, in favour of an anodyne amendment that spoke only of an increase in the prison building programme, strict enforcement of sentences and compensation for the victims of crime.[108] It was not only Iain Macleod – who rushed up to congratulate Rab the moment he had finished speaking – who felt that this had been Rab's finest hour.* Pushing his luck, the Prime Minister was to write not only to Rab but to his wife as well expressing his delight at what he, somewhat insouciantly, termed 'a real triumph'.[109]

For Rab, the vindication of the policy he had consistently pursued, while others (including the Prime Minister) had shown signs of wilting, was undoubtedly very gratifying. But it did not solve the problem of the gap left by the removal of two-thirds of his previous responsibilities. The first proposal made – and it surfaced, although not very prominently, even in the background Downing Street 'guidance' on the Cabinet changes – was that he would 'be available to assist the Prime Minister over a wide field of public duties and, in particular, to lead the ministerial group charged with the oversight of the Common Market negotiations'[110] (Britain's first application to join the EEC had been announced by the Prime Minister at the end of July). This project did not, however, prove to be a particularly fruitful one: there was already a double-banking relationship operating at the Foreign Office involving both Lord Home and Edward Heath – and in any case the negotiations, which were to drag on until January 1963, had not yet made sufficient progress for much 'oversight' to be required. In the months immediately following the

* Macleod had, in fact, refused to take the Chairmanship of the Party alone and had demanded the Leadership of the House as well as the price of moving from the Colonial Office. But he may well have felt a twinge of guilt. The day the Prime Minister capitulated to his demands and he got both jobs, he wrote a letter to Rab beginning, 'I have been so long a lieutenant of yours in my political career that I am particularly delighted to have the chance of carrying on work you have done with such distinction'. Butler Papers, G37.

1961 Party Conference, that may not have mattered much: the introduction of the Commonwealth Immigrants Bill, at the very beginning of the 1961–2 parliamentary session meant that even someone who was simply Home Secretary and nothing else had his hands pretty full. It was one Bill, however, out of whose passage through the Commons Rab got singularly little satisfaction: indeed, if anything, he made his personal 'lack of enthusiasm for some aspects of the measure' all too evident.[111] His attitude was, no doubt, partly determined by his own Indian childhood and imperial background, but it must also have owed something to the almost united hostility displayed by the quality Press towards the Government's proposals; for Rab, to be regularly and relentlessly attacked by such papers as *The Times*, the *Guardian* and *The Economist* was an entirely new experience – and he could be forgiven for not enjoying it.

But at least his parliamentary professionalism – except over a bad initial muddle as to whether or not citizens of the Republic of Ireland would be covered by the new immigration controls – did not desert him. The Bill, which had its Second Reading only on 16 November, was (despite having its Committee Stage on the floor of the Commons) safely in the Lords by February and on the Statute Book by the middle of April. Rab was almost certainly not sorry to be rid of it – even on the floor of the House he had appeared to his colleague at the Home Office, David Renton, far too eager to make concessions (explaining, when reproached, 'Oh, I had to do it to get the entire beastly clause through').[112] However, with the immigration battle behind him, he began to feel distinctly under-employed. It might, therefore, look as if Macmillan was guilty of a kindly gesture towards him in choosing precisely this moment to offer Rab a new assignment. Alas, any such suspicions can probably be laid to rest; for, as Rab was soon to discover, it was to the Secretary of the Cabinet, Sir Norman Brook, and not to the Prime Minister, that he owed the post that was to keep him employed – first half-time and then full-time – for the next fifteen months.

What seems to have agitated the Cabinet Secretary, and other members of the Downing Street staff, was the amount of unnecessary stress that was being placed on the Prime Minister. In particular, the substitution of Reginald Maudling for Iain Macleod at the Colonial Office had solved nothing: if anything, Maudling was showing greater tenacity in the cause of a fair constitution for Northern Rhodesia than his predecessor – and the relationship between him and Sandys (the Commonwealth Secretary) was even more strained than it had been between Sandys and Macleod. With his strong belief in ordered Government, Norman Brook began to suspect that there might be a structural fault in the system. The solution, he came to feel, lay in removing the inevitable tension between the two Cabinet Secretaries by uniting their contradictory functions – particularly manifest in their respective responsibilities, one for the Federal Government of the Central African Federation, the other for its dependent territories – under one senior ministerial head. The first indication that Rab had that such a proposal was even on the horizon was when he had two separate meals with Macmillan (the first a lunch at Buck's, the second a dinner at Smith Square) when he returned from his Christmas holiday, again spent on Mull:

> I saw at the first Cabinet that Harold was to have a sandwich lunch on Friday 12 January so I suggested lunch at Buck's, at which he jumped. He was most explicit at his pleasure at talking things over 'with his deputy' and said how few there were now, apart from David Kilmuir, with old-fashioned experience of politics. He said his main problem was dealing with the comparatively young and inexperienced.
>
> Of all the troubles facing the Government he seems still to be most personally influenced by Africa. He is astonished that, having taken so much trouble to change Macleod, the 'new priest', Maudling is so out-and-out for changing the Northern Rhodesian constitution. I was commissioned to see Macleod to whom I spoke of the importance of keeping things steady. I did not find him especially keen to give up all his new honours.
>
> On Tuesday I had Harold to dinner in Smith Square. In the development of gloom at the idea of possible resignations, he propounded the idea that I might become Colonial Secretary in the event of a break-up, with Reggie Buller* as Home Secretary. I have since played this down with the Chief Whip. The latter wouldn't mind me back as Leader of the House but thinks Thorneycroft could be Colonial Secretary. However, we all hope Maudling will stay.[113]

At that stage, therefore, the notion of Norman Brook's 'master plan' had clearly not been put to the Prime Minister. Six weeks later, however, it was a different story:

* Reginald Edward Manningham-Buller (1905–80). Conservative MP Daventry 1943–50, South Northants 1950–62. Solicitor-General 1951–4. Attorney-General 1954–62. Lord Chancellor 1962–4. Created 1st Viscount Dilhorne 1964.

I had several conversations with Harold Macmillan about what he finally described as 'my patriotic decision' to take on responsibility for the Central African Federation and the dependent territories. I remember best the last of the three. He quite clearly considers that this is the challenge of my present and future.

The genesis is old, dating over the last three years, or indeed since 1953 [when the Central African Federation was launched]. All this time the dichotomy between Colonial and Commonwealth Departments has been intense, leading to the threatened resignations of Iain Macleod and the recent doubts and perplexities of Reggie Maudling. Norman Brook, the Secretary of the Cabinet, put in a minute to the PM, suggesting the amalgamation of the two offices and recommending my name. He felt that the Prime Minister could not go on with the effort and anxiety involved. He thought the present system involved an unwarranted strain on Cabinet Government itself.[114]

The responsibility, therefore, for Rab's new incarnation – announced to a certain amount of derision in the Commons on 15 March in the presence of both the existing Commonwealth and Colonial Secretaries – plainly rested not with the head of Government but with the supreme mandarin of the Civil Service. That was not perhaps the ideal basis on which to embark upon an unchartered constitutional voyage. But Rab, though he had not at all reached for the job (suggesting, indeed, other candidates for it),[115] did start with certain advantages. In the first place he knew – and had established something of a personal relationship with – the now very much embattled Prime Minister of the Central African Federation, Sir Roy Welensky, with whom Macleod, in particular, had got on extremely badly.[116] They had first met in 1958, before Rab's marriage, when he had spent a holiday with some Courtauld relatives in the eastern highlands of Rhodesia: quite unpredictably they had hit it off (Welensky, an ex-boxing champion, was the opposite of an intellectual). Rab had seen something of him since then at the two Commonwealth Prime Ministers' Conferences Welensky had attended in London (as well as receiving long letters of grievance from him whenever he felt British policy was going astray in central Africa). Rab also knew from his Treasury days the Prime Minister of Southern Rhodesia, Sir Edgar Whitehead, who had been Finance Minister of the anomalous half-dominion when he had been Chancellor back in the early 1950s. The people he did not know were the black leaders in both Northern Rhodesia and Nyasaland – and it was to repair this omission that he planned a trip to the Federation, which took place between 11 and 27 May 1961.

It turned out, at least in terms of the white community, to be a distinct success – with even Welensky feeling 'encouraged to believe that Britain still had some desire to maintain close bonds between the Territories of the Federation'.[117] There were dangers, however, for Rab in this – as he had discovered before he left, finding himself besieged by various right-wingers (including his own pre-war and wartime PPS, Wing-Commander Sir Archibald James) with assorted plans for the dismemberment of Northern Rhodesia so that the whites might at least retain control of the Copper Belt. Rab, to his credit, remained not only sceptical but censorious of all such proposals, even though it was actively suggested to him that they might well provide 'a wonderful opportunity of cashing in with those Conservatives who might well be instrumental in forwarding my own personal interests'.[118]

There is no doubt, however, that his prospect of succeeding to the Leadership was still very much in Rab's mind. Indeed, his memo of two conversations with the Prime Minister in January included an almost excessive amount of attention to this topic – with Rab registering alarm, mingled with excitement, when Macmillan reflected, 'Either I shall decide to go before the Election, in which case it all falls on you, or it will be a year or two after the Election, in which case it will not be so certain.'[119] It is difficult, in fact, to resist the conclusion that Macmillan, by the year 1962, had come to regard Rab as a trout that he could tickle and play with at will, an impression reinforced by his presumably deliberate observation delivered later in the year, also in a private conversation, 'There is only one Minister now who could replace me and that is Alec Home.'[120]

For the time being, though, Rab could at least feel reasonably secure. On taking over his Central African responsibilities he had not had to vacate the Home Office: all he had done was to take on an additional staff – and an extra office for his Central Africa work, just across the road in Gwyddyr House, Whitehall. He would also perhaps have been less than human if he had not felt a certain sense of *schadenfreude* at the tribulations that had rapidly beset the man who had succeeded him as both Leader of the House of Commons and Chairman of the Party. Not only was Macleod getting very bad notices in his role as Leader of the House (a position which Rab had certainly not made any easier for him by stubbornly refusing to surrender the traditional Leader's room just behind the Speaker's chair);[121] as Chairman of the Party, Macleod was also becoming the victim of the Government's inevitable unpopularity after nearly three years in office. The Liberals had won the Orpington by-election in March, the Tories had lost a seat at Middlesbrough to Labour in June and on 12 July another by-election took place in the Labour marginal of Leicester North-East, where both the Conservative candidate's actual vote and his percentage share of the poll were halved.

The summer of 1962, in fact, saw the Government in very low water. Macmillan had never really recovered from the collapse of his 'Summit' diplomacy shortly after the 1959 election, the EEC negotiations were hanging fire, and there were increasingly angry rumblings from the Commonwealth over both that and the Commonwealth Immigrants Act. Worst of all, Selwyn Lloyd had contrived to give the impression of being not so much an Iron Chancellor as a wooden one, quite unable to show the qualities of flair or imagination which had carried Rab through his own difficult period in the early 1950s. It was against this background that Macmillan, sometime in midsummer, started reflecting on the need to make a change, at least at the Treasury. It was not a proposal that Rab initially opposed: he had never been a great admirer of Selwyn Lloyd and, like Macleod, he was worried by the general state of the Party's popularity, vividly focused by the findings of an opinion poll that the Central Office had specially commissioned on Leicester North-East in advance of the by-election result.

At the time, indeed, there was some suspicion that Rab was the instigator of what came to be known as 'the July Massacre', the act of prime ministerial autocracy by which Macmillan, in a single day, lopped off the heads of a third of his Cabinet.[122] In retrospect, that suspicion does not appear to have been well-founded – though Rab probably provided the occasion, but not the cause, for the swiftness and brutality with which Macmillan began to act on the evening of Thursday 12 July. That morning a 'leak' of the proposed Cabinet purge – remarkably accurate in most (though not all) particulars had appeared in the *Daily Mail*;[123] and Rab, through a chance conversation he had held on the previous day with Lord Rothermere, the paper's proprietor, was suspected to be the source of it.[124]

However, far from being the beneficiary of the most massive reshuffle of modern times – seven Cabinet Ministers, including the Chancellor of the Exchequer and the Lord Chancellor, were sacked overnight – Rab was more the victim of it. True, in the eventual official announcement he was given yet another new grand office, that of First Secretary of State, combined with an unofficial intimation (conveyed to the Lobby and faithfully reproduced in the newspapers on the morning of Saturday 14 July) that he would from now on in effect be Deputy Prime Minister. Those, however, who saw in that the fulfilment of all Rab's aspirations did not know their man: for the price was that he had had to sacrifice the one real job that he still held – Secretary of State for Home Affairs.

Any doubt of the reluctance that Rab felt to do so is adequately disposed of by a hand-written letter that he drafted, but may not have sent, to the Prime Minister that same week. It seems, admittedly, to have been written before the title '*First* Secretary of State' had been invented – but otherwise the substance of the case it made tended to be borne out by the events of the coming year:

> Dear Harold,
>
> Before we meet on Friday as arranged I ought shortly to put my anxieties about the plan you propose for me.
>
> 1) I understand from Norman Brook and others that there will be no precedence in the title Secretary of State. I will, therefore, lose my position as senior Secretary of State, as Home Secretary, and also all my connection with the Court and my duties with the Queen.
>
> 2) I am informed that no gazetted position as No. 2 is permitted.
>
> 3) The last time that arrangements were made with the Press to show that I was helping you very little came of it. I lost the Leadership of the House and chairmanship of the party – and the general impression was 'Butler Down'.
>
> 4) Since then the African appointment has tended to improve the situation but you said, most emphatically, when I took on Africa that I must *not* do it alone.
>
> 5) The latest proposal is that I become Secretary of State (*tout court*). I will to the public mind have no duties except Africa. Furthermore, without a classical office such as Lord President, I shall be out on a raft, as I was after Anthony Eden's decision in 1955. I know what this means: one has a personal assistant and inadequate staff to transact business.
>
> 6) I, therefore, think I shall be out on an African limb, as there has never yet been any clearly defined position for an undefined deputy.[125]

Apart from exposing the streak of self-pity which, as he came to his sixtieth birthday, was becoming an increasingly prominent element in Rab's make-up, the letter made shrewd political sense: yet, once again, when it came to the final decision, Rab proved to be putty in the Prime Minister's hands. On the evening of Friday 13 July, his successor at the Home Office was announced (he was Henry Brooke, who for the next two years was to show a total lack of sensitivity in what is always one of the most delicate jobs in Government); and, although on this occasion Macmillan kept his side of the bargain, by accompanying the publication of the formal Cabinet List with a *coda* explaining that Rab, as well as being First Secretary of State, would also be serving as Deputy Prime Minister – a constitutional innovation which at least excited the Lobby correspondents – the truth was that the whole arrangement was a piece of political nonsense from the start.

In the first place, Rab's continuing African responsibilities – he was to make two further lengthy trips to the Federation in the next twelve months as well as presiding over the Nyasaland Conference held in London in November – made it impossible for him to keep his old oversight of the home front, let alone function effectively as Deputy Prime Minister. The task he had been given in Africa was virtually to act as the receiver or liquidator for the Federation. It required 'all of his time and energy':[126] although as First Secretary of State he had been rewarded with an imposing new office in the Treasury – reputed to be the largest anywhere in Whitehall – he was seldom to be found in it and was far more often at work in the old headquarters of his Central Africa Office at Gwyddyr House. There, though he had an excellent Civil Service staff led by Mark Tennant and Duncan Watson,* it was necessarily – as Rab had foreseen – a small one: unlike at the Home Office, he was also without any junior Ministers to whom work could be delegated. But such assistance from support arms would probably not have been of much use in any case: the essence of Rab's role in central Africa was a diplomatic one – and that meant winning the confidence of all the parties concerned ranging from Dr Banda through Kenneth Kaunda to Sir Roy Welensky. It was something that, against all the odds, he achieved: within fifteen months of his original part-time appointment to the Central Africa Office, the Federation had been wound up, both Northern Rhodesia and Nyasaland had been established as the independent states of Zambia and Malawi (with only the dilemma

* Rab was to pay tribute to their 'remarkable capacities for work' in his autobiography and to add, 'In all my long experience of government office I never benefited from better briefs.' *The Art of the Possible*, p. 216.

of ceding full independence to Southern Rhodesia without majority rule remaining to haunt British Governments of the future). It was a formidable achievement; but its price – paid, perhaps appropriately, by Macmillan – was a Government that suddenly began to go badly adrift as the result of the absence of Rab's guiding hand at home.

THE LAST OF ENGLAND

15 The Second Leadership Struggle

By the late summer of 1962, one question dominated the minds of Macmillan and the majority of his Cabinet colleagues. The long Brussels negotiations to secure British entry into the EEC were, it seemed, about to be crowned with success – and the only apparent problem that remained was a political one. How could Europe be sold to the electorate as the great new challenge of the 1960s, answering, as it were, effectively and conclusively, Dean Acheson's wounding gibe about Britain having lost an empire and not yet found a role?

Rab, from the vantage point of his agricultural constituency in East Anglia, had never been an easy convert to the European cause – which may help to explain why Macmillan had sought to sterilise him by putting him in charge of the ministerial committee with oversight of the negotiations. It had not, as we have seen, turned out to be a particularly onerous responsibility – and in any case had done little initially to change Rab's own predominantly sceptical attitude. In fact, at the beginning of 1962 he was still plainly worried by the anxieties within his own constituency – noting that 'the simpler, down-to-earth farmers are all against it' and adding uneasily, 'My seat is fundamentally at stake.'[1]

His general sense of agnosticism was no secret to his colleagues – which, again, probably explains why Macmillan, as the negotiations appeared to be reaching their culmination, cut short an August shooting holiday in Yorkshire to have a long-planned dinner with Rab in London on the subject of Europe. At this dinner, once more at Buck's (a club of which they were both members), Rab, according to Macmillan, delivered a 'helpful, if somewhat belated, declaration' in favour of British entry, though warning 'that we might share the fate of Sir Robert Peel and his supporters'.[2] It is an account that, for once, Rab at least broadly confirms – admitting, with reference to that summer's Commonwealth Conference, 'I myself had to make a staunch decision to back the Common Market. This meant overcoming my anxieties on domestic agriculture and Saffron Walden.'[3]

A 'staunch' decision hardly sounds like a very enthusiastic one – and though Rab's Party Conference speech that year was given over to calming the fears of the agricultural elements within the Party,[4] he himself was never in favour of the Government putting its entire shirt on a horse before it even knew that it would be a runner. One of Rab's favourite maxims, borrowed from Talleyrand, was always *Surtout point de zêle* – and there was a great deal of zeal about that October at Llandudno, not all of which (like the campaign buttons pinned on Central Office girls saying simply 'Yes') he found to his taste. The Conference, in fact, turned out to be something of a false dawn – and not merely because of the ultimate collapse of the Common Market talks some three months later. From the moment the Conservatives left Llandudno almost everything started to go wrong in terms of both the Government's tactics and strategy.

To begin with, there was the strange affair of John Vassall,* the spy in the Admiralty. In the wake of his trial and conviction some wild allegations started to be flung about suggesting that, though an obvious homosexual, he had been protected by friends in high places. In its effort to rebut the charges, the Government made every mistake in the book – first of all encouraging the Security Commission to publish a White Paper[5] disclosing the harmless but faintly ridiculous correspondence that had passed between Vassall and the former Civil Lord of the Admiralty, T. G. D. Galbraith, who had since moved to be Under-Secretary to the Scottish Office (and whose resignation Macmillan accepted rather too hurriedly). Then, under pressure from the Opposition, the Government panicked again by resorting to the clanking machinery of a Judicial Tribunal under the 1921 Tribunals of Inquiry (Evidence) Act. The Radcliffe Tribunal, whose eventual report in April[6] was a wholesale indictment of the customs and practices of the trade of journalism (it had already sent

* J. W. C. Vassall was convicted of espionage and sentenced to eighteen years' imprisonment at the Old Bailey on 22 October. He had been a clerical officer both at the British Embassy in Moscow and in the office of the Civil Lord of the Admiralty in London.

two reporters to prison for contempt while it was sitting), seriously antagonised the whole of Fleet Street.

What part, if any, Rab played in this whole ill-advised procedure will presumably be established only when the official Government documents become available. But an interim assessment can only be that, because of his own preoccupation with Central Africa, he had little or nothing to do with it – certainly no documentation of his involvement survives in his own records. It is also hard, if not impossible, to believe that the entire affair would have been handled so maladroitly if he had still been in charge of the Home Office, with its traditional responsibility for security matters. (The same clumsy pattern was to be repeated – if in reverse order – a few months later, in a far more serious matter.)

The other blows that befell the Government that winter were, however, largely uncovenanted. The abrupt cancellation by the Kennedy Administration of the Skybolt nuclear delivery system knocked the stuffing out of Britain's defence policy in December. Then General de Gaulle's personal 'No' to Britain's application to join the Common Market in January destroyed the whole basis on which the Government had been conducting its foreign and Commonwealth policy. With a certain sense of lugubrious vindication, Rab subsequently recorded a leading journalist's view that 'the engine had fallen out of the entire Government strategy'[7] with the brutal ending of the Common Market negotiations.*

Rab, though, was to be spared the bitter aftermath of that, for on 27 January (two days before the talks in Brussels formally ended) he left on a tour of Central Africa, starting with a triumphal visit to Nyasaland, whose right to secession he had finally conceded in the Commons on 19 December.[8] However, before he departed on his second protracted African trip within six months, he had yet another dinner at Buck's with the Prime Minister, whom he found displaying 'all the pinkness of a caged lion'. Macmillan, showing perhaps an unappetising side of his character, remarked that he felt 'Gaitskell's illness was playing into his hands'[9] (the Leader of the Labour Party was at the time mortally ill in the Middlesex Hospital and finally died on 17 January). For once, however, the Great Manipulator was totally deceived: almost immediately after Gaitskell's death, a rebellion against Macmillan's continuing leadership started to

* Rab said as much in an interview with Anthony Wedgwood Benn on 20 February 1963, 'You know, the Common Market breakdown was a much bigger shock for us than you chaps realised.' Tony Benn, private papers, notes on interview with Rab, 20.2.1963.

build up within the Conservative Party in the Commons, increasing in momentum once the new Leader of the Opposition, Harold Wilson, was elected at the age of forty-six on 14 February.

By then Rab was back from Africa, and the first thing that struck him was the new mood of restiveness on the Tory benches. He was not, however, given much time to take consolation from it – for at their first meeting together on 21 February the Prime Minister went out of his way to make it clear that 'all the critics of himself covered me under their broad umbrella', driving the knife in further with the remark that 'the combination of the Kennedy image plus Harold Wilson at 46 is a potent force in favour of a younger man'.[10] Over the next few months Macmillan, in fact, became not so much the Great Manipulator as the Great Emasculator. If Rab never came out fighting from his corner, as the Prime Minister's authority and credibility visibly dwindled, it was largely because he had allowed himself to be cajoled into believing that they sank or swam together.

The first moment when Rab should have revised that estimate came on the morning of Friday 22 March. According to his own account, given some years afterwards, he found himself suddenly summoned by the Prime Minister to 'hold his hand' while they both waited in the House for John Profumo,* the Secretary of State for War, to make a Personal Statement as the first Order of Business that Friday morning. Rab, to be fair, was appalled – exclaiming on the telephone, 'Not on a *Friday morning* surely!' But Macmillan was obdurate, explaining that on the previous night on the floor of the House of Commons allegations had been made against the War Minister by three Labour MPs that needed to be rebutted straight away. Rab was still not convinced, arguing that all Profumo needed to say (and that in the fullness of time) was that he understood certain accusations had been made against him, that he demanded an inquiry and that, until it reported, he would wish to withdraw from his ministerial post.[11] If Rab's advice had been taken, the Government would have been spared a great deal of embarrassment, the Secretary of State for War the disgrace of being caught out in a lie to the House of Commons and Macmillan himself a wound to his reputation that was first to prove septic and ultimately fatal. However, the Prime Minister insisted that Friday morning that things were already on a pre-ordained course and Rab's advice had come

* John Dennis Profumo (1915–). Conservative MP, Stratford-upon-Avon 1950–63. Secretary of State for War 1960–3.

too late (a meeting between Profumo and five Government Ministers had in fact taken place in the small hours at which his Personal Statement had been hammered out). Considering what happened afterwards, there could hardly have been a more vivid illustration of all that the Government in general, and Macmillan in particular, had forfeited by losing Rab's influence from its central political counsels.

How great a part Rab played in the *dénouement* of the Profumo affair is, again, a matter of mystery. He was, actually, in charge of the Government when Profumo finally (and belatedly) sent his letter of confession and resignation to the Prime Minister on 4 June. But since all the preliminaries, following an official inquiry by the Lord Chancellor, had been handled by the Chief Whip and the Principal Private Secretary in Downing Street – and Macmillan was only as far away as Scotland (where Profumo's letter was sent direct to him) – it seems highly unlikely that Rab operated as anything more than a sidelines spectator. He did, however, speak to Macmillan on the telephone and was somewhat taken aback to hear him say he could 'hardly believe this was a major issue'[12] – a belief from which Rab must have disabused him, since the Prime Minister immediately came back to London.

In any event, Rab's main attention was almost certainly on other matters. At long last, his patient negotiation to bring about the voluntary dissolution of the Central African Federation was on the brink of fulfilment – and Rab was to leave for the Victoria Falls Conference just as the fallout from the eventual Profumo debate in the Commons (in which, on 17 June, twenty-seven Conservative MPs abstained from giving their support to the Prime Minister's handling of the episode) was beginning to have its impact on the Tory Party both in the House and in the country.

By the end of June, in fact, Macmillan was beginning to look not so much like 'a caged lion' as a seriously maimed one – and it was Rab's misfortune that he was not able to indulge his youthful inclination to be out and about at a time of political crisis. But, even before he left for Africa, after enduring a somewhat *mauvais quart d'heure* spent in taking Prime Minister's Questions, on 26 June (the Victoria Falls Conference itself lasted from 28 June to 4 July) he appears to have sensed from the general Commons atmosphere that any sudden, swift change in the Leadership would not necessarily be to his advantage. Indeed, on the Sunday after the Profumo debate his own most committed and influential journalistic supporter, William

Rees-Mogg* of the *Sunday Times*, wrote a revealing article urging patience on Conservative MPs, 'The first thing the Conservative Party needs, if it is to avoid destroying itself, is time.'[13] That was certainly Rab's own view; throughout the early stages of the crisis he was given full reports[14] on meetings of the 1922 Committee by his assiduous young PPS, Paul Channon† (the son of 'Chips' who had succeeded Ramsden in the job in 1960). He was not, therefore, altogether taken aback to receive a visit from the Chief Whip, Martin Redmayne,‡ and the joint Chairman of the Party organisation, Oliver Poole,§ inquiring whether he would be willing to serve in a new Government if one was formed.[15] The thrust of the question – and a similar one put to him earlier in the week at his own home by the Chairman of the 1922 Committee, John Morrison – plainly implied that his own chances of becoming Prime Minister were not rated very highly; and, indeed, throughout the early weeks of the protracted Leadership struggle the clear favourite to succeed (or displace) Macmillan was the 46-year-old Chancellor of the Exchequer, Reginald Maudling.

Rab appears to have been a good deal less put out by this than his friends might have expected. (It was, in fact, the view of one of his back-bench supporters that he should from the beginning have taken the position, '*Aut Caesar, aut nihil*'[16] but that was never Rab's way.) When he had been asked in an interview for the *Sunday Telegraph* only a few weeks earlier whether he wanted to be Prime Minister, he had replied, 'I am a great deal calmer about it than some people imagine'[17] – and his own attitude over the next few weeks seemed to bear that out.¶ He was, in fact, rather more

* William Rees-Mogg (1928–). Political and economic editor, *Sunday Times* 1961–3, deputy editor 1964–7. Editor, *The Times* 1967–81. Vice-Chairman, BBC 1981–6. Chairman, Arts Council 1982– . Knighted 1981.

† Henry Paul Guinness Channon (1935–). Conservative MP, Southend West 1959– . He became Rab's PPS within twenty-one months of entering the House of Commons, which he did at a by-election, succeeding to his father's old seat, in January 1959. Held various junior ministerial appointments before entering the Cabinet as Secretary of State for Trade and Industry in January 1986.

‡ Martin Redmayne (1910–83). Conservative MP, Rushcliffe, Nottingham 1950–64. Government Chief Whip 1958–64. Created life peer 1966.

§ Oliver Brian Sanderson Poole (1911–). Conservative MP, Oswestry 1945–50. Chairman Conservative Party 1955–7, Deputy Chairman 1957–9, Joint Chairman 1963, Vice-Chairman 1963–4. Created 1st Baron Poole 1958.

¶ In private Rab did not, however, display the same sang-froid. He had told Anthony Wedgwood Benn in February, 'Everybody always writes about me as a possible successor to Macmillan. When the Prime Minister's popularity slumps, which it often does, my name always pops up. Nobody ever writes about what I do. It is getting me down.' Tony Benn, private papers, notes on interview with Rab, 20.2.1963.

disturbed by the cloud of sexual scandal that was now threatening to envelop the entire Government – and it was in order to banish this that he agreed with the Prime Minister that there would have to be some form of judicial inquiry. The result – the commissioning of Lord Denning to inquire not only into the Profumo case but also, more generally, into 'Rumours affecting the honour and integrity of public life' – cannot help counting in retrospect as one of the more bizarre actions ever taken by a British Government; but at least it serves as evidence of the hectic nature of the atmosphere of the time – and may even explain why Rab found himself 'not altogether sorry to be going to Africa'.[18]

Rab probably never received adequate credit for the success of the Victoria Falls Conference. Its fate hung in the balance till the very end – Southern Rhodesia, where Winston Field had succeeded Edgar Whitehead as Prime Minister the previous December, made a determined last-minute bid to extract its own independence as the price of its support for the dissolution of the Federation; and only Rab's skill and experience as a negotiator procured the final agreement without yielding to Southern Rhodesia's demands. His colleagues in the Cabinet were certainly appreciative of all his diplomatic craftsmanship had achieved;[19] but somehow it was not the type of political endeavour to have much appeal to Tory backbenchers. *The Times*'s political correspondent may have called it 'a *tour de force* of political management and accommodation'[20] – but even Rab himself was to concede, 'I do not think that the whole episode has had much effect on the Conservative Party.'[21] (However, he did do his best to exploit it by appearing on 'Panorama' two days after his return.) In fact, it is possible that the settlement, which looked to some Tories far too much like a sell-out, may have been positively unhelpful. When Rab rose to inform the House of the agreement, it was only to be greeted by a swelling chorus of cheers from the Opposition benches (with the Labour spokesman on Commonwealth affairs going out of his way to congratulate him on his 'timely success'.[22] It was all, no doubt, good, clean parliamentary fun – but even the amused support of his opponents was a dubious blessing for Rab, given the reputation he had borne for 'milk and water socialism' ever since the days of the *Industrial Charter*.

However, he plainly found the atmosphere in the Conservative Party a great deal more reassuring on his return than it had been when he left. In his own words, 'The main reason for this is that the Prime Minister is feeling very well satisfied with himself and with events and there is no immediate likelihood of his deciding to go in a hurry.' The Chief Whip, Martin Redmayne, with whom he had an end-of-session talk, put the same point rather more graphically, 'Four or five weeks ago the chicken was coming out of the egg but now the shell is hardening up.'[23] Not that all the news was equally encouraging. Before Parliament rose for the summer recess, Rab had a second conversation with the Chairman of the 1922 Committee, who was still quite sure of 'the strong inclination of the younger back-benchers to get someone of their own age group': opinion, Major John Morrison felt, would 'crystallise around this as representing the greatest common factor'.[24] But one man who no longer seemed quite so confident of that was the young back-benchers' own champion – and here the story is probably best told in Rab's own words:

> I had a strange visit from Reggie Maudling about which I have not spoken to anybody. He started by saying that, if I got the job, could he continue at the Treasury, and then went on in a very friendly atmosphere to say that, if it went the other way, he could imagine no one he would wish more to have by him than me. As might be expected, the interview did not get very far. I said that I had been at the top of affairs and acting head of government long enough to have gained a certain calm of mind but I did not think we could carry the matter any further at present. I also said that, between us, there was no personal issue and that this was very fortunate.[25]

Game, set and match, one might have thought, to the older, more experienced hand – though all Rab's suavity apparently did not prevent Maudling from believing that he had secured his objective of getting his senior colleague to agree to serve under him.[26]

Elsewhere, however, a rather different estimate of the realities of the situation once more appeared under William Rees-Mogg's byline in the *Sunday Times*:

> Undoubtedly the temptation for the Prime Minister to fight the next election is stronger than it was. Yet in any dispassionate view the arguments have changed little – and that little goes in favour of his choosing to retire.
>
> About the successor I have much less doubt than I did six weeks ago. In that period Mr Maudling's support has relaxed and Mr Butler's has intensified. In a straight election in the Cabinet Mr

> Butler would have at least a two-to-one majority. I have heard of no member of the Cabinet who is more than a tepid supporter of Mr Maudling's claims.[27]

But if that was the case – and Rees-Mogg's estimate of Rab's support in the Cabinet, if a minor exaggeration, was not ultimately to prove far wrong – the question has to be asked why Rab chose to adopt the essentially delaying strategy that he did. The question has an even greater relevance as it was not until 16 July that a crucial amendment was carried, by a decisive majority of eighty, in the House of Lords,[28] to the Government's Peerage Bill.

In its original form this Bill would have allowed currently existing peers to renounce their titles only at the moment of the dissolution of the then Parliament. That might have posed no problems for Anthony Wedgwood Benn, who had steadfastly kept the loyalty of his own constituency in Bristol South-East (despite the fact that a Conservative had sat for the division since 1962 as the result of an electoral petition made to the Queen's Bench); but it did represent a serious obstacle for any Conservative peers who might wish to throw their hats into the ring. How would they be able to enter the existing House of Commons – let alone have enough time to secure parliamentary seats in the next one – if they were only qualified to do so from the moment Parliament was dissolved?

Whatever their motives – and at a time of great leadership turmoil in the Tory Party they were easy enough to guess – the majority of Tory peers appear to have thought that this was fundamentally unfair. Their amendment was not resisted by the Government in the Commons and, accordingly, when the Peerage Bill received the Royal Assent on 31 July it included a provision for any existing peer to renounce his peerage straight away (though this one-off option would automatically disappear after twelve months). The significance of this seemingly technical change over timing was not lost on the Tory Party. From 31 July onwards it meant that the Leadership question was no longer a contest between Rab and Maudling; from now on there were at least two lords in waiting whose claims the Party was entitled to consider.

From the beginning of the crisis over Macmillan's Leadership Rab had thus made a fundamental miscalculation. As Deputy Prime Minister, and indeed acting Prime Minister when Profumo eventually resigned, he had everything to gain by asserting his claims to the succession straight away. The newspaper headlines in the immediate aftermath of the Profumo debate had been lethal – 'Mac: The End',

'The Stag at Bay', 'The Lost Leader', 'A Broken Man Close to Tears'[29] represent just a sample from them. Yet Rab, with his renowned lack of instinct for the jugular, did nothing at all. He certainly saw Macmillan on the day following the Profumo debate – but the main part of their discussion centred on the form of inquiry that would be necessary in the wake of the charges that were now being hurled not only at the Government, but the judiciary too, in what had become a virtual Titus Oates climate of calumny and suspicion.

Rab, of course, owed Macmillan nothing; and it is therefore all the more astonishing that he did not take advantage of the Prime Minister's clearly feeble hold on the Leadership to issue an ultimatum – that, in the interests of the Party, he had to go and that even if the decision was not immediately made public, it must be taken straight away. Probably it was not in Rab's character to do so, a character that Macmillan understood all too well. However, it still seems extraordinary that Rab's only overt intervention in the aftermath of the Profumo debate should have been his 'Panorama' interview two days after his return from Africa, in which he found himself ambushed into discussing the Leadership – eventually coming up with the somewhat limp declaration, 'You want a mixture of youth and experience in guiding any party and there has, therefore, to be a collaboration between the senior ones and the junior ones, whatever is decided about the actual lead.'[30]

The sad truth was that, almost from the beginning, Rab succumbed to what appears to have been a fatal intimation of his own ultimate political defeat. Even before the end of July he was already conceding, 'To sum up the whole thing, it is no good thinking there is no life left if one is not elected Pope. One can always be a respected Cardinal.'[31] The fact that he should have invented this essentially defensive formulation* at the very height of the crisis tells its own tale of just how little Macmillan, even *in extremis*, had to fear from him.

And, in fact, by the end of July – just six weeks after his future as Prime Minister had been effectively written off – Macmillan had contrived, not least through the successful conclusion of the Test Ban Treaty initialled by Lord Hailsham in Moscow on 25 July, to restore his position. Rab himself was confronted with some inconvenient evidence of that when he presided over the Saffron

* The phrase, with embellishments, was to recur many times subsequently. It was first publicly used by Rab in a BBC radio interview in January 1965 and also featured in Rab's TV conversation with Kenneth Harris in July 1966.

32 In the Kremlin, as Foreign Secretary, negotiating with Khrushchev in 1964

33 Reginald Maudling, Rab and Alec Douglas-Home entering a Press conference at Conservative Central Office during the 1964 election

34 Rab with Iain Macleod, the man who had been his most loyal supporter, in October 1963

35 Rab walking through St James's Park on the day he left the Foreign Office, and Government service, for ever

Walden annual garden fête on 27 July in the grounds of his own home, Stanstead Hall. The occasion could hardly have opened more auspiciously. The constituency chairman, in introducing the Member, boldly asserted:

> It is the firm and solid conviction of people in this constituency, and in a great many others, that the wise, mature and experienced statesmanship that Mr Butler has recently displayed in Central Africa could be, and should be, employed in leading our party to victory at the next election.[32]

Alas, the best laid intentions sometimes go awry. In the audience, uninvited but vocal, was Randolph Churchill, one of the Prime Minister's most articulate defenders. Not only did he shout a resounding 'No, No!' to the chairman's introductory remarks: subsequently he ambushed Rab with the most embarrassing question possible, in the wake of a speech in which Rab (perhaps unwisely) had declared, 'Every single person should be prepared to sacrifice his or her own interests to the future and unity of the party . . . I am confident that we should all wish to express our gratitude to the Prime Minister.' If Rab intended these remarks to have a valedictory ring, they did not pass unchallenged. In no time Randolph Churchill was on his feet eager to establish the exact nature of Rab's own commitment of loyalty to Harold Macmillan. The answer that he eventually got, after a shrewd (and protective) effort by the constituency chairman to rule the question out of order, provided eloquent enough proof of the boxed-in position Rab had got himself into:

> I am asked whether or not I have advised the Prime Minister to lead our party into the next election. I must say perfectly frankly that Mr Macmillan has told me clearly that he intends to make up his own mind on this subject. And I should like to make it perfectly clear that I shall always remain loyal to the Prime Minister so long as he remains our leader and Prime Minister.[33]

Even given the ambivalent qualification implied in Rab's final remark, that answer marked the end of the first phase of Macmillan's struggle to survive. Whatever was going to happen, it was plain that there would be no overt challenge from Rab – and if he was not prepared to make one, it was hard to think of anyone else who now respectably could. In any event, the end of the parliamentary session on 2 August meant that the Prime Minister had secured a breathing space, even if there remained a time-bomb ticking away.

Rab had supported the Denning Inquiry into the Profumo affair and all its ramifications, if only in preference to the far more unwieldy (and uncontrollable) device of a Judicial Tribunal, following the unfortunate precedent of the Vassall episode. That he had doubts about the way it was finally handled is, however, indicated by a letter he received from his former faithful PPS, Hubert Ashton, in mid-September. Ashton's argument, arising from an earlier telephone conversation with Rab, was that if Lord Denning's Report was not immediately published, then 'the Labour Party and the country will assume that it is too damaging'.[34] Probably in that he was right; but Rab was not wrong either in regarding with personal distaste (and, indeed, a measure of political apprehension) the whole air of drama that ultimately attached to the Report's publication. The disagreement between him and Macmillan was a simple, even a minor, one: Rab favoured holding up releasing the Denning Report until Parliament returned (not least so that its contents might be protected by parliamentary privilege) while the Prime Minister felt that nothing was to be gained by delay and resolved to follow the Duke of Wellington's advice and 'publish and be damned'.[35] The queues of excited *voyeurs* who formed up outside the Stationery Office to await the document's release at midnight on 25 September proved perhaps that Rab's premonitions had some foundation. Whatever else he had done, Macmillan had at least ensured that the document would break all records in terms of Stationery Office sales.

In fact, though, Lord Denning's Report – written somewhat in the style of a Mills and Boon romance – gave the Government a relatively clean bill of health, even if it did inevitably raise questions about a lack of vigilance, particularly on the part of the Prime Minister. But here further misfortune occurred to blunt its central message. A full week before its official publication a suspiciously well-informed account of its security and scandal conclusions had appeared in the *Daily Mail* under the headline 'Ministers Cleared'.*[36] This necessarily meant that, when the *Mail*'s rivals got the actual report in their hands, they were determined to find a different angle. To the chagrin of Macmillan's supporters – and the delight of his critics – the Press, on the day of the Report's publication, virtually unanimously gave priority to the negative rather

* At least one of their colleagues was firmly convinced that Macmillan held Rab responsible for this leak. Somewhat compromisingly it appeared in the same paper, and under the byline of the same journalist, as the premature disclosure of the major Cabinet reshuffle fourteen months earlier. Lord Aldington, interview with the author, 16 January 1964.

than the positive aspects of Lord Denning's findings. That morning's newspaper headlines – 'Mac Blamed', 'Premier Failed', 'It's Dynamite'[37] – again told their own story. If the Profumo debate and the adverse reaction to Macmillan's performance in it had opened Round One of the Leadership crisis, the Denning Report and the hostile interpretation of its findings equally surely marked the beginning of Round Two.

Rab looked at first sight in an even stronger position at the beginning of Round Two in September than he had been at the start of Round One in June. True, both Hailsham and Home were now technically available as Leadership candidates – but neither had shown any public sign of being ready to leave the Lords (though Hailsham was soon to be warned by Macmillan to hold himself in readiness[38] while Home, on being invited to give his advice, had already bluntly told the Prime Minister that he ought to retire).[39] None of that, however, was known either to the British public or to Rab, with whom Macmillan by the end of September was operating on a distinctly arm's length principle: they had had one long talk over dinner at Chequers together on 11 September[40] but otherwise were to meet only to transact official business until they further discussed the prospects for the Party and the future of the Leadership on 7 October, the day before the Cabinet meeting held on the eve of the Party Conference. What, though, had transformed the situation from the point of view of Rab's long-term prospects was the bursting of the Maudling bubble: in truth, it had always been somewhat artificially inflated – largely through polls published in the *Daily Telegraph* during the months of June and July purporting to represent the views of Conservative MPs (but, in fact, deployed as a propaganda weapon by one of Macmillan's arch-critics, Lord Lambton)* – and now, with the House of Commons no longer sitting, the steam had gone out of the Chancellor's campaign. But if that was welcome news for Rab, it was perhaps even more reassuring tidings for the Prime Minister.

The principal element in Macmillan's strategy of protecting his own position had always lain in the skill with which he had ruthlessly used Rab as his own personal breast-plate. The cunning behind this defensive tactic consisted of more than his knowledge that Rab was

* Antony Claud Frederick Lambton (1922–). Conservative MP, Berwick-upon-Tweed 1951–73. Parliamentary Under-Secretary Ministry of Defence 1970–3. Renounced peerage as Earl of Durham 1970 and resigned from Government and House of Commons 1973 as consequence of a further sex scandal exposed by the *News of the World*. In 1963 he acted, in effect, as Maudling's campaign manager.

simply not the type of politician ever likely to rise up and strike him down: it also involved a recognition – as Rab was the first to acknowledge – that 'if you go on being No. 2 to No. 1 the idea really is to have something different: a number of people may feel the No. 2 is pretty good but what they want is someone new'.[41] Macmillan's single greatest achievement in terms of his own prospects of survival had been, after all the alarums and excursions of the summer, to get that position substantially restored before the Party Conference.

Of course, according at least to his own account, his mood had wavered[42] – hence his warning to Hailsham (which Rab was always afterwards to believe had 'badly unsettled' him)[43] to think in terms of making himself available for the eventual succession. But, significantly, even if his own version is accepted, the earliest date that Macmillan appears to have contemplated retirement was the New Year of 1964. Some doubt, moreover, is necessarily thrown on to how genuine that plan was by his obvious irritation with those – and they included Lord Home and Lord Poole – who urged him not only to act upon it but to accelerate it.

Rab, typically, took no such position. Indeed, when he was finally allowed a one-to-one audience with the Prime Minister, after an interval of exactly four weeks (during which various discussions, from which he had been carefully excluded, had taken place at Chequers), he contrived to leave Macmillan with the impression that he 'would clearly prefer me to go on'.[44] Here again, there is a direct conflict of evidence. For it was certainly Rab's intention to 'advise him [Macmillan] in all sincerity that it would be wiser for him to go' – and, as an additional proof of that sincerity, 'to offer my collaboration in joining in the choice of successor'.[45] Whatever the way the meeting between the two of them in reality went in Downing Street – Macmillan had just returned there after a two-year sojourn in Admiralty House, while No. 10 was being restored – proved, though, ultimately to be a matter of no great significance. For the very next day, Tuesday 8 October, was to demonstrate the sheer unpredictability of the roulette ball in politics.

One of the most dramatic days in the history of modern British Government opened at 10 a.m. with a Cabinet meeting, the first since 19 September when the Cabinet had last met to discuss the Denning Report and consider their reactions to it. There was, therefore, a heavy agenda and at noon Macmillan was forced to cut the official proceedings short and ask the Cabinet Secretariat (though not, significantly, the Cabinet Secretary himself, Sir Norman Brook) to withdraw in order to enable the Cabinet to proceed to a primarily political discussion. The objective here was that the Prime Minister should let his colleagues know what his intentions were for the future. The most, however, that he apparently said was, 'There has got to be a decision and I shall announce it at Blackpool'[46] (the venue of that year's Party Conference). He, then, himself withdrew leaving his colleagues understandably somewhat bewildered.* They were not, however, merely bewildered: those who sat near him (including Rab who sat next to him) were actively concerned.

It was quite clear to them from his pallor and demeanour that Macmillan was not well – an impression reinforced when, shortly before twelve o'clock, a glass of milky-looking fluid was brought in and set beside him. If it had been the Prime Minister's intention to announce at Blackpool (as most of them seem to have assumed) that he would be continuing in office, would he now be able to fulfil it? There was not, however, much time for discussion of that, or any other question, since most of the Cabinet members present were due to catch the lunchtime train from Euston to Blackpool. Before they did so, they were further unnerved by hearing Dilhorne, the Lord Chancellor, declare that, in the event of the Prime Minister deciding not to carry on, he would be available to help with any advice or guidance that might be needed over any Cabinet consultations as to a successor. Home then intervened to say very much the same thing – he was in no circumstances a candidate for the Leadership and, therefore, would be ready to assist in a similar way.[47] Wisely Rab, who had been left in charge of the meeting, whatever he may or may not have said to Macmillan the day before, offered no such undertaking.

It was not, though, until the evening that Rab realised just how totally things had been turned upside down. As the most senior Minister left in London, he had been invited to a cocktail party – primarily held for the Prime Minister's family and staff – to celebrate the renovation of No. 10. When he arrived, he was drawn to one side by Macmillan and told, for the first time, of the physical distress that the Prime Minister had been suffering. For the past twenty-four hours he had had acute difficulty in passing water and had been told that he was probably suffering from a prostate condition: the doctors thought that they might be able to 'patch him up' in order to enable him to make the speech at Blackpool on Saturday but it looked as

* Reginald Maudling was to reply later in October, when asked by Harold Macmillan whether he thought the Party would have backed him if he had gone through with his original plan, 'Frankly, Sir, I still don't know what your plan was.' Interview with the author, 21 November 1963.

if he must eventually have an operation. This conversation – which included an implicit hint that he might be asking Rab yet again to stand in for him for a month or two – took place at around 6 o'clock; but about half-an-hour later the news was worse. Macmillan, who had been going to and fro between his doctors and his guests, then told Rab that he had been advised that he must have the operation straight away, that he would be leaving for hospital that night and that Rab would have to deputise for him at the Conference.[48]

Significantly, at that stage nothing more was said – and it was always to be Rab's belief that Macmillan's statement of his intention to resign, which was composed on the following day in hospital before his operation but only finally released on the Thursday, had been virtually extracted from him by the principal of his two hospital visitors from the Cabinet. That visitor was Lord Home (the other was Lord Dilhorne) – and the Foreign Secretary, as has been noted, was the one Cabinet Minister with a consistent track record ever since mid-September of advocating the Prime Minister's early retirement. What is certain, therefore, is that when Rab wrote afterwards, '*I* would not have asked a wounded and sick man to make such a declaration at such a febrile time', he was not only measuring his words but suppressing a real suspicion: he was to conceal it perhaps less successfully when he wrote a few days later, 'A statement of the facts cannot stress too strongly that Alec Home obtained this and himself read it out.'[49]

It is only fair to say that there is no other evidence of any undue pressure being applied to the Prime Minister while he waited for the surgeon's knife the following day (unless perhaps it is Macmillan's own reported feeling, after he had fully recovered from the operation, that he might perhaps have made too precipitate a decision).[50] Where, however, Rab was totally right was in his conviction that 'the most important event in Blackpool was the message of the Prime Minister which Alec read to the conference on the Thursday afternoon'.[51] It converted a Party Conference into the nearest British equivalent of an American presidential convention – and that was ever afterwards to be the burden of Rab's complaint.

Admittedly, even before then he had found himself in a difficult, even anomalous, position. When he had arrived in Blackpool on the Wednesday afternoon he had boldly moved in to occupy the suite that had been booked for the Prime Minister; and he lost no time in asserting his rights even as a *locum tenens*. A meeting of the chief officers of the National Union was promptly summoned and persuaded to offer him the invitation, in lieu of the Prime Minister, to address the Party's annual rally – in those days still held, after the Conference proper was over, on the Saturday afternoon. With rather more difficulty, a dozen of his own Cabinet colleagues were, an hour or so later, prevailed upon to permit him to accept the invitation – some of them, including one of Rab's subsequent most stalwart supporters, Sir Edward Boyle, felt that it would be rather more seemly that year if there were no traditional Leader's speech or, at least, if it was delivered in an abbreviated form at the end of the Saturday morning session.

Rab, however, correctly perceiving that any denial of such a role to him would, in effect, mean that a public judgment had been passed on his qualifications for the Leadership, displayed a firmness bordering on stubbornness[52]: he insisted on speaking at the rally and would be satisfied with nothing less. It may well be, of course, that this stand of his – which surprised even his closest friends like Macleod and Boyle – had something to do with a piece of knowledge in his possession that was not yet available to them. When exactly Rab learned of Macmillan's intention to announce his retirement remains not wholly clear; but he certainly knew of it when the dozen Cabinet members, already in Blackpool, gathered in his room in the Imperial Hotel at 6.30 p.m. on the evening of Wednesday 9 October. That was more than could be said for the rest of them – including the most notable absentee from the meeting, Lord Hailsham, who had rushed off to the neighbouring constituency of Morecambe and Lonsdale to deliver a typically boisterous speech including a 'Get well, quick' message to the Prime Minister who, his audience was assured, would 'come back soon'.[53]

At least two members of the Cabinet, however, knew better than that – Rab and Lord Home (who had, in fact, seen Macmillan in hospital at 10.30 a.m. that morning). The delay in making any public announcement – the news was not formally given to the Conference until 5 p.m. the following day – seems to have been largely determined by two factors: first, Macmillan's insistence that he must inform the Queen, then at Balmoral, in writing of his intention and that nothing at all should be said until she had signified her approval,[54] and, secondly, by a more curious decision, again traceable to Macmillan, that the proper way to announce the news would be for Home to read a message from him to the Conference. Admittedly, Home – purely by chance – was that year's President of the National Union, the voluntary body of Conservative Party workers under whose auspices the annual Tory Conference formally meets; and, slightly strangely, it had been he, and not Rab (still in London till lunchtime on the Wednesday), who had been summoned on the same Wednesday morning to the Prime Minister's bedside in the King Edward VII hospital in Marylebone. Still, Rab was not alone in wondering why, if the announcement could be delayed for twenty-four hours, it could not have been delayed even further until the Conference was safely over: he fully shared 'the dismay' of at least one of his Cabinet colleagues, Henry Brooke, that 'so electric a statement *inviting* consultations of the choice of a successor'[55] should have been delivered in the midst of the always excitable atmosphere of the annual gathering of the Tory clans.

The timing and nature of Macmillan's announcement (it specifically included the expression of a hope on his part for 'the customary processes of consultation to be carried on within the party about its future leadership')[56] were, however, no accident. As has been noticed, he had already broached the question of the eventual succession with Lord Hailsham – and, given that Hailsham was initially very much the Macmillan family's candidate,[57] the choice of Party Conference week to declare the vacancy was undoubtedly intended to put a fair wind in his sails: Hailsham had, after all, been the darling of the Conference ever since his bell-ringing speech at Brighton in 1957. But what of the Prime Minister's selection of an emissary? Again, it is hard to believe that it was not also a matter of calculated design. Since Rab was acting Prime Minister and was deputising for the Party Leader at the Conference, the conventional course would surely have been to allow him to break any news that had to be given – conceivably even in his Saturday afternoon speech, thereby allowing at least the Conference itself to take place free of the fevered climate of Leadership speculation that necessarily overtook it once Home had delivered Macmillan's message on the Thursday afternoon.

No such considerations, though, played any part in Macmillan's own game plan. That, indeed, seems to have had one prime negative objective: to ensure that, whatever else happened, there would be no question of any simple bodily assumption of Rab into the Leadership. From that point of view, it is possible that the real skill of Macmillan's strategy lay in the cunning with which he had persuaded Rab to walk into a trap. As we have seen, at the time the decision had to be made as to who, if anyone, would speak at the annual rally, Rab alone of those at Blackpool knew of the circumstances in which such a speech would have to be delivered: all his colleagues thought he would be speaking merely as a stand-in – only he was armed with the knowledge that, by the time he came to make the speech, he would inevitably be regarded as a declared candidate for the succession. He was certainly justified in sensing that if he passed such an opportunity up, it would necessarily reflect badly on his confidence in his own leadership abilities; on the other hand, he had been forced – by the way in which Macmillan had arranged matters – to make his own bid for the Leadership on ground that was certainly not of his choosing and before an audience whose feelings about him as Macmillan's successor were likely to stop some way short of overt enthusiasm. (The challenge confronting Rab was made even more demanding by the fact that, in getting his way on his right to address the annual rally, he had had to barter a speech he was due to deliver winding up a debate on Party policy on the Thursday morning – and his Saturday afternoon performance thus became his one and only contribution to the Conference.)[58]

To meet the challenge, Rab had at his disposal, since the address by the Prime Minister at the end of the Party Conference was always regarded as more than a purely Party occasion, the services not only of the Central Office staff but also of the Downing Street secretariat. It turned out to be a mixed blessing: the relationship between a politician and his speech-writers is necessarily very individual – and in inheriting a draft that had been prepared for Macmillan, Rab was probably worse off than he would have been if he had started from scratch. Nevertheless, as he himself always afterwards maintained, 'great pains'[59] were taken in preparing the speech and it does, in fact, even today *read* pretty well.

That did not, though, prove true of its delivery, which was flat and uninspiring.[60] It was, of course, the first time Rab had undertaken such an exercise: the speeches he had made in Conference debates – where his aim had usually been to argue, persuade or even to bamboozle – offered no real training for the kind of revivalist, declamatory sermon that, in the Macmillan era, had come to be associated with the annual Party rally. Nor was Rab himself perhaps in the most confident of moods. In the lunchtime break between the ending of the morning session and the 2 p.m. start of the annual rally Rab and his wife had lunched in their hotel suite with the Homes: Lord Home intimated that he thought it only right to let Rab know that he would be seeing his doctor in London the following week. There was no need for him to say any more: the point could scarcely have been more plainly made that he, too, now considered himself a contender for the succession. The timing of Home's seemingly casual remark was, no doubt, coincidental; but given that he was to be chairman of the mass meeting that afternoon – and indeed in introducing Rab was to be greeted with tumultuous applause – the impact of such news can hardly have been anything but unsettling. The public ordeal, for someone like Rab who had always been a parliamentary rather than a platform speaker, would have been difficult enough in any circumstances: the personal background to it made it all the more daunting – something, presumably, that Home overlooked when he commented some years later, 'It was rather a pity really that he just had this one sort of failure, which anyone can have.'[61]

At least, though, with the speech behind him, Rab could escape from Blackpool. He did so with evident relief (ever afterwards the Imperial became simply in his vocabulary 'that awful hotel');[62] it was, in fact, the last Tory Conference that Rab was to attend – and he never displayed the slightest sense of deprivation at missing the ones which followed. If he had had his successes down the years at them, the Conferences themselves ranked probably, at best, in his mind as necessary tribal tribulations to be endured with as much patience and fortitude as one could muster. The last thing certainly, in Rab's view, that they should ever be concerned with was the Leadership of the Party.

Yet in October 1963, from whatever motive, that was what Macmillan had brought about. Any hopes that Rab may have retained that, with the Conference over, 'the normal processes of consultation' would revert to their time-honoured pattern of a new Leader emerging gradually and decorously were soon dashed. At Blackpool he had been particularly offended by 'the urgency' with which the supporters of Hailsham – and, in the last phase, of Home – had appeared determined to 'bring things to a head'.[63] The fact that this was a calculated tactic was brought home to Rab when his own constituency agent happened to overhear a telephone conversation between Martin Redmayne, the Government Chief Whip, and the Principal Private Secretary at No. 10 in which Redmayne openly castigated Rab for trying to 'hold things up'.[64] There was something to the charge: if Macmillan's strategy was to hurry things along, Rab's was to slow them down – and each for a very obvious reason. The Prime Minister, having brought the Conference into play, did not want to see its influence over the choice dissipate. Rab, on the other hand, had every motive for wanting to put the greatest distance possible between the events of Blackpool and the eventual end of the consultation process. Both, in fact, had their minds on a single date – Thursday 24 October, when the House of Commons was due to resume its 1962–3 session and Rab's (or even Maudling's) position would undoubtedly be strengthened at the expense of Home's or Hailsham's. It was in Macmillan's interests to get the choice made well before then: it was in Rab's to try to spin things out so that the voices of MPs, once more assembled together at Westminster, could be thrown into the equation.

Whatever the weakness of his earlier tactical appreciations, Rab grasped this point from the moment of the Party's return from Blackpool. In a move of unusual decisiveness, he vetoed a proposed visit by Dilhorne, the Lord Chancellor, to the Prime Minister's bedside on the Sunday immediately following the Conference – explaining that he had 'checked with the hospital and found that Macmillan is not capable of more than three or four minutes of concentration'.[65] Rab himself merely rested at home at Stanstead – trying to lower the temperature by having his picture taken in a leisurely posture sitting on a chintzy sofa and explaining to a pertinacious reporter that the day for him had been 'much as usual' and refusing to enter into any discussion at all about his prospects of the succession.[66]

What, however, he found himself quite unable to do was to damp down the general mood of public excitement and expectation that had built up as a result of the drama at Blackpool. Daily the newspapers carried the bookmakers' odds on what inevitably were called 'The Tory Leadership Stakes' – and, though the results were generally gratifying for Rab (he remained the bookies' favourite throughout the week, as he also was in a public opinion poll published by the *Daily Express* on the Wednesday),* such manifestations of public popularity did nothing at all to help him in his overall strategy of trying to make sure the final decision was not a rushed one. Indeed, even by the Sunday evening Rab seems to have recognised that that cause was a lost one – noting ruefully that 'the Lord Chancellor has joined the Great Urgency movement' and diagnosing accurately that its general objective was to see to it 'that Macmillan should resign this week'.[67]

The next day, however, Rab seems to have felt that he had been thrown something of a life-line – at least in terms of the measured deliberation with which he believed 'the customary processes of

* The figures were Butler 39½ per cent, Hailsham 21½, Maudling 11, Home 9½. Among Tory voters alone Rab's lead was not quite so decisive but still impressive enough, Butler 38, Hailsham 27, Maudling 10½, Home 10. Significantly, Rab's greatest lead was with Labour voters, where his margin over Hailsham was 25½ per cent.

consultation' should proceed. As chairman of the first Cabinet held after Blackpool, it fell to him to read out to his colleagues an elaborate memorandum composed by the Prime Minister recommending the procedures that Macmillan thought ought to be followed in taking soundings within the Party. Rab himself received the document only when he went to see Macmillan in hospital just before the Cabinet meeting that Tuesday morning (though he had had some advance notice of its general contents the previous evening in a minute sent to him by the Prime Minister);[68] it is possible, therefore, that what put him off his guard was the sheer complexity of the scheme it put forward (for the first time in history Macmillan was recommending four separate tracks of consultation, taking in not just the Cabinet and MPs but peers and the National Union as well). If Rab, however, believed that this would necessarily take a good deal of time, his belief was soon to be confounded: indeed, in his message to the Queen (though not, perhaps significantly, in his minute to Rab) Macmillan had specifically mentioned Thursday 17 October as the date by which he hoped to have 'the result' available to him from all four separate channels.[69]

The members of the Cabinet who assembled under Rab's chairmanship in No. 10 on the morning of Tuesday 15 October had, however, no inkling of the pace with which events would now move. Even the attention given to Macmillan's minute appears to have been somewhat perfunctory: it was taken as the last item on the agenda and in agreeing to it as 'the right procedure',[70] no one seems to have realised the extent to which total control of the situation had been handed over to a sick, if determined, outgoing Prime Minister with a major operation only a week behind him. Certainly, the notion that this would be the last occasion on which members of the Cabinet would meet collectively together before a new Prime Minister was installed does not appear to have been present in anyone's mind.

It is probable that Rab made an error in not summoning the Cabinet afresh on the morning of Thursday 17 October, for at least then there would have been a chance of the Cabinet asserting its own authority rather than allowing itself to be effectively bypassed. As it was, the first intimation that the *dénouement* was at hand reached Rab via a phone call from the Lord Chancellor that Thursday morning. It was a piece of intelligence that he – again probably mistakenly – kept to himself: faithful Government servant to the end, he simply carried on with routine business, presiding that morning over a meeting of Ministers in No. 10 called to consider some difficult questions that had arisen over the Kenya constitutional conference then being held at Lancaster House. Two of the Ministers present at this meeting were Maudling and Macleod (both being ex-Colonial Secretaries) and it could have provided an ideal opportunity for Rab to have corralled them into a council of war: typically, however, Rab concentrated on the business in hand and said nothing to either of them about events that he, at least, now knew to be imminent. (It is possible, of course, that Rab thought things were going his way but, if so, he displayed a striking lack of suspicion about Macmillan, who had told him, only the previous day, that he felt 'my succession would not make enough difference between his regime and the ncxt'.)[71]

For their part, the Chancellor and the Chairman of the Party proved to be a good deal more alert. Macleod had got some whiff of the *coup de main* Macmillan was planning through a phone call made at breakfast time that morning to his wife by a close friend of the Lord Chancellor's wife.* Once their meeting under Rab at No. 10 was over, Macleod lost no time in imparting the news he had been given to Maudling. They talked for an hour together in the Chancellor's room at the Treasury, where they were soon joined by the President of the Board of Trade, Frederick Erroll† (the Chancellor's own closest friend in the Cabinet). The eventual upshot was a phone call, made just before one o'clock by Maudling on behalf of the three of them, to the Lord Chancellor suggesting that he convene a meeting of Ministers to discuss the whole question of the Leadership. Lord Dilhorne was, however, extremely resistant to the idea, claiming that it would only prove 'divisive' and pointing out that he was due back in any event that afternoon at the King Edward VII hospital, where he had spent a good part of the morning. Maudling rang again ten minutes later. This time he asked merely that the Cabinet should have an opportunity of reviewing the procedures Macmillan was proposing to follow in bringing the Party's views to the attention of the Queen. Dilhorne refused again.[72]

It was, no doubt, significant that at this stage neither Maudling

* Although Macleod never divulged the name of the source of this information, all the evidence points to it having been Ava, Lady Waverley, the widow of Churchill's wartime Chancellor of the Exchequer.

† Frederick James Erroll (1914–). Conservative MP, Altrincham and Sale 1945–64. President of Board of Trade 1961–3. Minister of Power 1963–4. Created 1st Baron Erroll of Hale 1964.

nor Macleod made any effort to associate Rab with their last-ditch attempt to reassert the role of the Cabinet in the decision-making process. The reason for that was that Maudling had not yet quite finally abandoned his own Leadership aspirations[73] – and both he and Macleod had understandably assumed at lunchtime that an immediate decision could only mean one in favour of Rab.[74]

They both learned how wrong that assumption was within the next few hours – Macleod from a phone call made to him that afternoon by William Rees-Mogg of the *Sunday Times* and Maudling through a conversation his Private Secretary had had that lunchtime in the Cabinet Office Mess with a member of the Downing Street secretariat. Both pointed unhesitatingly towards the fact that the choice had already been made, and that that choice was Lord Home.

The same news had by then reached Rab – indeed, he was the source of William Rees-Mogg's own information.[75] Yet beyond making one phone call to his most ardent newspaper champion, Rab showed a marked reluctance to exert himself. In the various agitated consultations between Ministers that took place that afternoon and evening (the celebrated 'midnight meeting' at Enoch Powell's house was merely a continuance of a gathering that had started off at 5 p.m. in Iain Macleod's flat) Rab had no direct involvement at all. He worked quietly in Downing Street till six o'clock, then walked across Whitehall to his Central Africa office in Gwyddyr House, where he spent half-an-hour before being driven not home to Smith Square but to the St Ermin's Hotel near St James's Park Station, where he and his wife were staying while 3 Smith Square was being repaired and redecorated. There he made his sole concession to the drama of the day by allowing himself to be photographed sitting out on the hotel veranda with his wife as the evening shadows drew in.[76]

Rab's character had always, of course, included a strong fatalistic streak – something that he was inclined to associate with his early upbringing in India. It is hard, however, to think of any other leading politician who would have behaved at such a time in quite the passive way that Rab did. He distanced himself from all the 'cabals' and intrigues that were going on – receiving information about them but steadfastly refusing to take any initiatives of his own. Although rumours were to circulate that he had attempted to get in touch directly with Macmillan, in fact, he made no effort to do so. The limit of his intervention was a telephone call to the Lord Chancellor (not initiated until early on the Friday morning) urging him to seek the Prime Minister's authorisation to convene a meeting of the three other main candidates for the succession before any final decision was taken in favour of Home. To this request, as Rab was bleakly to record in his memoirs, 'no reply was vouchsafed'.[77]

In any event, such a meeting eventually did take place (though without the Lord Chancellor) – and, since it ended with the formal agreement on the part of both Maudling and Hailsham to serve under Rab, it should have resolved the whole crisis. That it failed to do so – indeed, was not even given the chance of providing the solution to the ten-day-old deadlock – was entirely due to Macmillan's refusal to be deterred from his own pre-ordained course. Even as Rab, Hailsham and Maudling – along with Macleod (present in his capacity as Chairman of the Party) – were meeting together in Rab's office in the Treasury, Home was already on his way to the Palace: by the time the meeting broke up, he had agreed to try to form a Government, although he had not yet kissed hands on appointment as the Queen's First Minister. The question may legitimately be asked why, if a sick 69-year-old outgoing Prime Minister felt so certain of the constitutional correctness of the advice he was proffering, it needed to be implemented with quite such precipitate haste: equally properly, a query arises as to the uncritical alacrity with which the Palace fell in with both the nature and timing of Macmillan's scheme.*

Neither objection, however, provided ideal ground on which a Conservative could fight – least of all one possessing Rab's own respect for the constitution and the Royal Prerogative. Once Home had been to the Palace – and been entrusted with the responsibility of seeing whether he could form a Government – all the cards were in his hands. Probably the only chance Rab ever had of successfully challenging Home's right to succeed lay in the immediate organisation of a 'quadrilateral' meeting in which the Prime Minister-designate would have been compelled to confront his three principal rivals, each of whom could successively have made clear his refusal to serve under him. Faced with such a three-way ultimatum, Home might well have had to withdraw. However, it was not to be. That very afternoon Rab found himself invited to visit Home in No. 10 and, probably unwisely, consented to go by himself. The memo he wrote later that same day provides its own evidence of just what a

* Iain Macleod, as a loyal monarchist, forbore to raise this second point in his famous *Spectator* article of 17 January 1964. The omission was repaired one week later by Paul Johnson writing in the *Spectator*'s traditional rival, 'Was the Palace to Blame?', *New Statesman* (24 January 1964).

forlorn cause any prospect of a successful rebellion had already become:

> I saw Lord Home this afternoon. He said that everything depended upon my decision and that of the Chancellor of the Exchequer. In one case it would be the Foreign Office and the other the Treasury. I said that I must reserve my position on two grounds: first, as to whether it was right to go back to a hereditary peer at the present time and, second, as to whether he could command enough unity in the Cabinet.
>
> On the first point I said much depended on character: if he could get himself across to the public, he could make up for the difficulties of the Upper House but that they still remained and spoilt the image of modernisation. On the second count, I had attempted to make some efforts to get people together this morning and the Lord Chancellor telephoned the hospital but we received no reply. The thing had been rushed and there had not been sufficient consideration of the difficulties. It was now up to him to make an effort to secure the necessary unity. He said he would do this by a series of interviews and possibly a meeting later. I gave him the particulars of the Ministers who were unwilling to go on and he took down their names and said he would see them.
>
> I said that I was honoured by any suggestion he had made for me but would like to see him later in the evening when I had the answer to the question of unity. I said that I was, of course, not presuming that I personally would have all the support. One had to be as modest as possible. I was only trying to seek a solution, which would obtain the maximum unity. We decided to leave the matter until I met him again.[78]

The interview cannot have been an easy one for either man, but Rab himself plainly stopped some way short of open defiance. One trouble, of course, was that Rab simply lacked the buccaneering attitude to politics that his friends and supporters now wished to instil into him. When Enoch Powell later talked of having handed him 'a loaded revolver'[79] – or Macleod of having 'put the golden ball in his lap, if he drops it now, it's his own fault'[80] – they were speaking a language that was alien to Rab's whole outlook and character. It is only right to add that there were others outside the then power struggle at the top of Tory politics who felt that Rab should have fought harder to assert his claim. They included his own oldest friend, Geoffrey Lloyd, who sat up with him into the small hours of Saturday morning, finally telling him at around 3 a.m., 'If you're not prepared to put everything to the touch, you don't deserve to be Prime Minister.'[81]

By then, however, it was almost certainly too late. The united front displayed by Home's rivals had, in fact, begun to crack at the long-planned and long-delayed 'quadrilateral' meeting which finally took place just after dinner on the Friday evening. Hailsham, to the ill-concealed irritation of Maudling[82] and perhaps the private disappointment of Rab, had shown distinct signs of wavering: although Rab still refused to commit himself that night, he returned to the St Ermin's Hotel with a firm conviction that nothing was to be gained by holding out any longer – and the next morning accepted the Foreign Office from Home, to be followed within the hour by Maudling agreeing to stay at the Treasury. Well before noon the new Prime Minister had kissed hands at the Palace (his day of triumph being marred only by the resolute refusal of both Macleod and Powell to take office under him).

Curiously, Rab's own sense of disappointment on this occasion seems to have been less intense than it had been in 1957. In part that was, no doubt, due to a feeling that he had made almost, as it were, a voluntary renunciation – that the job could still have been his if he had decided to insist upon it: he seems, in fact, to have found a good deal of consolation in the reflection that, despite the

pleas of his friends and the entreaties of his wife,* he had held back from deliberately imperilling the unity of the Party. There was, however, another factor at work, too – perhaps most vividly expressed in Rab's own statement delivered some years afterwards, 'You see I had against me such a terrific gent . . . if I had had the most ghastly walrus I might have done something.'[83] Leaving tactfully aside whom the description 'ghastly walrus' was supposed to fit, there can be no doubt of the feeling of genuine friendship between Rab and Home: they had, after all, known each other for over thirty years (Home had first been elected to the House of Commons only two years after Rab), they had both been disciples of Neville Chamberlain (though Rab tended to carry the taint of that association far more indelibly than Home) and they had been close colleagues together in the Cabinet ever since Eden formed his ill-fated Government in April 1955 (so close, indeed, that, as we have seen, it was to Home that Rab instinctively turned for help just two years earlier when he felt he was being badly treated by Macmillan). Certainly, the view commonly attributed to Lloyd George that 'there can be no friendship at the top' is hard to sustain in face of the letter that Rab received from the new Prime Minister within three days of his formally moving into No. 10:

22 October 1963

My dear Rab,

Until now my heart has been too full to dare to write to you and Mollie. Never in my wildest dreams did I think that circumstances could ever conspire to bring me to hurt even in the tiniest degree one of my friends. And when, of all the people in the world, it had to be you, my misery was complete.

I would like to say how deeply grateful I am for your loyalty and to express my unstinted admiration for your courage. Now that we have been put to the test, perhaps the most precious thing is that friendship and loyalty holds.

I only hope that I can be of some small help to one who will increasingly have the hopes of the world resting on his shoulders.

* In the public eye at least Mollie Butler became the most poignant figure of the week. She behaved with great dignity but never sought to disguise the distress she felt on behalf of her husband. Her loyalty found its most eloquent expression in a statement she made on the Friday to the *Daily Mail*, 'My husband would have made the best Prime Minister in the world. I know he would.' More surprisingly, Lord Home's own mother provided some support for her sentiments, being quoted in the *Daily Herald* as saying, 'I thought it would be Mr Butler. He deserved it, don't you think?'

My love and understanding to Mollie.

Yours ever,

ALEC[84]

To that letter Rab replied the same day:

22 October 1963

Dear Alec,

Mollie and I were very touched by your letter. I was not anxious to compete again this time in circumstances which could lead to my rejection. But Harold's illness and the acting leadership of the Government, combined with the duties I had to perform in Blackpool, brought forward a great deal of support, both popular and otherwise. So it would not have been human to go into a monastery.

I am proud to takc on the Foreign Office. I asked Harold for the reversion in 1957. It has always been an ambition of mine and I do feel the weight of the responsibility.

It was you who made me feel I was wanted. If it had not been for that, Mollie and I would have resigned ourselves to a rather lonely wilderness.

So now our love to you both,

RAB[85]

Of all commentators covering this second Tory Leadership contest William Rees-Mogg had a strong claim to be considered the most astute and best informed. Yet when ten days previously he had declared, with typical trenchancy, 'The Conservatives have ceased to be gentlemen without becoming democrats',[86] he had plainly failed to allow for one factor: that, in the 1960s, at the summit of the Tory Party, old habits died hard.

16 The Foreign Office

It was over twenty years since Rab had left the Foreign Office and his return, if hardly in triumph, to take charge of the Department in which he had once been a humble Parliamentary Under-Secretary, undoubtedly brought him some satisfaction. He knew, of course, that his reign as Foreign Secretary was unlikely to match in duration the three-and-a-half years he had spent serving Halifax and Eden between 1938 and 1941; but the fact that an election was due in twelve months at most never seemed to be his prime preoccupation. The past, indeed, tended to count with him far more than the future. Try as he might, Rab could never quite settle, even to his own satisfaction, the question of whether, in allowing Home to become Prime Minister, he had done the right thing: the consequence was that his doubts, increasingly, were communicated to others. Certainly, his ministerial colleagues at the Foreign Office (headed by Lord Carrington* but amounting to four in total) grew all too accustomed to having the 1963 Leadership battle reopened during their discussions with him – even if all such exercises generally ended with a plea for reassurance along the lines of 'I believe I was right not to split the party, don't you?'[1]

That was a view, understandably, that the Government backbenches were only too eager to endorse. Rab was not present on the day MPs came back to Westminster for the ceremony of Prorogation, since on Thursday 24 October he was already engaged

* The 6th Baron Carrington (1919–). UK High Commissioner in Australia 1956–9. First Lord of the Admiralty 1959–63. Minister without Portfolio (attached to the Foreign Office) and Leader of the House of Lords 1963–4. Leader of Opposition, House of Lords 1964–70 and 1974–9. Secretary of State for Defence 1970–4. Secretary of State for Energy 1974. Secretary of State for Foreign and Commonwealth Affairs 1979–82. Secretary-General of NATO 1984– .

on his first official duty as Foreign Secretary – attending a meeting of Western European Union held at The Hague. However, he received a full account of the prevailing mood on the Tory side of the House from his youthful PPS, Paul Channon, who had made it his business to be 'out and about', just as Rab himself had always liked to be at moments of political tension when he was a young man. Channon's report, in any event, could hardly have been more consoling:

> Your own stock has never been higher and Member after Member came up to me saying how wonderfully you have behaved and how you have saved the party. They are all unanimous in your praise.[2]

Making every allowance for the natural loyalty of a PPS, that does appear to have been a fair assessment of the immediate reaction within the Tory Party. Yet Rab was the hero of the back-benches not through anything he had done but rather through what he had stopped short of trying. Alas, as the next twelve months were to demonstrate, that kind of debt of gratitude in politics can be a rapidly diminishing asset.

To begin with, however, Rab won glowing notices, not least for his performance in his new role. Meeting his French opposite number, Couve de Murville, for the first time at The Hague, he was reported to have made an immediate impression on that notably unexcitable figure by conversing with him in fluent French[3] – something quite beyond the powers of Edward Heath during the long-drawn-out Brussels negotiations. Within the Foreign Office, too, he was said to have lost no time in making a favourable impact, with officials being particularly impressed by the speed and thoroughness with which he did his 'boxes'.[4] In getting to grips with his new Department, Rab enjoyed one piece of good fortune: the need for the new Prime Minister to be elected to the House of Commons meant that he could concentrate exclusively on his new domain, since Cabinet meetings were rarely called and Parliament itself did not reassemble until 12 November.

On the eve of Parliament's return, Rab had, however, to endure, for the second time, the ordeal of submissively saluting his successful rival. Fresh from his convincing by-election victory at Kinross and West Perthshire, Sir Alec Douglas-Home was duly elected leader of the Conservative and Unionist Party at 'a Party meeting' held again in the gloomy *ambience* of Church House on the morning of 11

November 1963. Rab was spared the indignity of actually placing his former opponent's name in nomination – that duty fell on Lord Carrington, in his capacity as Leader of the House of Lords – but, as in 1957, he was required to demonstrate his sportsman's credentials by making the seconding speech. He does not appear to have found it a wholly easy exercise – and there was something perhaps consciously perverse in his characterisation of the Prime Minister as 'looking and being ageless'.[5]

The House of Commons itself was not to hear the new Foreign Secretary until half-way through the Debate on the Address – and it cannot be pretended that Rab's first foreign affairs speech, delivered on a Friday morning, ranked as a particularly spectacular début (though he did raise a few wry smiles with one of his opening sentiments, 'I know that I shall greatly profit by the Prime Minister's own experience and great skill as Foreign Secretary in conducting my own duties as Foreign Secretary in succession to him').[6] All along the fear had been that Sir Alec would want to continue as his own Foreign Secretary – and Rab's diplomatic guile deceived no one. However, the Prime Minister's three weeks' enforced absence campaigning in Scotland had enabled Rab to establish his own claim to be running an independent fiefdom, not least in the eyes of the Cabinet Office and the Civil Service. When his wife declared in a newspaper interview, just a month after he took over at the Foreign Office, that in her view he 'stood head and shoulders above everyone else'[7] in the Government, she was, whether she knew it or not, merely reflecting the conventional Whitehall wisdom.

Rab brought to his new duties not only a first-class mind but a talent, rare among Ministers, for organising – and indeed economising upon – the use of his own time. He carried away from the Foreign Office, as he had done from no other Government Department that he had headed, a full engagement diary of his various interviews and appointments. Although a sedentary life, it was certainly not a slack one. A typical day in January 1964, for instance, went as follows:

10.00 a.m.	Sir Patrick Dean (UK Representative at the UN)
10.30	Cabinet, No. 10
1.00 for 1.15 p.m.	Lunch with Donald Tyerman (Editor, *The Economist*)
3.00	Eldon Griffiths (Prime Minister's speech-writer)
3.30	Duncan Sandys (Commonwealth

	Secretary)
4.10	Turkish Ambassador (first call)
4.20	Bulgarian Minister (first call)
4.30	Congolese Chargé (first call)
4.40	Michael King (*Daily Mirror*)
5.00	Sir C Rowe
5.30	Sir William Luce (Political Resident in Persian Gulf)
8.00	Dinner with Prime Minister – No. 10[8]

It was the kind of schedule, involving frequent switches of attention, that provided Rab with just the sort of challenge that he relished. And, indeed, if any incarnation in his ministerial life provided him with the *solatium* for never having been Viceroy of India, it was probably the year that he spent as Secretary of State for Foreign Affairs. It was not merely the imposing nature of his official surroundings – though Rab gloried in the grandeur of his office with its massive portrait of George III opposite his desk, its enormously high ceiling complete with hanging chandelier and its magnificent views over both St James's Park and Horse Guards Parade. More to the point was the feeling the job gave him of being 'in touch', not just with the preoccupations of one country but with the concerns of the world. It was a measure of Rab's immediate sense of involvement that, within a month of his appointment, he should have moved into the Foreign Secretary's official quarters at No. 1 Carlton Gardens, abandoning his own now redecorated home in Smith Square (something he had never done during his four years as Chancellor of the Exchequer).

Initially, Rab – whose own views on 'abroad' were always a little ambivalent – managed to keep foreign trips down to a minimum. He did not accompany the Prime Minister to President Kennedy's funeral held on 25 November in Washington, deputising instead for Sir Alec in moving the adjournment of the House in tribute to the slain President on the same day.[9] He made a brief visit to Germany and France in December and another to Denmark in January; but his first major excursion as Foreign Secretary was a transatlantic trip, when he accompanied the Prime Minister to Ottawa and Washington from 9 to 14 February.

For Rab it was probably not a wholly agreeable experience. No Foreign Secretary is ever seen to best advantage when he travels as part of the official entourage of the head of Government: for one thing, all arrangements are firmly in the hands of No. 10 and, for another, media attention focuses on the star of the show and barely, if at all, on the supporting player. It was, therefore, a shrewd precaution on Rab's part to see to it that he should have at least one day of the trip to himself. Leaving Sir Alec in Ottawa, he flew to New York on 11 February first to hold discussions with Adlai Stevenson, the US Ambassador to the United Nations, and then with U Thant, the UN Secretary-General. The main item on the agenda was a proposal for an international peace force for Cyprus, not necessarily UN-run but commanding the backing of at least some of the main European powers. It was not a suggestion about which the Secretary-General of the United Nations could be expected to feel wholly enthusiastic; but Rab's meeting with U Thant appears to have been at least cordial and civilised.[10]

That was more than could be said for the Prime Minister's and the Foreign Secretary's encounter the next day with President Johnson in the White House: the new President appears to have fascinated Rab but also to have repelled him – certainly, the indelible impression he left was of a somewhat vulgar political operator. In the course of one dinner party, held at the White House, LBJ contrived to hand Mollie Butler five separate examples of his own signature – grabbing anything within reach (menu cards, table *placements*, even books of matches) and submitting them to the imprint of the presidential autograph.[11] It says much for the Foreign Secretary's wife's self-possession that she should have managed to stow them all away, one by one, into her handbag without betraying a sense that anything in the least untoward was occurring; but then, if Rab was, at best, neutral about foreign travel, Mollie was strongly in favour of it, not least for the unexpected experiences it brought.[12]

In his year at the Foreign Office Rab embarked on only one really extensive trip. That took place from 26 April to 7 May 1964 and embraced three separate foreign capitals (Washington, Tokyo and Manila in the Philippines) in the space of twelve days. Its diplomatic purpose was none too clear at the time and today inevitably looks even more obscure: nevertheless it did offer the Foreign Secretary a political dividend. Self-effacing to a fault in the era of a new Prime Minister, he had not made a major speech in the Commons since November – and there was a growing feeling on the Government benches that he was treating his tenure of the Foreign Office as a period of 'self-imposed exile'.[13] At least a three-nation tour gave an impression of activity – even if it did seem to be somewhat bizarrely directed, given that the major tension points of British foreign policy at the time concerned Cyprus and the Yemen. The original occasion for Rab going to Washington was, though, to attend a Central Treaty Organisation meeting – and Turkish membership of CENTO provided, no doubt, part of the reason for Rab's decision to participate in the annual get-together of what was already a somewhat fragmented alliance.

His second visit to Washington became, however, memorable for something quite else – a face-to-face confrontation with Lyndon Johnson in the White House, during which the sale of British Leyland buses to Cuba provoked the President into producing a wad of dollar bills and a barbed inquiry as to whether Britain was really so hard up that it needed to trade with Cuba: why didn't the British Government simply cancel the contract and send the bill straight to him at his Texas ranch, asked LBJ, fingering dollar notes as he posed the question.[14] If the President's intention had been to humiliate his guest, he had chosen the wrong man: Rab was to dine out many times on the story in London – the gurgles of delight with which he re-created the scene were proof of the genuine pleasure that he always found in experiencing the more eccentric examples of human behaviour.[15]

Neither Tokyo nor Manila could compete with Washington in that respect – though the visit to Japan had its own irritant legacy for the Foreign Office. While in Tokyo, Rab had gone shopping and had bought himself a camera; a routine visit by a Customs official to the Foreign Office on 8 May, following the Secretary of State's return, produced a demand for a cheque for £7 4s 7d to be made payable to 'the Collector of Customs, London'. For some reason, this invoice enraged Rab, who threatened to write direct to the Chancellor protesting against so outrageous an impost – 'It is really bad to charge a sum nearly as big as the camera itself.' For twenty-four hours despondency reigned in the Private Office but finally Rab was prevailed upon to have second thoughts. There is no doubting the air of relief with which, a day later, a minute was written on the original Customs and Excise demand declaring, 'Discussed matter personally with S of S who has decided not to write to the Chancellor.' Instead, thanks to Rab's Assistant Private Secretary, a letter went off that same day to 'The Custom House, London' dutifully enclosing the Foreign Secretary's cheque for £7 4s 7d.[16]

Rab allowed himself, in fact, to be taken more and more into the care and protection of his Private Office,* and it may have been this

* He had an excellent Private Office staff consisting of Nicholas Henderson, Tom Bridges and Nicholas Fenn, each of whom later distinguished himself in the Diplomatic Service.

which permitted the idea to take root that he had simply grown weary of the political battle and was content now to live his life above it. Nor was that an impression fostered only by his enemies: no sooner had he returned from Manila than he received a surprisingly sharply worded letter from Paul Channon warning him that a great deal had gone on in his absence (in particular with regard to Party opinion on Cyprus and the Yemen) and suggesting strongly that it 'would be a great help if you saw the officers of the Foreign Affairs Committee in the reasonably near future'.[17] What, in fact, had happened was that on both flash-points (with their post-colonial overtones) Rab had allowed the Commonwealth Secretary, Duncan Sandys, to make the running: there was, as a result, some doubt as to what Foreign Office policy actually was. That may have exercised Rab's colleagues in the Commons and, indeed, exasperated the serious newspapers: it did not bother Rab one little bit. Regarding both problems as virtually intractable, he was more than content to play for time – and if that meant keeping the Foreign Office view opaque, then at least it was not the FO that was rushing in and making a fool of itself.

From the mandarins' point of view, there was a good deal to be said for Rab's attitude; from the working politician's, there was somewhat less. Politicians, after all, always want definite answers, even when solutions are not available – and Rab was offering neither. Indeed, he sometimes seemed during the spring and summer of 1964 to be providing the Tory Party with strangely little sense of direction in any context. He was no longer making great policy speeches and held firmly aloof from all partisan battles, like the running struggle in the Commons over the Resale Price Maintenance Bill. With his voluntary renunciation of his position as Deputy Prime Minister, once Alec Douglas-Home came to office, he had retained membership of only one Cabinet committee, that on Overseas and Defence Policy (which he could hardly avoid); otherwise his performance was very much that of a pro-consul presiding over his own corner of the Whitehall empire and not particularly caring about what went on elsewhere.

One factor, of course, that had not helped Rab through all this time was the constant harking back, by others as much as by himself, to the events of the previous autumn. It may have been very much in the Conservative Party's interest for them to be forgotten – but there were too many participants with axes to grind for that to be possible. First, early in January, there came Randolph Churchill's paperback panegyric to Macmillan called *The Fight for the Tory*

Leadership which, in turn, provoked Iain Macleod's scourging review in the *Spectator* entitled simply 'The Tory Leadership' (Rab was sent both in advance of publication, though Churchill's manuscript was ignored[18] while Macleod's galley proofs were carefully put in the Foreign Secretary's weekend bag).[19] Worse, memoirs continued to appear from relics of the Macmillan era, with one at least (the autobiography of the former Lord Chancellor, Lord Kilmuir)* proving not only unhelpful for the Government in general but unsettling for a number of its members individually. It was scarcely surprising if Rab opted for a certain detached demeanour.

The Conservative Party, however, insisted on misunderstanding his position. The same Tory MPs, who had acclaimed his self-sacrifice in October, had come by the spring to regard him almost as a non-playing member of Sir Alec Douglas-Home's team. Nor were their suspicions totally without foundation. A letter Rab wrote to Sir Glyn Jones, the Governor of Nyasaland, on learning that the colony he had allowed to secede from the Central Africa Federation was finally proceeding to its independence celebrations, reveals all too clearly just how easily the mantle of the disinterested elder statesman was slipping on to his shoulders:

> Politically, I have no particular news to give you. There is quite a feeling of euphoria that we shall make quite an easy victory but I fear this is being propagated by those who have not great experience of politics. I think it will be extremely difficult to conquer the feeling of a change being necessary. It could be done if we could wait long enough for the PM and others to get across in the country, but it cannot be done very quickly.[20]

As those words suggest, Rab was a strong protagonist – in the one real battle within the Home administration – of the general election being postponed till October. This set him at odds with his most powerful surviving ally from the events of the previous October, the Chancellor, Reginald Maudling; but the perspective, no doubt, was different as viewed from the Foreign Office rather than as seen from the Treasury. Certainly, there seems to have been total conviction in Rab's Cabinet stand that the Government's one hope of salvation lay in clinging on to the bitter end.

* The Earl of Kilmuir, *Political Adventure* (Weidenfeld & Nicolson, 1964). The book revealed an astonishing streak not merely of vanity but of malice in one who had generally been regarded as a rather pedestrian politician. Paradoxically, Kilmuir's one contribution to the British political lexicon had been the phrase, 'Loyalty is the Tories' secret weapon.'

His relationship with Alec Douglas-Home remained cordial, if (on his side) slightly condescending. One young journalist who went to see him for the first time in January was startled to hear him describe the Prime Minister as 'an amiable enough creature – I'm afraid he doesn't, you know, understand economics or even education at all'.[21] But the necessary public courtesies, at least, were observed – with Rab, for the second time, paying fulsome tribute to the Prime Minister's unrivalled experience in a foreign affairs debate he both opened and wound up in the Commons in June. Again, it was in no sense a dramatic occasion, although Rab's opening speech did end with the announcement that he would shortly be paying an official visit to the Soviet Union.[22]

In the event, the visit, which did not take place till the very end of July, proved something of an anti-climax. The Russians, who had already received the Leader of the Opposition and his Shadow Foreign Secretary at the beginning of June, were quite sophisticated enough in their knowledge of British politics not to be disposed to do any serious business with the representative of a Government destined to face its rendezvous with the voters in two or three months. Rab was granted the privilege of an audience with Khrushchev, thus becoming the last Western statesman to see him before his fall from power (on, as events transpired, the very day of the British general election). But, as Rab himself bleakly recorded in his memoirs, he was confronted with 'an absolute negation' of any hopes he had nurtured for an international breakthrough.[23] The most noteworthy incident of the visit turned out to be the question he posed on his second day in Moscow to an understandably bewildered Rector of Moscow University, 'Tell me, Vice-Chancellor, is this university state-aided?'[24] No one, though the representatives of the British Press all heard it, was ever quite sure whether the query was wholly naïve or whether it did not conceal some subtle deadpan purpose on Rab's part.

Once back from Moscow, Rab left almost at once for the Isle of Mull, where his planned summer holiday was inconveniently curtailed by the continuing Cyprus crisis and the imminence of the general election.* Rab returned to London on Monday 17 August though, significantly, he seems to have been given very little

* One of the other demands on Rab's time during his final weeks at the Foreign Office was sitting for an official portrait, painted by Allan Gwynne-Jones. The original hangs in Pembroke College, Cambridge, while a copy of it by the artist – suitably touched up by Rab's own brushwork to give the cheek-bone 'a more elegant line' – is in the possession of Lady Butler of Saffron Walden.

encouragement to co-operate in the Conservative Party's electoral preparations. He had been a somewhat desultory attender at the Party's 'steering committee' – charged with the task of producing the Conservative 1964 manifesto – and, according to one of his colleagues, had 'perceptibly lost status and heart'[25] in the eyes of the Party organisation ever since his rejection for the Leadership the previous autumn. It was, therefore, hardly a surprise to the political world (though it does seem to have been a shock to Rab) when the American magazine *Newsweek* carried a story suggesting that, even if Alec Douglas-Home won the election, Rab would no longer be sitting round the Cabinet table after it, since he 'planned to quit politics for an academic post'.[26] From Rab's point of view, such speculation could hardly have been more unfortunately timed, and he moved quickly to stamp on it – issuing a statement on the same day as *Newsweek* appeared in London insisting that there was 'absolutely no truth' in its report.[27] It was an honest enough denial at the time in so far as it affected Rab's own intentions; but it was also a good deal too sweeping since, unknown to Rab, his Foreign Office role had already been promised by the Prime Minister to Christopher Soames in any subsequent Government that he formed.[28]

The mere fact that such a private understanding existed – and it must presumably have been known to one or two others as well (though certainly not to Rab) – does a good deal to explain the remarkably restricted part Rab was offered in the 1964 election campaign. He had, by pre-arrangement, delivered a radio Party political broadcast just before the campaign proper opened but after that was hardly seen or heard of again. He had a non-speaking role at the presentation of the Conservative manifesto on 18 September, took part in only one Central Office Press conference and made a single, fleeting, three-minute appearance in just one of the Conservative Party's five television election broadcasts. Moreover, until he made a foray into the north-east just a week before polling day, even his personal campaigning had been confined to one journey to the south-west and to constituencies neighbouring on his own in East Anglia.

It was, no doubt, an awareness of the strange neglect with which the former architect of Conservative victories was seeming to be treated that led the *Daily Express* to suggest sending its star writer, George Gale, to cover the Foreign Secretary on the stump (an admirable exercise of a similar kind had, in fact, appeared a week earlier in a then Labour paper under James Cameron's byline).[29]

The original idea was that Gale also should report on Rab in his own constituency but the Foreign Office, which still assumed responsibility for its Secretary of State even at election time, obligingly pointed out that there might be more interest (and, indeed, novelty) in following the Foreign Secretary up to Tees-side, where he was due to speak at two meetings on the evening of Thursday 8 October. Consequently, just after lunch on 8 October, Gale joined Rab on the two o'clock train from King's Cross to Darlington, tactfully leaving him at first to work through his boxes in his reserved compartment.

According to Gale's own recollection, it was about an hour into the journey that he joined Rab in his compartment, finding him in distinctly reflective and ruminative mood. At least half the piece that Gale subsequently wrote – and which was published in the *Express* the next morning[30] – dwelt on the odd phenomenon of Rab's virtual invisibility in the campaign. As such, it was a perfectly legitimate example of journalistic observation – and one, given its failure to offer Rab even a modest share of the limelight, that the Conservative Central Office could hardly complain about. What, however, caused apoplexy in the Tory high command were the remarks that Rab himself was quoted as having made – remarks that to anyone who knew Rab had a ring of total authenticity.

They were all typically irreverent but only one had the clear potential for real trouble – and that was Rab's assent to Gale's own proposition that the election, even if it was still very close, might yet slip away from the Tories in the last few days. In any terms, with just a week to go before the voters went to the polls, that had to count as a catastrophic own-goal; and it was hardly surprising that Rab's colleagues – particularly those bearing the responsibility for maintaining party morale – were enraged by it. Not all of them may have gone as far as Randolph Churchill who charged in the *Evening Standard* the next afternoon that Rab had 'uttered his own death-wish and death-warrant'[31] – but there were certainly those, without any knowledge of the secret arrangement that Sir Alec Douglas-Home had made, who from now on doubted whether Rab could expect to hold any office (let alone retain the Foreign Office) in a re-elected Conservative Government.

How serious, though, had Rab's indiscretion really been? All his life he had made a habit of talking extraordinarily frankly to the Press and his very candour had normally afforded him a cast-iron form of protection. Probably, given the atmosphere and timing of this particular interview, he should have exercised greater caution –

and he was certainly careless in having no witness present apart from his detective (who proved understandably reluctant to be dragged into any of the inevitable recriminations that followed). On the other hand, Rab was surely entitled to plead that politicians seldom do themselves much good by simply whistling defiantly in the dark: he had given his own honest appraisal of the way he felt things were going – and where was the harm in that? In fact, he was entitled to add something else. On the train to Darlington he had said nothing markedly different concerning general election prospects from the view he had expressed at his one appearance at the Conservative Party's Press conferences five days earlier: even then he had spoken openly of detecting 'a strong undercurrent to Labour'.[32] That had certainly produced some puzzled frowns in the Central Office but it had not led to any great explosion of anger: indeed, some of the more sophisticated of the Tory Party's *apparatchiks* had come to see in it evidence that the old hand had not lost its cunning. When some notably gloomy Gallup Poll figures came out the next day, Rab was even congratulated on having done his best to pre-empt their effect.

On this second occasion, however, no such excuses were forthcoming. Rab was simply seen as having let the side down and for the remaining six days of the campaign he was very much in the dog-house. Fortunately, he had no cause to be in London (even the demands of the Foreign Office had to make way for the requirements of his constituency during the final phase of the campaign): and he was able to beat a dignified retreat to Stanstead and Saffron Walden. It was always in Rab's nature to run slightly scared so far as his constituency was concerned – and in his own view he had cut things rather fine by continuing to work at the Foreign Office (at least during the day) right up to the last week of the campaign. He had nothing, however, to feel particularly apprehensive about. On polling day East Anglia proved itself one of the less volatile regions of the country and in his final parliamentary election Rab was returned with a majority of 4,955* which, while down on his 1959 majority of 6,782, was still comfortable enough.

The overnight results – Rab's own, according to Saffron Walden's custom, was not declared until the next morning – had been sufficiently gloomy for Rab to go to bed with the melancholy premonition that his Government career was now finally at its end. True, he was only sixty-one but, if the likely new Labour Government

* The figures were R. A. Butler (Con.) 20,610, M. Cornish (Lab.) 15,655, F. Moore (Lib.) 5,539.

under Harold Wilson was to run anything like its allotted span, it was hard to think there was much realistic hope of his returning to office at the age of sixty-five; nor, of course, had the way in which he had been pointedly cut out from any prominent part in the Conservatives' national campaign provided him with any reassurance as to his long-term future. The morning, however, brought a flickering hope of reprieve: not only was the result in Saffron Walden surprisingly good – so were the returns from most of the county constituencies. The Labour Party General Secretary's rash overnight forecast that Harold Wilson would 'have a majority of at least 30 seats'[33] soon began to look decidedly dicey: by lunchtime it was doubtful if he would have a majority at all. But by 2.45 p.m. when Meriden in the Midlands fell to Labour, to be swiftly followed by Labour holding on to Brecon and Radnor, giving the new Government its overall majority, it was clear even to Alec Douglas-Home that the game was up. By 3.30 p.m. he was at the Palace and half-an-hour later Harold Wilson (if with a majority of only four) was the country's new Prime Minister.

Rab, once his own count was over, had gone straight to the Foreign Office. There he took his leave of his Private Secretaries, making them an eloquent speech on the theme of how he envied their continuing careers in the Government service before leaving by a side-entrance to walk alone across St James's Park to his flat in Carlton Gardens from which he was soon to be also dispossessed. He had first become a Minister over thirty-two years earlier so the wrench – which he must have realised would now be permanent – cannot have been anything but painful.

But almost immediately there was a surprise. For Rab, given his background of service to the Crown and his allegiance to the family as an institution, it must have been a gratifying one. Sir Alec Douglas-Home, who alone among his colleagues appears to have taken his railway carriage interview in good part,[34] promptly proposed to him that he should accept an Earldom in his Resignation Honours. The offer, of course, may have been double-edged: Sir Alec, as has been noted, had not foreseen any great role for Rab had he succeeded in winning the election. But, in defeat, the offer was none the less generous – and Rab was undoubtedly touched by it. It was, after all, the rank of the peerage that traditionally went to ex-Prime Ministers – and to Rab it must have appeared as an effort to compensate him for the dual disappointments he had suffered in being robbed of his Downing Street inheritance. It, therefore, says much for Rab's basic lack of susceptibility to flattery

36 Rab knocking on the wicket gate at Trinity on 7 October 1965

37 Listening to Harold Wilson accepting an honorary degree at Essex University, of which Rab was Chancellor from 1962 until his death

38 Mollie and Rab with her daughter, Susie (*left*), and their grandchildren; Stanstead Hall in the background

that he should, after an initial period of hesitation, have resolved to refuse it. The terms in which he eventually did so could hardly have been more forthright:

> *21 October 1964*
>
> My dear Alec,
>
> I was deeply touched by your suggestion that, in recognition of my many years of service, I should accept an Earldom in another place.
>
> This should be a great honour to me and my family. It so happens that my family, on the Cornish side, has served in Parliament on and off since the earliest days, and this would be a distinguished honour.
>
> I feel, however, that this is not the time to leave the Commons. If it was an expanding moment of my career, I might take a different line, but there are so many difficulties ahead that I think they ought to be faced and that I should not, so to speak, retire. I am very attracted by the idea of helping you over the foreign scene, and this will be a great personal pleasure to me.
>
> Yours ever,
>
> RAB[35]

It was almost certainly not the reply that Home had hoped for – as he now found himself forced to demonstrate by moving to deprive Rab of the one institutional link with the Conservative Party Organisation that he had held for twenty years. When the new dispositions for the organisation of the Central Office were announced, it was revealed (if only to the closer students of Conservative Party Kremlinology) that Rab had lost not only his leadership of the Conservative Party's Advisory Committee on Policy to Edward Heath but had forfeited the chairmanship of the Conservative Research Department as well. The latter disclosure, admittedly, was oblique – *The Times*, for example, carrying the story under the dual headline, 'Sir Michael Fraser to be deputy chairman of the Tory Party – Speculation over Mr Butler's future role'.[36] But Rab, at least, was in no doubt as to what was meant, as a somewhat more stilted note he wrote to the new Leader of the Opposition within ten days of the election result made only too clear:

> Thank you for your suggestions about my future, which as I have told you I much appreciate. I shall be glad to help with the wide implications of the foreign scene in Opposition in the Commons.

> I would like to add that I should be glad to put my experience at the disposal of any younger man you may choose to take charge of the policy outlook of the party. I have enjoyed exerting influence in this sphere for many years and think this is the right time for you to make a fresh appointment.[37]

In fact, that was not at all Rab's view – and it was some tribute to his historic influence over at least the policy arm of the Conservative Party that the new Leader of the Opposition should have deliberately refrained from making any alternative political appointment as chairman of the Conservative Research Department (Sir Michael Fraser was to hold *de facto* control of the Department until he assumed the actual chairmanship in 1970). But Rab's humiliations were not yet over. When the formal protocol list of the Shadow Cabinet was published, it was found to be presented in an entirely new form: there was no longer 'a pecking order' and Rab was simply listed as being the senior of the three Shadow Ministers concerned with Foreign Affairs compared with twelve involved in Home Affairs. For the former Deputy Prime Minister, and First Secretary of State, that was – at least in Westminster terms – a dramatic relegation.

As always, Rab put a brave face on adversity. He continued to conduct himself as the number two figure in the Party, even though there seemed to be little inclination on the part of the Opposition leadership to make use of his talents: he was not even, for example, invited to take part in the Debate on the Address – a striking omission for the Opposition's chief Foreign Affairs spokesman. He delivered only one Commons speech, opening a foreign affairs debate on 16 December, in the first two months running up to the Christmas recess.[38] That was, as events turned out, not only his début from the Opposition front-bench after thirteen years in Government: it was also his swan-song in any Commons debate.

The reason for that lay in a sudden request which reached Smith Square in the week before Christmas, saying that the new Labour Prime Minister would very much like to see Rab as soon as it could be arranged. It was not, in fact, very easy to arrange: Rab was out shooting at Stanstead and all efforts to contact him during the day failed. Sensing, however, that it must be a matter of some urgency, Mollie Butler resourcefully arranged for a car to meet her husband at Liverpool Street (where he was due to return on an evening train) and to take him straight to No. 10. It was there, in his shooting clothes with his dog, Bella, on a lead, that Rab found himself asked by the Prime Minister whether he would consider accepting the

Crown Appointment of the Mastership of Trinity College, Cambridge.

It cannot have been a complete shock – the current Master (the distinguished scientist, Lord Adrian) was known to be retiring and Rab's name had already been mentioned in a number of newspaper articles as a possible candidate for the post.* Nor were Wilson's motives all that hard to fathom: he had never made any secret of his belief (fully shared by the Liberal Leader, Jo Grimond)†[39] that, if Rab had led the Tories into the 1964 election, there would have been a Conservative victory – so removing him permanently from the political scene plainly had its attractions. The difficulty lay with securing Rab's assent: it was, after all, only two months since he had turned down an Earldom from his own Party Leader – and yet here was a Labour Prime Minister making exactly the same effort to ensure his departure from active politics.

There was, though, clearly a distinction between the two offers. Being an Earl might be very grand – but it was not actually a job: running a large college, on the other hand, clearly gave one something to do – and it was that sense of being constructively engaged that Rab had missed most since leaving Government in October. His eventual answer, therefore, was almost certainly predetermined; characteristically, however, Rab refused to be rushed into a decision and it was three weeks before a letter went off to Downing Street accepting the Prime Minister's invitation.[40]

The formalities, complicated by the death of Sir Winston Churchill at the age of ninety on 24 January 1965, took a further three weeks to complete. But on the evening of Sunday 31 January a formal Press Notice was released from No. 10 saying simply:

> The Queen has been graciously pleased to approve that the Right Hon. Richard Austen Butler, CH, MA, MP be appointed to the Mastership of Trinity College, Cambridge, in succession to Lord Adrian, OM, FRS, MA, MD, FRCP who retires on 30 June 1965.
>
> The Queen has also been graciously pleased to approve that the

* The first time the idea was floated was in the Atticus column of the *Sunday Times* the very Sunday after Sir Alec Douglas-Home became Prime Minister. Since the story predicted that the offer would be made by Harold Wilson (still at that stage Leader of the Opposition) and accepted by Rab (only just appointed as Foreign Secretary) it ranked as an uncannily accurate gossip column piece of prediction. Nicholas Tomalin in the *Sunday Times* (20 October 1963).

† Joseph Grimond (1913–). Liberal MP, Orkney and Shetland 1950–83. Leader of the Liberal Party 1956–67. Created life peer 1983.

> dignity of a Barony of the United Kingdom for Life be conferred upon Mr Butler.[41]

Even with the bonus of the life peerage thrown in, the announcement meant only one thing: after thirty-six years in the Commons, Rab had cut the painter with politics. From now on, like God and the Queen, he would be expected to be 'above Party'. It would have been astonishing if he had felt no regrets – but they did not last long. If any single event liberated Rab from wistful nostalgia, it was probably a ceremony, that he could not resist attending, some six months later. On 2 August 1965 he was once again present in Church House – only this time not having to make a speech but rather to be a passive spectator to the anointing of Edward Heath as Tory Leader in place of Sir Alec Douglas-Home. 'Today', he was wryly to comment that evening, 'I attended the tribal *levée* when, with shouts of exultation, the new Leader was applauded and Alec Home was thanked.'[42] It is hard somehow to detect in those words the reaction of someone still pining for the life of politics.

17 *Master of Trinity*

One of the by-products of Rab's return to academic life – after nearly forty years – was that he was able, while still very much alive, to read for himself the kinds of appraisal of a career that are normally reserved for an obituary. The announcement of his appointment to the Mastership of Trinity provoked a torrent of tributes, some active, like the various presentations made to him by his constituency, the National Union and the Research Department, and others passive, if scarcely less generous, as reflected in the testimonials that appeared in a host of newspapers and periodicals. It is no disparagement of the former to suggest that Rab was probably even more touched by the latter. True, the warmer assessments tended to come from the less partisan elements of the Press (with the more vociferous Conservative newspapers, like the *Daily Mail*, displaying a marked measure of restraint); elsewhere, however, there was no holding back. *The Times* declared that all his life Rab had been 'a progressive and a force for good',[1] the *Observer* that the Conservative Party 'owed him an enormous debt',[2] *The Economist* that those who blocked his way to the top had, for the most part, been 'small-minded or emotional men',[3] while to the *Spectator* he was, quite simply 'the architect of the Tory years 1951–64'.[4]

The only snag was that the common thread running through all such judgments was the implicit suggestion that Rab's life was now, to all intents and purposes, over. It was hardly surprising, therefore, if in contemplating his future at Cambridge, Rab should initially have given way to a certain melancholy. 'You know,' he remarked to his wife at one moment during the eight months that elapsed between the news of his appointment and their joint arrival at Trinity, 'this is going to be a very small pond indeed compared to London' – to which Mollie had the good sense to reply, 'Yes, but to that pond will come all sorts of distinguished birds and fishes' (only to be rewarded with the cheerless comment, 'But it won't be the same').[5]

At least the period of Rab's gradual withdrawal from politics was a busy one. First of all came his introduction to the House of Lords, a piece of ceremonial that Rab enjoyed and which took place on 24 February only just over three weeks after his life peerage was announced. The one difficulty here, though, was that it provided the occasion for a further bout of tributes – with the *Sunday Express*, for example, striking an almost elegiac note in its comment that it could only be 'a moment for sadness, the moment that takes Rab Butler away for ever among the elder statesmen'.[6]

Next, perhaps mercifully, came the business of getting Rab's successor at Saffron Walden elected to the House of Commons. Yet here the Master-designate found himself in a delicate position. Although the candidate the local Conservatives chose – the old capital punishment abolitionist, Peter Kirk (defeated at Gravesend in the October 1964 general election) – met with Rab's full approval, there was a problem about the degree of support he could properly afford to his successor. In the House of Lords Rab had already taken his seat on the cross-benches, the place normally reserved for those peers without any formal Party allegiance. He had done so, not because he had ceased to be a Conservative, but rather because he had prudently thought it right to 'keep aloof from the fray', at least until he had 'discovered how far an involvement in party politics would conflict with what is expected of a Master of Trinity'.[7]

This high-minded posture provided, however, an irresistible temptation for both the Labour and Liberal candidates to make trouble – and they were each soon drawing attention to Rab's minimal participation in the campaign. Rab had spoken at Peter Kirk's formal adoption meeting but there was originally no intention on his part to involve himself any further in the election after that. A mischievous charge by the Labour candidate that he was 'fed up with his old party'[8] forced Rab, however, to think again. In the last week of the campaign he made a surprise appearance at an election meeting held in his local town of Halstead and, mounting the platform, called for 'a thumping majority' for his successor.[9] Whether this last-minute intervention was decisive or not can only be a matter of conjecture; but at least Rab had the satisfaction of seeing his successor elected to Parliament with a majority of nearly 3,500* – no mean achievement,

* Peter Kirk's majority was 3,493 compared with Rab's one of 4,955 five months earlier. Both the Labour Party and the Liberals fielded the same candidates who had fought in the general election, with the latter on this occasion losing his deposit.

given that the Labour Party had at first had high hopes of winning the seat.

Rab's real worry, however, remained Trinity. The cordial reception given to his appointment by the national Press had not been entirely reflected within Cambridge itself. When Rab's nomination as a possible successor to Lord Adrian was still merely a matter of rumour, one left-wing Fellow of Trinity, Peter Laslett, had done his best to head it off, by pointedly remarking, 'We're not here to cushion the fall of failing politicians, that's not what the Mastership is for'[10] – and, inevitably, that comment was now remembered. An equally sour note was struck by a don at another college in a letter to the *Cambridge Review*:

> May I offer my sympathy to Mr Butler on his appointment to the management of the Siberian power station masquerading as Trinity College? I feel certain that this was the post that he (like Marshal Bulganin) always wanted in his heart of hearts. It is interesting to hear him say so in public. But does the Press seriously expect us to fall for this line?
>
> Yours faithfully,
>
> BILL SUTHERLAND
>
> *St Catharine's College*[11]

Dons, it is well known, delight to bark and bite – but Trinity had not, in fact, been treated with any great tact or consideration by No. 10. The Prime Minister's Private Secretary for Appointments had paid just one visit to the college ahead of the announcement; and he seems to have taken soundings only from two or three members of the Governing Body. Apart from one seemingly innocent query, 'Would it be difficult if someone who was not a Trinity man was to be appointed?' (to which anyway he was firmly told 'Yes' by the Vice-Master of the college), he had given absolutely nothing away. Nor did the college get any advance warning of the announcement – the Vice-Master, Professor Patrick Duff, received a letter from No. 10 indicating that the choice had fallen on Rab only after he had already read the news in that morning's papers.[12] All things considered, it was perhaps fortunate for Rab that a long tradition of Cambridge courtesy dictated that the only immediate comment made on behalf of Trinity, turned out to be as restrained as it was, 'I have', declared the Vice-Master, 'been reading in the Press about the appointment. We shall be very glad to see Mr Butler here.'[13]

Yet, even in saying that, Professor Duff was bravely concealing a collegiate sense of shock. It was not Rab's own academic qualifications, or lack of them, that bothered Trinity; it was simply the fact that, for the first time in 250 years, the college was to have a Master who was not himself a Trinity man.* That was why none of the newspaper rumours suggesting Rab might be appointed had been taken seriously within the college itself: in the sheltered atmosphere of the Fellows' Parlour it simply did not seem conceivable that even a Labour Government would dare to depart from what had become an established, almost hallowed, tradition of the Master always being chosen from among the college's own alumni.

How far Rab was sensitive to the extent to which the traditionalists at Trinity had been offended by his appointment was never wholly clear. But there was perhaps a trace of his being conscious of the college's susceptibilities in his decision to emphasise his family connection right from the start. On his first visit to the college as Master-designate on 3 March he did not rest content merely with dining with the outgoing Master, Lord Adrian; he also lunched with his second cousin, Sir James Butler, a Fellow of the college since 1913 and the son of the great Henry Montagu Butler, who had reigned in the Master's Lodge from 1886 to 1918.[14] Since he had never been particularly close to J. R. M. Butler, that was probably intended to be seen as a deliberate gesture of obeisance to Trinity's own household gods.

Inevitably, the limbo period till 7 October 1965, when Rab (by now even looking episcopal) formally took possession of his new academic see, was not an easy one. Rab, for the moment, was neither one thing nor the other: no longer an active politician nor yet the involved head of a Cambridge House. If anything, it was a time for clearing the decks – and, almost as a signal that he now expected his life totally to change, Rab resolved even to abandon Stanstead Hall, the home in his constituency in which he had lived ever since taking it over from his father-in-law some thirty years earlier. Stanstead was leased to Essex University, which planned to use it as flats for visiting academics: the arrangement, initially at least, appeared to set the seal on Rab's own association with the new pre-Robbins university of which he had been Chancellor since its foundation in 1962. (Essex University was ultimately to find Stanstead too expensive to keep up – and too remote from its central

* In proposing the health of the outgoing Master, Dr G. M. Trevelyan, in 1951, the then Vice-Master, Professor H. A. Hollond, had specifically stated, 'I am sure that what any Fellow of Trinity wants in a Master is, first, that he should be a Trinity man.' *Trinity College Annual Record* (1950–1), p. 10.

campus at Colchester – and returned it to Rab, who then sold it for use as a nursing-home, in 1970.)

For the rest, the summer of 1965 was very much a season for farewells and leave-taking – though Rab and Mollie did manage to get away on a three-week holiday to Greece, where they visited Rhodes and toured the Peloponnese, driving their own car. But at least Rab was still not pining for the life that he had left behind: a pressing invitation from Harold Wilson that he should take on the chairmanship of a new National Committee for Commonwealth Immigrants met with a firm, if polite, refusal, with Rab pleading 'preoccupation with work at Trinity'.[15]

As the date for their formal arrival drew nearer, both Rab's and Mollie's thoughts centred more and more on Trinity. The Master's Lodge at Trinity is more like a stately home than a private house, but in the fourteen years that Lord and Lady Adrian had lived there, it had 'hardly seen a lick of paint'.[16] Mollie – while leaving the formal Elizabethan Great Drawing-Room more or less as it was – was determined to set her own imprint on the rest of the house:* that meant constant supervision of the redecoration of the Lodge, which started the moment the Adrians left at the end of June. Even so, when Rab and Mollie began the long process of moving in at the end of September, 'the water supply went wrong and the whole hall had to be dug up for the pipes to be got at, just as we arrived'.[17]

It was not, however, in Rab's nature to allow himself to be distracted by small domestic complications of that kind. His own attention was focused, almost exclusively, on the installation ceremony and the speech he was expected to make to the assembled Fellows and Scholars in Hall that same evening.

As a politician Rab may never have had a great sense of theatre but he had, down the years, developed a definite taste for pageant. The ceremonial aspect of his own inauguration at Trinity, therefore, appealed to him. Capped and gowned, he was required to knock three times on the wicket gate of Trinity in order to gain admission: even then, it was not immediately granted – with the head porter instead popping his head round the gate and inquiring, 'Who are you, sir?' On getting the reply, 'I am Lord Butler, the appointed Master of Trinity College', the porter promptly shut the gate, pausing only to take the Crown's Letters Patent from Rab's hands. In accordance with ancient tradition, the Letters were then taken to

* Its greatest glory became the Small Drawing-Room, where the Impressionist paintings that Rab had inherited a life interest in from Sam Courtauld – a Renoir, a Monet, a Boudin, a Manet and a Cézanne – were all hung.

the Chapel to be examined by the Vice-Master and Fellows. Only when they had satisfied themselves as to their authenticity were the two doors of the Great Gate flung open and Rab admitted, to be conducted straight away to the Chapel and symbolically seated in the Master's stall, after making the statutory promises.

It was a piece of mummery that not every politician would have found it easy to bring off; but Rab (though he was not quite action perfect – he knocked, with a glass paperweight, four times on the gate instead of three and, with a politician's instinct, vainly tried to shake hands with the Vice-Master the moment he was allowed in)[18] seemed perfectly at home with it. It was, of course, to some extent in the blood: his great-uncle had, after all, been through exactly the same ordeal eighty years earlier and Rab's own father, in his time, had also been Master of a Cambridge college (if a much smaller, and less grand, one than Trinity). Rab's performance, though, fully earned the credit that even the most prominent critic of his appointment was prepared to concede him: writing in his diary that night, Peter Laslett, the same Trinity Fellow who had warned the college against being used 'to cushion the fall of failing politicians', was fair-mindedly to comment that 'Rab cut rather a good figure'.[19]

Almost instinctively, that soon seemed also to be the judgment of the entire college. True, Rab's first speech – delivered on the evening of his installation – disappointed some of its hearers; but that was probably because they either expected too much of a politician or, alternatively, had been spoilt by the standards set by an academic (Lord Adrian had the reputation of being one of the best speakers in Cambridge). At least, though, Rab had one piece of reassurance to offer. He was aware, he said, that 'the Master is no longer a Venetian Doge but the chairman of a constitutional council'.[20] He looked forward to taking a lively interest in the college's affairs but it would only be in a strictly constitutional role.*

The precise nature of any college's internal government system tends to be a secret it keeps very much to itself. The executive arm at Trinity has been, however, for many years the College Council – not, as its title almost implies, a random collection of distinguished individuals recruited on the pattern of the governors of a public school, but rather a small, tightly-knit group of professional dons

* The only overt breach of Trinity's constitution which Rab opened up, lay in his insistence on being allowed to keep his dog, Bella, in the Master's Lodge. The college rules stipulated that no dog was allowed to be kept in college: Rab overcame this prohibition by having Bella officially classified as a cat.

with a shared appetite for administration. If the Master has any opportunity for influence, it lies in the way he chairs and steers this particular committee: with fourteen members – nine elected for three-year terms and five ex-officio, comprising the Vice-Master, Senior Tutor, two Bursars and the Master himself – it functions more like the board of a public company than, say, the Greater Chapter of a cathedral. Certainly, in Trinity's case, the Mammon analogy is apposite. Easily the best endowed educational institution in the country, the college owned, even by the half-way stage of Rab's Mastership, seventy-six shops, fifteen warehouses, six factories and 16,000 acres of farmland[21] (to say nothing of an undeclared investment in development land – an investment which was to provide it with an entirely new level of prosperity once the expansion of the port of Felixstowe and the development of the Cambridge Science Park came on stream in the mid-1970s):[22] its annual investment income in 1974–5 was already touching £1 million (ten years later it was to be some six times that).[23]

Rab, with his experience of the Treasury and of the board of Courtaulds (of which from 1 January 1966 he, once again, became a director) took to this side of his new duties with avidity.* The College Council meeting, held at 11.15 a.m. every Friday in term-time, was soon entrenched as the most important engagement in his weekly diary; he proved an admirable chairman, conducting business with a great deal more dispatch than his predecessor, under whom meetings had frequently dragged on until after lunch (something unheard of in Rab's day). He displayed a miraculous ability to summon up agreement – 'Even in a body adamant for faction he could induce consensus.'[24] This was an even more remarkable gift, since there was often no sign that he had been paying any great attention – he could still, however, 'arouse himself from a distant absorption, which might have been a nap, and with a "Well, I think we are agreed" produce a formula which disarmed dissent'.[25]

If that had been all there was to it, Rab's legend would hardly have reached out into all the corners of the college. He started off, of course, with some advantages: unlike most Heads of Houses, he arrived in Cambridge as already a national figure – but that, so far as the young are concerned, can often be as much a handicap as an

* Here Rab represented a sharp contrast to his great-uncle, Henry Montagu Butler, of whom it was written, 'Presiding at the Council was a duty in which Dr Butler took little pleasure, and for which perhaps he was not altogether fitted.' J. R. M. Butler, *Henry Montagu Butler: Master of Trinity College, Cambridge, 1886–1918* (Longmans, 1925), p. 34.

asset. Rab's political attributes were put to the test during the student troubles of the late 1960s; if Trinity emerged largely unscathed from them, the credit within the college was largely thought to belong to him. Probably his most public success was an Open Meeting of the entire college which took place in the middle of the Lent Term of 1969. Other Masters would, no doubt, have thought it far too dangerous – and the meeting, with the dons sitting on the dais and the students facing them below, might well have seemed doomed to end in some form of confrontation. That it did not do so was largely due to Rab: 'big, burly and imposing, Rab was in his real element – smiling all the time but never perturbed'.[26] Even when one of the younger firebrands rushed up from the body of the Hall and tried to seize the microphone, it had no effect on the Master, 'he merely very mildly, but audibly, said, "I'm afraid you can't do that because, you see, I am chairman of this meeting," and the lad wasn't deflated but he desisted'.[27]

The meeting was a triumph for Rab – and the college, or at least the senior members of it, had no doubt as to why, 'one of the bits of luck we had was that when a political head was needed, we actually had such a person'.[28] But the Open Meeting – unprecedented in the college's 400-year history – was not just an example of an experienced hand being able to exhibit all the arts of political skill. Rab was always adept at picking up vibrations, and he gathered from that meeting that things could not go on at Trinity as they always had done. One practical consequence was that the rules for closing the Trinity gates were immediately changed. Undergraduates, instead of being locked out at midnight, were permitted to come in freely till 2 a.m. But that was only the initial item in a programme of reform that went on throughout Rab's Mastership. Joint meetings were promptly started between representatives of the College Council and the College Union (the democratic title by which the JCR Committee is known). Before Rab left, this process had led to the admission of women guests initially at lunch, then at dinner and, eventually, the decision to admit women as members of the college first as Fellows in 1975, then as postgraduate students in 1976 and finally, after in fact Rab had gone, in Michaelmas term 1978 as undergraduates.

Rab was not the progenitor of any of these changes – indeed, his Senior Common Room colleagues suspected that he was a reluctant convert to most of them. But, as he had always shown in politics, when a tide was irresistible, he saw no point in opposing it: only a major structural reform in Trinity's admissions system seems to have caused him any real anxiety. Traditionally, Trinity had operated very much like Eton – with individual tutors, of whom there were eventually six (five for undergraduates, and one for postgraduate students), enjoying much the same rights as Etonian housemasters in deciding who was, and who was not, admitted to the college. Rab apparently regarded the radicals' assault on this practice as an attack on the very ark of the covenant – even threatening, at a College Meeting, that he 'simply could not go on as Master if it was carried'.[29] It *was* carried and, before he left, Rab was to be heard boasting to his last commemoration dinner that he took pride in the fact that 'many changes have been made in the past thirteen years'.[30]

That was, no doubt, par for the course – for the great characteristic of Rab's political career had always been his instinct to make the best of things, even if they had not occurred quite as one had wanted. Naturally, there were those among the more conservative Trinity Fellows – just as there had been among the more reactionary elements in the 1922 Committee – who felt let down by this apparent display of flexibility on Rab's part. It, therefore, says a good deal for his personal qualities, as opposed to his policy attitudes, that, when the moment came for all the Fellows to decide whether or not they wished to prolong his tenure of the Mastership beyond the normal retiring age of seventy, they should have decided to do so unanimously. At a meeting, held some six months ahead of Rab's initial retirement date in 1973, 91 (out of 118) Fellows were present and 91 voted in favour of an extension of Rab's term of office to the last permissible point under the statutes, his seventy-fifth year.[31] (Possibly even more remarkably, Rab and his wife also received a letter signed by all the senior college staff saying how pleased they were by the Fellows' decision.)

But by then, of course, Rab had become very much the personification of Trinity. In the Lodge he and Mollie may have maintained the standards of a different age – keeping both a butler and a chef – but the college, which had always rather liked grandeur, saw no harm in that: indeed, it tended to take a certain pride in it – 'we had a kind of slippered duke in the Lodge for 13 years, and it was lovely'.[32] Nor was Rab's style in any way that of an aloof grandee – he thought nothing of popping in and joining the undergraduates in the college bar (an amenity which he was responsible for introducing); and every Sunday morning some fifty junior members of the college (accompanied, if they liked, by girlfriends) would be invited to the Lodge for a drinks party. The Lodge was very much Mollie's own province, and, over the span of thirteen years, more than 3,000

Trinity undergraduates probably acquired their lasting criterion for gracious living from the atmosphere which she created: there would always be flowers (masses of them), there would often be music and, above all, there would be her uncanny knack for remembering not only names but also for recalling exactly what each individual guest's interests were, thereby making the shyest and most diffident undergraduate feel almost instantly at home.

Inevitably a certain glamour rubbed off on the Lodge from the three years the Prince of Wales spent in the college, between 1967 and 1970. Rab seems to have played no part in the decision to send Prince Charles to Trinity: he was not present at the famous royal advisers' dinner party held at Buckingham Palace on 22 December 1965 to consider the Heir to the Throne's further education after Gordonstoun;[33] and the first he appears to have known of the decision to offer Prince Charles to Trinity was when the Queen wrote to him in the autumn of 1966[34] asking whether the college would be prepared to accept him. The go-between for all the arrangements was Robin Woods,* then Dean of Windsor, himself a Trinity man who also had two sons in the college: after Charles had gone down, Rab was publicly to refer to the Dean as having been 'a great help to us in introducing the Prince of Wales to Trinity'.[35]

It is possible, however, that it was Rab himself who served as the most powerful magnet. Certainly, from the Royal Family's point of view, it made sense – once the decision had been narrowed down to Cambridge University – to choose a college with a head who had experience both of politics and of the world; and it cannot exactly have been a liability either that Rab, through his long periods of understudying Macmillan (including regular Tuesday evening audiences at the Palace), was probably the only college Master known at all well to the Queen. In any event, Trinity was extremely proud of its royal catch – and the Prince's arrival, just two years after his own, provided Rab with the final proof that in moving to Trinity he had done the right thing.

There was always a distinctly nostalgic element in Rab's attitude towards the Royal Family (he would, for example, talk about 'the Court' as if it were a constitutional concept that still had political meaning); and there is no doubt that the notion of playing Melbourne to the Heir to the Throne was something that pleased him enormously. How far that relationship actually came into being

* Robert Wilmer Woods (1914–). Dean of Windsor 1962–70. Domestic Chaplain to the Queen 1962–70. Bishop of Worcester 1970–81.

at Trinity it is hard to say. Certainly, Rab was one of the formative influences upon Prince Charles – but probably only one among many. There is some evidence, indeed, that Rab may have seemed almost too ready to play the role of guide and mentor; the awareness that the Master was holding three-quarters of an hour available for advice every evening cannot always have been an easy or comfortable thought for the Heir Apparent to live with. Throughout his three years at Trinity Charles had his own key to a side-entrance to the Master's Lodge, giving him direct access to a private staircase that led straight to Rab's study; and he was also, of course, a frequent guest on social occasions – it was at a Lodge dinner party that he initially met, and was immediately charmed by, Lucia Santa Cruz, the daughter of the Chilean Ambassador in London, who was assisting Rab with research on his memoirs. This friendship was certainly not discouraged within the Master's Lodge – though the notion put about some years afterwards that Rab had acted as a kind of Pandarus to the couple[36] was deeply resented on both sides and may even have led to a certain cooling in Rab's relationship with the Palace, though not with the Prince.

And in this special course of history we've made up for you, I become Prime Minister.

However, in 1970 when the Prince went down, such recriminations were far in the future – and Cambridge's local newspaper was probably perceptive in regarding the award of the Garter to Rab in April 1971 as a token of royal appreciation for all that he had done in seeing the Prince successfully through his Cambridge career.[37] Charles's academic honours had been satisfactory but not exceptional: he had got a 2:1 after his first year in Archaeology and Anthropology followed, after the distractions of the Investiture and a term at Aberystwyth, by a 2:2 in History in 1970 – but his real triumph had lain in his ability to lead a relatively normal student life. He had played the cello in the college orchestra, he had taken an active part in the Trinity Dramatic Society (in particular, in revues it put on in the Lent Terms of 1969 and 1970) and, above all, he had saved Rab from going to the Tower – the standing joke between them was that the Master would be sent there if the Prince failed to take a degree of any sort.[38] There seems, indeed, no room to doubt that when Charles left Trinity in June 1970, he did so with genuine gratitude for all Rab had tried to do on his behalf: if the relationship was not kept up,* it was possibly because the Royal Family, now anxious to turn the Prince of Wales into a sailor, never intended that it should be.†

The departure of the Prince meant, necessarily, that Trinity fell a little in public visibility; but there does not appear to have been much sense of 'Ichabod' in Rab's own life. He had always, in fact, taken care to preserve its metropolitan end, with Mollie and him normally spending the middle part of each week in London: he spoke, admittedly, seldom in the House of Lords but he still retained from his political life the desire to 'keep in touch'. As a general rule, he would be in London on Wednesdays and Thursdays, returning to Trinity in good time for the College Council meeting on Fridays. This pattern continued even after 3 Smith Square was sold (to William Rees-Mogg) in 1970, since Rab and Mollie immediately moved to a large and airy flat in Whitehall Court. However, most of their entertaining was still done in the Lodge and invitations to dine there (or in Hall at feasts) came to be much prized among politicians of both major Parties. A notable absentee from such convivial gatherings was Harold Macmillan – but then Mollie took a strong line about that and would not have him to stay in her home

* Rab and Mollie were invited to the Prince of Wales's wedding in July 1981 but otherwise seem to have seen singularly little of him once he left Trinity.

† The Prince had only come to Trinity, Rab discovered afterwards, because his father considered him 'too immature' for the Services.

(on the one occasion when Rab's former rival visited Trinity he was made to sleep in the Judges' Suite, which forms a kind of annexe to the Lodge).[39] Other political guests, however, were always welcome, regardless of Party – and it was perhaps after dinner round the fire talking to former political colleagues or opponents that Rab would come most into his own.[40]

By the time Rab was half-way through his reign at Trinity, the young men in college could hardly have been expected to remember him as an active politician, though that deficiency was soon made up by the publication in 1971 of *The Art of the Possible*. Widely acknowledged as the best political autobiography since Duff Cooper's *Old Men Forget* in 1953, it was not by any means exclusively Rab's own work. In addition to the research done by Lucia Santa Cruz, the shaping of the material – and indeed the actual casting of the narrative – owed a great deal to the literary skill of Peter Goldman.* However, the book remains a model of its kind and fully deserved the critical acclaim with which it was received. If any one aspect of that gave Rab especial pleasure, it was perhaps the frequent comparisons that were drawn, and always in his favour, with the six-volume autobiography that Harold Macmillan was just in the process of completing. To some degree that, indeed, appears to have been the object of the exercise – and the motive for the notably laconic style that Rab chose to adopt.† Enoch Powell was not alone in finding the sheer economy of the writing among the book's most attractive attributes.[41]

With his book safely written and published, Rab did very little other outside work once he was established at Trinity. He would occasionally deliver a lecture (he gave the Romanes Lecture at Oxford in 1966 on 'The Difficult Art of Autobiography'), from time to time he would make a visit to universities abroad (including to Witwatersrand in South Africa in 1969), as well as presiding regularly over ceremonial occasions connected with the two English universities of which he was Chancellor, Sheffield and Essex. Public duties,

* Peter Goldman (1925–). Director of Conservative Political Centre 1955–64. Conservative candidate, Orpington by-election 1962. Director, Consumers' Association 1964–86.

† Rab's four-paragraph preface includes the revealing sentence, 'I have eschewed the current autobiographical fondness for multi-volume histories and have preferred a single book which is not too heavy for anyone to hold up and doze over in bed', *Art of the Possible*, p. xi. Any doubt as to whom that arrow was aimed at should perhaps be resolved by the last sentence of Rab's own review of Harold Macmillan's fourth volume, *Riding the Storm*, 'Altogether this massive work will keep anybody busy for several weeks.' *Cambridge Evening News* (24 April 1971).

however, he steadfastly refused, until in June 1972 he, somewhat surprisingly, surrendered to the blandishments of Reginald Maudling and accepted the chairmanship of a joint Home Office/DHSS Departmental Committee on Mentally Abnormal Offenders.[42] It proved to be a thankless task – the Committee's report took three years to produce and was hardly, if at all, acted upon by the new Labour Government. The most Rab got out of it was an extremely cordial letter from the new Secretary of State at the Department of Health and Social Security, Barbara Castle, who wrote personally to tell him that she regarded it as 'an excellent Report' and to thank him for 'what I fear must have been a somewhat arduous three years' work'.[43] She forbore to mention, even if she knew, that it would prove to be largely wasted work as well. The Report was eventually published in October 1975[44] but fell victim to inter-departmental and inter-professional rivalries and jealousies.

After that (and, understandably, in the light of that experience) Rab took on no more Whitehall assignments – he would turn up every year for the Garter Ceremony at Windsor in June but that was about as far as his official life went. And the truth was, of course, that he was not getting any younger. His seventieth birthday was celebrated with a grand dinner party for 210 people in the Lodge on 9 December 1972, at which he made a short speech which was a great success; but before his next birthday he was to receive a sharp reminder that speaking engagements, at least if not adequately prepared for, can become a hazard for the elderly. In November 1973 he had agreed to present the annual Booker Prize for Fiction at a dinner held at the Café Royal in London. He made the mistake of going to it straight from a cocktail party and, battling with a cold as well, arrived perhaps not in the most clear-headed of states. He insisted, however, on making a speech – and at some length: unfortunately, his remarks included two profoundly unsuitable jokes, especially in a gathering of publishers where jests about Jews are liable to be not merely publicly offensive but personally wounding as well. The result was humiliation – in which admiration for the prize-winner, J. G. Farrell and his novel, *The Siege of Krishnapur*, was all but obliterated as 'astonished guests squirmed'[45] as a result of Rab's remarks. The postscript was this sad and revealing paragraph published a week later in the *Jewish Chronicle*:

> Lord Butler told the *Jewish Chronicle* on Tuesday of his sincere regrets, adding that telling the jokes had been a mistake on his part. He had always been a supporter of Israel and had no intention

of embarrassing Jewish people. He had been asked to speak before the prize award was announced and the chairman had told him to tell some anecdotes. 'It was unfortunate that I chose these two stories and I express my regrets,' he said.[46]

There were still, however, public appearances that Rab could carry off, even if they tended to be more and more on his own home ground. On 3 June 1974 the Cambridge Union, to mark the anniversary of his own presidency fifty years earlier, made him the first former President to become an honorary member in its entire history: Rab, who was cheered all the way to the Despatch Box, responded with a reminiscent speech, expressing his debt of gratitude for all he had learnt about debating from the Cambridge Union Society and affirming his total confidence in its future.[47] He was becoming, too, now that he had found his own style and broken free from the shadow cast by his predecessor, a much more successful speaker at Trinity commemoration dinners: no doubt, his audiences had got used to him but he had also begun to 'get the feel' of them, too. The very inconsequential nature of his remarks – to say nothing of his often unpredictable use of language – had come to be seen as an intrinsic part of his charm. It was, therefore, a disappointment to the whole college when in 1975, for the first time in ten years, illness prevented the Master from appearing at the commemoration dinner, held by tradition on the last Friday of the Lent Term.[48] Rab had bronchitis, an ailment that was to return to trouble him the following spring. In April 1976 he was abroad, taking a Greek cruise, when what had started off as a mere chest complaint developed into congestion of the lungs. There was a fear of pneumonia setting in, so Rab was rushed to a hospital in Athens and then flown home (where he made a speedy recovery).[49]

On the whole, Rab enjoyed remarkably good health during his thirteen years at Trinity. He certainly put on weight – often lingering over port in the Combination Room after dinner longer than was good for him (and sometimes explaining that he was forced to do so because 'Mollie has some concert raging away in the Lodge').*[50] He also acquired a curious habit of making his way to the Lodge drinks-tray and helping himself to a touch of vodka every morning before breakfast – something that Mollie was for a long time quite unaware of (it was an innovation in his life-style that seems to have

* Rab was distinctly unmusical. At concerts in the Lodge, when he did attend them, he would insist when he got impatient on snapping his hunter watch open and shut to the distraction of the audience and the embarrassment of his wife.

arisen from a foolish relative informing him that it was the custom with schnapps in Scandinavia). Yet his popularity with the college grew, if anything, with every year that passed. And so did his own feeling of being at home at Trinity. It was certainly believed in the college, even when he reached his seventy-fifth year in December 1977 that, had it been remotely possible under the statutes, he would have liked to have gone on.[51]

Rab, however, was sufficient of a realist to know that that was out of the question. Already in 1976 he had begun to make his dispositions. Gatcombe Park, the one property he had inherited outright from his father-in-law, he sold that summer to the Queen. The transaction, designed by the Queen to provide a home (and a farm) for Princess Anne and Captain Mark Phillips, did not provide Rab with complete satisfaction. 'The Royal Family, you know,' he was heard to remark more than once, 'drive a very hard bargain.'[52] Nevertheless, the capital (at least some £500,000) he acquired from the sale enabled him to make provision for his retirement. In November 1976 it was disclosed that Rab had bought Spencers at Great Yeldham in Essex, the house in which Mollie had lived until the death of her first husband in 1959. Characteristically, Rab described it as 'a small Georgian house, with a little bit of ground – not enough to farm; it's not too big for an older couple'.[53] In fact, it was a 24-room, three-storey, eighteenth-century house set in seventy acres of parkland with two 300-yard drives leading to a country lane. When, at the dinner to welcome Rab's successor, Sir Alan Hodgkin,* held at Trinity in October 1978, the Vice-Master referred to having received a phone call from 'the old Master talking from the frontiers of Essex, where he lives in a log cabin', he was rewarded with one of the largest laughs of the evening.[54]

But by then, of course, Trinity had got to know all Rab's foibles. A relationship that had begun with a wary anticipation had ended with warm affection. Once again, in the summer of 1978, Rab found himself doing the round of fond farewells. On 4 June all the junior members of the college, numbering some 650, were invited to a farewell garden party held for the Master and his wife in the Fellows' Garden; two days later there was a similar occasion, though not quite so crowded, given by the college staff and pensioners; ten days after that it was the turn of the Trinity MPs to entertain Rab – and fourteen out of nineteen of them made the journey to Cambridge

* Alan Lloyd Hodgkin (1914–). Fellow of Trinity 1936–78, Master 1978–84, Fellow 1984– . Joint winner of Nobel Prize for Medicine 1963. OM 1983. Sir Alan had been the only visible internal rival when Rab was appointed in 1965.

in order to honour him at a dinner in the Old Kitchen; finally, on the night of Saturday 17 June, both Rab and Mollie were the guests of honour at a farewell dinner held in Hall at which all the college's Fellows were their hosts. On each occasion presentations were made and speeches were delivered – but of the latter only one line seems to have stuck in anyone's memory: it came from Rab and it appears to have been used more than once. No one, however, minded about that – for what Rab said was, 'I would rather have been here than continued my political career.'[55] By Trinity, quite rightly, that was regarded as the ultimate compliment.

For Rab the previous thirteen years had, in fact, been a good deal more than the benign twilight that he may originally have envisaged. He had taken not just to the panoply and pomp of his office but, even more, to the institution and the people whom he served. He had had, of course, his disappointments: it was an open secret that he had hoped to build a theatre for the college and that the twin hostel development which finally went up on the site he had had in mind was an altogether more modest venture than he would have liked (even if one of the hostels was called 'Butler House').[56] Like most Masters, he had grand ideas about masonry and would have preferred a more imposing monument. But, given that a major architectural development was underway when he arrived – and, furthermore, had already been named 'The Wolfson Building' in honour of the project's main benefactor – Rab accepted, philosophically enough, that this was not to be. In its place, he had, in any event, built a different kind of memorial – in the minds and memories of a dozen successive generations of Trinity graduates.

Rab was under no illusion, when he left Trinity, that it was 'the young men' whom he would miss most: indeed, in the week of his departure, he said – revealing his penchant for the slightly surprising turn of phrase – 'From now on, I fear, we shall only have cows to stroke.'[57] The thing, he remarked in a newspaper interview, he was most afraid of was 'being lonely' – explaining, 'When we wake up in the morning here we look out and see people; what we shall do when we wake up at Yeldham and see only cows out of the windows, I don't know.'[58]

In fact, the retirement outlook was hardly as bleak as that. Rab still had, after all, his London flat in Whitehall Court as well as Frachadil, his white farmhouse home on the Isle of Mull, which had become far more important to him than Gatcombe Park ever was. There he could both paint and fish – painting, of course, had been his hobby for years, ever since he used to set up his easel alongside

Churchill's, but fishing was something he had come to only late in life, finding, as he once casually commented to a slightly amused Mollie, an almost sexual pleasure 'in the tug you get on the line'.[59]

It was, therefore, a wise move of Mollie's to decide that they should spend the summer holidays of 1978 on Mull, just as they had always done while they had been at Trinity. A slight shadow was cast over that year's August holiday by the discovery just before they left that Rab was suffering from polyps in the intestines. The doctors did not, however, insist on any immediate action, and all went well on Mull until Rab contracted a chill: the island doctor summoned to Rab's bedside then, somewhat disconcertingly, established that Rab was also suffering from a heart condition known as 'fibrillation' (which meant the heartbeat was uneven). The return from Mull was, consequently, a good deal less cheerful than the journey up – Rab's heart trouble necessarily meant that there were additional anxieties about any surgery which might be necessary to remove the polyps. In November Rab eventually went into Addenbrooke's Hospital, Cambridge where a colonoscopy was performed and then a further investigation under general anaesthetic which established that the polyps were not malignant and that surgery would not be necessary.

Rab's original intention had been, once free of the inhibitions of the Mastership of Trinity, to play a much fuller part in politics – in particular by speaking regularly in the House of Lords (during his thirteen years at Cambridge he had made only infrequent speeches, and these generally on matters concerned with education or on questions affecting Trinity's own interests, like the Labour Government's British Transport (Docks) Bill in 1976 that threatened the growth of the Port of Felixstowe).* The doubts about his health, combined with the imminence of an election, persuaded him, however, to hold his hand (like most shrewd political observers, he expected the general election to be called in the autumn of 1978 and was surprised when the new Labour Prime Minister, James Callaghan,† postponed it).[60] The prevailing pre-election atmosphere

* Rab made two uncharacteristically belligerent speeches opposing the passage of this Bill before it eventually foundered. *Lords Hansard*, 22 June 1976, cols 193–8 and 22 October 1976, cols 1708–13.

† Leonard James Callaghan (1912–). Labour MP, South Cardiff 1945–50, South-East Cardiff 1950–83, South Cardiff and Penarth 1983– . Chancellor of the Exchequer 1964–7. Home Secretary 1967–70. Foreign Secretary 1974–6. Prime Minister 1976–9. Leader of the Opposition 1979–80.

still struck him, however, as providing an inappropriate climate for his own political re-entry: he was not, in fact, to deliver any speech in the House of Lords until after Margaret Thatcher* had won the May 1979 election and become Prime Minister.

The election campaign itself Rab observed only from the sidelines. Once Edward Heath fell from the Tory Leadership in 1975, there were few direct links with Rab's own era at the top of the Tory Party; and it was not perhaps wholly a coincidence that his guests at Cambridge had tended to be drawn almost as much from the Labour Government as from the Conservative Opposition. Margaret Thatcher's appointment of Lord Thorneycroft as Party Chairman meant, though, that he still had a line to one old colleague very much in operational charge of the conduct of the campaign; and Rab was occasionally in touch with him, and the Central Office, during the five weeks that divided the defeat of the Callaghan Government in the Commons (on 28 March 1979) from the day (3 May) that the nation went to the polls. It was symbolic, however, of the ease with which he had settled into an elder statesman's role that his first action, once the votes had been counted, should have been to ring up James Callaghan and congratulate him 'for being so magnanimous' a loser.[61]

Rab's own connections with the new Prime Minister were hardly close: they had served in the same Government together from 1961 to 1964; but there was an obvious gulf between being First Secretary of State or Foreign Secretary and occupying the humble position of Joint Parliamentary Under-Secretary at the Ministry of Pensions and National Insurance. They had, though, a rather surprising subsequent link: Rab's second son, Adam, Conservative MP for Bosworth since 1970, had throughout Margaret Thatcher's period as Leader of the Opposition been one of her two Parliamentary Private Secretaries (and was now a junior member of her Government); it cannot, therefore, have been wholly a surprise when Rab and Mollie found themselves summoned to lunch at Chequers on the Sunday before Christmas in 1979. An engagement entered into with the best of motives on both sides proved something less than a success. Rab had arrived with the impression that the Prime Minister wished to listen to his advice; instead he was throughout given the

* Margaret Hilda Thatcher (1925–). Conservative MP, Finchley 1959– . Secretary of State for Education 1970–4. Leader of the Opposition 1975–9. Prime Minister 1979– .

benefit of her own views.* No further invitation was ever issued; nor, perhaps, would it have been accepted if one had been forthcoming.[62]

In any event, all prospects of Rab being counted 'one of us' were soon foreclosed. He had not, as has been seen, spoken at all in the House of Lords since leaving Trinity. When he finally did so on 25 February 1980, it was not in order to support the Government but rather to criticise it. One of the earliest measures of the first Thatcher administration was an Education (No. 2) Bill – a piece of legislation primarily designed to introduce 'assisted places' into fee-paying schools. In addition, however, it contained a number of clauses intended to bring about financial savings – and one of them (Clause 23) was designed to empower local authorities to charge parents for the school buses in which their children, especially in rural areas, went to school.

To Rab this represented a frontal attack on the central principle ('free secondary education for all') of his 1944 Education Act; and he resolved to resist it with all the power at his command. His first speech on the Bill's Second Reading in the Lords was relatively temperate, if a little mischievous. Not only did he suggest to the Government that, if they withdrew their 'assisted places' scheme, they would automatically save the money they were planning for local authorities to collect from parents for school buses; he also made a point of advertising his own allegiance to the comprehensive principle (disclosing, to the Government's discomfiture, that it was he himself who had insisted on including the word 'comprehensive' in the 1943 White Paper).[63] It was hardly surprising that the general drift of his remarks persuaded even the *Daily Telegraph* to headline its story the next day, 'Butler Attacks Changes in His Education Act'.[64]

However, Rab's main assault came on the Bill's Committee Stage some two and a half weeks later. He had, as he explained, deliberately absented himself from the debate on most other clauses on the Committee Stage in order not to raise a false impression that he was motivated by 'small political reasons' – adding that he had even voted, rather against his own inclination, in favour of 'the disband-

* Their conversational styles anyway were very different. They had previously met at the by-election held at Saffron Walden following Peter Kirk's death in 1977. Their encounter then in the cattle market had gone reasonably well – but when Rab, shortly afterwards, met Margaret Thatcher at a Buckingham Palace reception his opening teasing gambit was to say, 'You remember that great black bull we saw together, well I've bought it for you.' The horror on Mrs Thatcher's face, who took the remark seriously, had apparently to be seen to be believed.

ment' of the free milk and meals services which he himself had initiated some thirty-six years earlier; but when it came to charging fares for transporting children to schools in the public sector, he had to draw the line. It was a clear breach of the undertakings that he had given to the religious denominations (especially the Roman Catholics) in negotiating the passage of the 1944 Act; it was also a betrayal of the undertakings given by local authorities in a guidance paper issued to the Churches in 1950. The House was, therefore, being asked to go back on a double pledge – and he, for one, would not do it. He would oppose the clause for the same reason that Martin Luther gave to the Diet of Worms in refusing to recant his beliefs – 'I can do no other.'[65]

In the House of Lords, that ranked as stirring stuff and an almost equally stern speech from the Duke of Norfolk, on behalf of the nation's Roman Catholics, effectively sealed Clause 23's fate. In a division it was knocked out of the Bill by a majority of almost two to one, by 216 votes to 112.* It was, as *The Times* remarked the following morning, the 'first important defeat for the Government since the general election'.[66] As the principal instrument of that defeat Rab had not, of course, endeared himself to his former colleagues; but he had, in what was virtually his last parliamentary performance,† enhanced his reputation for independence and fair-mindedness with the British public.

After that striking political victory, Rab had just two more years to live. They were years, on the whole, spent quietly – diabetes had been diagnosed in May 1979 and a skin condition, which had persisted since the mid-1950s, grew gradually worse. Within limits, however, Rab was able to lead a full, if not very active, life: in August 1980 he and Mollie went to Mull for the last time but that autumn found him back in hospital, this time at Papworth because of anxiety about his heart. There was to be no more foreign travel – in September 1979 Rab had made his final visit abroad to deliver the Sotheby Lecture at the Metropolitan Museum in New York – but he was kept busy working on a further volume of memoirs‡ and

* Five days later it was announced in the Commons that the Government had abandoned the scheme for charging for school buses. *Hansard* (18 March 1980), cols 209–17.

† Rab continued to attend the House of Lords through the spring and summer of 1980, but, though he intervened two or three times, he never made another full speech.

‡ *The Art of Memory* (Hodder, 1982) was published six weeks after Rab's death. A collection of essays about nine friends and contemporaries, it lacked the sparkle and charm of his earlier work, *The Art of the Possible*.

by sitting at Spencers for another portrait, this time commissioned for the National Portrait Gallery and painted by a thirty-year-old artist named Margaret Foreman. He was back in Papworth Hospital twice in the first two months of 1981, and even journeys to London became progressively more difficult. His doctors had earlier been concerned about his weight and the strain that put upon his heart; but this became less a cause for anxiety as both his frame and his face seemed to shrink visibly. The medical advice was still, however, that he should take exercise and it was with that objective in mind that he and Mollie went for a three-week holiday at Aldeburgh in late August 1981; the winds along the sea-front, though, proved biting and Mollie soon became especially concerned about Rab's colour. A local doctor, summoned to the hotel, diagnosed chronic anaemia and Rab was rushed by ambulance to the Evelyn Nursing Home in Cambridge for a massive blood transfusion. It was there that the discovery belatedly was made that Rab was, after all, suffering from cancer of the colon, and Mollie was warned that there could be no question of an operation, since his heart would not withstand it.

Rab's last public appearance was at the National Portrait Gallery for the unveiling of the Margaret Foreman portrait on the evening of 13 January 1982. He was unable to mingle with the company but instead received individual guests sitting down, rather as if he were a Viceroy at the centre of a Durbar. One aspect of the occasion which gave him particular pleasure was that the Arts Minister of the time, who was present representing the Government, was none other than his own last PPS, Paul Channon – and a number of his other old friends from politics paid him the compliment of turning up, too. It was, in fact, a remarkably cheerful gathering – with Rab, although looking very frail, talking eagerly about a holiday that he and Mollie were planning to take in Switzerland.

It was not, of course, to be. Although Rab never knew that he was suffering from cancer (Mollie had been encouraged by the doctors to keep it from him), his condition after his final public outing rapidly deteriorated. Back at Spencers he became increasingly an invalid. Soon he was in the charge of nurses round the clock, though the most devoted care came from Mollie herself. He remained mentally alert until the last few days but, for fear of alarming him, the family was not summoned until his doctor had disclosed there was no hope. He slipped into unconsciousness early in the morning of Sunday 7 March, dying the next day in the late evening in what was already his eightieth year.

His death, which had taken place, as he had wished, at home surrounded by his family, was not announced until the afternoon of Tuesday 9 March. It brought instant tributes on radio, on television and in the newspapers – with *The Times* the next morning yielding him the ultimate accolade of carrying no other obituary.[67] The funeral, deliberately devised as primarily a constituency (and Essex) occasion, was held the following Saturday at the parish church of St Mary the Virgin in Saffron Walden. A far grander, and more formal, national service of thanksgiving followed some three weeks later, on Monday 5 April 1982 in Westminster Abbey, and was attended by virtually every public dignitary in the land. The Prime Minister and the Prince of Wales were present. Lord Carrington, who had that morning resigned as Foreign Secretary as a result of criticism of the Government's inability to prevent the Argentine invasion of the Falklands, read one of the lessons, and the Archbishop of Canterbury and the Cardinal-Archbishop of Westminster each took part in the service. An unusually perceptive address was delivered by the Rev. Harry Williams of the Community of the Resurrection, who had been Dean of Trinity for the first four years of Rab's reign as Master. Possibly the most thought-provoking reflection in it was contained in the following passage:

> It is – or was – a pulpit commonplace that if in a crucial and irrevocable matter a man makes a decision which he believes to be morally wrong, then he cannot expect afterwards to live in perfect peace with himself. What is less widely appreciated is that if in a crucial and irrevocable matter a man makes a decision which he believes to be morally right, then he by no means has an automatic guarantee of peace. On the contrary, the result may well be persistent inner turmoil. Because of its continuing cost we can repent the good we have chosen as much as, perhaps more than, we repent of the evil.[68]

No one in the vast congregation, which included both Harold Macmillan and Lord Home, had the slightest doubt what message Father Harry Williams meant to convey. Rab may have been 'the uncrowned Prime Minister' – but at least in Westminster Abbey he had finally achieved, if posthumously, the vindication of a moral coronation.

18 *The Man and the Legend*

Some thirty years before his own death, Rab wrote a note of condolence to a fellow MP, belonging to the opposite side of the House, whose wife had just died. Rab's own letter does not survive, but the reply, for understandable reasons, was preserved among his own records:

9 July 1952

My dear Butler,

I hope you will excuse me dictating this reply to your extremely nice letter. About the only thing which makes life tolerable at this sort of moment is the kind of thoughts which prompted you to write.

I hope it will not embarrass you if I tell you something now. For quite a number of years, half-jokingly and half-seriously, my wife had maintained that you were her favourite politician. We were dining in the House last Wednesday night, a few hours before she was struck down, when she maintained this to a group of Labour MPs who were sitting round her. When one of them asked why she held this strange view, she replied: 'I'd like Dick one day to have the same sort of position inside the Labour Party as Rab Butler has in the Tory Party, even though he's unpopular.'

I think you will have an inkling of what she meant, and the fact that she meant it made me more pleased to get your letter than I can tell you.

Yours sincerely,

DICK CROSSMAN[1]

It was an exceptional tribute to come from a member of an opposing Party, even if the MP who wrote it was, just two years later, to take a rather different line in print. Arguably, the most serious attempt ever made to demolish Rab's non-partisan reputation came in the shape of a *New Statesman* profile, published in the spring of 1954. Entitled 'The Ideologist of Inequality',[2] it raised fundamental and, as was only to be expected from Crossman, typically iconoclastic questions about Rab's right to be regarded as the liberal voice of the Tory Party. Given the rough and tumble of politics, the very nature of the assault provided its own evidence of the standing Rab had already won for himself, not merely with the uncommitted voter but even with staunch Labour supporters, such as Crossman's second wife.

The *New Statesman* profile, coming from the pen of the best journalist in the Labour Party (and one who shared Rab's own donnish background), was, however, a thoroughly serious piece of writing. In it Crossman correctly identified a number of strands that went to comprise Rab's personal outlook and political make-up. Noting 'his contempt for the Blimps of his own party', the profile went on to pay him full credit for the way in which he had been 'quick to recognise the passing of Imperial power in India and indeed throughout the Empire'. Nor did that sort of realism, in face of the irreversible tide of history, simply apply abroad:

> The art of government, in his view, is to yield to the forces of change and then to harness them in time to prevent the disintegration of authority, whether in domestic politics or in international relations. In his eyes, there is no last ditch which is really worth fighting for if, by surrendering it, you can retain control of the situation.

But what was that 'control' about? Here Crossman might seem to have been on more controversial ground. He argued that Rab, as a good Platonist, was really concerned with an effort to perpetuate a society 'controlled by an élite and within a firm framework of authority'. Thus the challenge facing Conservatism in the twentieth century, viewed from Rab's own perspective, was 'not to oppose public ownership or planning or the Welfare State but to use them in an effort to maintain the differences of wealth and status which are essential to stability'.[3]

There was probably some part of that indictment to which Rab would have been willing to plead guilty. He would hardly, for example, have denied that he was dedicated to seeing that the traditional organic nature of British society continued for as long as possible. In that sense, he was – as Enoch Powell once eloquently noted – 'a real Tory',[4] and certainly not any forerunner of the New Radical Conservatism introduced by Margaret Thatcher. But, traditionalist though Rab unquestionably was, he remained also a progressive modern Conservative. He left very little by way of a personal political testament behind him; but what evidence there is both substantiates and modifies Crossman's vision of him as the political equivalent of the little Dutch boy with his finger in the dike.

In contradiction to the myth often propagated about him, Rab did not have any great tribe of disciples. However, when he was a young man, and before he even had a foothold in national politics, he engaged in a long and revealing correspondence with a fellow Cambridge undergraduate, almost three years his junior, who (like him) subsequently went on to a career of great eminence. The most notable thing about the letters he then wrote to Patrick Devlin – many of them from his world tour of 1926–7 – is the light they throw on the constancy of his political attitudes through more than fifty years.

Even before he was twenty-five, Rab was much exercised by the thought that capitalism might only too easily be responsible for bringing about its own downfall. 'Capitalists and employers in industry must *give* slowly and surely or be *taken from*.' It was the same story with education: 'Cambridge undergraduates have privileges which modern times will *take from* them unless they *give* some and come half-way to meet . . .'[5] Nor was it simply a question of economic advantages. 'Caste', he asserted even more boldly to Devlin, 'is the bane of India and the luxury of England – India must learn from Burma to lessen this bane and England to indulge less freely in this luxury.'[6] And, here again, the disturbed premonitions of a settled order of society just about to be overthrown were never far away: 'The privileged have got to have a damned good reason to be so or else take their share at the trough.'[7]

Those were by no means the normal instinctive reflexes of a Tory of the 1920s – but their primary interest lies in the vein of total consistency (the Education Act, the *Industrial Charter*, the pre-Robbins polytechnic revolution) that they reveal in Rab's Conservatism. To claim that he went through his political life fighting what was in effect a perpetual rearguard action may be over-dramatic; but certainly he understood, better than any other Tory of his time, that an orderly retreat in face of social and economic pressures must always be preferable to putting the whole system at risk by resorting to the defiance of the Winter Palace.

Inevitably this readiness to bend made him a slightly suspect figure with his own Party, though not with the public at large. He was never a doctrinaire and had little use for the dogmatic assertions and ideological excesses of the New Radical Conservatism of the 1970s and 1980s. Its representatives, in turn, had little patience with him, coming to regard him as no better than a secret socialist who had been allowed to roam for too many years within the Party's doctrinal citadel. Some of this hostility had even surfaced by the time he died in 1982 – with one apologist of the New Right roundly accusing him of always being 'content to work within the existing consensus without seeking to change it', of having consistently 'viewed the problems of government as managerial rather than political', and of never having been willing 'to fight for any distinctive point of view'.[8]

The fact that there should be such a striking correlation between those charges and the ones mounted almost thirty years earlier (if from the opposite political standpoint) by Richard Crossman might be thought to lend them a certain force. But, in truth, they both left out of account what was perhaps Rab's most prominent characteristic as a politician – his feeling for the continuity of history and, above all, his sense of allegiance to what for him was a living English tradition of the true art of government. He expressed this perhaps most vividly in his own memoirs, in seeking to rebut the accusation that he was somehow a covert fellow-traveller of socialism:

> I had derived from Bolingbroke an assurance that the majesty of the State might be used in the interests of the many, from Burke a belief in seeking patterns of improvement by balancing diverse interests and from Disraeli an insistence that the two nations must become one. If my brand of Conservatism was unorthodox, I was committing heresy in remarkably good company.[9]

It was an effective riposte – even if it does go some way to proving the validity of the other charge sometimes made against Rab: that he was by nature and instinct a man of government and neither by taste nor by temperament a warrior in the political battle at all. For that reason, it has sometimes been asked[10] whether he was not more cut out to be a Civil Servant than a politician – but the answer to that is not a simple one. True, he lacked entirely the vulgar streak that often goes with political success – ruefully telling an interviewer on one occasion that he felt in retrospect he might have been wrong ('I may have paid for it') not to include any 'personal revelations or personal statements' in his crucial speech at the Blackpool Conference in 1963.[11] But he made up for that deficiency with something else: an uncanny sixth sense for 'the feel' of a political decision – seldom, if ever, shared by the more extrovert or exhibitionistic of his colleagues and, indeed, hardly required in the then reticent ranks of the Civil Service.

Again, however, this singular gift of his led to misunderstanding. It was largely responsible for the reputation he acquired for indecisiveness. It was often Rab's habit before he took a decision to try it on for size, to live with it for a day or two, just as if he had already made it, and then to cast it off, like a suit of clothes, if he found he didn't feel at home with it.[12] Naturally, this technique puzzled, and indeed irritated, some starchier Civil Servants, at least until they got used to it (Rab may have had 'a Rolls-Royce mind' – one of his own favourite phrases – but it was by no means as smooth or orderly as his Private Office would have liked). Nor could its workings always be accurately forecast.

There is, for instance, the story told by his last Principal Private Secretary, Sir Nicholas Henderson, of the National Day cocktail party due to be given by the Moroccan Ambassador. Twice during the day at the Foreign Office, Rab had inquired whether his Private Secretary felt he really ought to put in an appearance – only to be told helpfully that it was absolutely unnecessary. No sooner, however, had Rab got home than the phone rang in the Private Office – and the same query was put again and given an identical answer. That, it seemed, was that – until the next morning a suggestion was made to Rab that, perhaps, he ought to write to the Moroccan Ambassador to apologise for his unavoidable absence of the night before. 'Oh, I went,' replied Rab airily, provoking mystification all round.[13] (In fact, though, he had done no more than run true to form: he had lived with an interim decision, not found it altogether comfortable, and accordingly had simply altered it.)

For the most part Rab got on very well with Civil Servants, particularly the young men who worked with him in his various Private Offices, four of whom eventually became either Head of the Home Civil Service or Secretary of the Cabinet.* Whatever price they paid for their chief's indecision was more than made up for by his other penchant for indiscretion – with even Henderson reluctantly admitting, 'I learned more in one year from Rab about political life than I did from anyone else I have served for however long.'[14] Rab

* Lord Armstrong, Lord Bancroft, Lord Trend and Sir Robert Armstrong.

39 On the Isle of Mull. His holidays there – at Frachadil – became very important to Rab

40 The last outing at the hustings. Rab at the Saffron Walden by-election in July 1977

41 Rab and Mollie at home in Whitehall Court

42 The past and the future: Rab with Margaret Thatcher

never believed in building a Chinese wall between a Minister and his official subordinates. Even his scribbles on official minutes – 'No. 10 seems to be going mad'[15] or 'Tell him to go to hell' (this about the Chairman of one of the five clearing banks)[16] – were modified neither by caution nor by inhibition; and sometimes his sense of fun would simply get the better of him, as when on a memorandum he approved of, instead of formally expressing thanks, he would simply draw a little Valentine – a heart with an arrow going through it pointing directly towards the initials of the writer.[17]

Rab's somewhat solemn public demeanour was thoroughly misleading. What those who worked most closely with him chiefly remember about him was his light-heartedness – the chortle of glee sometimes reaching its *crescendo* in a great crow of delight as he found himself confronted by some grotesque piece of political pomposity or human pretentiousness. In private, he was a very funny man, with a highly developed sense of the ludicrous – and, like most people with a sense of humour (and it was humour Rab possessed rather than wit), he knew how to laugh at himself. 'You'd like a little whisky?' he once remarked to a newspaper visitor. 'My wife's not here and she said I mustn't make tea. I'm afraid I've never really got the hang of boiling a kettle.'[18]

A lot of that, of course, was put on – but, as he grew older, Rab began to take a particular pleasure in the stories that were told about him. The majority of these tended to arise from 'Rabisms', those ambiguous, double-edged remarks which, even on reflection, no one could ever be quite sure were deliberate or not. A quintessential 'Rabism' is contained in a letter Rab sent in 1975 to a former member of the Conservative Research Department, an MP, explaining why, to his great regret, he would not be able to be present at the formal gathering to mark the retirement from politics of Lord Fraser of Kilmorack (as Sir Michael Fraser had by then become). It was a model letter of its kind, apart from its first sentence. That read, either through misfortune or design, 'There is no one I would rather attend a farewell meeting for than Michael.'[19] To this day no one is certain whether that was intentional or some sort of accidental *double entendre*. The suspicion, however, must remain (if only because Rab had earlier said something similar at Trinity – 'Mollie and I are so glad to have got here in time to see you leave')[20] that, by then, a touch of mischief was contributing to the careful honing of such phrases in advance.

No doubt, such remarks had started off innocently enough – for, as Michael Fraser himself once wrote 'like many very clever people,

Rab was rather naïf about the simpler aspects of life'.[21] It is possible, though, to believe in the self-defence mechanism of an essentially modest, even insecure, man. Rab always had more than his fair share of self-doubt and, on finding that the droll way he put things was considered funny by other people, he may well have resolved to capitalise upon it. Certainly, by the time of his retirement, when he would cheerfully make remarks like, 'Would you like to take this book on fishing to bed with you?' (referring, with a characteristic gurgle, to the memoirs of Lord Home), it was hard to accept that he did not know exactly what he was doing.[22]

The origins of that sort of comic, whimsical phraseology went back, after all, a very long way. The boy at Marlborough who had announced, 'Tomorrow is another half-holiday on account of some sportsman, St Luke the Evangelist, I believe'[23] had remained faithful, not least in his irreverence, to the end.

Was it, perhaps, that irreverence which deprived him of the Leadership of the Tory Party?* If so, it was a harsh judgment on the part of his colleagues – though one should never underestimate the resentment of the stupid at being teased by the clever. What, however, can be said, and on the authority of as distinguished a Tory historian as Lord Blake, is that in blocking the claims of Rab to the Prime Ministership, Harold Macmillan 'did a lasting disservice to his party'.[24]

Rab himself put it more modestly. 'I think', he wrote in the summer of 1965, before his translation to Trinity, 'I could have made quite a tolerable leader for the Conservatives.'[25]

* This was the view of at least one shrewd outside observer of the British political scene. In his Introduction to the American edition of *The Art of the Possible* Professor J. K. Galbraith commented admiringly on Rab's ability to look on 'his own role and that of others with ill-concealed amusement'. He then took the point further by raising the question of whether this was not also the secret of why Rab never became Prime Minister, leaving little doubt of his own inclination to believe that it was, 'He could never view himself with the terrible solemnity of the truly determined politician. And the determined men, for their part, are always a little suspicious of those who are amused. So it is the solemn men who make it.' *The Art of the Possible* (Gambit Publishers, Boston, Mass.), 1972, p. x.

Notes and References

1 FOUNDING FATHERS

1 Ian Bradley, 'Cambridge Without a Butler: Like a Master Without a Servant', *The Times* (24 July 1978).
2 There is an interesting *Dictionary of National Biography* (hereafter *DNB*) entry on Weeden Butler. Also on his other son, and George Butler's brother, Weeden Butler II, who succeeded his father as headmaster of the Chelsea School.
3 *DNB* essay, by Walter Sydney Sichel.
4 The private Butler genealogical tree, compiled by the late Dr Audrey Richards, Honorary Fellow of Newnham College, Cambridge, includes an illuminating note on Spencer Perceval Butler. He is said to have had 'to get up each day at about 5 a.m., make himself tea on one of the little spirit stoves known then as "Etnas", get from [his home in] Harrow to Wembley, from Wembley to Baker Street, Baker Street to Charing Cross and hence to his office in Chancery Lane'. Recording his family reputation for testiness, Dr Richards charitably adds, 'It is not surprising that he may have appeared rather irritable of an evening!'

2 CHILD OF THE EMPIRE

1 Iris Portal, interview with the author, 19–20 September 1980.
2 Family Papers held by Rab's sister, Dorothy Middleton. Letter from Ann Butler to Monty Butler dated 23.7.1909.
3 Ibid.
4 Ibid. Letter from Ann Butler to Monty Butler dated simply 'Tuesday' but from internal evidence written on 14.8.1909.

5 Conversations with the author 1979–81. His sister, Iris's recollections remain, however, more exact – 'We were the poor relations.' Interview with the author, 19–20 September 1980.
6 Butler Papers, Trinity College, Cambridge, D48 Part 1.
7 Butler Papers, A65.

3 MARLBOROUGH AND CAMBRIDGE

1 See *DNB* entry on Dr Cyril Norwood in 1951–60 vol., p. 773.
2 Butler Papers, Trinity College, Cambridge, D48 Part 2, letter dated 18.10.1916.
3 Ibid., letter dated 5.7.1917.
4 Butler Papers, A67. Referred to in a letter from Ann Butler to Rab dated 23.4.1918.
5 Ibid., letter from Ann Butler to Rab dated 19.9.1918.
6 Butler Papers, D48 Part 2, letter dated 11.11.1918.
7 Ibid., D48, letter dated 27.10.1918.
8 Iris Butler, contribution to *East and West*, ICR Monograph, Series no. 16, Institute for Cultural Research (1978).
9 Butler Papers, D48 Part 2, letter dated 22.3.1920.
10 Ibid., letter dated 27.11.1920.
11 Butler Papers, D48 Part 3, letter dated 22.1.1921.
12 Butler Papers, D48 Part 4, letter dated 20.8.1921.
13 Ibid., letter dated 3.9.1921.
14 Butler Papers, A65, letter dated 25.9.1921.
15 Ibid., letter dated 7.5.1924.
16 *Cambridge Review* (11 November 1921).
17 Butler Papers, D48 Part 4, letter dated 8.11.1921.
18 *Cambridge Review* (19 May 1922).
19 Butler Papers, D48 Part 6, letter dated 7.3.1923.
20 Ibid., letter dated 4.2.1923.
21 Ibid., letter dated 19.2.1923.
22 Butler Papers, D57, letters from Kathleen Buchanan Smith dated respectively 'Rab's Room Pembroke Tuesday 6 March' and 'St Giles, Chesterton Lane, Cambridge Wednesday 7 March'.
23 Butler Papers, D48 Part 6, letter dated 17.7.1923.

4 THE COURTAULD CONNECTION

1 Butler Papers, Trinity College, Cambridge, D48 Part 6, letter dated 15.7.1923.
2 Ibid.
3 Ibid.

4 Ibid., letter dated 24.10.1923. Rab's initial reaction to having accepted the invitation was, admittedly, not exactly romantic – 'got soaked coming back to evening chapel'.
5 S. L. Courtauld, *The Huguenot Family of Courtauld*, 3 vols (privately printed 1957, 1966 and 1967).
6 Butler Papers, D48 Part 6, letter dated 6.11.1923.
7 Percy Cradock (ed.), *Recollections of the Cambridge Union, 1815–1939* (Bowes & Bowes, 1953). Essay by R. A. Butler, p. 119.
8 Butler Papers, D48 Part 6, letter dated 6.11.1923.
9 R. A. Butler, *The Art of the Possible* (Hamish Hamilton, 1971), p. 16.
10 Butler Papers, D48 Part 7, letter dated 13.3.1924.
11 Ibid., letter dated 12.3.1924.
12 Butler Papers, A65, letter from Greenwood Court, Simla dated 7.7.1924.
13 Butler Papers, D48 Part 7, letter dated 2.7.1924.
14 Ibid., letter dated 23.7.1924.
15 Ibid., letter dated 30.7.1924.
16 Butler Papers, A9.
17 Ibid., letter dated 11.5.1925.
18 Butler Papers, A65, letter dated 21.6.1925.
19 Ibid.
20 Ibid., letter dated 12.7.1925.
21 Butler Papers, D48 Part 9, letter dated 6.8.1925.
22 Dorothy Middleton, interview with the author, 1 November 1982. The need to provide for Rab was apparently the reason given for neither of his sisters going to university.
23 Butler Papers, D48 Part 9, letter dated 11.8.1925.
24 Ibid.
25 Butler Papers, A65, letter dated 16.11.1925.
26 Butler Papers, D48 Part 11, letter dated 24.6.1926.

5 THE ROAD TO WESTMINSTER

1 Butler Papers, Trinity College, Cambridge, A65, letter dated 13.2.1926.
2 Butler Papers, D48 Part 12, letter dated 27.1.1927.
3 Butler Papers, A13.
4 Butler Papers, A10.
5 Butler Papers, A14, letter to Rab from Samuel Courtauld dated 1.7.1927.
6 R. A. Butler, *The Art of the Possible* (Hamish Hamilton, 1971), p. 22.
7 The *Herts and Essex Observer* (4 November 1927):

Retirement of Mr Foot Mitchell, MP
Adoption of Prospective Candidate

A meeting of the Saffron Walden Division Conservative Association was held at the Conservative Club, Saffron Walden on Saturday afternoon in connection with the retirement at the end of the present Parliament of Mr W. Foot Mitchell, the Member for the Division.

The following resolution, proposed by Mr F. S. H. Judd, and seconded by Mr S. Moger, was carried unanimously:

> That this meeting of the Saffron Walden Conservative Association desires to express its deepest regret at the contemplated retirement of Mr Foot Mitchell at the expiration of the present Parliament, and to record its great appreciation of the services he has rendered to this Division and to the Conservative cause.

A further resolution – that this meeting of the Saffron Walden Conservative Association concurs with the recommendation of the Central Council that Mr R. A. Butler be invited to become our prospective candidate upon Mr Foot Mitchell's retirement – was also carried unanimously.

After the meeting tea was served in the Parish Room.

8 Letter from Will Coote, 'Humorous Entertainer', to Rab dated 15.3.1928, Rab Books, Trinity College, Cambridge, 1.
9 Undated 1928 cutting headed 'Walden Liberal Association' from *Herts and Essex Observer*, Rab Books, 1.
10 Rab Books, 1.
11 Private Papers of late Canon W. G. Howard.
12 Rab Books, 1.
13 *The Art of the Possible*, p. 24.

6 A PRO-BALDWIN BACK-BENCHER

1 *Hansard* (30 October 1929), cols 199–203.
2 *The Times* (31 October 1929).
3 'Politicians and Politics', *Sunday Express* (3 November 1929).
4 R. H. S. Crossman, *The Myths of Cabinet Government* (Harvard University Press, 1972), Introduction, p. xxiii.
5 *The Times* (27 May 1930).
6 *The Times* (28 May 1930).
7 BBC Radio Profile, 29 June 1978.
8 Butler Papers, Trinity College, Cambridge, D48 Part 14, MS diary note dated 4.11.1930 (sent to Monty Butler).
9 Ibid.
10 Ibid.
11 Ibid., letter from Rab to his parents dated 4.3.1931.
12 Ibid., letter dated 23.4.1931.
13 Ibid., letter from Rab to Sam Courtauld dated 14.7.1931.
14 Ibid., letter from Rab to his parents dated 24.9.1931.

15 Ibid., letter dated 29.7.1931.
16 Ibid. The letter did, in fact, go on to mention the possibility of 'a breakdown of the ordinary party system for the moment' – but it was, after all, written on the day before the Report of the May Economy Committee (which effectively precipitated the crisis) was published.
17 Ibid., letter dated 26.8.1931.
18 Ibid., letter dated 4.3.1931.
19 Ibid., letter dated 19.3.1931.
20 Ibid., letter dated 4.3.1931.
21 Ibid., letter dated 30.8.1930.

7 APPRENTICED TO INDIA

1 Butler Papers, Trinity College, Cambridge, D48 Part 14, letter dated 28.8.1931.
2 Butler Papers, D48 Part 12, letter dated 3.2.1926.
3 Butler Papers, A65, letter dated 17.11.1929.
4 Butler Papers, D48 Part 14, letter dated 28.8.1931.
5 Ibid., letter dated 30.8.1931.
6 Butler Papers, A65, letter dated 23.9.1931.
7 Butler Papers, D48 Part 14, letter dated 10.9.1931.
8 Ibid., letter dated 17.9.1931.
9 *Daily Mail* (7 September 1931). Winston Churchill was reviewing Sir Harcourt Butler's book, *India Insistent* (1931).
10 Butler Papers, A65, letter dated 28.7.1931.
11 Butler Papers, D48 Part 14, letters dated 24.6.1931 and 2.7.1931 respectively.
12 Butler Papers, A65, letter dated 13.8.1930.
13 Butler Papers, D48 Part 14, letter dated 1.10.1931.
14 Butler Papers, letter preserved in Rab Books, 2, dated 2.11.1931.
15 Butler Papers, D48 Part 14, letter dated 5.11.1931.
16 *Essex Weekly News* (8 January 1932).
17 'Social and Personal', *Times of India* (2 February 1932).
18 Butler Papers, G4, letter from Sir Samuel Hoare dated 20.5.1932.
19 Ibid.
20 Ibid., note to Secretary of State dated 13.9.1932.
21 Keith Middlemas and John Barnes, *Baldwin* (Weidenfeld & Nicolson, 1969), p. 688.
22 Viscount Templewood, *Nine Troubled Years* (Collins, 1954), p. 70.
23 Ibid., p. 71.
24 Ibid., p. 72.
25 Recorded conversation with the author, 20 June 1978.
26 *Daily Express* (30 September 1932).
27 Butler Papers, B8, telegram dated 1.10.1932.

28 Butler Papers, G1, letter dated 7.10.1932.
29 *Hansard* (29 March 1933), col. 1011.
30 Butler Papers, H45, with Gov. of India Act File, letter dated 10.5.1933.
31 Butler Papers, G39, letter from Rab's former Private Secretary, Sir Algernon Rumbold, dated 22.3.1962.
32 Butler Papers, A155, letter from J. S. Courtauld dated 19.7.1933 (forwarded to Rab by Lord Brabourne 21.7.1933).
33 Butler Papers, A65, letter dated 19.6.1932.
34 *Evening News* (15 May 1933).
35 Butler Papers, D48 Part 15, letter dated 6.7.1933.
36 Butler Papers, H45, with Gov. of India Act file, letter dated 9.4.1933.
37 Brabourne Collection, India Office Library, F97 20B, letter dated 5.10.1934.
38 Butler Papers, H45, with Gov. of India Act File, letter dated 23.3.1933.
39 Brabourne Collection, F97 20C, letter dated 2.5.1934.
40 Ibid., letter dated 19.4.1934.
41 Ibid., letter dated 26.4.1934.
42 Ibid., letter dated 15.6.1934.
43 Brabourne Collection, F97 20B, letter to Lord Brabourne dated 14.12.1934.
44 Butler Papers, G6, diary notes dated 'July 20th–21st 1935' and headed 'Full Description of the Baldwin Visit and Talking with Him.' There are some revealing discrepancies between the contemporary version and that given by Rab in *The Art of the Possible* (Hamish Hamilton, 1971), p. 30. In particular the last sentence in the book version – 'Then you will be on the path to Leader of the Conservative Party' – does not appear in the original diary notes.
45 Brabourne Collection, F97 20A, letter dated 27.11.1935.
46 Butler Papers, A169, letter dated 9.4.1935, addressee unknown.
47 *The Art of the Possible*, p. 61.
48 Brabourne Collection, F97 20A, letter dated 12.12.1935.
49 *The Art of the Possible*, p. 61.
50 Butler Papers, *Hindustani Times* (10 December 1935). Rab Books, 3.
51 Brabourne Collection, F97 21, letter dated 3.12.1936.
52 Brabourne Collection, F97 20A, letter dated 19.12.1935.
53 Brabourne Collection, F97 21, letter dated 21.12.1936.
54 Ibid., letter dated 3.2.1937.
55 Ibid., letter dated 7.3.1937.
56 Butler Papers, letter from Neville Chamberlain dated 26.5.1937. Rab Books, 3.
57 Butler Papers, letter dated 26.5.1937. Rab Books, 3.
58 Ibid.

8 APPEASEMENT AND THE FOREIGN OFFICE

1 Brabourne Collection, India Office Library, F97 22B, letter dated 23.2.1937.
2 Butler Papers, Trinity College, Cambridge, letter dated 3.6.1937. Rab Books, 3.
3 Ibid., letter from Ernest Brown dated 26.5.1937.
4 Brabourne Collection, F97 22B, letter dated 5.2.1938.
5 R. A. Butler, *The Art of the Possible* (Hamish Hamilton, 1971), p. 61.
6 Brabourne Collection, F97 22B, letter dated 22.11.1937.
7 Ibid., letter dated 12.2.1938.
8 Brabourne Collection, F97 21, letter dated 3.2.1937.
9 Brabourne Collection, F97 22B, letter dated 23.2.1938.
10 Ibid., letter dated 23.2.1938.
11 Ibid., letter dated 2.3.1938.
12 Ibid., letter dated 3.12.1937.
13 *Glasgow Herald* (26 February 1938).
14 *Daily Mail* (29 July 1938).
15 Butler Papers, A25, letter to Anthony Butler dated 22.10.1938.
16 Butler Papers, D48 Part 16, letter dated 29.9.1938.
17 *Hansard* (5 October 1938), col. 453.
18 *The Art of the Possible*, p. 72.
19 *Hansard* (5 October 1938), col. 371.
20 *Hansard* (5 October 1938), col. 548.
21 *Bristol Evening Post* (15 November 1938).
22 Brabourne Collection, F97 22B, letter dated 24.4.1938.
23 Ibid.
24 *The Art of the Possible*, p. 76.
25 Butler Papers, G10, letter dated 28.1.1939.
26 Brabourne Collection, F97 22B, letter dated 22.4.1938.
27 *The Art of the Possible*, p. 77. The alleged contemporary 'Diary' entry from which Rab there quotes no longer survives among the Butler Papers.
28 Butler Papers, G11, typed notes dated in pencil June 1939.
29 Ibid.
30 *The Times*, leading article (1 April 1939).
31 *The Art of the Possible*, p. 78.
32 Ibid., p. 79.
33 Martin Gilbert, *Winston S. Churchill*, vol. v, *1922–1939* (Heinemann, 1976), p. 1073.
34 Butler Papers, G11.
35 Ibid., typed notes headed 'September 1939'.

36 Ibid.
37 Ibid.
38 Iris Portal, interview with the author, 17 January 1983.
39 Butler Papers, G11, typed notes headed 'September 1939'.

9 CHURCHILL COMES TO POWER

1 Butler Papers, Trinity College, Cambridge, G10.
2 Butler Papers, G11, letter from R. G. Hunt dated 24.12.1940.
3 Ibid., document headed 'Narvik' dated 11.1.1940.
4 Ibid.
5 Ibid., letter dated 22.12.1940.
6 Butler Papers, G13, diary note dated 7.5.1940.
7 Ibid., diary note dated 8.5.1940.
8 Ibid., diary note dated 13.5.1940.
9 Ibid., diary note dated 14.5.1940.
10 Ibid., diary note dated 15.5.1940.
11 Ibid.
12 Recorded conversation with the author, 20 June 1978.
13 Butler Papers, G13, diary note dated 15.5.1940.
14 Martin Gilbert, *Winston S. Churchill*, vol. VI, *1939–1941* (Heinemann, 1983), p. 55.
15 Ibid., pp. 72–3.
16 Ibid., pp. 402, 404, 411–13, 418, 421.
17 *Daily Express* (11 September 1965).
18 W. M. Carlgren, *Swedish Foreign Policy During the Second World War*, trans. Arthur Spencer (Ernest Benn, 1977). See also Mallet's telegram to the Foreign Office, PRO, Foreign Office Papers 800/322.
19 Gilbert, *Churchill*, vol. VI, pp. 598–9.
20 This document no longer survives in the Foreign Office official papers. Rab, however, kept a personal copy of it which was never even transferred to Trinity. Its full text reads:

Cypher telegram to Mr Mallet, (Stockholm).
Foreign Office. 23rd June, 1940. 2.00 p.m.
No. 534 DIPP.

Your telegram No. 748.

Swedish Minister who called here today agrees with Mr Butler that statement attributed to him in your telegram is quite inaccurate. Swedish Minister further informed Mr Butler that he telegraphed on his own responsibility on 20th June to Minister for Foreign Affairs that in his view His Majesty's Government's attitude had certainly not had time to crystallise 'awaiting French events and results of secret session'. These the Swedish Minister said had been his own views, and he certainly had no authority for these from Mr Butler.

He said that he thought that the Swedish Minister for Foreign Affairs had derived an exaggerated impression and he was very surprised that the matter should have been put to the Foreign Affairs Committee of the Riksdag who incidentally were sworn to secrecy and should not speak to Press.

For your private information, M. Prytz told Mr Butler that he could not help thinking that certain interested parties in Sweden had mixed themselves up in this affair in an attempt to cause mischief.

I trust you will continue to prevent any further exaggerations.

21 PRO, Foreign Office papers 800/322, folios 278–81.
22 Ibid.
23 Butler Papers, G13, typed diary note dated 'August 1940'.
24 Ibid., diary note dated 27.7.1940.
25 Ibid., letter to Mrs Portal dated 3.9.1940.
26 Ibid.
27 Ibid.
28 Ibid., letter to Mrs Portal dated 6.1.1941.
29 Ibid., note headed 'The Diplomatic Corps' dated 17.12.1940.
30 Halifax diary, 25.11.1940, quoted in *The Diaries of Sir Alexander Cadogan* (Cassell, 1971), p. 337.
31 Butler Papers, G13, diary note dated 22.12.1940.
32 Ibid.
33 *The Times* (23 December 1940).
34 *Evening Standard* (17 January 1941), *Daily Herald* (18 January 1941), *The People* (19 January 1941).
35 *Daily Telegraph* (6 February 1941).
36 Butler Papers, G12, note from Secretary of State dated 8.1.1941.
37 Butler Papers, G13, diary note dated 14.4.1941.
38 Ibid.
39 Foreign Office Papers 371/26224, minute dated 24.1.1941.
40 Butler Papers, G13, diary note dated 8.4.1941.

10 BOARDED TO EDUCATION

1 R. A. Butler, *The Art of the Possible* (Hamish Hamilton, 1971), p. 87. Rab's visit to Baldwin in which he records he drove down thinking about the prospect of going to the Board of Education, took place on 6.6.1941.
2 For example, *Evening News* (21 July 1941). The story is also mentioned in the Dalton diaries, where Rab is said to have been offered the Colonial Office in January 1941, but only on the condition that he went to the House of Lords. Dalton, however, is merely reporting a Lobby correspondent's tale and offers no corroboration of his own. Ben Pimlott (ed.), *The Second World War Diary of Hugh Dalton, 1940–5* (Jonathan Cape, 1986), p. 155.

3 Butler Papers, Trinity College, Cambridge, G13, diary note dated 8.5.1941.
4 Ibid., minute dated 2.7.1941.
5 *The Times* (21 July 1941).
6 Butler Papers, D48 Part 17, letter dated 9.1.1941.
7 Lord Butler, *The Art of Memory* (Hodder & Stoughton, 1982), p. 152.
8 Butler Papers, G13, diary note dated 'August 1941'.
9 Ede Diaries, British Library, additional MS 59690, diary entry dated 22.7.1941.
10 Ibid., diary entry dated 1.8.1941.
11 *Hansard* (17 February 1870), cols 439–40.
12 Ede Diaries, British Library, additional MS 59690, diary entry dated 15.8.1941.
13 PRO, Ed. 136/215.
14 Butler Papers, G13, minute from WSC dated 13.9.1941.
15 *The Art of the Possible*, p. 95.
16 Butler Papers, G13, letter from Sir Maurice Holmes dated 16.9.1941.
17 Ede Diaries, British Library, additional MS 59692, diary entry dated 30.1.1942.
18 Butler Papers, G13, letter dated 8.10.1941.
19 F. A. Iremonger, *William Temple: Archbishop of Canterbury* (Oxford University Press, 1948), p. 569.
20 Butler Papers, G13, diary note dated 7.1.1941.
21 Ede Diaries, British Library, additional MS 59692, diary entry dated 20.1.1942.
22 Ibid., diary entry dated 4.2.1942.
23 Ibid., diary entry dated 14.1.1942.
24 Ibid., diary entry dated 5.1.1942.
25 Ede Diaries, British Library, additional MS 59690, diary entry dated 20.10.1941.
26 Butler Papers, G15, letter dated 2.4.1943.
27 *Hansard* (16 June 1942), col. 1416.
28 *Manchester Guardian* (17 June 1942).
29 Ede Diaries, British Library, additional MS 59692, diary entry dated 12.2.1942.
30 Ede Diaries, British Library, additional MS 59693, diary entry dated 17.3.1942.
31 Ede Diaries, British Library, additional MS 59694, diary entry dated 22.6.1942.
32 Ibid.
33 *The Art of the Possible*, p. 106.
34 Ede Diaries, British Library, additional MS 59695, diary entry dated 15.9.1942.
35 Ibid., diary entry dated 6.10.1942.
36 Ibid., diary entry dated 16.9.1942.

37 *The Times* (9 October 1942), *Manchester Guardian* (10 October 1942).
38 *The Times* (2 November 1942).
39 *The Art of Memory*, p. 159.
40 Ede Diaries, British Library, additional MS 59695, diary entry dated 11.11.1942.
41 Ibid.
42 Ibid., diary entry dated 26.10.1942.
43 Butler Papers, G15, diary note dated 9.9.1943.
44 Ibid.
45 Butler Papers, G14, letter dated 6.2.1942.
46 Recorded conversation with the author, 20 June 1978.
47 Butler Papers, G14, draft pencilled letter dated 19.11.1942.
48 Ede Diaries, British Library, additional MS 59695, diary entry dated 7.12.1942.
49 *The Art of the Possible*, p. 1.
50 *Hansard* (8 September 1942), cols 77–80.
51 Ede Diaries, British Library, additional MS 59695, diary entry dated 13.1.1943.
52 *Observer* (20 December 1942).
53 Ede Diaries, British Library, additional MS 59695, diary entry dated 16.9.1942.
54 This whole account is based on a ten-page note Rab wrote at the time entitled 'A Visit to Chequers', Butler Papers, G15. It is reproduced with some minor variations in *The Art of the Possible*, pp. 109–16.
55 *Hansard* (29 July 1943), cols 1826–7.
56 *Lords Hansard* (4 August 1943), cols 1005–6.
57 *The Art of Memory*, p. 161.
58 *The Times* (26 October 1943).
59 *The Times* (25 November 1943).
60 *Hansard* (19 January 1944).
61 *Daily Telegraph* (29 March 1944).
62 Butler Papers, G15, note dictated by Rab some time in April 1944.
63 *The Art of the Possible*, p. 121.
64 Butler Papers, G15, note dictated by Rab some time in April 1944.
65 Ede Diaries, British Library, additional MS 59698, diary entry dated 29.3.1944.
66 *Daily Telegraph* (20 January 1944).
67 *Hansard* (12 May 1944), col. 2247.

11 REMAKING THE TORY PARTY

1 John Ramsden, *The Making of Conservative Policy* (Longman, 1980), p. 96.
2 Ibid., p. 97.

3 *Daily Telegraph* (9 August 1941).
4 Ramsden, *The Making of Conservative Policy*, p. 98.
5 Butler Papers, G15, diary note dated 9.9.1943.
6 Ibid.
7 Butler Papers, G16, diary note dated 8.9.1944.
8 Ibid., letter dated 13.9.1944.
9 R. A. Butler, *The Art of the Possible* (Hamish Hamilton, 1971), p. 127. Rab's claimed reply – 'That doesn't really affect me at all, for if we have an early election there isn't going to be a Conservative Government' – can probably safely be regarded as apocryphal, or at least an example of *esprit d'escalier*.
10 *The Memoirs of Lord Chandos* (Bodley Head, 1962), p. 327.
11 For example, *Yorkshire Post* (26 May 1944), 'It will fall to Mr Butler to carry through Mr Bevin's reallocating manpower scheme. Time will show whether he will be equal to the complicated tasks that lie before him.'
12 Butler Papers, G17, letter dated 5.6.1945.
13 *The Art of the Possible*, p. 128.
14 Ibid., p. 129.
15 Butler Papers, G17, letter from James Stuart dated 5.8.1945.
16 Private Papers of Lord Devlin, letter from Rab dated 8.7.1945.
17 Stanley Wilson, *The Mayor and the Matron* (Precision Press, 1971), Foreword by Lord Butler, p. 1.
18 Butler Papers, A65, letter from Sir Monty Butler dated 26.7.1945.
19 BBC TV Programme 'Reputations – R. A. Butler' first transmitted on BBC2, 13 July 1983.
20 *Hansard* (17 August 1945), cols 191–208.
21 J. F. S. Ross, *Parliamentary Representation* (Eyre & Spottiswoode, 1948), p. 247.
22 Butler Papers, G17, letter from Lord Baldwin dated 12.8.1945.
23 Butler Papers, H33, letter from Rab to Sir Joseph Ball dated 9.10.1946.
24 *The Times* (18 December 1945).
25 Conservative Party Archive, Bodleian Library, Oxford, Box 600/01, letter to Aubrey Jones dated 12.1.1946.
26 Butler Papers, H33, letter from Rab dated 13.4.1946 and from Ralph Assheton dated 18.4.1946.
27 Butler Papers, D32, letter ('Personal and Confidential') from Stanley Baldwin dated 20.4.1937.
28 There is a most revealing similarity between the 'Workers Charter' section of the *Industrial Charter* and a lecture that Sam Courtauld had delivered to an industrialists' conference at Oxford in 1942. The text of the lecture is preserved in the Butler Papers, G14, transcript dated 22.8.1942.
29 Harold Macmillan, *Tides of Fortune* (Macmillan, 1969), p. 302.
30 *The Art of the Possible*, p. 145.

31 Reginald Maudling, *Memoirs* (Sidgwick & Jackson, 1978), pp. 45–6.
32 1947 Conservative Party Conference Report, p. 52.
33 *Daily Telegraph* (3 October 1947).
34 *The Art of the Possible*, p. 146.
35 Butler Papers, H92, letter from Lord Woolton dated 24.8.1947.
36 Ibid., copy of memo dated 5.5.1947.
37 Ibid., letter from Harold Macmillan dated 9.5.1947.
38 Ibid., letter from Oliver Stanley dated 11.5.1947.
39 Butler Papers, H33, the final document, following an early draft by the Chairman of the Party, was sent by Rab to Lord Woolton, who did not amend it.
40 Ibid., original document dated 7.3.1949.
41 *The Times*, Correspondence Column (3, 7, 9, 10, 11, 12 March 1949) and almost every day for the rest of the month.
42 *Daily Dispatch* (19 March 1949).
43 Butler Papers, L104, letter from Eden dated 27.3.1949.
44 Butler Papers, H33, memo addressed to Butler by Woolton dated 1.4.1949.
45 Ramsden, *The Making of Conservative Policy*, p. 137.
46 Ibid., p. 139.
47 Peterborough column, *Daily Telegraph* (16 July 1949).
48 1949 Conservative Party Conference Report, p. 96.
49 *The Times* (15 October 1949).
50 Interestingly, one of those who led the clamour in favour of such moves at the Tory Party Conference in October was a young Cambridge undergraduate named Norman St John-Stevas: 1949 Conservative Party Conference Report, p. 93.
51 Alan Bullock, *Ernest Bevin, Foreign Secretary, 1945–51* (Heinemann, 1983), p. 712.
52 Ramsden, *The Making of Conservative Policy*, p. 142.
53 David Clarke, interview with the author 1 October 1984.
54 Ramsden, *The Making of Conservative Policy*, p. 142.
55 *The Art of the Possible*, p. 153.
56 *Sunday Times* (5 February 1950).
57 Butler Papers, L104.
58 Butler Papers, G22.
59 Ibid.
60 Ibid., letter dated 4.8.1950.
61 1950 Conservative Party Conference Report, p. 63.
62 *The Art of the Possible*, p. 155.
63 J. D. Hoffman, *The Conservative Party in Opposition, 1945–51* (MacGibbon & Kee, 1964), p. 202.
64 1950 Conservative Party Conference Report, p. 112.
65 Ibid., p. 113.
66 Rab Letter Books, Conservative Party Archive, Bodleian Library,

Oxford, 1 September–30 December 1950, Rab's letter to Lady Violet dated 9.11.1950.

67 1950 Conservative Party Conference Report, p. 113.
68 Peterborough column, *Daily Telegraph* (26 April 1949).
69 Chandos, *Memoirs*, p. 269.
70 *The Times* (14 March 1951).
71 Rab Letter Books, Conservative Party Archive, 1 January–30 April 1951, letter dated 5.4.1951.
72 J. W. Wheeler-Bennett, *King George VI: His Life and Reign* (Macmillan, 1958), p. 792.
73 *The Art of the Possible*, p. 155.
74 *Daily Mail* (4 October 1951).

12 HIGH NOON AT THE TREASURY

1 BBC Radio Profile, 29 June 1978.
2 Recorded interview with the author, 20 June 1978.
3 Anthony Seldon, *Churchill's Indian Summer* (Hodder & Stoughton, 1981), p. 555. Rab is reported there to have told Piers Dixon, son of the diplomat, Sir Pierson Dixon, in late 1950, that he expected to be Chancellor in any future Conservative administration. See also *The Memoirs of Lord Chandos* (Bodley Head, 1962), p. 342.
4 Dept of Western MSS, Bodleian Library, Oxford, MS Woolton 3, diary entry dated 22.12.1955.
5 Recorded interview with the author, 20 June 1978.
6 Dept of Western MSS, MS Woolton 3, diary entry dated 22.12.1955.
7 Ibid.
8 *The Diaries of Hugh Gaitskell, 1945–1956*, ed. Philip M. Williams (Jonathan Cape, 1983), p. 305.
9 *Gaitskell Diaries*, p. 305.
10 R. A. Butler, *The Art of the Possible* (Hamish Hamilton, 1971), p. 156.
11 Butler Papers, Trinity College, Cambridge, G24, letter dated simply 'December'.
12 *The Art of the Possible*, p. 156.
13 BBC TV interview with Keith Kyle. Originally transmitted in 1971 and repeated in 1982.
14 *The Art of the Possible*, p. 157.
15 PRO, CAB 128, CC (51) 1.
16 Ibid.
17 *Hansard* (7 November 1951), cols 197–209.
18 *Hansard* (29 January 1952), cols 40–62.
19 PRO, CAB 128, CC (52) 8, and CC (52) 9.
20 PRO, CAB 128, CC (51) 23.

21 PRO, CAB 128, CC (52) 7 and CC (52) 8.
22 *Listener* (31 January 1952), p. 163.
23 House of Lords, Beaverbrook Papers, Box C57, letter dated 15.1.1952.
24 *Hansard* (25 February 1952), col. 719.
25 The Cabinet records relating to 'Operation Robot' are extremely sparse. The narrative given here is based principally on the accounts given in two books: the Earl of Birkenhead, *The Prof in Two Worlds* (Collins, 1961) and Arthur Salter, *Slave of the Lamp* (Weidenfeld & Nicolson, 1967). There is also a good deal of detail based on oral history in Seldon, *Churchill's Indian Summer*, pp. 171–3 and some rather more sketchy comment in *The Art of the Possible*, pp. 158–60. Sam Brittan's *Steering the Economy: the Role of the Treasury*, 2nd edn (Penguin, 1971) gives perhaps the best concise account of the economic issues involved (pp. 195–200). A much fuller one is in Alec Cairncross, *Years of Recovery* (Methuen, 1985), pp. 234–71.
26 Butler Papers, G24, undated note on crested prime ministerial paper.
27 *The Art of the Possible*, p. 159.
28 PRO, CAB 129, C (52) 217 and 223.
29 'The Professor Knows All the Answers' – Spotlight column by A. J. Cummings, *News Chronicle* (8 August 1952).
30 Butler Papers, G24, letter to Rab from Sir Edward Bridges dated 12.8.1952.
31 Ibid., letter addressed 'Dear Prime Minister' dated 'August 1952'.
32 Ibid., letter to Rab dated 14.8.1952.
33 *Hansard* (11 March 1952), col. 1305.
34 Dept of Western MSS, Bodleian Library, MS Woolton 25.
35 Ibid., letter from Churchill dated 22.3.1952.
36 *The Times* (12 March 1952).
37 Butler Papers, G24: letter from the producer (Grace Wyndham Goldie) dated 15.7.1952 in which the phrase appears, 'You made history'.
38 PRO, CAB 128, CC (52) 80.
39 *Daily Telegraph* (20 September 1952).
40 *The Times* (8 October 1952).
41 1952 Conservative Party Conference Report, p. 48.
42 *Sunday Times* and *Observer* (12 October 1952).
43 Butler Papers, A67, letter to Rab from Sir Monty dated 16.6.1952.
44 Butler Papers, G25, letter to Rab from Sir John Archibald Ruggles-Brize dated 28.11.1952 – 'I am so sorry for your worry about your wife's illness.'
45 Maurice Webb in *Reynolds News* (28 December 1952) and Frederick Ellis in the *Daily Express* (31 December 1952).
46 Butler Papers, G25.
47 *Hansard* (14 April 1953), col. 33.
48 Political Diary, *Observer* (19 April 1953).

49 Sir Robert Armstrong, interview with the author, 9 April 1985.
50 Political Diary, *Observer* (19 April 1953).
51 *Sunday Times* (12 October 1952).
52 Butler Papers, G26, diary note headed '24 June 1953'.
53 Ibid., pencilled diary note untitled and undated.
54 Ibid.
55 Ibid.
56 *The Art of the Possible*, p. 169.
57 Butler Papers, G26, pencilled diary note untitled and undated.
58 *The Art of the Possible*, p. 169.
59 Ibid.
60 *The Art of the Possible*, p. 170.
61 Butler Papers, G26, letter from Jane Portal.
62 *Hansard* (29 June 1953), col. 28.
63 PRO, PREM 783/188.
64 *The Times* (29 June 1953).
65 c.f. 'Butler's Gag on Churchill Stroke', *Guardian* (2 January 1985).
66 Sir John Colville, interview with the author, 4 June 1985.
67 See Robert Lacey, *Majesty* (Hutchinson, 1977), pp. 247–9, and James Margach, *The Abuse of Power* (W. H. Allen, 1978), p. 85.
68 BBC Radio Profile, 29 June 1978.
69 Manuscript note of a conversation between Lord Cherwell and Lord Plowden passed to the author in 1979.
70 Butler Papers, G26, letter from Brigadier (later Sir) Ralph Rayner, Conservative MP for Tavistock 1935–66, dated 12.7.1953.
71 *Hansard* (21 July 1953), cols 211–27.
72 c.f. Obituary in the *Observer* (14 March 1982): 'I may never have known much about ferrets or flower-arranging – but one thing I did know was how to govern the people of this country.'
73 *The Art of the Possible*, p. 171.
74 *The Times* (17 November 1953).
75 Butler Papers, G26, letter from Sir Alan Lascelles dated 20.11.1953.
76 Ibid., letter from Stanford Cade dated 7.12.1953.
77 Butler Papers, A9, letter from Sydney to Rab dated 24.9.1954.
78 *Sydney Sunday Telegraph* (24 January 1954).
79 *The Times* (9 January 1954).
80 *The Art of the Possible*, p. 172.
81 Butler Papers, G46, letter from Sydney to Rab dated 9.1.1954.
82 Ibid., letter from Sydney to Rab dated 1.1.1954.
83 *The Times* (3 February 1954).
84 *Hansard* (2 February 1954), col. 209, intervention by Fred Lee MP.
85 *The Economist* (13 February 1954).
86 Ibid.
87 *The Art of the Possible*, p. 170.
88 *Hansard* (6 April 1954), col. 218.
89 *Hansard* (6 April 1954), col. 381.

90 Dept of Western MSS, Bodleian Library, MS Woolton 3, diary entry dated 6.4.1954.
91 Ibid.
92 Butler Papers, G27, MS diary note dated 11.3.1954.
93 *Hansard* (24 May 1954), col. 154. The actual vote was 280–166.
94 *Hansard* (24 May 1954), col. 100.
95 PRO, CAB 128, CC (54) 39.
96 Butler Papers, G27, typed copy memorandum dated 16.6.1954.
97 *Hansard* (8 July 1954), cols 2347–9.
98 PRO, CAB 128, CC (54) 48. Confidential Annex.
99 Harold Macmillan, *Tides of Fortune* (Macmillan, 1969), pp. 536–7.
100 PRO, CAB 128, CC (54) 52. Confidential Annex.
101 Butler Papers, G27, letter to Eden dated 15.8.1954.
102 Ibid., draft letter by Churchill accompanied by covering note opening, 'Please have a look at this version', dated 18.8.1954.
103 Ibid., carbon copy only.
104 BBC Radio Profile, 29 June 1978.
105 Butler Papers, G27, letter to Vincent Massey dated 24.8.1954.
106 *The Art of the Possible*, p. 125.
107 Butler Papers, G27, letter from Cherwell dated 17.6.1954.
108 Butler Papers, A9, letter from Sydney to Rab dated 28.9.1954.
109 Ibid., letter from Sydney to Rab undated but probably *circa* October–November 1954.
110 *Manchester Guardian* (9 October 1954).
111 Butler Papers, B24, letter to Rab from Lady Violet Bonham Carter dated 10.12.1954.
112 Butler Papers, L105, letter to Sydney from Winston Churchill dated 27.11.1954.
113 PRO, T 172/2055.
114 *The Times* (10 December 1954).
115 Dept of Western MSS, MS Woolton 3, diary entry dated 22.12.1954.
116 *Hansard* (24 February 1955), cols 1453–9.
117 Harold Wincott, 'Mr Butler's Restrictions and the Coming Budget', *Listener* (3 March 1955), p. 364.
118 Anthony Eden, *Full Circle* (Cassell, 1960), p. 278. The Prime Minister also did not help Rab by announcing in the House of Commons on 3 May the total abolition of purchase tax on non-woollen cloths and domestic textiles, at a further cost to the Exchequer of £6 million a year. When the announcement was made, contradicting his own defence of the 25 per cent tax only five days earlier, Rab was reported to have looked on with 'a reddened face'. *Manchester Guardian* (4 May 1955).
119 Political Diary, *Observer* (27 February 1955).
120 Butler Papers, B25, letter from Mr Justice Devlin.
121 *Listener* (21 April 1955), p. 687, text of the Budget Broadcast.
122 Dept of Western MSS, Bodleian Library, MS Woolton 3, diary entry dated 6.4.1955.

123 Portrait Gallery, *Sunday Times* (24 April 1955).
124 *The Art of the Possible*, p. 180.
125 *Hansard* (25 July 1955), cols 825–7. The only practical measure Rab announced was to increase the deposit rate on goods bought on hire purchase.
126 Butler Papers, G28, undated MS diary note but apparently written in December 1955.
127 Peterborough column, *Daily Telegraph* (19 October 1955).
128 Cassandra column, *Daily Mirror* (20 October 1955). Its author was William Connor. He was knighted a year before his death in 1967.
129 Macmillan, *Tides of Fortune*, p. 688. Eden, according to this account, offered him the Chancellorship on 23.9.1955.
130 Ibid., p. 692. Macmillan reproduces the letter he sent to Eden on 24.10.1955.
131 *Hansard* (26 October 1955), col. 211.
132 *Daily Telegraph* (27 October 1985).
133 Butler Papers, G28, letters from Reginald Maudling and Sir Humphrey Mynors, both dated 26.10.1955.
134 His friends were later to complain to Hugh Gaitskell about it – saying that Rab had been 'greatly upset'. *Gaitskell Diaries*, pp. 422 and 449.
135 *Hansard* (27 October 1955), col. 401.
136 *The Art of the Possible*, p. 180. See also Peterborough column, *Daily Telegraph* (1 November 1955).
137 Political Diary, *Observer* (30 October 1955).
138 *Hansard* (1 November 1955), col. 797.
139 Butler Papers, G28, MS diary note.
140 Macmillan, *Tides of Fortune*, p. 680.
141 Butler Papers, G28, MS diary note.
142 Political Diary, *Observer* (25 December 1955).
143 Macmillan, *Tides of Fortune*, p. 694.
144 *Manchester Guardian* (22 December 1955).

13 LEADER IN LIMBO

1 Dept of Western MSS, Bodleian Library, Oxford, MS Woolton 3, diary entry dated 24.10.1955. The man who delivered the warning to Rab was Harry Crookshank.
2 Ibid.
3 Harold Macmillan, *Tides of Fortune* (Macmillan, 1969), p. 693.
4 Butler Papers, Trinity College, Cambridge, G28, letter from Lady Eden to Rab dated 30.12.1955.
5 *Observer* (8 January 1956). The story was not written by its political correspondent, Hugh Massingham.
6 *The People* (8 January 1956). This paper changed its headline half-way

through the night to 'Eden: I mean to stay' – an apparent concession to Downing Street's unprecedented official denial of its original story as 'false and without any foundation whatever'.

7 *Manchester Guardian* (9 January 1956).
8 William Clark, *From Three Worlds* (Sidgwick & Jackson, 1986), p. 153.
9 Clark, *From Three Worlds*, p. 153. The word 'devilishly' does not appear in the book but is in the original manuscript diary.
10 Clark, *From Three Worlds*, p. 155.
11 A full two months after his unfortunate comment at Heathrow about his being resolved 'to support the Prime Minister in all his difficulties', Rab was at it again. In a speech to the quarterly meeting of the National Union of Conservative and Unionist Associations held in London on 15 March he, once more, somewhat condescendingly remarked in reference to Eden, 'We see a great deal of each other and we support each other in all the troubles that occur.' *Daily Herald* (16 March 1956).
12 Political Commentary, *Spectator* (30 December 1955).
13 Butler Papers, G30, letter from Sir Edward Boyle to Rab dated 2.1.1956.
14 *The Economist* (4 February 1956).
15 *Hansard* (26 January 1956), col. 362.
16 Leader column, *Manchester Guardian* (15 February 1956).
17 *Hansard* (16 February 1956), col. 2643.
18 *Hansard* (16 February 1956), col. 2645.
19 c.f. F. M. Cornford, *Microcosmographia Academica* (Bowes & Bowes, 1908). 'The Principle of Unripe Time' is discussed on p. 24.
20 *Hansard* (16 February 1956), col. 2644.
21 Leading article entitled 'The Decisive Step', *Spectator* (24 February 1956).
22 *Hansard* (16 February 1956), col. 2635.
23 *Hansard* (21 June 1956), col. 1752.
24 *Daily Express* (24 June 1956).
25 *The Economist* (17 March 1956).
26 John Colville, *The Churchillians* (Weidenfeld & Nicolson, 1981), p. 179.
27 Sir John Colville, interview with the author 4.6.1985.
28 *Spectator* (16 March 1956).
29 *Daily Mail* (3 July 1956).
30 *Hansard* (3 July 1956), col. 1167.
31 Clark, *From Three Worlds*, p. 162.
32 Leader entitled 'Interval', *The Times* (4 August 1956).
33 Clark, *From Three Worlds*, p. 166.
34 Philip Ziegler, *Mountbatten* (Collins, 1985), pp. 537–8.
35 Anthony Eden, *Full Circle* (Cassell, 1960), p. 557.

36 1956 Conservative Party Conference Report, p. 124.
37 *Hansard* (13 November 1956), cols 882–3. Rab repeated his announcement that he had 'unhesitatingly supported' the Suez venture the following month, *Hansard* (6 December 1956), col. 1575.
38 Clark, *From Three Worlds*, p. 171. Diary entry dated Wednesday 8 August. The question of Israeli intervention, and the uses to which it could be put, is also more guardedly referred to by Macmillan himself in the fourth volume of his memoirs, *Riding the Storm* (Macmillan, 1971), pp. 111–12.
39 Recorded interview with the author, 20 June 1978.
40 Hannan Swaffer column, *The People* (28 October 1956).
41 Column headed 'It was Mr Butler's Day' by Randolph Churchill, *Evening Standard* (12 October 1956). Also *The Economist* (13, 20 October 1956). A leading article in the latter issue, looking back on the Conference, went so far as to comment, 'If one reads the signs aright, the real message of Llandudno was not "more Conservatism more quickly", but "More Butlerism more briskly".'
42 Lord Molson, interview with the author 1 July 1985.
43 R. A. Butler, *The Art of the Possible* (Hamish Hamilton, 1971), p. 192.
44 Selwyn Lloyd, *Suez 1956* (Jonathan Cape, 1978), p. 176.
45 Recorded interview with the author, 20 June 1978.
46 Rab used the phrase twice in the hearing of a visitor staying the weekend at Stanstead in October 1956: information passed to the author in 1985. The source wishes to remain anonymous.
47 *The Art of the Possible*, p. 195.
48 *News Chronicle* (7 November 1956).
49 Reginald Maudling, *Memoirs* (Sidgwick & Jackson, 1978), p. 64.
50 Clark, *From Three Worlds*, p. 209. Diary entry headed 'Sunday 4 November'.
51 Ibid., p. 202. Diary entry headed 'Wednesday 31 October'.
52 Ibid., p. 213. Rab's letter is there described as 'typically convoluted'.
53 *Daily Herald* (20 November 1956).
54 *The Art of the Possible*, p. 194.
55 *Hansard* (22 November 1956), cols 1943–4.
56 Butler Papers, G30, the letter, dated 22.11.1956, is in Birch's own handwriting.
57 Ibid., the note is dated 'Thursday evening' so it was probably written after the meeting, starting at 6.30 p.m., was over.
58 Enoch Powell, recorded interview with the author 1 February 1983.
59 *Manchester Guardian* (23 November 1956).
60 Column by 'A Student of Politics', *Sunday Times* (25 November 1956).
61 Nigel Fisher, *Harold Macmillan* (Weidenfeld & Nicolson, 1982), p. 170.
62 *The Art of the Possible*, p. 195.

63 David Carlton, *Anthony Eden* (Allen Lane, 1981).
64 Butler Papers, G30, letter from George Humphrey dated 18.12.1956.
65 Carlton, *Eden*, p. 459.
66 Beaverbrook Papers, House of Lords, BBK C58, letter from Bracken to Beaverbrook dated 23.1.1957.
67 *Forward* (14 December 1956).
68 *The Economist* (22 December 1956).
69 Ibid.
70 The Earl of Kilmuir, *Political Adventure* (Weidenfeld & Nicolson, 1964), p. 283.
71 *The Times* (10 January 1957). The bulletin was signed by Evans and two specialists, Sir Gordon Gordon-Taylor, a celebrated surgeon, and Thomas Hunt, a noted gastroenterologist, and Dr Ralph Southward, the Edens' own family doctor.
72 Butler Papers, G31, MS diary note probably written February 1957.
73 Ibid. According to Rab there was 'an altercation' between the Chancellor and the Prime Minister's doctor, Sir Horace Evans.
74 Ibid.
75 BBC Radio Profile, 29 June 1978.
76 Butler Papers, G31, letter from Sir Horace Evans to Rab dated 14.1.1957.
77 Ibid., memo of 'confidential exchange with the Chief Whip' dated 22.2.1957.
78 Lead 'Note of the Week' headed 'By Whose Choice?', *The Economist* (12 January 1957).
79 Iris Portal, interview in BBC TV 'Reputations' programme 13 July 1983.
80 *Daily Express* (10 January 1957). c.f. Harold Macmillan's own statement in the fourth volume of his memoirs, 'I could not go to see even intimate friends or I would seem to be canvassing for support.' *Riding the Storm*, p. 184.
81 Sir John Colville, interview with the author 4 June 1985.
82 *Daily Sketch* (11 January 1957).
83 Maudling, *Memoirs*, pp. 64 and 126.
84 Butler Papers, G31, letter to Rab from Lord Beaverbrook dated 23.1.1957.
85 Iain Macleod, 'The Tory Leadership', *Spectator* (17 January 1964).
86 Butler Papers, G31, diary note probably written February 1957.

14 THE YEARS OF POOH-BAH

1 Butler Papers, Trinity College, Cambridge, G31, typed note dictated by Rab dated 18.4.1957, headed 'Diverse Reminiscences Ending with Suez'.

2 Charles Hill, *Both Sides of the Hill* (Heinemann, 1964), pp. 208–9. The journalist was Derek Marks, political correspondent (and later editor) of the *Daily Express*.
3 Private information. One phone call, initiated at lunchtime, simply began, 'Our beloved Monarch has sent for Harold.'
4 Harold Macmillan, *Riding the Storm* (Macmillan, 1971), p. 186.
5 R. A. Butler, *The Art of the Possible* (Hamish Hamilton, 1971), p. 196.
6 *Daily Express* (11 January 1957). Front-page story by Derek Marks and John May.
7 *The Times* (23 January 1957).
8 Ibid.
9 Butler Papers, G31, letter from Mrs Elaine Kellett dated 23.1.1957.
10 Ibid., letter from Commander Robert Allan, MP, dated 23.1.1957.
11 *Sunday Express* (13 January 1957). See also *Evening Standard* (11 January 1957).
12 Westminster Commentary by Taper, *Spectator* (1 February 1957).
13 Ibid.
14 *The Art of the Possible*, p. 202.
15 Auberon Waugh, *Sunday Telegraph* (12 April 1981).
16 Butler Papers, G31, letter signed by J. E. S. Simon but written on behalf of Pat Hornsby-Smith as well dated 19.7.1957.
17 Cross-Bencher column, *Sunday Express* (31 March 1957).
18 Butler Papers, G32, letter from the Marquess of Salisbury dated 19.3.1957.
19 *Hansard* (13 March 1957), cols 1141–55.
20 Cmnd 645 published on 2 February 1959.
21 *Daily Mail* (7 January 1958).
22 *The Times* (6 January 1958).
23 *Daily Telegraph* (7 January 1958). Rab apparently made the remark as an impromptu comment after opening the new offices of the Jewish Board of Guardians in St Pancras.
24 *Hansard* (3 February 1958), cols 815–30.
25 *Scotsman* (8 February 1958).
26 Butler Papers, G32, letter dated 12.5.1958.
27 Ibid., memorandum to the Prime Minister dated 11.11.1957.
28 Harold Macmillan, *Pointing the Way* (Macmillan, 1972), p. 5.
29 Butler Papers, G32, typed five-page Note headed 'Top Secret' and addressed to the Prime Minister.
30 Butler Papers, G34, diary note dated 6.6.1958.
31 *Evening Standard* (21 February 1958).
32 *Daily Mirror* (22 February 1958).
33 Leader, *Manchester Guardian* (22 February 1958).
34 Butler Papers, G34, private memo to the Prime Minister.
35 Butler Papers, G32, copy of letter to the Prime Minister from 'Home Office, Whitehall'.

36 Ibid., Prime Minister's personal minute dated 28.6.1958.
37 Ibid., typed copy of memorandum to Sir Charles Cunningham dated 27.8.1958.
38 1958 Conservative Party Conference Report, pp. 100–2.
39 Note headed 'Onward from Blackpool', *The Economist* (18 October 1958).
40 1958 Conservative Party Conference Report, pp. 121–4.
41 Cmnd 247. The Report had been published on 4.9.1957.
42 Lord Renton, interview with the author, 15 October 1985.
43 *Hansard* (26 November 1958), cols 366–7.
44 *Daily Telegraph* (27 January 1959).
45 *Hansard* (29 March 1957), cols 1491–1581.
46 Note headed 'Obscenity for a Select Committee', *The Economist* (6 April 1957).
47 *Hansard* (16 December 1958), cols 992–1005.
48 Butler Papers, G34, letter from Roy Jenkins dated 9.8.1959.
49 Leading article headed 'Dr Gallup's Tranquilliser', *The Economist* (19 September 1959).
50 *The Art of the Possible*, p. 198.
51 Butler Papers, G34, letter from Sir Henry Willink, Master of Magdalene College, Cambridge, dated 13.2.1959. The colleges concerned were St John's and Jesus.
52 Iris Portal, interview with the author, October 1982.
53 Butler Papers, G34, the letter from D. M. M. Carey in the Faculty Office of the Archbishop of Canterbury dated 9.10.1959 begins, 'I wish to acknowledge the receipt of the Application Form for a Special Licence duly completed and signed by yourself. By the same post, I have also received letters from Mrs Courtauld's mother, the Rector of Great Yeldham and the Rector of Ashwell, the last named consenting to the use of his Church.'
54 *Daily Telegraph* (5 October 1959).
55 *The Economist* (21 September 1957, 5 April 1958).
56 'A Political Notebook', *News of the World* (11 September 1959), which bears all the imprints of having been inspired by Rab.
57 Note headed 'The Cabinet Reshuffle', *The Economist* (17 October 1959).
58 Transcript of interview with Lord Butler recorded for BBC2 'Reputations' programme on Iain Macleod in summer 1981.
59 *The Times* (15 October 1959).
60 Butler Papers, G34, the letter was sent out from the Home Office.
61 Recorded interview with Lady Butler of Saffron Walden, 17 March 1984.
62 *Saffron Walden Weekly News* (23 October 1959).
63 *The Times* (3 and 4 September 1959).
64 Butler Papers, G34, undated copy of 'Personal and Confidential' letter addressed to Viscount Kilmuir.

65 *The Times* (23 October 1959).
66 *Hansard* (5 November 1959), cols 1180–5.
67 *Guardian* (6 November 1959), front-page story headed 'Floggers Flourish Their Birches'; the sub-head was 'Mr Butler at His Best'.
68 *Hansard* (5 November 1959), cols 1196–9.
69 *The Times* (6, 18 and 20 November 1959).
70 *Hansard* (18 November 1959), cols 1246–56.
71 *Daily Telegraph* (20 November 1959).
72 *Daily Sketch* (4 December 1959). The story was written by Guy Eden, its political correspondent, who was normally friendlily disposed toward Rab.
73 *Hansard* (16 December 1959), cols 1531–42.
74 *Daily Sketch* (18 December 1959). The article again was by Guy Eden.
75 *Lords Hansard* (16 December 1959), col. 458. Speech by Earl Winterton.
76 *Lords Hansard* (16 December 1959), col. 475. Speech by Viscount Kilmuir.
77 Butler Papers, G35, letter from Rab to Macmillan 27.1.1960.
78 Philip Ziegler, *Mountbatten* (Collins, 1985), p. 681.
79 Butler Papers, G35, 'Prime Minister's Personal Telegram' dated 3.2.1960.
80 Ziegler, *Mountbatten*, p. 682.
81 Butler Papers, G35, drafts of both statements with MS amendments are to be found on Rab's own files.
82 Ibid., typed note prepared for Macmillan on his return.
83 Macmillan, *Pointing the Way*, p. 161.
84 Butler Papers, G35, 'note' dated 9.3.1960.
85 Ibid.
86 *The Times* (26 May 1960).
87 *Hansard* (11 May 1960), cols 426–91.
88 Macmillan, *Pointing the Way*, p. 228.
89 Butler Papers, G35, the minute is addressed 'Prime Minister' and dated 2.7.1960.
90 Ibid., letter to Rab from James Ramsden MP dated 'Tue night'. That Ramsden was a strong advocate of Rab going to the Foreign Office is proved by an earlier letter from him dated 24.4.1960.
91 *Hansard* (24 June 1960), cols 1490–8.
92 *New Statesman* (13 October 1961), the vision was recalled in its 'Spotlight on Politics' column.
93 'Student of Politics' column, *Sunday Times* (16 October 1960).
94 'Spotlight on Politics' column headed 'Mr Macleod's Escape', *New Statesman* (23 June 1961).
95 *Daily Mail* (1 November 1960, 10 March 1961). The first poll, organised by Gallup, showed 35 per cent of Conservative voters favouring Rab, the second, an NOP one, 46 per cent. In neither poll did the

runner-up – Selwyn Lloyd and Duncan Sandys respectively – enjoy a rating of more than 10 per cent.

96 *The Times* (14 April 1961).
97 Ibid., 12 April 1960.
98 *Hansard* (26 April 1960), col. 421.
99 *Daily Express* (20 April 1961). Rab's chief tormentor was reported to have been 'mild-looking, motherly Mrs Ruby Frith' who 'eyed him squarely' and said, 'Let him be a man and bring back corporal punishment for young offenders.'
100 *The Times* (19 June 1961).
101 *The Times* (24 June 1961).
102 Harold Macmillan, *At the End of the Day* (Macmillan, 1973), p. 9.
103 Butler Papers, G36, copy of circular letter dated 17.2.1961.
104 Ibid., two successive ones went out at Christmas 1960 and Easter 1961.
105 Butler Papers, G37, the letter signed by Philip Woodfield of the Prime Minister's secretariat is dated 14.7.1961.
106 Ibid., some time in October Rab wrote a fourteen-page handwritten memorandum revealingly called 'Description of Changes in the Government 1961 and Techniques of the Prime Minister'. The narrative given here is largely based on it.
107 Ibid., MS original of letter marked 'Strictly Private' and addressed to the Earl of Home. Dated 1.10.1961, the letter does not appear to have been sent.
108 1961 Conservative Party Conference Report, pp. 64–77. The amendment had been moved by a young Bow Group barrister named Geoffrey Howe.
109 Butler Papers, G37. The typed letter to Rab speaks of 'a real triumph', the hand-written letter to Mollie merely of 'Rab's triumph'. The first is dated 12.10.1961, the second 13.10.1961.
110 *Scotsman* (10 October 1961).
111 'Student of Politics' column, *Sunday Times* (19 November 1961).
112 Lord Renton, interview with the author, 15 October 1985.
113 Butler Papers, G38, MS diary note dated 24.1.1962.
114 Ibid., MS note headed 'The African Choice' dated 10.3.1962.
115 Ibid. Rab's slightly surprising alternative candidates were Julian Amery and Peter Thorneycroft.
116 Sir Roy Welensky, *4,000 Days* (Collins, 1964), pp. 161–2.
117 Ibid., p. 339.
118 Butler Papers, G38, diary note of conversation with Sir Archie James and others marked 'Private' and dictated 4.4.1962.
119 Ibid., diary note dated 24.1.1962.
120 Ibid., diary note dated 10.11.1962.
121 Nigel Fisher, *Iain Macleod* (Andre Deutsch, 1973), p. 203.
122 'Spotlight on Politics' column, *New Statesman* (20 July 1962).

123 *Daily Mail* (12 July 1982). The story, the 'splash' in all editions, was written by the paper's political correspondent, Walter Terry, never a confidant of Rab's.
124 *Time and Tide* (20 July 1962).
125 Butler Papers, G39, undated MS letter – presumably written in the week beginning 8 July. This is a shortened version of the original in which there is much repetition and an even stronger flavour of self-pity.
126 Butler Papers, G38, MS diary note dated 1.12.1962.

15 THE SECOND LEADERSHIP STRUGGLE

1 Butler Papers, Trinity College, Cambridge, G38, MS diary note dated 24.1.1962.
2 Harold Macmillan, *At the End of the Day* (Macmillan, 1973), p. 128.
3 Butler Papers, G38, MS diary note dated 23.10.1962.
4 1962 Conservative Party Conference Report, pp. 52–4. Rab also produced, for once, a resounding phrase, 'For the Labour Party 1,000 years of history books. For us the future.'
5 Cmnd 1871.
6 Cmnd 2009.
7 Butler Papers, G40, reference to article by James Margach in the *Sunday Times*, MS note dated 7.3.1963.
8 *Hansard* (19 December 1962), cols 1266–8.
9 Butler Papers, G40, diary note headed 'Macmillan at 6 Years PM' and dated 8.1.1963.
10 Ibid., MS note of two conversations with the Prime Minister dated 7.3.1963, the day of the second of them.
11 BBC Radio Profile, 29 June 1978.
12 BBC TV Interview with Kenneth Harris, *Listener* (28 July 1966).
13 'Mending the Eggshells', William Rees-Mogg, *Sunday Times* (23 June 1963).
14 Butler Papers, G41, two such reports – one dated 27.6.1963 and the other 3.7.1963 – survive in typescript, though another covering the immediate post-Profumo meeting of the 1922 Committee is missing.
15 Butler Papers, G40, 'Confidential Note' dictated 21.6.1963.
16 Ibid., letter from Charles Fletcher-Cooke MP to Mollie Butler dated 18.7.1963.
17 The interview was with Hugh Massingham who, at the end of 1962, had transferred his allegiance there from the *Observer*. It was never published.
18 Butler Papers, G40, typewritten 'Note' dated 21.6.1963.
19 Macmillan, *At the End of the Day*, p. 331.
20 *The Times* (27 July 1963).

21 Butler Papers, G40, 'Confidential Note' dated 12.7.1963.
22 London Letter, *Guardian* (10 July 1963).
23 Butler Papers, G40, second 'Confidential Note' dated 31.7.1963.
24 Ibid.
25 Ibid.
26 Maudling certainly expressed this view in an interview he gave to D. R. Thorpe, the prospective biographer of Selwyn Lloyd. Note of interview given April 1975.
27 Article by William Rees-Mogg entitled 'Generating Victory,' *Sunday Times* (28 July 1963).
28 *The Times* (17 July 1963). The actual voting was 105–25.
29 The headlines come, respectively, from the *Daily Mail*, *Daily Mirror*, *Daily Herald* and *Daily Telegraph*.
30 *The Times* (9 July 1963).
31 Butler Papers, G40, 'Confidential Note' dated 31.7.1963.
32 'Spotlight on Politics' column, *New Statesman* (2 August 1963).
33 Ibid. The article was written by the author, who attended the meeting.
34 Butler Papers, G40, letter from Sir Hubert Ashton dated 19.9.1963.
35 Macmillan, *At the End of the Day*, p. 448.
36 *Daily Mail* (19 September 1963).
37 The headlines all appeared in Conservative newspapers – respectively the *Daily Sketch*, the *Daily Telegraph* and the *Daily Express* – on 26 September 1963.
38 Randolph S. Churchill, *The Fight for the Tory Leadership* (Heinemann, 1964), p. 95.
39 Kenneth Young, *Sir Alec Douglas-Home* (Dent, 1970), p. 159. It is only fair to say that what is clearly Home's own version of a conversation held at Chequers on 14 September finds no corroboration in Macmillan's own account of the same event, *At the End of the Day*, p. 494. Nor does he record Home giving him any firm advice to go when they subsequently met, again for dinner at Chequers on 6 October. Ibid., p. 498.
40 R. A. Butler, *The Art of the Possible* (Hamish Hamilton, 1971), pp. 238–40. See also Macmillan, *At the End of the Day*, p. 494.
41 BBC Radio Profile, 29 June 1978.
42 Macmillan, *At the End of the Day*, pp. 491–500.
43 BBC Radio Profile, 29 June 1978.
44 Macmillan, *At the End of the Day*, p. 499.
45 Butler Papers, G40, MS diary note afterwards dated (by Rab) 'week before Blackpool', but in fact written during the week of the Conference (probably 6 October 1963).
46 Churchill, *The Fight for the Tory Leadership*, p. 97. The account given here of the Cabinet meeting is largely based on Churchill's book – accurately described by Iain Macleod, one of the participants, as 'Mr Macmillan's trailer for the screenplay of his memoirs'. 'The Tory Leadership', *Spectator* (17 January 1964).

47 Young, *Sir Alec Douglas-Home*, pp. 161–2. Home's intervention is also confirmed, if obliquely, by Iain Macleod in his *Spectator* article of 17 January 1964.

48 *Sunday Times* (13 October 1963). Its main Insight political feature, written by James Margach and Clive Irving, was almost too transparently based on information supplied by Rab.

49 Butler Papers, G40, MS and typed notes both dated merely 'October 1963'. From internal evidence the former would appear to have been written on 13 October and the latter dictated on 20 October.

50 See also Reginald Bevins, *The Greasy Pole* (Hodder & Stoughton, 1965), p.34, and Anthony Sampson, *Macmillan: a Study in Ambiguity* (Allen Lane, 1967), p. 250.

51 Butler Papers, G40, MS note dated 'October 1963'.

52 Lord Boyle of Handsworth, interview with the author, 23 September 1980.

53 *The Times* (10 October 1963).

54 Macmillan, *At the End of the Day*, pp. 502–3.

55 Butler Papers, G40, typed note probably dictated 20.10.1963.

56 *The Times* (11 October 1963).

57 Churchill, *The Fight for the Tory Leadership*, p. 108.

58 *Daily Express* (10 October 1963).

59 *The Art of the Possible*, p. 243.

60 *Sunday Telegraph* (13 October 1963). Peregrine Worsthorne commented on his 'limp and faltering voice' and judged that his 'lofty, statesmanlike address' was delivered 'only at the price of disappointing his audience'. Other Press comments were less harsh but none was ecstatic, apart from that of the Television Critic of the *Sunday Times*, Maurice Wiggin, who, watching the performance on the screen, judged it 'the most rational and sensitive political speech I have heard in my dozen years watching television', *Sunday Times* (13 October 1963).

61 BBC 'Reputations' Programme, 13 July 1983, interview with Lord Home.

62 Conversations with the author, 1979–82.

63 Butler Papers, G40, MS note probably dated 13.10.1963.

64 Ibid.

65 Ibid.

66 *Daily Telegraph* (14 October 1963).

67 Butler Papers, G40, MS note probably dated 13.10.1963.

68 Macmillan, *At the End of the Day*, pp. 509–10.

69 Macmillan, *At the End of the Day*, p. 511.

70 Rab's minute to Macmillan dated 15.10.1963. It is quoted by Macmillan, *At the End of the Day*, p. 510.

71 *The Art of the Possible*, p. 246.

72 Interview with Sir Derek Mitchell, at the time Maudling's Private Secretary, 7.9.1985.

73 *The Art of the Possible*, pp. 246–7.
74 Iain Macleod, 'The Tory Leadership', *Spectator* (17 January 1964).
75 The source was an indirect one. The intelligence was supplied to William Rees-Mogg by a colleague on the *Sunday Times*.
76 *Daily Express* (18 October 1963). The caption read, 'The Butlers last night. She sees the strain in her husband's face. And he sees the shadow of defeat.'
77 *The Art of the Possible*, p. 248.
78 Butler Papers, G40, memo headed 'Secret' dated 18.10.1963.
79 Thames Television, 'The Day before Yesterday', first transmitted in October 1970. Quoted in Susan Barnes, *Behind the Image* (Jonathan Cape, 1974), p. 70.
80 'Reputations', BBC2, 13 July 1983. Powell quoted Macleod in his interview.
81 Ibid. Interview with Geoffrey Lloyd.
82 Interview with Reginald Maudling 21.11.1963: Maudling's actual phrase was that 'Quintin, having started the day by buzzing about like a fly in a bottle, simply capitulated.'
83 BBC Radio Profile, 29 June 1978.
84 Butler Papers, G40, hand-written letter on No. 10 writing paper.
85 Ibid., Rab's letter survives only in a handwritten draft.
86 *Sunday Times* (13 October 1963), article entitled 'The Week of Wounding'.

16 THE FOREIGN OFFICE

1 Lord Carrington, interview with the author, 1 June 1981.
2 Butler Papers, Trinity College, Cambridge, G40, letter to Rab from Paul Channon dated 25.10.1963.
3 *Daily Mirror* (25 October 1963). Its report on the Hague meeting was headed 'Friends Again – Thanks to Rab'.
4 *Yorkshire Post* (24 October 1963). Diary paragraph entitled 'Rab impresses'.
5 *The Times* (12 November 1963). Home was, in fact, just six months younger than Rab.
6 *Hansard* (15 November 1963), col. 502.
7 *Sunday Express* (17 November 1963). The interview was with Susan Barnes, later, as Susan Crosland, the wife of a Foreign Secretary.
8 Butler Papers, F101, typed sheet headed 'Secretary of State's Engagements'. The details given are for 9.1.1964.
9 *Hansard* (25 November 1963), cols 35–8.
10 *Birmingham Post* (20 February 1964).
11 Nicholas Henderson, *The Private Office* (Weidenfeld & Nicolson, 1984), p. 58.

12 Lady Butler of Saffron Walden, interview with author, 1 February 1986.
13 *Yorkshire Post* (16 April 1964). Diary paragraph headed 'Mr Butler in Exile'. See also 'London Letter', *Guardian* (14 April 1964).
14 R. A. Butler, *The Art of the Possible* (Hamish Hamilton, 1971), p. 256.
15 The story, or a version of it, eventually surfaced in print in the *Daily Mirror* (31 January 1968) as part of a profile of Lyndon Johnson.
16 Butler Papers, E20/1, the letter from the Customs was dated 13.5.1964 and the letter enclosing the Foreign Secretary's cheque, signed by his Assistant Private Secretary, was sent on 15.5.1964.
17 Butler Papers, G42, letter from Paul Channon to Rab dated 6.5.1964.
18 Butler Papers, C33, Churchill wrote to Rab on 15.11.1963 enclosing his manuscript and asking if he would 'scribble any comments and suggestions in the margin' – a request that Rab appears to have disregarded.
19 Butler Papers, G43, the galley proofs were accompanied by a most elegant letter from Macleod in which he wrote, 'I think now (although the establishment will be livid) that the truth must be told and it must in fact be made clear that you were the rightful choice.' Letter to Rab dated 15.1.1964.
20 Butler Papers, E20/3, letter to Sir Glyn Jones dated 9.3.1964.
21 Interview with the author at the Foreign Office, 28 January 1964.
22 *Hansard* (16 June 1964), cols 1126–39.
23 *The Art of the Possible*, p. 258.
24 Lord Carrington, interview, BBC2 'Reputations' programme, 13 July 1983. The incident is also referred to in Henderson, *The Private Office*, pp. 78–9.
25 D. E. Butler and Anthony King, *The British General Election of 1964* (Macmillan, 1965), note, p. 88.
26 'The Periscope' column, *Newsweek* (24 August 1964).
27 *The Times* (19 August 1964).
28 Lord Soames, interview with the author, 19 June 1985.
29 *Sun* (1 October 1964). The piece, headed 'The Night the Lights Went Out All Over Saffron Walden', is partially reproduced in *The Art of the Possible*, p. 25.
30 *Daily Express* (9 October 1964). Gale's report, headed 'On Tour Yesterday, the Man on the Edge of Things', extraordinarily, appeared on p. 9.
31 Column headed 'Randolph's Teleview', *Evening Standard* (10 October 1964).
32 *Observer* (4 October 1964).
33 *Sun* (16 October 1964). The General Secretary was Sir Len Williams, who later became Governor-General of Mauritius.
34 Henderson, *The Private Office*, p. 84.
35 Butler Papers, G42.

36 *The Times* (23 October 1964).
37 Butler Papers, G42, letter from Rab to Sir Alec Douglas-Home dated 26.10.1964.
38 *Hansard* (16 December 1964), cols 401–15.
39 It was one of Rab's proudest boasts that both rival Party Leaders said the same thing to him in the immediate aftermath of the 1964 election: conversations with the author 1979–82.
40 Butler Papers, C34, Rab's letter dated 11.1.1965 survives only in a handwritten rough draft.
41 Butler Papers, C34, the Press Notice was sent to Rab for approval before it was issued.
42 Butler Papers, G45, Rab wrote the comment on a piece of paper and attached it to the copy of the letter of sympathy he sent to Alec Douglas-Home.

17 MASTER OF TRINITY

1 Leader entitled 'Lord and Master', *The Times* (1 February 1965).
2 Comment headed 'Great Educator', *Observer* (7 February 1965).
3 *The Economist* (6 February 1965). Its leading article made an exception for Harold Macmillan – whose opposition to Rab's succession was, however, dismissed as 'the last infirmity of the old *poseur*'.
4 *Spectator* (5 February 1965). The judgment appeared in its 'Quoodle' column written by the editor, Iain Macleod.
5 Lady Butler of Saffron Walden, interview with the author, recorded 17 March 1984.
6 *Sunday Express* (21 February 1965), comment headed simply 'Rab'. See also *Daily Telegraph* (20 February 1965), Leader headed again 'R.A.B.'
7 Peterborough column, *Daily Telegraph* (6 March 1965).
8 *Cambridge Evening News* (17 March 1965).
9 London Letter, *Guardian* (18 March 1965).
10 News feature by Ivan Yates, *Observer* (7 February 1965).
11 *Cambridge Review* (13 February 1965).
12 Professor Patrick Duff, interview with the author, 19 February 1986.
13 *Cambridge Evening News* (1 February 1965).
14 *Cambridge Evening News* (4 March 1965).
15 Butler Papers, Trinity College, Cambridge, G44, MS note on top of first page of long letter from Prime Minister dated 23.7.1965. The chairmanship eventually went to the then Archbishop of Canterbury, Dr Michael Ramsey.
16 Lady Butler of Saffron Walden, recorded interview with the author, 17 March 1984.
17 Ibid.

18 *Cambridge Evening News* (8 October 1965).
19 Peter Laslett, Diary, entry for 7.10.1965.
20 *Trinity College Annual Record* (1964–5), p. 20. Rab also announced that he would be resigning his position as High Steward to the University lest it led to any conflict with his position as Head of a House. He retained his post as High Steward to the City of Cambridge.
21 'An Education for Land Tycoons', *Sunday Times* (5 January 1975).
22 *Cambridge Evening News* (10 March 1975).
23 *Cambridge University Reporter* (19 February 1986), p. 306.
24 J. A. Weir, 'Lord Butler', *Cambridge Review* (7 May 1982).
25 Ibid.
26 Peter Laslett, Diary, entry for 26.2.1969.
27 J. A. Weir, recorded interview for BBC2 'Reputations' programme, 13 July 1983.
28 Robert Robson, interview with the author, 19 February 1986.
29 Ibid.
30 *Trinity College Annual Record* (1977–8), p. 13.
31 *Trinity College Annual Record* (1972–3), p. 29.
32 Weir, 'Lord Butler'.
33 Anthony Holden, *Charles, Prince of Wales* (Weidenfeld & Nicolson, 1979), p. 135.
34 All Lord Butler's royal correspondence is closed for 100 years. This letter was, however, specifically referred to by Rab in conversation with the author.
35 *Trinity College Annual Record* (1971–2), p. 5.
36 *Daily Mirror* (17 August 1979).
37 *Cambridge Evening News* (23 April 1971).
38 Private information.
39 Lady Butler of Saffron Walden, recorded interview for BBC2 'Reputations' programme, 13 July 1983.
40 Peter Laslett, interview with the author, 19 February 1986.
41 'R. A. B. the Greatest of the Might-Have-Beens', *Daily Telegraph* (12 July 1971).
42 *Cambridge Evening News* (29 June 1972).
43 Butler Papers, G46, letter from Barbara Castle to Rab dated 27.8.1975.
44 Cmnd 6244.
45 Londoner's Diary, *Evening Standard* (29 November 1973).
46 *Jewish Chronicle* (7 December 1973). The paper's diarist commented in the same issue, 'Lord Butler's explanation of his poorly judged "Jew boy" joke at the leading literary occasion of the year is so innocent that there is no choice but to accept it.'
47 *Cambridge Evening News* (4 June 1974).
48 *Trinity College Annual Record* (1974–5), p. 5. Rab's written speech, which he had prepared, was read for him by the Vice-Master, Professor J. A. Gallacher.

49 *Cambridge Evening News* (19 April 1976).
50 Lady Butler of Saffron Walden, recorded interview for BBC2 'Reputations' programme, 13 July 1983.
51 Robert Robson, interview with the author, 19 February 1986.
52 Conversations with the author, 1979–82.
53 *Cambridge Evening News* (2 November 1976).
54 *Trinity College Annual Record* (1977–8), p. 10.
55 Ibid., p. 7.
56 Ibid., p. 6.
57 Recorded interview with the author, 20 June 1978.
58 *Cambridge Evening News* (20 June 1978).
59 Lady Butler of Saffron Walden, recorded interview with the author, 17 March 1984.
60 *Cambridge Evening News* (15 May 1979).
61 Ibid.
62 Private information. The lunch was on 23 December 1979.
63 *Lords Hansard* (25 February 1980), cols 1043–52.
64 *Daily Telegraph* (26 February 1980), lead story on parliamentary page.
65 *Lords Hansard* (13 March 1980), cols 1218–24.
66 *The Times* (14 March 1980).
67 *The Times* (10 March 1982).
68 *Trinity College Annual Record* (1981–2), pp. 43–4.

18 THE MAN AND THE LEGEND

1 Butler Papers, Trinity College, Cambridge, G24.
2 *New Statesman* (3 April 1954). The profile, though unsigned, was the work of R. H. S. Crossman.
3 Ibid. The profile is reproduced in *New Statesman Profiles* (Phoenix House, 1957). It also appears in Crossman's own book, *The Charm of Politics* (Hamish Hamilton, 1958).
4 Enoch Powell, 'Portrait, R. A. Butler – the Last of the True Tories', *Now!* (14–20 March 1980).
5 Private papers of Lord Devlin, letter from Rab in Australia dated 7.5.1927.
6 Ibid., letter from Rab in New Zealand dated 28.5.1927.
7 Ibid., letter from Rab in Australia dated 7.5.1927.
8 Jonathan Sumption, 'An Old Tory and the New Toryism', *Sunday Telegraph* (14 March 1982).
9 R. A. Butler, *The Art of the Possible* (Hamish Hamilton, 1971), p. 134.
10 For example by Paul Johnson, 'Their Obedient Servant', *New Statesman* (1 August 1975).
11 Kenneth Harris, *Conversations* (Hodder & Stoughton, 1967), p. 53.

12 Lord Carrington, interview with the author, 12 June 1980.

13 Nicholas Henderson, *The Private Office* (Weidenfeld & Nicolson, 1984), p. 73.

14 Ibid., p. 82.

15 Butler Papers, G46, handwritten scribble to Sir Bernard Gilbert, Second Secretary, H.M. Treasury, dated 10.3.1955.

16 Ibid., scrawl on letter from A. W. Tuke, chairman of Barclays Bank, dated 19.12.1955 and sent to Derek Mitchell (then Private Secretary to the Permanent Secretary of the Treasury).

17 Ibid., Ian Bancroft was the most regular recipient of this signal mark of favour.

18 John Mortimer, *In Character* (Penguin, 1984), p. 126.

19 Letter dated 21.6.1975. The dinner, commemorating Lord Fraser's nearly thirty years of service with the Conservative Party was held in the House of Commons on 28.7.1975.

20 Private information. The remark was made to a retiring Clerk of the Works and caused some offence.

21 *Ancient and Modern History Magazine*, no. 4 (Autumn 1982).

22 Kenneth Rose, 'Albany at Large', *Sunday Telegraph* (14 March 1982).

23 See p. 12.

24 'Grand Old Man – Robert Blake on Harold Macmillan's Services and Disservices', *London Review of Books* (1 May 1980).

25 Private document passed to the author 20 July 1980.

Bibliography

PRIMARY SOURCES

The principal primary source for this narrative has been the collection of Lord Butler's own papers kept at Trinity College, Cambridge. They span the whole of his life, from his christening to his funeral, and must rank as one of the more remarkable biographical archives for any twentieth-century politician. Lord Butler donated the papers to the college, just after he had ceased to be Master, in July 1978.

The Brabourne Collection, preserved at the India Office Library in London, was also of material assistance to me in writing Chapters 7 and 8. Part of it consists of the regular correspondence which passed between Rab and Lord Brabourne from 1933 to 1939: it provides invaluable source material for the politics both of India and Britain in the 1930s.

The Chuter Ede Diary, in the Department of Manuscripts at the British Library is, again, a most useful contemporary record. For Chapter 10 it afforded me some unique insights into the struggle which preceded the passing of the 1944 Butler Education Act.

The Woolton Papers and Diary, kept in the Department of Western Manuscripts at the Bodleian Library, Oxford, served a similar purpose in the writing of Chapters 11 and 12. Woolton may not always have been an objective observer (particularly of Rab) but at least he was an insider on many of the events I was attempting to describe. The Conservative Party Archives in the Bodleian also helped me with Chapters 10 and 11.

The Public Record Office at Kew provided a rewarding, if sometimes frustrating, quarry for the periods when Rab was in government. Given the exigencies of the thirty year rule (which only ex-Prime Ministers and ex-Ministers of the Crown appear to be given a licence to disregard), its usefulness was exhausted for me by the time Rab ceased to be Chancellor in 1955. I was fortunate, though, in having sight of Robert Rhodes James's

Anthony Eden (Weidenfeld & Nicolson, 1986) – with its splendidly comprehensive documentary account of Suez – just before this book went to press.

I am also much indebted to Lord Devlin and Mr Tony Benn – both of whom made available to me those parts of their own private papers having a relevance to Rab. Mrs Iris Portal and Mrs Dorothy Middleton (Rab's sisters) were equally forthcoming with family documentary and photographic evidence as to Rab's childhood.

BOOKS BY AND ABOUT RAB

Rab's own autobiography, *The Art of the Possible* (Hamish Hamilton, 1971), is far the most illuminating source for Rab's own views and attitudes: if sometimes elliptical in content, it is always evocative in tone. The only other book Rab wrote, *The Art of Memory* (Hodder & Stoughton, 1982), is revealing only as to his attitudes towards other people: apparently modelled on Winston Churchill's *Great Contemporaries*, it matches that work in neither verve nor anecdote.

There have been four previous biographical studies of Rab. The first was Ralph Harris's *Politics without Prejudice: A Biography of R. A. Butler* (Staples, 1956), a workmanlike account of Rab's rise to the Chancellorship and (considering Lord Harris of High Cross's later career at the Institute of Economic Affairs) a surprisingly warm endorsement of his tenure of that office. The second attempt at an assessment of Rab, published almost simultaneously, was Francis Boyd's 'political monograph', *Richard Austen Butler* (Rockliff, 1956), which, despite its brevity, has the merit of displaying a sympathetic but shrewd judgment of Rab at that stage of his career, together with a real understanding of the post-war Conservative Party. A third biographical study, produced some nine years later by a Cambridge contemporary, Gerald Sparrow's *'R.A.B.' – Study of a Statesman* (Odhams, 1965), is a good deal less successful: it is neither reliable on fact nor penetrating in interpretation. Patrick Cosgrave's *R. A. Butler: An English Life* (Quartet, 1981), is less a full-length portrait than a biographical essay. It contains some small errors of fact but admirably captures the various traits and quirks of Rab's character.

GENERAL

Addison, Paul, *The Road to 1945* (Jonathan Cape, 1975).
Barnett, Correlli, *The Audit of War* (Macmillan, 1986).
Bevins, Reginald, *The Greasy Pole* (Hodder & Stoughton, 1965).
Birkenhead, Earl of, *The Prof in Two Worlds* (Collins, 1961).
——, *Halifax: The Life of Lord Halifax* (Hamish Hamilton, 1965).
——, *Walter Monckton* (Weidenfeld & Nicolson, 1969).
Blake, Robert, *A History of Rhodesia* (Eyre Methuen, 1977).
——, *The Conservative Party from Peel to Thatcher* (Methuen, 1985).
Boyd-Carpenter, John, *Way of Life* (Sidgwick & Jackson, 1980).
Brittan, Sam, *The Treasury under the Tories, 1951–64* (Penguin, 1964).
——, *Steering the Economy: the Role of the Treasury*, 2nd edn (Penguin, 1971).
Bullock, Alan, *Ernest Bevin, Minister of Labour* (Heinemann, 1967).
——, *Ernest Bevin, Foreign Secretary* (Heinemann, 1983).
Burridge, Trevor, *Clement Attlee: a Political Biography* (Jonathan Cape, 1985).
Butler, D. E., *The British General Election of 1951* (Macmillan, 1952).
——, *The British General Election of 1955* (Macmillan, 1955).
Butler, D. E., and King, Anthony, *The British General Election of 1964* (Macmillan, 1965).
Butler, D. E., and Rose, Richard, *The British General Election of 1959* (Macmillan, 1960).
Cairncross, Alec, *Years of Recovery* (Methuen, 1985).
Carlton, David, *Anthony Eden* (Allen Lane, 1981).
Chandos, Viscount, *The Memoirs of Lord Chandos* (Bodley Head, 1962).
Churchill, Randolph, *The Rise and Fall of Sir Anthony Eden* (MacGibbon & Kee, 1959).
——, *The Fight for the Tory Leadership* (Heinemann, 1964).
Clark, William, *From Three Worlds* (Sidgwick & Jackson, 1986).
Colville, John, *Footprints in Time* (Collins, 1976).
——, *The Churchillians* (Weidenfeld & Nicolson, 1981).
——, *The Fringes of Power: Downing Street Diaries, 1939–55* (Hodder & Stoughton, 1985).
Cooper, Duff, *Old Men Forget* (Hart-Davis, 1953).
Cradock, Percy (ed.), *Recollections of the Cambridge Union, 1815–1939* (Bowes & Bowes, 1953).

Cross, J. A., *Sir Samuel Hoare: a Political Biography* (Jonathan Cape, 1977).
——, *Lord Swinton* (Oxford, 1982).
Crossman, R. H. S., *The Myths of Cabinet Government* (Harvard University Press, 1972).
Dalton, Hugh, *The Fateful Years, Memoirs, 1931–45* (Muller, 1951).
——, *High Tide and After, Memoirs, 1945–60* (Muller, 1962).
Dilks, David (ed.), *The Diaries of Sir Alexander Cadogan* (Cassell, 1971).
Eden, Anthony, *Full Circle* (Cassell, 1960).
——, *Facing the Dictators* (Cassell, 1962).
Egremont, Lord, *Wyndham and Children First* (Macmillan, 1968).
Evans, Harold, *Downing Street Diary: the Macmillan Years, 1957–63* (Hodder & Stoughton, 1981).
Fairlie, Henry, *The Life of Politics* (Methuen, 1968).
Feiling, Keith, *The Life of Neville Chamberlain* (Macmillan, 1946).
Fisher, Nigel, *Iain Macleod* (Deutsch, 1973).
——, *Harold Macmillan* (Weidenfeld & Nicolson, 1982).
Gilbert, Martin, *Winston S. Churchill*, vol. V, *1922–1939* (Heinemann, 1976).
——, *Winston S. Churchill,* vol. VI, *1939–1941* (Heinemann, 1983).
Halifax, Earl of, *Fulness of Days* (Collins, 1957).
Harris, Kenneth, *Attlee* (Weidenfeld & Nicolson, 1982).
Harvey, John (ed.), *The Diplomatic Diaries of Oliver Harvey* (Collins, 1970).
Hearnden, Arthur, *Red Robert: a Life of Robert Birley* (Hamish Hamilton, 1984).
Henderson, Nicholas, *The Private Office* (Weidenfeld & Nicolson, 1984).
Hill, Lord, *Both Sides of the Hill* (Heinemann, 1964).
Hoffman, J. D., *The Conservative Party in Opposition, 1945–51* (MacGibbon & Kee, 1964).
Holden, Anthony, *Charles, Prince of Wales* (Weidenfeld & Nicolson, 1979).
Home, Lord, *The Way the Wind Blows* (Collins, 1976).
Howard, Anthony, and West, Richard, *The Making of the Prime Minister* (Jonathan Cape, 1965).
Howarth, T. E. B., *Prospect and Reality: Great Britain, 1945–1955* (Collins, 1985).
Hutchinson, George, *The Last Edwardian at No. 10* (Quartet, 1980).
Iremonger, F. A., *William Temple* (Oxford University Press, 1948).
James, Robert Rhodes (ed.), *Chips: the Diaries of Sir Henry Channon* (Weidenfeld & Nicolson, 1967).
James, Robert Rhodes, *Anthony Eden* (Weidenfeld & Nicolson, 1986).
Johnson, Paul, *The Suez War* (MacGibbon & Kee, 1957).

Kilmuir, Earl of, *Political Adventure* (Weidenfeld & Nicolson, 1964).
Lacey, Robert, *Majesty* (Hutchinson, 1977).
Lloyd, Selwyn, *Suez 1956* (Jonathan Cape, 1978).
Macleod, Iain, *Neville Chamberlain* (Muller, 1961).
Macmillan, Harold, *Memoirs III, Tides of Fortune* (Macmillan, 1969).
——, *Memoirs IV, Riding the Storm* (Macmillan, 1971).
——, *Memoirs V, Pointing the Way* (Macmillan, 1972).
——, *Memoirs VI, At the End of the Day* (Macmillan, 1973).
Margach, James, *The Abuse of Power* (W. H. Allen, 1978).
Maudling, Reginald, *Memoirs* (Sidgwick & Jackson, 1978).
Middlemas, Keith, and Barnes, John, *Baldwin* (Weidenfeld & Nicolson, 1969).
Moran, Lord, *Winston Churchill: the Struggle for Survival, 1940–55* (Constable, 1966).
Morgan, Janet (ed.), *The Backbench Diaries of Richard Crossman* (Hamish Hamilton and Jonathan Cape, 1981).
Morgan, Kenneth, *Labour in Power, 1945–1951* (Oxford University Press, 1984).
Mortimer, John, *In Character* (Penguin, 1984).
Nicolson, Nigel, *People and Parliament* (Weidenfeld & Nicolson, 1958).
Nicolson, Nigel (ed.), *Harold Nicolson, Diaries and Letters, 1930–9* (Collins, 1966).
——, *Harold Nicolson, Diaries and Letters, 1939–45* (Collins, 1967).
——, *Harold Nicolson, Diaries and Letters, 1945–62* (Collins, 1968).
Pimlott, Ben, *Hugh Dalton* (Jonathan Cape, 1985).
Pimlott, Ben (ed.), *The Second World War Diary of Hugh Dalton, 1940–5* (Jonathan Cape, 1986).
Punnett, R. M., *Front-Bench Opposition* (Heinemann, 1973).
Ramsden, John, *The Making of Conservative Policy* (Longman, 1980).
Raymond, John (ed.), *The Baldwin Age* (Eyre & Spottiswoode, 1960).
Ross, J. F. S., *Parliamentary Representation* (Eyre & Spottiswoode, 1948).
Salter, Arthur, *Memoirs of a Public Servant* (Faber, 1961).
——, *Slave of the Lamp* (Weidenfeld & Nicolson, 1967).
Sampson, Anthony, *Macmillan: a Study in Ambiguity* (Allen Lane, 1967).
Seldon, Anthony, *Churchill's Indian Summer* (Hodder & Stoughton, 1981).
Shuckburgh, Evelyn, *Descent to Suez* (Weidenfeld & Nicolson, 1986).
Sissons, Michael, and French, Philip (eds), *Age of Austerity* (Oxford Paperbacks, 1986).
Skidelsky, Robert, *Oswald Mosley* (Macmillan, 1975).
Stuart of Findhorn, Viscount, *Within the Fringe* (Bodley Head, 1967).
Taylor, A. J. P., *Beaverbrook* (Hamish Hamilton, 1972).
Templewood, Viscount, *Nine Troubled Years* (Collins, 1954).

Thomas, Hugh, *The Suez Affair* (Weidenfeld & Nicolson, 1967).
Thorpe, D. R., *The Uncrowned Prime Ministers* (Dark Horse, 1980).
Trethowan, Ian, *Split Screen* (Hamish Hamilton, 1984).
Vansittart, Lord, *The Mist Procession* (Hutchinson, 1958).
Watkinson, Harold, *Turning Points: a Record of Our Times* (Michael Russell, 1986).
Welensky, Sir Roy, *4,000 Days* (Collins, 1964).
Wheeler-Bennett, J. W., *King George VI: His Life and Reign* (Macmillan, 1958).
——, *John Anderson, Viscount Waverley* (Macmillan, 1962).
Williams, Philip M., *Hugh Gaitskell* (Jonathan Cape, 1979).
Williams, Philip M. (ed.), *The Diary of Hugh Gaitskell, 1945–1956* (Jonathan Cape, 1983).
Woolton, Lord, *Memoirs of the Rt Hon. Earl of Woolton* (Cassell, 1959).
Young, Kenneth, *Sir Alec Douglas-Home* (Dent, 1970).
Young, Kenneth (ed.), *The Diaries of Sir Robert Bruce Lockhart, 1915–1938* (Macmillan, 1973).
——, *The Diaries of Sir Robert Bruce Lockhart, 1939–1965* (Macmillan, 1980).
Ziegler, Philip, *Mountbatten* (Collins, 1985).

Index

Notes: Rab = Richard Austen Butler
n. = note